Beyond the Crossroads
Change and Innovation in Dental Education

ADEA Commission on Change and Innovation
in Dental Education

American Dental Education Association
Washington, D.C.

American Dental Education Association
1400 K Street, NW, Suite 1100
Washington, DC 20005
Phone: 202-289-7201
Fax: 202-289-7204
publications@adea.org
www.adea.org

ISBN 978-0-9820951-3-3

Additional copies of this book are available from ADEA at the address above.

Printed in the United States of America.

A major component of the work of the ADEA Commission on Change and Innovation in Dental Education (ADEA CCI) has been the development of a series of commissioned papers originally published in the *Journal of Dental Education* from 2005 to 2009. All 22 papers in the series appear in this special volume, *Beyond the Crossroads: Change and Innovation in Dental Education*. The intent of these papers was to stimulate self-assessment and reflection on the status of academic dentistry and to consider ways to enhance the preparation of our next generation of practitioners. This volume was produced by the American Dental Education Association and is being disseminated throughout the dental education community to stimulate dialogue about the future directions of dental education. Its publication is an opportune time to summarize the purpose of this series of invited papers within the broader context of a national initiative to explore the future directions of dental education.

The Board of Directors of the American Dental Education Association (ADEA) in 2004 identified curriculum development to address the public's evolving oral health care needs as a key strategic direction of the Association. Then-ADEA President Eric J. Hovland created the ADEA Commission on Change and Innovation in Dental Education (ADEA CCI) in 2005 to coordinate ADEA's efforts to assist the academic community in the development of educational models necessary to prepare general dentists for twenty-first century practice. From 2005 to 2008, we had the privilege of working with the ADEA CCI Oversight Committee to facilitate its activities. Under the best of circumstances, exploring, stimulating and implementing education enhancements is an arduous task fraught with countless pitfalls. One of the complexities in moving toward consensus about needed change is the number of stakeholders within the educational component of the dental profession. Many organizations and constituencies influence the goals, structure, and implementation of dental education in the United States, including faculty and administrators at academic dental institutions, organizations that represent the interests of practitioners, the dental specialty organizations, the dental licensure community, the Commission on Dental Accreditation, the ADA Council on Dental Education and Licensure, the Joint Commission on National Dental Examinations, and ADEA itself. Historically, these groups have operated independently when developing policies and regulations that affect the education of future practitioners. The core philosophy of ADEA CCI is that effective innovation in dental education is most likely to occur when stakeholder organizations work together to reach agreement on fundamental goals and strategies to pursue these goals. ADEA CCI was created to be the forum in dental education where these constituencies could meet, agree on desired goals, and coordinate efforts to move forward.

Over the past four years, the meetings of these constituencies within the framework of ADEA CCI has stimulated a number of initiatives: (1) a special ADEA Council of Sections Task Force, chaired by Dr. Gerald N. Glickman, developed an updated set of competencies for the entry-level general dental practitioner which provide a benchmark for predoctoral dental education; these "Competencies for the New General Dentist" were adopted by the ADEA House of Delegates in April 2008, (2) a network of dental school faculty Liaisons to ADEA CCI was established to provide a mechanism for disseminating information about new educational and assessment strategies to the schools, and national ADEA CCI Liaison Conferences in 2007 and 2008 were attended by more than 100 representatives from 45 schools each year, (3) ADEA CCI members collaborated with the Commission on Dental Accreditation (CODA) to develop a modified set of predoctoral education accreditation standards, currently under review by dental communities of interest until May 2009, which emphasize important themes of ADEA CCI— cultivation of critical thinking, self-assessment, and capacity for self-directed, lifelong learning among our dental students, (4) through an ADEA CCI Task Force on Student Outcomes Assessment, the first-ever national investigation of competency assessment strategies by U.S. dental schools was conducted in 2008 with participation by nearly 1,000 course directors at 50 schools; the findings are published in one of the articles in this volume (Albino et al), (5) the first-ever national assessment of dental school faculty members' perception of the academic work environment was conducted with participation by nearly 2,000 academicians and the findings are also published in this volume (Haden et al), (6) ADEA CCI recommended exploration of an alternative format for the National Board Dental Examinations including consideration of a single blended examination that integrates basic, behavioral, and clinical sciences, and (7) as evidenced by this volume, ADEA CCI sponsored a series of commissioned articles to stimulate new ways of thinking about the curriculum, teaching and learning strategies, student assessment, educational leadership, and academic environment and quality of faculty work-life.

The papers in this volume are organized into six themes: (1) Background; (2) Visions of the Future; (3) Finding, Cultivating and Retaining Faculty; (4) Assessing Students' Progression toward Competence; (5) Leadership in Academic Dentistry; and (6) Reflections. From the papers included in the Mission chapter, you will learn the origins and purpose of ADEA CCI and review the compelling reasons for exploring alternatives to current educational practices in the "Case for Change" by Dr. Marsha A. Pyle. The "Competencies for the New General Dentist" place new emphasis on cultivation of our students' capacity for critical thinking, self-assessment, self-directed learning, and critical appraisal of the research literature in support of the central ADEA CCI theme: **developing lifelong learners who provide evidence-based care to meet the needs of society.** These new competencies are intended to provide a framework by which academic dental institutions can analyze their curricula and stimulate inclusion of educational experiences to facilitate development of critical thinking and skills needed for lifelong learning throughout dentists' careers.

The four papers in the "Visions of the Future" chapter encourage reflection about dental education over the next 20 years – what could or should dental education look like in 2030? Four questions are addressed in this chapter. Dr. Maxwell H. Anderson addresses the question of influence on dental education by the evolving oral health needs and expectations of the public and potential scenarios for evolution of the health care delivery system in this nation. Dr. N. Karl Haden responds to the question of whether academic dental institutions can create an environment that is more consistent with the academic culture found in other sectors of higher education, including more emphasis on cultivation of "habits of the mind" among both students and faculty: critical thinking, self-assessment, and self-directed learning. Dr. Anthony M. Iacopino asks: what will be the influence on dental curriculum of the escalating sophistication

of scientific inquiry and information dissemination, driven by nanoscience and rapid leaps in imaging and computing systems, and the consequent new understandings of disease etiologies and mechanisms that are now emerging? In the final paper in this chapter, Prof. William D. Hendricson examines how current teaching and learning strategies compare to research about developing students' capacities for critical thinking, problem-solving, and self-directed learning, and how our curricular methods stack up against the evidence.

The chapter on "Finding, Cultivating and Retaining Faculty" focuses on the heart and soul of dental schools—the faculty. The six papers in this chapter address questions that are central to sustaining excellence in dental education. Dr. Haden describes and analyzes the findings of the nationwide study of faculty members' perceptions of academic work-life in dental schools. This study, conducted by ADEA CCI, is the largest and most comprehensive investigation of what faculty members think about their job responsibilities, relationships with colleagues and students, and working conditions conducted to date in any component of health professions education. Three papers in this chapter, by Dr. Cathy A. Trower, Dr. Carroll-Ann E. Trotman, and Dr. Charles N. Bertolami, consider what dental schools will need to do to create an environment that is attractive to dental professionals who desire to pursue teaching and scholarship, with particular emphasis on creating an institutional culture and work climate necessary to attract and retain younger dentists. The papers in this chapter by Dr. Frank W. Licari and Prof. William D. Hendricson address the critical issue of faculty development, including mechanisms to provide "planned" career growth for our faculty and building a culture that values and supports faculty members' attainment of capacities needed for new teaching and learning techniques. These papers emphasize that curriculum reform and adoption of more effective teaching strategies is heavily dependent on faculty development. Case studies of major initiatives to reform health professions education indicate these efforts are doomed to failure unless accompanied by extensive professional development using "hands-on learning" strategies.

The chapter titled "Assessing Students' Progression toward Competence" includes a comprehensive review of competency assessment strategies currently employed by dental schools and concludes that most dental schools still rely on standard techniques to evaluate dental students, including heavy reliance on multiple-choice testing, and have not adopted a number of assessment innovations that are used by other health professions education programs. This paper, which was developed by the ADEA CCI Task Force on Student Outcomes Assessment, also includes a review of the literature on student assessment in dental education, an examination of the principles of assessment in competency-based education, and a description of evaluation techniques that are endorsed by assessment experts as appropriate for measurement of several aspects of overall professional competence. A companion paper by Dr. Gene A. Kramer provides a toolbox of 17 assessment methods, with discussion of the applications, advantages, and disadvantages of each technique and designation of specific evaluation methods that are appropriate for each of the "Competencies for the New General Dentist." Dr. Laura M. Neumann and Dr. R. Lamont MacNeil describe innovations in the national board examinations and review the methodology for exam construction and validation.

The papers in the chapter on "Leadership in Academic Dentistry" by Dr. Geralyn D. Crain, Dr. Peter A. Cohen, and Dr. Lisa A. Tedesco were designed to promote consideration of factors that influence the outcomes of change initiatives in higher education and encourage reflection about the type of leadership that is needed for academic dental institutions to evolve rather than "tread water." In the concluding "Reflections" chapter, Dr. Karen F. Novak and Dr. Huw F. Thomas provide their thoughts on what this series of papers has meant to them, from their respective positions as a mid-career dental school faculty member and a dental school dean.

The papers in this volume were developed and written from scratch by the 42 individuals listed below, who gave generously of their time, insights, and expertise. Unlike symposia or conference proceedings published in academic journals that are developed from transcripts of presentations, the lead authors and co-authors were invited to develop original contributions to address designated topics or issues. The individuals are a reflection of the "central forum" mission of ADEA CCI. Members of the dental community—faculty and academic leaders, organized dentistry, the licensure community, and other components of higher education outside of dental education—are all represented. These individuals devoted considerable time to creating original papers and serving as reviewers, sounding boards, and sources of information over the past four years.

Individuals Contributing to the ADEA CCI Series as Authors and Co-Authors

Affiliations reflect positions at the time of authorship.

- Dr. Judith E. N. Albino, University of Colorado School of Dental Medicine and Academy for Academic Leadership
- Dr. Eugene L. Anderson, American Dental Education Association
- Dr. Maxwell H. Anderson; Anderson Dental Consulting
- Dr. Sandra C. Andrieu, Louisiana State University School of Dentistry
- Dr. Charles N. Bertolami, New York University College of Dentistry and 2008–2009 President, American Dental Education Association
- Dr. Lina M. Cardenas, University of Texas Health Science Center at San Antonio Dental School
- Dr. Gregory Chadwick, East Carolina University School of Dentistry
- Ms. Jacqueline Chmar, American Dental Education Association
- Dr. Peter A. Cohen, Wichita State University College of Health Professions
- Dr. James R. Cole II, Commission on Dental Accreditation
- Dr. Geralyn D. Crain, University of Missouri-Kansas City School of Dentistry
- Dr. Edward A. Funk, University of Texas Health Science Center at San Antonio Dental School
- Prof. Mary C. George, University of North Carolina at Chapel Hill School of Dentistry
- Dr. Gerald N. Glickman, Baylor College of Dentistry
- Dr. Joel F. Glover, American Dental Association
- Dr. Jerold S. Goldberg, Case School of Dental Medicine
- Dr. N. Karl Haden, Academy for Academic Leadership
- Prof. William D. Hendricson, University of Texas Health Science Center at San Antonio Dental School and Academy for Academic Leadership
- Dr. Lindsey C. Henson, University of Minnesota School of Medicine
- Dr. Bruce D. Horn, Joint Commission on National Dental Examinations
- Dr. Anthony M. Iacopino, University of Manitoba Faculty of Dentistry
- Dr. Kenneth L. Kalkwarf, University of Texas Health Science Center at San Antonio Dental School

- Dr. Gene A. Kramer, American Dental Association
- Dr. Frank W. Licari, University of Illinois at Chicago College of Dentistry
- Dr. R. Lamont MacNeil, University of Connecticut School of Dental Medicine
- Dr. Cyril Meyerowitz, Eastman Dental Center, University of Rochester School of Medicine and Dentistry
- Dr. Laura M. Neumann, American Dental Association
- Dr. Karen F. Novak, University of Kentucky College of Dentistry
- Dr. Marsha A. Pyle, Case School of Dental Medicine
- Dr. Richard Ranney, University of Maryland Baltimore College of Dental Surgery and Academy for Academic Leadership
- Dr. William F. Rose, University of Texas Health Science Center at San Antonio Dental School
- Dr. Ridley O. Ross, University of Texas Health Science Center at San Antonio Dental School
- Dr. Kathleen Roth, American Dental Association
- Dr. Lisa A. Tedesco, Emory University Graduate School and Rollins School of Public Health
- Dr. Huw F. Thomas, University of Alabama at Birmingham School of Dentistry
- Dr. Carroll-Ann E. Trotman, University of Maryland Baltimore College of Dental Surgery
- Dr. Cathy A. Trower, Harvard University Graduate School of Education
- Dr. Richard W. Valachovic, American Dental Education Association
- Dr. Adriana Vargas, University of Texas Health Science Center at San Antonio Dental School
- Dr. Richard G. Weaver, American Dental Education Association
- Dr. Ronald L. Winder, Joint Commission on National Dental Examinations
- Dr. Stephen K. Young, University of Oklahoma College of Dentistry

In closing, we would like to share the perspectives and reflections of several members of ADEA CCI. This group of individuals, representing many facets of our profession and academic dentistry, was first assembled in 2005 and given a daunting charge: stimulate the educational community to engage in a national dialogue about how we collectively propose to develop the next generation of dental professionals for our nation. In the course of just four years, this group of dedicated individuals, demonstrating great pride in their profession, has indeed stimulated appraisal of what we're doing now to educate dental students and what we could do in the future. Here are comments from some of these individuals about the work of the ADEA Commission on Change and Innovation in Dental Education, concluding with our reflections on the work of this Commission.

As the thought leader for dental education, the American Dental Education Association (ADEA) provides excellent service to its members. The papers in *Beyond the Crossroads: Change and Innovation in Dental Education* represent not only another valuable service to members, but include what I consider the most important work undertaken by the Association. This work, conducted under the aegis of the ADEA Commission on Change and Innovation in Dental Education (ADEA CCI), will greatly influence the vitality and future of dental education. Because of how strongly I feel about the importance of ADEA CCI's work, I made the promotion of its work my highest priority as ADEA President for 2009-10. The 22 papers in *Beyond the Crossroads: Change and Innovation in Dental Education* include a wide range of topics, ideas, and strategies for improving educational processes and content at our member schools. Some of the papers describe the rationale for ADEA CCI itself and the need for educational reform. One paper espouses eight *Principles of Dental Education* that provide a clear template for shaping the dental curriculum of the future, as well as new accreditation standards. Others develop ideas about enhancements in curriculum, faculty development, and student assessment. Still others outline the importance of strategic partnerships with entities outside of dental schools and allied and advanced dental education programs. First published as individual articles in the *Journal of Dental Education* in over past three years, the papers collectively promote a greater understanding of ADEA CCI and educational reform. Compiling the articles into this single comprehensive volume creates an easily accessible and extraordinary resource for many years to come. I am pleased that ADEA and ADEA CCI have made these resources available, and am confident that as our members read them, they will engage in thoughtful dialogue about the future of dental education.

—Dr. Ronald J. Hunt
Harry Lyons Professor and Dean, Virginia Commonwealth University
ADEA 2009-2010 President

As a member of ADEA CCI and having been involved in dental education for over 25 years, I have come to recognize that dental education still remains at a crossroads with respect to many of the tenets originally espoused in the 1995 Institute of Medicine report on dental education. ADEA CCI has and must continue to help lead the way to address the challenges that our dental graduates in 2009 and beyond will face. Within our own dental school environments and cultures, there must be impetus for systemic change to deliver contemporary dental education in a way that is exciting, rewarding, and effective for all stakeholders. Within our dental school curricula, there must be transparency between disciplines and continuous integration of the clinical sciences with the biomedical sciences so that our graduates are more than able to understand the complexities of patient care and practice quality dentistry as an integral member of the total health care team. This landmark volume represents the spirit of the current as well as the future climate in dental education and represents a must-read for anyone with an interest and concern about dental education. In conjunction with the papers, the recently approved Competencies for the New General Dentist were developed with many of these aforementioned principles in mind, and I hope that through the ongoing efforts of ADEA CCI and all of the dental education community that our students will be more than well-prepared to be outstanding caregivers and academic leaders in the future.

—Dr. Gerald N. Glickman
Chair, Department of Endodontics
Baylor College of Dentistry
President, American Academy of Endodontics
Chair, ADEA Council of Section Task Force on Competencies for the New General Dentist

The work of ADEA CCI as manifest in the *Beyond the Crossroads: Change and Innovation in Dental Education* has served as a source of important reflection on the future direction of dental education. The diverse topics, authors, and contributions have touched upon a vast group of core concepts for contemporary pedagogical approaches. It is clear that ADEA CCI has provided a comprehensive view of the educational landscape of the future through these papers. They have fostered discussion, motivation, angst, and inspired vision for what dental education may become. The momentum for change and improvement in our educational system has promoted significant creativity and innovation already. How we continue to move the profession forward into the future depends on the imagination and creativity that *Beyond the Crossroads* articles and the other initiatives of ADEA CCI engender in each individual and collectively within each dental education institution.

—Dr. Marsha A. Pyle
Associate Dean for Education,
Case School of Dental Medicine

There are many important concepts for dental educators in the papers that follow in this volume. Most of these messages have been discussed in dental education for many years. Many have already been implemented individually or collectively in dental schools throughout the United States. The time has come for significant change in dental education as suggested in these manuscripts. Wherever our discussions for change lead us, there are a few important and basic concepts that I feel should be considered:

- Dental education must remain current. New concepts in treatment and patient management, evidence based, should be incorporated into the curriculum in a timely fashion. Faculty should teach evidence-based dentistry, and students should consider the concept second nature by graduation.
- The most common procedures performed in the general practice of dentistry should be emphasized in the teaching of clinical sciences. Less common procedures should be de-emphasized or included in the curriculum as time or opportunity permit.
- Ethics and professionalism should be emphasized on the first day of dental education and every day thereafter.
- Problem solving, critical thinking, and self-directed learning should be integrated into all curricula.

- Lifelong learning should be a goal for all students, and faculty must teach students how to learn.
- Each school should carefully consider moving some of the basic sciences into the undergraduate curriculum and replacing them with clinical sciences in the dental school curriculum.

—*Dr. Ronald L. Winder*
Pediatric Dentist, Tulsa, Oklahoma
Joint Commission on National
Dental Examinations

Dental education has been witness to the birth of a major policy report during every decade since the 1926 William J. Gies report. Each report reverberates with concerns about a set of challenges facing dental education. The reports come and go, while familiar challenges remain. This volume may look like more of the same, destined to fall dead-born from the press. However, the manuscripts in *Beyond the Crossroads: Change and Innovation in Dental Education* have already enlivened debate and initiated important changes through ADEA CCI. Because ADEA CCI includes representatives from major stakeholder groups and dental education oversight agencies, new ideas have been heard by agents of change. For example, as this volume goes to press, significant recommendations to the predoctoral dental education accreditation standards are available for public comment. ADEA CCI members played important roles in the development and dialogue about these updated standards. Actions to improve the national boards are under way. On the local level, ADEA hears frequent reports of exciting innovations at dental schools across the United States and Canada. As dental school administrators, faculty, students, and staff explore changes necessary to meet a dynamic educational, societal, and health care environment, *Beyond the Crossroads: Change and Innovation in Dental Education* will serve as an unparalleled guide to the rapidly evolving ecology of dental education.

—*Dr. N. Karl Haden*
President, Academy for Academic Leadership

The activities of ADEA CCI as reflected in the manuscripts in *Beyond the Crossroads: Change and Innovation in Dental Education* are a significant step toward creating a culture of change and innovation in the dental education community. The first step toward improvement is often developing an awareness of the issues and building a case for change. These papers raise the sensitive issues and ask the difficult questions to start the dialogue. The ball is rolling, and hopefully it will encourage all with an interest in improving dental education and ultimately oral health to join in the discussion, whether their interests are in the curriculum, assessment tools, community-based learning, critical thinking, faculty development, etc.—there are many areas to explore. ADEA CCI has primed the pump, and now it's time to involve a broad range of stakeholders from the education, research, and practicing communities, as well as industry and the public, to build a broad-based consensus for long-lasting change.

—*Dr. Gregory Chadwick*
Associate Dean for Planning and
Extramural Affairs, East Carolina University
School of Dentistry

ADEA CCI was born out of a comment at the 2004 Forum on Predoctoral Dental Education—"The only thing we know about the future of dentistry is that it will be different than today." That statement stimulated ADEA CCI discussions of how dental schools could do a better job of creating graduates with the characteristics of lifelong learners, ready to flourish in a changing environment. The papers in *Beyond the Crossroads: Change and Innovation in Dental Education* provide the background to trigger academic discussions of the qualities that dental students should develop during their educational years. The papers also give dental faculty members a starting point to develop teaching strategies to facilitate the development of these qualities. ADEA CCI has been encouraged by the reception the papers have received from ADEA CCI Liaisons, dental faculty members and administrators, and individuals across the spectrum of health care education. I want to thank ADEA CCI for the inspiration and guidance they brought to this project—and the authors for doing the heavy lifting of preparing these excellent papers. We all look forward to the implementation of the principles brought forward in the papers by dental schools as they initiate curricular changes to enhance each of their students' ability to become **lifelong learners providing evidence-based care to meet the needs of society**.

—Dr. Kenneth L. Kalkwarf
Dean, University of Texas Health Science
Center at San Antonio Dental School
Chair, ADEA Commission on Change and
Innovation in Dental Education, 2005-08

—Dr. Stephen K. Young
Dean, University of Oklahoma College of
Dentistry
Chair, ADEA Commission on Change and Innovation in Dental Education, 2008-present

—Prof. William D. Hendricson
Assistant Dean, Educational and
Faculty Development
University of Texas Health Science Center at
San Antonio Dental School
Academy for Academic Leadership
ADEA CCI Member
Beyond the Crossroads: Change and Innovation in Dental Education *Coordinator*

Acknowledging all members, past and present, of the ADEA Commission on Change and Innovation in Dental Education (ADEA CCI) Oversight Committee

As of February 4, 2009

Current ADEA CCI Members

Chair

Dr. Stephen K. Young
Dean, University of Oklahoma
College of Dentistry

Dr. Sandra C. Andrieu
Associate Dean for Academic Affairs
Louisiana State University School of
Dentistry

Dr. Carol A. Aschenbrener
Executive Vice President
Association of American Medical
Colleges

Dr. Gregory Chadwick
Representing the American Dental
Association Foundation
Associate Dean for Planning and
Extramural Affairs
East Carolina University School of
Dentistry

Dr. Gerald N. Glickman
Chair, Department of Endodontics
Baylor College of Dentistry

Prof. Tami Grzesikowski
Dean, College of Health Sciences
St. Petersburg College

Prof. William D. Hendricson
Assistant Dean, Educational and
Faculty Development
University of Texas Health Science
Center at San Antonio Dental School

Dr. Bruce Horn
Representing the Joint Commission
on National Dental Examinations
Tulsa, Oklahoma

Dr. Ronald J. Hunt
ADEA 2008–2009 President-elect
Dean, Virginia Commonwealth
University School of Dentistry

Dr. Steven M. Lepowsky
Associate Dean for Education and
Patient Care
University of Connecticut School of
Dental Medicine

Dr. Laura M. Neumann
Representing the American Dental
Association
Senior Vice President of Educational
and Professional Affairs, American
Dental Association

Dr. Michael J. Reed
Representing the Commission on
Dental Accreditation
University of Missouri-Kansas City

Dr. Lisa A. Tedesco
Dean and Vice Provost, Academic
Affairs - Graduate Study
Emory University

Dr. Russell Webb
Representing the American Dental
Association Board of Trustees
Upland, California

Dr. Richard W. Valachovic
ADEA Executive Directive

Past ADEA CCI Members

Dr. Kenneth L. Kalkwarf
ADEA Past President
Dean, University of Texas Health
Science Center at San Antonio Dental
School

Prof. Mary C. George
Director, Allied Dental Education
Programs
University of North Carolina at
Chapel Hill School of Dentistry

Dr. Cyril Meyerowitz
Director, Eastman Dental Center
University of Rochester School of
Medicine and Dentistry

Dr. James R. Cole
Represented Commission on Dental
Accreditation
Oral and Maxillofacial Surgeon
Albuquerque, New Mexico

Dr. Joel F. Glover
Represented American Dental
Association Board of Trustees
General Practitioner
Reno, Nevada

Dr. Jerold S. Goldberg
Dean and Interim Provost
Case School of Dental Medicine

Dr. Marsha A. Pyle
Associate Dean for Academic Affairs
Case School of Dental Medicine

Dr. Ronald L. Winder
Represented Joint Commission on
National Dental Examinations
Pediatric Dentistry of Tulsa,
Oklahoma

Dr. Michael C. Alfano
Executive Vice President
New York University

ADEA Staff and Consultants

Dr. Eugene L. Anderson
Associate Executive Director and
Director,
ADEA Center for Educational Policy
and Research

Ms. Lisa A. Fanning
ADEA Director of Grant Programs

Dr. Ifie M.F. Okwuje
ADEA Director of Analysis

Ms. Faduma Hayir
ADEA Program Coordinator

Dr. N. Karl Haden
President, Academy for Academic
Leadership

Dr. Judith E. N. Albino
Academy for Academic Leadership

Dr. Richard G. Weaver
Former Associate Director, ADEA
Center for Educational Policy and
Research

Ms. Jacqueline Chmar
Former ADEA Program Associate

Table of Contents

ADEA Commission on Change and Innovation in Dental Education

Kenneth L. Kalkwarf, D.D.S.; N. Karl Haden, Ph.D.; Richard W. Valachovic, D.M.D., M.P.H.

Dr. Kalkwarf is Dean, Dental School, University of Texas Health Science Center at San Antonio, and Chair of the ADEA Commission on Change and Innovation in Dental Education; Dr. Haden is Associate Executive Director and Director of the Center for Educational Policy and Research, American Dental Education Association; and Dr. Valachovic is Executive Director, American Dental Education Association. Direct correspondence and requests for reprints to Dr. Kenneth Kalkwarf, Dean, Dental School, University of Texas Health Science Center, 7703 Floyd Curl Drive, San Antonio, TX 78229-3900; 210-567-3160 phone; 210-567-6721 fax; kalkwarf@uthscsa.edu.

"It's easier to move a cemetery than to change a curriculum." When these words were originally spoken, dental education probably wasn't the focus. However, numerous authors and speakers over the past twenty years are convinced that these words describe the reality of curriculum reform in a contemporary dental school. The literature, conference proceedings, and private conversations are replete with discussions of the frustration that arises when significant curriculum change is attempted, along with commiseration about efforts toward major curriculum reform that ended up as minor schedule tweaking. In 1995, the Institute of Medicine (IOM) reported a variety of challenges in dental education: individual courses and curriculum reflect past dental practice rather than current and emerging practice and knowledge; clinical education does not sufficiently incorporate the goal of comprehensive care, with instruction focusing too heavily on procedures; linkages between medicine and dentistry are weak; and the curriculum is crowded with redundant material, often taught in disciplinary silos. The IOM also identified a fundamental pedagogical dichotomy in the curriculum: "basic and clinical science teaching do not stress the basic sciences as a relevant foundation for clinical practice."[1] A decade after the IOM study, these problems still persist in dental education.

A number of recent articles have been published that identify obstacles to and strategies for change in dental education.[2-6] Kassebaum et al. found that 86 percent of dental schools characterized their curriculum as traditional discipline, lecture-based, or largely discipline-based with few interdisciplinary courses.[6] The obstacles to change are numerous: the need to convert clinical education to a general practice-based comprehensive care model, only to find an inadequate number of academic general dentists who can serve as role models; the desire to eliminate "outdated" clinical approaches only to have faculty from the various specialist disciplines successfully argue that their interpretation of accreditation standards is that all students must demonstrate achievement of discipline-based competencies that are "above and beyond" the skill set of an entry-level general dental practitioner; a desire to move to an active-learning, problem-based approach only to have some faculty members make a case that they have no background or training to be a facilitator and bring forth the pervasive assumption that national boards

Editor's Note: A number of important issues and initiatives regarding dental education—including access to care, diversity in dental education, curriculum reform, national licensure examination, and faculty shortages—are on the current discussion and debate agenda at the national level. In an effort to give ADEA members and other JDE readers the benefit of important individual perspectives on matters likely to have significant impact in the immediate future, with this issue the journal is launching a new section titled "Perspectives." The articles in this section are meant to be thought-provoking, perhaps even provocative, in an effort to stimulate ongoing debate and sharing of ideas. These articles will not be peer-reviewed, and within reason, there is no limit to their length. I eagerly encourage individuals at all levels in dental academia to participate in this forum; doing so has the potential of providing a valuable service to our profession and community. In this issue, Dr. Kenneth Kalkwarf and his coauthors present their perspectives on the ADEA Commission on Change and Innovation in Dental Education.

test only "facts" that can best be delivered in a lecture format. Kassebaum et al., for example, found that 87 percent of schools use either National Board results or National Board exam content as a basis to evaluate the effectiveness of the school curriculum.[6] The list goes on to include attempts to integrate basic science and clinical science instruction, move parts of the curriculum into prerequisites, and provide more sequential education in the context of an educational continuum.

The American Dental Education Association (ADEA) has explored a number of strategies to assist dental schools in developing curricula, standardizing curricula with contemporary concepts, aligning educational methodology to focus on the development of core competencies, and fostering curricular innovation. Among the Association's initiatives are "Curriculum Guidelines," with the first set published in 1986 and the last in 1993; "Competencies for the New Dentist," approved by the American Association of Dental Schools House of Delegates in 1997; the publication of best practices that include innovations in curricula; and open forums on dental school curricula at the ADEA annual sessions. The ADEA Council of Deans considered new directions in curricula at its November 2004 meeting. The ADEA Council of Sections provided the catalyst for the most recent ADEA initiative to engage the communities of interest to investigate systemic change that will advance and sustain curricular reform and innovation.

At its interim meeting in October 2003, the ADEA Council of Sections presented and discussed a proposal to develop foundation knowledge guidelines and revise the ADEA "Competencies for the New Dentist." In March 2004, the ADEA Board of Directors considered the proposal and concluded that it provided an opportunity to engage all communities of interest in a dialogue about foundation knowledge, clinical competencies, and the relationship between foundation knowledge and clinical competencies—all in the larger context of systemic change for major curricular innovation. As a means to build upon and move forward the Council of Sections proposal, the ADEA Board of Directors concluded that the Association should hold a Forum on the Predoctoral Dental Curriculum to involve all the major stakeholder groups required for a systemic change. This forum took place on October 21, 2004. It included representatives from the American Dental Association (ADA), Commission on Dental Accreditation (CODA), Council on Dental Education and

Licensure (CDEL), Joint Commission on National Dental Examinations (JCNDE), ADEA Council of Deans, ADEA Council of Sections, academic deans, and others.

There are a number of ways to conceptualize curricular reform in dental education. What is lacking in most proposals for innovation is a single Archimedean leverage point by which to shift the entire system. Based on feedback from the ADEA Forum on the Predoctoral Dental Curriculum, a lever for systemic change could be created by involving all communities of interest in the development of a new document: "Competencies for the New General Dentist." This document would include foundation knowledge linked to competencies that encompass the desired entry-level skills for a general dentist who is prepared to serve the public's oral health needs. As envisioned by the forum participants, this document would provide a common reference for the development of new curricula, the construction of National Board examinations, the update and revision of CODA standards, and the reform of the clinical licensure process—processes, tasks, and outcomes that should be intertwined in a well-orchestrated professional development and credentialing pathway that is based upon the official curriculum model for the dental accreditation process: that is, competency-based education.[7,8]

The forum recommended that the ADEA Board of Directors engage groups inside ADEA, as well as across the dental and health care communities, to contribute to the development of the "Competencies for the New General Dentist" under the leadership of an oversight committee. The ADEA Board of Directors accepted this recommendation, and in April 2005 ADEA President Eric Hovland appointed the oversight committee—the Commission on Change and Innovation in Dental Education. With the October 21, 2004 forum as a model, the commission represents the various components of ADEA as well as advanced education, the licensure community, the ADA, CODA, CDEL, JCNDE, and other areas of health care education. President Hovland appointed Dr. Kenneth L. Kalkwarf, ADEA President-Elect and Dean, University of Texas Health Science Center at San Antonio Dental School, to chair the commission. The commission held its inaugural meeting on May 12, 2005.

Work on the document "Competencies for the New General Dentist" began on June 8, 2005. With the oversight of the commission, an ADEA Council of

Sections Task Force met to begin the development of a new set of competencies along with accompanying descriptions of appropriate foundation of knowledge. In its oversight capacity, the commission charged this task force to construct the competences for a new general dentist as an interdisciplinary model with thematic units rather than discipline-specific courses and to identify foundation knowledge for each competency as well as the knowledge that should be a prerequisite to admission to dental school. As documents are developed, the commission will distribute them to a broad array of the communities of interest, including other health professions, and the various ADEA councils for input.

"Competencies for the New General Dentist" is not the endpoint of the ADEA process, but the reference point for innovative change. Curriculum guidelines are envisioned to delineate the specifics underlying clinical competencies and foundation knowledge. This information will prove useful in determining appropriate prerequisites to dental school admission as well as identifying curricula that are extraneous to education for entry into the profession of a new general dentist. Through its councils, ADEA will engage its membership in workshops and forums to explore new educational and assessment methodologies, to identify best practices in curriculum as models, and to create a dynamic model and process to assist dental schools in curricular innovation. With the guidance of the commission, ADEA is developing a communications plan to engage faculty, students, administrators, and communities of interest in the change effort.

The ADEA Commission on Change and Innovation in Dental Education presents a unique opportunity for ADEA to work with its members, CODA, CDEL, JCNDE, and the clinical licensure examining community to initiate meaningful, systemic change into dental education. Working together through the commission, these groups will provide a conduit for continuous innovation to prepare the new general dentist for the challenges of the twenty-first century.

REFERENCES

1. Field MJ, ed. Dental education at the crossroads: challenges and change. Institute of Medicine Report. Washington, DC: National Academy Press, 1995.
2. Dharamsi S, Clark DC, Boyd MA, Pratt DD, Craig B. Social constructs of curricular change. J Dent Educ 2000; 64:603-9.
3. Hendricson WD, Cohen PA. Oral health care in the 21st century: implications for dental and medical education. Acad Med 2001;76:1181-205.
4. Bertolami CN. Rationalizing the dental curriculum in light of current disease prevalence and patient demand for treatment: form vs. content. J Dent Educ 2001;65:725-35.
5. DePaola DP, Slavkin HC. Reforming dental health professions education: a white paper. J Dent Educ 2004; 68:1139-48.
6. Kassebaum DK, Hendricson WD, Taft T, Haden NK. The dental curriculum at North American dental institutions in 2002-03: a survey of current structure, recent innovations, and planned changes. J Dent Educ 2004;68:914-31.
7. Smith SR, Dollase R. AMEE guide no. 14: outcome-based education—planning, implementing, and evaluating a competency-based curriculum. Med Teacher 1999;21:15-22.
8. Grussing PG. Currricular design: competency perspective. Am J Pharm Educ 1987;51:414-9.

The Case for Change in Dental Education

ADEA Commission on Change and Innovation in Dental Education: Marsha Pyle, D.D.S., M.Ed.; Sandra C. Andrieu, Ph.D.; D. Gregory Chadwick, D.D.S.; Jacqueline E. Chmar, B.A.; James R. Cole, D.D.S.; Mary C. George, R.D.H., M.Ed.; Gerald N. Glickman, D.D.S., J.D.; Joel F. Glover, D.D.S.; Jerold S. Goldberg, D.D.S.; N. Karl Haden, Ph.D.; William D. Hendricson, M.A., M.S.; Cyril Meyerowitz, D.D.S., Ph.D.; Laura Neumann, D.D.S.; Lisa A. Tedesco, Ph.D.; Richard W. Valachovic, D.M.D., M.P.H.; Richard G. Weaver, D.D.S.; Ronald L. Winder, D.D.S.; Stephen K. Young, D.D.S.; Kenneth L. Kalkwarf, D.D.S.

Abstract: This article introduces a series of white papers developed by the ADEA Commission on Change and Innovation (CCI) to explore the case for change in dental education. This preamble to the series argues that there is a compelling need for rethinking the approach to dental education in the United States. Three issues facing dental education are explored: 1) the challenging financial environment of higher education, making dental schools very expensive and tuition-intensive for universities to operate and producing high debt levels for students that limit access to education and restrict career choices; 2) the profession's apparent loss of vision for taking care of the oral health needs of all components of society and the resultant potential for marginalization of dentistry as a specialized health care service available only to the affluent; and 3) the nature of dental school education itself, which has been described as convoluted, expensive, and often deeply dissatisfying to its students.

Dr. Pyle is Associate Dean for Education, Case School of Dental Medicine; Dr. Andrieu is Associate Dean for Academic Affairs, Louisiana State University School of Dentistry; Dr. Chadwick is Associate Vice Chancellor for Oral Health, East Carolina University; Ms. Chmar is Policy Analyst, American Dental Education Association; Dr. Cole is a member of the Commission on Dental Accreditation; Prof. George is Associate Professor, Department of Dental Ecology, University of North Carolina School of Dentistry; Dr. Glickman is Chair, Endodontics, Baylor College of Dentistry; Dr. Glover is a member of the Board of Trustees, American Dental Association; Dr. Goldberg is Dean, Case School of Dental Medicine; Dr. Haden is President, Academy for Academic Leadership; Mr. Hendricson is Assistant Dean, Educational and Faculty Development, University of Texas Health Science Center at San Antonio Dental School; Dr. Meyerowitz is Director, Eastman Dental Center, University of Rochester School of Medicine and Dentistry; Dr. Neumann is Associate Executive Director for Education, American Dental Association; Dr. Tedesco is Vice Provost for Academic Affairs in Graduate Studies and Dean, Graduate School, Emory University; Dr. Valachovic is Executive Director, American Dental Education Association; Dr. Weaver is Director, Center for Educational Policy and Research, American Dental Education Association; Dr. Winder is a member of the Joint Commission on National Dental Examinations; Dr. Young is Dean, College of Dentistry, University of Oklahoma; and Dr. Kalkwarf is Chair of the Commission on Change and Innovation in Dental Education, President of the American Dental Education Association, and Dean of the University of Texas Health Science Center at San Antonio Dental School. Direct correspondence to Dr. Marsha Pyle, Associate Dean for Education, Case School of Dental Education, 10900 Euclid Avenue, Cleveland, OH 44106-4905; 216-368-3968 phone; map6@po.cwru.edu. Reprints of this article will not be available.

Key words: dental school, dental education, curriculum, dental students

The rationale for curricular change in dental education is compelling. Financing of higher education will remain a challenge for the foreseeable future, which is critical because dental education is among the most expensive university programs. Budget constraints alone present multifaceted difficulties, ranging from those associated with student diversity and pipeline issues to infrastructure. The ability to recruit and retain faculty, and to ensure the quality of faculty worklife, is increasingly difficult. The curriculum at most dental schools is based on a model of educational delivery that is at least fifty years old, while emerging science, technology, and disease patterns promise to change oral health care significantly. Finally, while dental education is subject to the winds that are changing higher education, dental practice also exists in a tumultuous health care system that demands reform in the face of an aging and more ethnically and racially diverse population.

These issues have led some to question the underpinnings of educational practice and learning in general. Others question the ability of the profession to sustain itself as a learned profession that contributes to the mission of research by creating new knowledge in the university setting. As an introduction to some of dental education's major challenges, this article is a first step in initiating a new dialogue about the need for transformation in dental education and in galvanizing deliberate action for change and innovation.

The Environment of Higher Education and Health Care

The global perspective on trends in dental education is characterized by financial difficulties and by loss of vision for the profession. A number of dental schools are facing financial difficulty due to external and internal forces in their environments.[1] Both private and public dental schools experienced increases of just over 50 percent in expenses from 1991 to 2001.[2] Ultimately, these threats may wipe out dental schools' ability to contribute to the research mission of their parent universities. The importance of science, research, and scholarship in guiding change in dental education cannot be minimized. Otherwise, the profession risks its own de-evolution to a vocational school program, losing its hallmark as a learned professsion.[3,4] New approaches to dental school curricula must create ways to enhance the level of inquiry, research experience, and the applications of relevant science to clinical problems within academic dentistry and the dental practice community.

Most critical to the need for change is the profession's apparent loss of vision for taking care of the oral health needs of society. Today, there is an increasing chasm between the principles that we teach in dental school and the core values that define the profession. The profession is evolving toward promotion of high-end specialized clinical services to the individuals who can afford them, while the complexity of disease across all populations continues to grow. This type of professional isolation disregards demographic trends in the population, diminishes dentistry's role in primary care, allows for marginalization of the profession, and hinders incorporation of dental care models into other health professions. The risk of isolation and marginalization is becoming reality.

The Need for Curricular Change and Innovation

Much has been written about the crisis in health care and, occasionally, dentistry's role in it.[5,6] Much of what has been said about the crisis in health care is analogous to dental education. Specifically, dental education could be described as "convoluted, expensive, and often deeply dissatisfying to consumers."[6] What do these adjectives mean?

- *Convoluted*: The curricula of dental education have been characterized as overcrowded, unmanageable, inflexible, disjointed, irrelevant, and lacking in effective connectivity among basic science, behavioral science, and clinical science applications. Further, the system is permeated by a culture that supports memorization of factual knowledge over reasoning based on evidence and critical thinking skills.

- *Expensive*: The cost of dental education leaves many students with significant debt that limits options upon graduation and thus may influence practice choices. This obstacle contributes to the declining ability of the profession to recruit recent graduates into academic careers and to attract young dentists into primary dental care to respond to the growing oral health needs of a diverse population of patients. The cost may also limit access to dental education for a diverse population of applicants, with the result that dental school is primarily limited to affluent students.

- *Dissatisfying to consumers:* Students quickly learn the survival game of dental school, often buying into the "test file" approach to learning in response to extreme academic loads. Passive learning environments fail to challenge students' ability to grow intellectually and to become critical thinkers and lifelong learners.

Historical reports suggest that established, evidence-based, basic elements of curriculum organization and delivery have never capitalized on educational theory.[7,8] As early as the 1930s, cognitive-social psychologists espoused experiential learning environments that tie together an integrative perspective combining experience, perception, cognition, and behavior.[7] These theories suggest that experiential learning creates the opportunity for deep learning on higher order levels. Jerome Bruner suggested that the purpose of education is to create levels of curiosity and skills in inquiry, rather than memorization of factual knowledge.[8]

These approaches to learning have yet to be institutionalized in dental education, perhaps because changing the usual way we design and deliver curricula causes anxiety, and perhaps because doing what we know is easy. If students are to move from memorization of facts to an integrated experiential approach, then current educational programs will need to reassess their goals, workload, relevancy, efficiency, and effectiveness. To move away from an educational environment that rewards memorization and survival game strategies, students must have time to reflect and think about their learning. This will demand a different approach to traditional educational formats and a complete reorganization of the educational competencies and content delivery. It has been suggested that a "natural critical learning environment" must be created that fosters reasoning from evidence, improves thinking, and develops inquiry skills.[9]

What Will Lead to Systemic Change in Dental Education?

Often, wide-ranging, systemic change in organizations occurs in response to obvious crises.[10] Belief systems color perceptions of change requirements, expected impact, and outcomes. A new perspective on the future must acknowledge that the status quo cannot sustain the organization, and leaders must model the vision for change, allay the anxiety that change brings, and deal with resistance.[10]

Historical reports informing the profession and public have long recommended system-wide change.[11-14] Yet, few outcomes in dental education suggest meaningful change has occurred. Fresh approaches by leaders to remove barriers to systemic change that allow new business models and innovations to emerge may provide the impetus for the preservation of dentistry as a learned profession. Equally needed are forces for change that will sustain dentistry as a source of new knowledge, discovery, and innovation. Serious focus on the didactic classroom curriculum, clinical and supporting didactic preclinical learning experiences, and pedagogy will be required to sustain vitality in dental education and research.

The implication here, clearly, extends to faculty capacity and capability as well. As recruitment and retention of faculty become more difficult, existing faculty are asked to do more—and often with less. Workloads are increasing, and the quality of faculty worklife is in jeopardy. The exodus of new faculty and the likely acceleration in retirements will strain scholarship and make existing models of teaching and learning unsustainable in an environment of reduced resources. Faculty work and reward systems must be reframed in light of emerging realities.

Over the next year, the ADEA Commission on Change and Innovation (CCI) will develop a series of white papers to explore in detail the case for change in dental education. CCI will seek to build consensus within the educational community about new directions that will strengthen dental education and the profession, so that graduates of academic dental institutions enter the profession competent to meet the oral health needs of the public throughout the twenty-first century and to function as an important member of an efficient and effective health care team. CCI's first white paper, "Educational Strategies Associated with Development of Problem-Solving, Critical Thinking, and Self-Directed Learning," follows in this issue of the *Journal of Dental Education*. Future white papers will address such topics as the quality of faculty worklife; student learning and pedagogy; emerging science and the dental school curriculum; financing higher education; and the impact of the changing health care system on dental education.

There are compelling reasons for change in dental education, *now*. The opportunity to shape the destiny of this learned profession must proceed beyond conversation through leadership to action. If this does not occur, external forces will be likely to force change, wanted or unwanted.

REFERENCES

1. Bailit HL, Beazoglou TJ, Formicola AJ, Tedesco L, Brown LJ, Weaver RG. U.S. state-supported dental schools: financial projections and implications. J Dent Educ 2006;70(3):246-57.
2. American Dental Association. 2000-2001 survey of predoctoral dental education. Chicago: American Dental Association, 2002.
3. Bertolami CN. The role and importance of research and scholarship in dental education and practice. J Dent Educ 2002;66(8):918-24.
4. Bertolami CN. Disquieting change, extraordinary challenge. J Dent Res 2002;81(5):366.
5. Gladwell M. The moral hazard myth. The New Yorker, August 29, 2005.
6. Christensen CM, Bohmer R, Kenagy J. Will disruptive innovations cure health care? Harv Business Rev 2000;Sept-Oct:102-12.
7. Kolb DA. Experiential learning: experience as the source of learning and development. New York: Prentice Hall, 1984.
8. Bruner JS. Toward a theory of instruction. Cambridge: Harvard University Press, 1966.
9. Bain K. What makes great teachers great? Chronicle of Higher Education, April 9, 2004, B7-B9.
10. Aschenbrener CA. Understanding change theory and practice. SELAM Newsletter 2002;5(2):5-9.

11. Feld MJ, ed. Dental education at the crossroads: challenges and change. An Institute of Medicine Report. Washington, DC: National Academy Press, 1995.

12. Oral health in America: a report of the surgeon general. Department of Health and Human Services, USPHS. At: www.nidcr.nih.gov/sgr/execsumm.htm. Accessed: February 15, 2006.

13. American Dental Association, Health Policy Resources Center. Future of dentistry. Chicago: American Dental Association, 2001.

14. Institute of Medicine. Health professions education: a bridge to quality. Washington, DC: The National Academies Press, 2003.

Competencies for the New General Dentist
(As approved by the 2008 ADEA House of Delegates)

Preamble

The general dentist is the primary oral health care provider, supported by dental specialists, allied dental professionals, and other health care providers. The general dentist will address health care issues beyond traditional oral health care and must be able to independently and collaboratively practice evidence-based comprehensive dentistry with the ultimate goal of improving the health of society. The general dentist must have a broad biomedical and clinical education and be able to demonstrate professional and ethical behavior as well as effective communication and interpersonal skills. In addition, he or she must have the ability to evaluate and utilize emerging technologies, continuing professional development opportunities, and problem-solving and critical thinking skills to effectively address current and future issues in health care.

As used in this document, a "competency" is a complex behavior or ability essential for the general dentist to begin independent, unsupervised dental practice. Competency includes knowledge, experience, critical thinking and problem-solving skills, professionalism, ethical values, and technical and procedural skills. These components become an integrated whole during the delivery of patient care by the competent general dentist. Competency assumes that all behaviors are performed with a degree of quality consistent with patient well-being and that the general dentist can self-evaluate treatment effectiveness. In competency-based dental education, what students learn is based upon clearly articulated competencies and further assumes that all behaviors/abilities are supported by foundation knowledge and psychomotor skills in biomedical, behavioral, ethical, clinical dental science, and informatics areas that are essential for independent and unsupervised performance as an entry-level general dentist. In creating curricula, dental faculty must consider the competencies to be developed through the educational process, the learning experiences that will lead to the development of these competencies, and ways to assess or measure the attainment of competencies.

The purpose of this document and the proposed foundation knowledge concepts are to:

- Define the competencies necessary for entry into the dental profession as a general dentist. Competencies must be relevant and important to the patient care responsibilities of the general dentist, directly linked to the oral health care needs of the public, realistic, and understandable by other health care professionals;

- Reflect (in contrast to the 1997 competencies) the 2002 Institute of Medicine core set of competencies for enhancing patient care quality and safety, and illustrate current and emerging trends in the dental practice environment; they are divided into domains, are broader and less prescriptive in nature, are fewer in number, and, most importantly, will be linked to requisite foundation knowledge and skills;

- Serve as a central resource, both nationally for the American Dental Education Association (ADEA) and locally for individual dental schools, to promote change and innovation in predoctoral dental school curricula;

- Inform and recommend to the Commission on Dental Accreditation standards for predoctoral dental education;

- Provide a framework for the change, innovation, and construction of national dental examinations, including those provided through the Joint Commission on National Dental Examinations and clinical testing agencies;

- Assist in the development of curriculum guidelines, both nationally for ADEA and locally for individual dental schools, for both foundation knowledge and clinical instruction;

- Provide methods for assessing competencies for the general dentist; and

- Through periodic review and update, serve as a document for benchmarking, best practices, and interprofessional collaboration and, additionally, as a mechanism to inform educators in other health care professions about curricular priorities of dental education and entry-level competencies of general dentists.

Domains

1. **Critical Thinking**
2. **Professionalism**
3. **Communication and Interpersonal Skills**
4. **Health Promotion**
5. **Practice Management and Informatics**
6. **Patient Care**
   A. **Assessment, Diagnosis, and Treatment Planning**
   B. **Establishment and Maintenance of Oral Health**

The statements below define the entry-level competencies for the beginning general dentist.

1. Critical Thinking

Graduates must be competent to:

1.1 Evaluate and integrate emerging trends in health care as appropriate.
1.2 Utilize critical thinking and problem-solving skills.
1.3 Evaluate and integrate best research outcomes with clinical expertise and patient values for evidence-based practice.

2. Professionalism

Graduates must be competent to:

2.1 Apply ethical and legal standards in the provision of dental care.
2.2 Practice within one's scope of competence and consult with or refer to professional colleagues when indicated.

3. Communication and Interpersonal Skills

Graduates must be competent to:

3.1 Apply appropriate interpersonal and communication skills.
3.2 Apply psychosocial and behavioral principles in patient-centered health care.
3.3 Communicate effectively with individuals from diverse populations.

4. Health Promotion

Graduates must be competent to:

4.1 Provide prevention, intervention, and educational strategies.
4.2 Participate with dental team members and other health care professionals in the management and health promotion for all patients.
4.3 Recognize and appreciate the need to contribute to the improvement of oral health beyond those served in traditional practice settings.

5. Practice Management and Informatics

Graduates must be competent to:

5.1 Evaluate and apply contemporary and emerging information including clinical and practice management technology resources.
5.2 Evaluate and manage current models of oral health care management and delivery.
5.3 Apply principles of risk management, including informed consent and appropriate record keeping in patient care.
5.4 Demonstrate effective business, financial management, and human resource skills.
5.5 Apply quality assurance, assessment, and improvement concepts.
5.6 Comply with local, state, and federal regulations including OSHA and HIPAA.
5.7 Develop a catastrophe preparedness plan for the dental practice.

6. Patient Care

A. Assessment, Diagnosis, and Treatment Planning

Graduates must be competent to:

6.1 Manage the oral health care of the infant, child, adolescent, and adult, as well as the unique needs of women, geriatric, and special needs patients.

6.2 Prevent, identify, and manage trauma, oral diseases, and other disorders.

6.3 Obtain and interpret patient/medical data, including a thorough intra/extra oral examination, and use these findings to accurately assess and manage all patients.

6.4 Select, obtain, and interpret diagnostic images for the individual patient.

6.5 Recognize the manifestations of systemic disease and how the disease and its management may affect the delivery of dental care.

6.6 Formulate a comprehensive diagnosis, treatment, and/or referral plan for the management of patients.

B. Establishment and Maintenance of Oral Health

Graduates must be competent to:

6.7 Utilize universal infection control guidelines for all clinical procedures.

6.8 Prevent, diagnose, and manage pain and anxiety in the dental patient.

6.9 Prevent, diagnose, and manage temporomandibular disorders.

6.10 Prevent, diagnose, and manage periodontal diseases.

6.11 Develop and implement strategies for the clinical assessment and management of caries.

6.12 Manage restorative procedures that preserve tooth structure, replace missing or defective tooth structure, maintain function, are esthetic, and promote soft and hard tissue health.

6.13 Diagnose and manage developmental or acquired occlusal abnormalities.

6.14 Manage the replacement of teeth for the partially or completely edentulous patient.

6.15 Diagnose, identify, and manage pulpal and periradicular diseases.

6.16 Diagnose and manage oral surgical treatment needs.

6.17 Prevent, recognize, and manage medical and dental emergencies.

6.18 Recognize and manage patient abuse and/or neglect.

6.19 Recognize and manage substance abuse.

6.20 Evaluate outcomes of comprehensive dental care.

6.21 Diagnose, identify, and manage oral mucosal and osseous diseases.

APPENDIX
Glossary of Terms

Competency: a complex behavior or ability essential for the general dentist to begin independent, unsupervised dental practice; it assumes that all behaviors and skills are performed with a degree of quality consistent with patient well-being and that the general dentist can self-evaluate treatment effectiveness.

Critical thinking: the process of assimilating and analyzing information; this encompasses an interest in finding new solutions, a curiosity with an ability to admit to a lack of understanding, a willingness to examine beliefs and assumptions and to search for evidence to support these beliefs and assumptions, and the ability to distinguish between fact and opinion.

Curriculum guidelines (content): the relevant and fundamental information that is taught for each category of foundation knowledge; these are to be used as curriculum development aids and should not be construed as recommendations for restrictive requirements.

Domain: a broad, critical category of activity for the general dentist.

Emerging technologies: current and future technologies used in patient care, including technologies for biomedical information storage and retrieval, clinical care information, and technologies for use at the point of care.

Evidence-based dentistry: an approach to oral health care that requires the judicious integration of systematic assessments of clinically relevant scientific evidence relating to the patient's oral and medical condition and history integrated with the dentist's clinical expertise and the patient's treatment needs and preferences.

Foundation knowledge and skills: the basic essential knowledge and skills linked to and necessary to support a given competency; these would serve to help guide curriculum in dental schools, assist educators in removing irrelevant, archaic information from current curricula, aid in including important new information, and help test construction committees develop examinations based upon generally accepted, contemporary information.

General dentist: the primary dental care provider for patients in all age groups who is responsible for the diagnosis, treatment, management, and overall coordination of services related to patients' oral health needs.

Health promotion: public health actions to protect or improve oral health and promote oral well-being through behavioral, educational, and enabling socioeconomic, legal, fiscal, environmental, and social measures; it involves the process of enabling individuals and communities to increase control over the determinants of health and thereby improve their health; includes education of the public to prevent chronic oral disease.

Informatics: applications associated with information and technology used in health care delivery; the data and knowledge needed for problem-solving and decision making; and the administration and management of information and technology in support of patient care, education, and research.

Interprofessional health care: the delivery of health care by a variety of health care practitioners in a cooperative, collaborative, and integrative manner to ensure care is continuous and reliable.

Management: includes all actions performed by a health care provider that are designed to alter the course of a patient's condition; such actions may include providing education, advice, treatment by the general dentist, treatment by the general dentist after consultation with another health care professional, referral of a patient to another health care professional, and monitoring the treatment provided; it may also include providing no treatment or observation.

Patient-centered care: the ability to identify, respect, and care about patients' differences, values, preferences, and expressed needs; relieve pain and suffering; coordinate continuous care; listen to, clearly inform, communicate with, and educate patients; share decision making and management; and continuously advocate disease prevention, wellness, and promotion of healthy lifestyles, including a focus on population health.

Problem-solving: the process of answering a question or achieving a goal when the path or answer is not immediately obvious, using an acceptable heuristic or strategy such as the scientific method.

Special needs care: an approach to oral health management tailored to the individual needs of people with a variety of medical conditions or physical and mental limitations that require more than routine delivery of oral care; special care encompasses preventive, diagnostic, and treatment services.

Educational Strategies Associated with Development of Problem-Solving, Critical Thinking, and Self-Directed Learning

ADEA Commission on Change and Innovation in Dental Education: William D. Hendricson, M.A., M.S.; Sandra C. Andrieu, Ph.D.; D. Gregory Chadwick, D.D.S.; Jacqueline E. Chmar, B.A.; James R. Cole, D.D.S.; Mary C. George, R.D.H., M.Ed.; Gerald N. Glickman, D.D.S., J.D.; Joel F. Glover, D.D.S.; Jerold S. Goldberg, D.D.S.; N. Karl Haden, Ph.D.; Cyril Meyerowitz, D.D.S., Ph.D.; Laura Neumann, D.D.S.; Marsha Pyle, D.D.S., M.Ed.; Lisa A. Tedesco, Ph.D.; Richard W. Valachovic, D.M.D., M.P.H.; Richard G. Weaver, D.D.S.; Ronald L. Winder, D.D.S.; Stephen K. Young, D.D.S.; Kenneth L. Kalkwarf, D.D.S.

Abstract: This article was developed for the Commission on Change and Innovation in Dental Education (CCI), established by the American Dental Education Association. CCI was created because numerous organizations within organized dentistry and the educational community have initiated studies or proposed modifications to the process of dental education, often working to achieve positive and desirable goals but without coordination or communication. The fundamental mission of CCI is to serve as a focal meeting place where dental educators and administrators, representatives from organized dentistry, the dental licensure community, the Commission on Dental Accreditation, the ADA Council on Dental Education and Licensure, and the Joint Commission on National Dental Examinations can meet and coordinate efforts to improve dental education and the nation's oral health. One of the objectives of the CCI is to provide guidance to dental schools related to curriculum design. In pursuit of that objective, this article summarizes the evidence related to this question: What are educational best practices for helping dental students acquire the capacity to function as an entry-level general dentist or to be a better candidate to begin advanced studies? Three issues are addressed, with special emphasis on the third: 1) What constitutes expertise, and when does an individual become an expert? 2) What are the differences between novice and expert thinking? and 3) What educational best practices can help our students acquire mental capacities associated with expert function, including critical thinking and self-directed learning? The purpose of this review is to provide a benchmark that faculty and academic planners can use to assess the degree to which their curricula include learning experiences associated with development of problem-solving, critical thinking, self-directed learning, and other cognitive skills necessary for dental school graduates to ultimately become expert performers as they develop professionally in the years after graduation.

Mr. Hendricson is Assistant Dean, Educational and Faculty Development, University of Texas Health Science Center at San Antonio Dental School; Dr. Andrieu is Associate Dean for Academic Affairs, Louisiana State University School of Dentistry; Dr. Chadwick is Associate Vice Chancellor for Oral Health, East Carolina University; Ms. Chmar is Policy Analyst, American Dental Education Association; Dr. Cole is a member of the Commission on Dental Accreditation; Prof. George is Associate Professor, Department of Dental Ecology, University of North Carolina School of Dentistry; Dr. Glickman is Chair, Endodontics, Baylor College of Dentistry; Dr. Glover is a member of the Board of Trustees, American Dental Association; Dr. Goldberg is Dean, Case School of Dental Medicine; Dr. Haden is President, Academy for Academic Leadership; Dr. Meyerowitz is Director, Eastman Dental Center, University of Rochester School of Medicine and Dentistry; Dr. Neumann is Associate Executive Director for Education, American Dental Association; Dr. Pyle is Associate Dean for Education, Case School of Dental Medicine; Dr. Tedesco is Vice Provost for Academic Affairs in Graduate Studies and Dean, Graduate School, Emory University; Dr. Valachovic is Executive Director, American Dental Education Association; Dr. Weaver is Director, Center for Educational Policy and Research, American Dental Education Association; Dr. Winder is a member of the Joint Commission on National Dental Examinations; Dr. Young is Dean, College of Dentistry University of Oklahoma; and Dr. Kalkwarf is Chair of the Commission on Change and Innovation in Dental Education, President of the American Dental Education Association, and Dean of the University of Texas Health Science Center at San Antonio Dental School. Direct correspondence to William Hendricson, Assistant Dean, Educational and Faculty Development, University of Texas Health Science Center at San Antonio School of Dentistry, 7703 Floyd Curl Drive, San Antonio, TX 78229-3900; 210-567-0436 phone; Hendricson@uthscsa.edu. Reprints of this article will not be available.

Key words: dental education, critical thinking, self-directed learning, curriculum

In 2004, the Board of Directors of the American Dental Education Association (ADEA) identified curriculum development to meet the changing needs of oral health care as one of the Association's strategic directions. Nearly every Council within ADEA, including Deans, Sections, Faculties, Allied Dental Program Directors, and Hospitals and Advanced Education Programs, has created an initiative related to curricular change in recent years. In 2005, then-ADEA President Eric Hovland created the ADEA Commission on Change and Innovation in Dental Education (CCI) as the Association's primary mechanism to lead and coordinate ADEA's efforts to assist in the development of curricula for the twenty-first century. The CCI is chaired by Dr. Kenneth Kalkwarf, Dean of the Dental School at the University of Texas Health Science Center at San Antonio, and 2006-07 President of ADEA.

A number of organizations and stakeholders influence the goals, scope, structure, and directions of dental education in the United States. Most of these groups operate independently of each other in adopting policies, positions, and regulations that affect dental education. The underlying philosophy of the CCI is that effective change and innovation in dental education can take place only when each of the component organizations agrees on fundamental improvements to dental education. To provide a forum for building such consensus, CCI was created to be the focal meeting place in dental education where these constituencies—including dental educators and administrators and representatives from organized dentistry, the dental licensure community, the Commission on Dental Accreditation, the ADA Council on Dental Education and Licensure, and the Joint Commission on National Dental Examinations—can come together with the purpose of coordinating efforts to improve dental education and thereby the oral health of the public. While recognizing the diversity of dental school missions, the CCI has engaged a special ADEA Council of Sections task force to provide a benchmark for predoctoral dental education by preparing an updated set of competencies for the entry-level general dental practitioner. The CCI will pursue a variety of other initiatives, including faculty development programs focused on curricular change and innovation. During 2006-07, the CCI will publish a series of white papers to address critical considerations in curricular innovation. The preamble to this series, "The Case for Change in Dental Education," appears in this issue of the *Journal of Dental Education*. Subsequent publications and reports from the CCI will address additional factors influencing the dental landscape, including the influence of emerging science on curriculum, access to dental education and oral health care, dentistry and dental education in the context of the evolving health care system, best practices for faculty development, and strategies for assessment.

This first white paper reviews evidence related to the fundamental curricular question: What are best practices for helping dental students acquire the capacities to function as an entry-level general dentist? Three issues are addressed, with special emphasis on the third item:

1. What constitutes expertise, and when does an individual become an expert?
2. What are the differences between novice and expert thinking?
3. What educational best practices can help our students acquire the mental capacities associated with expert function, including critical thinking and self-directed learning?

1. What Constitutes Expertise, and When Does an Individual Become an Expert?

The primary mission of dental school is to produce an entry-level general practitioner who has the capacity to function independently without supervision. The cornerstone of professional practice is the application of thought processes that allow dentists to recognize pertinent information in a patient's presentation, make accurate decisions based on deliberate and open-minded review of available options, evaluate outcomes of therapeutic decisions, and assess their own performance. Before delving into the cognitive processes that allow dentists to "do what they do," a few notes about the novice to expert continuum are warranted to provide a context for the following discussion of expertise.

The process of developing the capacity for expert thought and skillful on-the-job performance typically extends well beyond the temporal confines of in-school education.[1] In the 1980s, the Dreyfus brothers popularized the five-stage development continuum that consists of novice, advanced beginner, competent, proficient, and expert.[2] An individual in training for a professional role evolves from a true neophyte (a beginner; derived from the term "novice" used in religious orders) through a series of stages where capacities are gradually and progressively enhanced by trial and error learning and successive approximation supported by timely and corrective coaching. The "safe practitioner stage," in which an individual can perform the core tasks associated with a professional role and solve commonly encountered problems without assistance, is often equated with being "competent"—the launching point for acquiring the fluid, seamless, accurate, and flexible performance that is the hallmark of true expertise.

There has been considerable debate among educational psychologists and cognition specialists, much of it semantic in nature, about whether the desired graduate of professional education should be competent, proficient, or even possessing some aspects of expertise. How long it takes to acquire true expertise also has been the source of much debate among cognitive scientists. The most frequent answer to this question by many of the investigators referenced in this article is a conditional "five to ten years depending on many factors." These factors include the inherent difficulty of the skills the individual is attempting to acquire, the frequency of practice, opportunities for progressively increasing levels of challenge and responsibility in work after completion of formal school-based training, and the availability of a mentor to serve as a coach and role model.[3-4] Thus, for purpose of clarification, this article takes the "long view" of expertise over the entire development continuum and will focus on how to best prepare students to ultimately reach a level of expertise. All experts on expertise believe that the "seeds must be sown" during the in-school phase of professional education. Graduates from dental school will rarely have the capacity to function as true experts immediately upon graduation, but hopefully are competent entry-level performers who can provide the fundamental skills associated with general dentistry and are well on their way to achieving expertise with practice and refinement over the next several years.

Based on research from aeronautics, athletics, computer science, engineering, mathematics, phys-ics, the military, and industrial settings, cognitive psychologists have identified six components of expertise (see Figure 1). Components 1, 2, and 3 are developed by overt practice and do not simply develop spontaneously with maturation. Component 4 (rapidly accessible and problem-focused knowledge) can be developed with frequent practice in problem-solving simulations.[5-11] Components 5 and 6 are largely dependent on an individual's personality (composure and confidence) and may not be amenable to development through training although positive attributes can be reinforced and rewarded.

Figure 2 displays the characteristic behavior of novices and experts while trying to solve an ill-structured problem where the solution is not immediately obvious and the outcome is not certain. The primary goal of the dental curriculum is to facilitate students' transition from the left side of the figure, which represents classic novice approaches to problem solving, to the right side, which depicts the mental processes and behavior we hope will be ultimately instilled in our graduates.[12,13]

2. What Are the Differences Between Novice and Expert Thinking?

Advances in brain imaging technology such as positron emission tomography and functional magnetic resonance imaging have allowed neurophysiologists to investigate brain functions during cognitive, perceptual, and psychomotor tasks.[14-15] Based on these technological breakthroughs, obser-

1. Pattern recognition: ability to discern pertinent information (i.e., "connect the dots")

2. Anticipatory guidance: ability to think ahead and anticipate outcomes and problems

3. Ability to accurately reflect on performance and modify behavior to improve outcomes

4. Knowledge that is quickly retrievable, useful, and situation-specific

5. Ability to maintain personal composure so that emotions do not hinder decision making

6. Confidence to make decisions even when conditions are ambiguous and outcomes uncertain

Figure 1. Six components of expertise

Novice Behavior	Expert Behavior
Rule bound; tries to implement textbook approaches	Adapts to circumstances; not locked into one particular strategy
Slow and hesitant; lacks confidence in decisions	Fast and fluid; confident about decisions; optimistic
Looks for help or even "bails out"; overwhelmed by uncertainty and ambiguity of the situation	Takes charge and provides leadership even when situation is ambiguous and outcome uncertain
Cannot access pertinent knowledge quickly	Quickly retrieves needed knowledge by largely subconscious recall of pertinent information
Slow "trial and error" efforts to solve the problem using one approach at a time; slow to recognize when strategies are not working	Settles on "best course of action" after quick review of options but willing to change course quickly if results are not satisfactory
Singular: concentrates on own needs and own discomfort in ambiguous situation; inefficient; does not manage time or resources well	Multi-task: can simultaneously study the problem and also coordinate work of others
Focus: surface features of the problem	Focus: underlying problem source
Flawed thinking: • Premature closure—makes decisions too fast • Anchoring—stubbornly supports poor decisions • Faulty synthesis—2 + 2 = 6 • Ignores or doesn't recognize important data	Accurate: makes correct decisions Avoids flawed thinking

Figure 2. Characteristic behaviors of novices and experts during problem solving

vational studies that document the overt behaviors of neophytes and experienced practitioners during situations that require problem solving, and content analysis of the information-seeking steps and decision-making processes employed by trainees and practitioners, cognitive psychologists and educators have converged on a model of the way individuals structure and use information at different stages along the novice to expert continuum. Expert practitioners, represented by the right side of Figure 3, have integrated neural networks that facilitate instantaneous retrieval of chains of information relevant to task performance or problem assessment.[16-25] In contrast, novice learners, represented by the left side of Figure 3, struggle to assemble isolated bits of information, depicted by the symbols within the columns. Novices employ an inefficient trial and error approach because they lack pre-existing networks that allow fast retrieval of pertinent information. The student may have encyclopedic information (i.e., "book smarts"), but this information is compartmentalized and largely unlinked to other topics. To develop problem-solving ability, students must convert the unorganized static information (i.e., bits of data) they have "sponged" from textbooks and lectures into the interlinked chains of networked knowledge, defined as information that has meaning, value, and recognized utility and which an individual can explain in his or her own words.[21,26-28]

3. What Educational Best Practices Can Help Our Students Acquire Mental Capacities Associated with Expert Function?

Cognitive psychologists categorize "knowledge" into three areas: 1) declarative knowledge, 2) procedural knowledge, and 3) an ill-defined gray zone between declarative and procedural knowledge that includes the reasoning skills often described as critical thinking and problem solving. In the health professions, critical thinking and problem solving are often loosely defined as clinical reasoning, diagnostic thinking, or clinical judgment.

Declarative Knowledge

Declarative knowledge consists of two memory components. The first is explicit memory that individuals overtly retrieve by sending a message to the brain; this is thus called "dial-up" knowledge as in dialing a phone to send a message. Explicit memory includes memories that contain factual information such as names, places, dates, terminology, and past events an individual has personally experienced that may have emotional components.

For explicit (dial-up) knowledge, seven elements are associated with effective learning:[25,29-33]

1. Communication of learning objectives for each class session;

2. Organization of the subject matter in a manner that makes sense to the learner;
3. Frequent in-class activity such as writing notes, analyzing problems, or answering questions;
4. Use of mnemonics to aid memorization of factual information;
5. Frequent in-class quizzing with immediate feedback on response correctness;
6. Total amount of "time on task" including in-class activities and personal study time; and
7. Summary of key points to remember ("take-home messages") at the end of each lesson.

The second component of declarative knowledge is generalizable rules that guide an individual's behaviors. These rules are embedded in subconsciously retrieved memory, known as implicit memory, so that the guiding action happens automatically without overt thought, as implied by the phrase "functioning on automatic pilot."[11,17,25] Implicit memory is called pop-up memory because these guiding rules

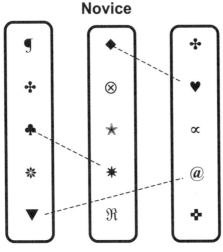

Novice

Vertical—compartmentalized

Lack of linkages requires inefficient trial and error search and slow retrieval

Data

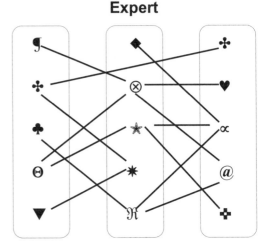

Expert

Horizontal—networked

Dense neural networking allows quick scan and rapid retrieval

Knowledge

Source: Hendricson WD, Kleffner JH. Assessing and helping challenging students: why do some students have difficulty learning? J Dent Educ 2002;66(1):43-61.

Figure 3. Information storage in novices' and experts' memory

literally "pop" into consciousness without active retrieval when cueing stimuli are detected. Implicit memory consists of past experiences that influence our current behavior—for example, memory of how a particularly tricky restoration was successfully handled on a previous patient. Implicit memories are subconsciously blended into our thought formation and are usually instantly available. Implicit memory includes most of the unique mental skills that are the hallmarks of expertise: subconscious pattern recognition based on an accumulation of prior exposures to the same stimuli, coping responses (previously successful actions that kick in when certain stimuli are encountered), alertness for signals that indicate a coming event, alertness for deviations from established patterns, and ability to anticipate future actions. The last three capacities are called anticipatory guidance.

Five strategies develop implicit (pop-up) memory:[17,32,34-37]

1. Simulations in which students apply decision making for both well-defined, frequently seen problems and ill-structured, rarely encountered problems;
2. Prospective simulations in which students practice anticipatory guidance by analyzing scenarios to predict likely problems and then develop coping strategies;
3. Retrospective critique of case scenarios in which actions are reviewed to identify errors as well as exemplary performance;
4. Self-assessment of performance in comparison to best practice benchmarks; and
5. Written or verbal reflection on the meaning of experiences, especially how to avoid errors.

Procedural knowledge is the "how to do things" component of memory and is divided into discrete (isolated action) performance and continuous action performance. A discrete procedure has definite start and stop points, predictable and easily measured outcomes, and a finite series of steps that do not tax the memory limits (i.e., three to seven steps). Continuous procedures involve an ongoing series of actions that need to be coordinated with continuous monitoring of the environment: driving a car, for example, or in dentistry, the precise placement and movement of a handpiece. Engagement of multiple senses to "read" the environment is critical in continuous procedures, and the metacognitive centers of the brain are critical to success. Metacognition is the process of internal self-review that allows an individual to assess "how things are going" and modify actions based on this personal critique.[38]

Six strategies help individuals develop procedural skills:[25,39-47]

1. Practice describing, visualizing, or drawing the desired end-product;
2. Comparing the desired outcome to examples of outcomes that are not acceptable;
3. Observing task performance by an expert who explains procedures as they are executed;
4. Frequent hands-on practice with prompting (i.e., tips) and correction by a coach;
5. Feedback that allows error correction early in the learning process; and
6. Analysis of their own work process and products to compare how their techniques and outcomes correspond to best practice standards.

Development of Problem-Solving and Critical Thinking Skills

Best practice strategies for helping students learn the reasoning skills of problem solving and critical thinking remain a source of conjecture, particularly with regard to critical thinking. Research in the health professions has been based on observations of novices and experts "in action," analysis of their respective decision-making steps and accuracy, assessment of dysfunctional behaviors during problem solving, and theoretical speculation about the cognitive mechanisms involved in clinical reasoning.[12,48-50] Most of this research has occurred in medicine and nursing where some findings suggest a linkage between critical thinking capacity and soundness of clinical judgment although the generalizability of these outcomes is limited by the nature of the assessment instruments as subsequently discussed.[51] The dental education literature is fundamentally devoid of research on the cognitive components of clinical decision making. However, research on these complex skills has been stronger in aeronautics, engineering, the mathematical sciences, and performance disciplines such as dance, music, and athletics; findings from these disciplines appear to translate to the decision making by health care providers.[52]

For clarification, critical thinking and problem solving are seen by cognitive psychologists as intertwined mental capacities, and many investigators have recently merged these two concepts into a single construct labeled by terms such as reflective judgment or deliberative assessment. Critical thinking is the reflective process in which individuals assess a situation or evaluate data by using mental capacities characterized by adjectives such as compare, analyze, distinguish, reflect, and judge. Halpern defined critical thinking as "an assessment process in which all assumptions are open to question, divergent views are sought and analyzed, and inquiry is not biased or directed by predetermined notions."[53] Kurfiss described critical thinking as "the rational response to questions that can't be answered definitively and for which all the relevant information may not be available."[54] Michael Scriven and Richard Paul of the National Council for Excellence in Critical Thinking Instruction describe a "critical thinker" as an individual who

- raises questions and problems, formulating them clearly and precisely,
- gathers and assesses relevant information,
- comes to well-reasoned conclusions and then tests them against relevant standards,
- thinks open-mindedly about alternative systems of thought or alternative perspectives, and assesses their assumptions, implications, and practical consequences, and
- communicates effectively with others in determining solutions to complex problems.[55]

Critical thinking clearly underlies the components of expertise described in Figures 1-3.

The noted educator and psychologist Benjamin Bloom said that critical thinking "is the opposite of making judgments based on unexamined assumptions or untested hypotheses."[56] Much of the research on critical thinking has focused on the willingness and disposition of individuals to engage in reflective and analytical thought. Dewey observed that "possession of knowledge is no guarantee for the ability to think well—an individual must desire to think."[57] Cultivating a disposition to think critically appears to be a key component in developing the thought processes and approach to problem solving that constitutes "expertise."[58] A panel of experts on critical thinking commissioned by the American Philosophical Association identified the following dispositions as essential for critical thinking: inquisitiveness, open-mindedness, willingness to be systematic and thorough when exploring problems, capacity and willingness to be analytical when considering evidence, desire to seek truth including asking difficult or troublesome questions that challenge assumptions or conventional wisdom, willingness to continue inquiries even if outcomes do not support one's self-interests or preconceived opinions, willingness to trust the soundness of one's reasoned judgments after review of the evidence, and maturity, which includes recognition that many problems are ill structured and difficult to assess, responses may have to be

implemented without complete certainty, and there may be more than one best response.[59] Because of the strong personality component underlying these dispositions, there is debate among critical thinking experts about the degree to which these traits can be cultivated in students if they are not already present at the time of admission to the academic program. In addition, questions have been raised about the capacity of available critical thinking measurement instruments to assess the type of clinical reasoning required by health care providers. Concerns also have been raised about the psychometric properties of commonly used critical thinking inventories such as the Watson Glaser Critical Thinking Appraisal and the Cornell Critical Thinking Test, which are narrow in scope, measure thinking about well-structured problems, and do not meet the Standards for Educational and Psychological Testing set by the American Psychological Association.[60]

Problem-solving is the "action-end" or implementation component of the overall critical thinking process—in other words, "where the rubber meets the road." John Dewey originally described the components of the deliberative assessment process that encompasses the intertwining of critical thinking and problem solving in 1933, and this process, represented in Figure 4, still underlies the reflective judgment process advocated in many disciplines including the health professions.[8,49,61,62]

The capacity for self-directed learning (SDL) is required to implement the reflective judgment process and underlies many of the dispositions needed for critical thinking. SDL is the ability to direct and regulate one's own learning experience.[63,64] Essentially the same educational strategies have been proposed to develop critical thinking and self-directed learning. These best practices include providing students with frequent opportunities to use the reflective judgment process described in Figure 4 to analyze problems presented in case scenarios or during the elaborate simulations employed by the aeronautics industry and the military.[65-68] The data seeking and analysis required to accomplish the reflective judgment process are thought to help students acquire SDL skills in a "learn by doing" approach, and there is evidence that students who routinely use this process to explore problems develop more sophisticated SDL than do students in lecture-based curricula.[69] Implementation of this reflective judgment process with emphasis on student-directed exploration of the literature represents the core elements of problem-based learning, which has been employed widely as a curriculum

- Identify the issues and facts in a problem or dilemma.

- Identify and explore causal factors.

- Retrieve and assess knowledge needed to appraise response options and guide actions.

- Compare the strengths and limitations of options.

- Skillfully implement the option most likely to resolve the problem.

- Monitor implementation and outcomes and modify the strategy/action as needed.

- Candidly appraise the outcomes of actions, both positively and negatively.

Figure 4. Reflective judgment process involved in problem analysis and resolution

model in medical and nursing education with generally positive acceptance by faculty and students, but to a much lesser extent in dental education.[70,71]

In addition to simulation-driven learning experiences that require application of the reflective judgment process, four additional educational strategies have been associated with enhancement of critical thinking skills:[25,51,54,72]

1. Frequent use of questions by instructors that require students to analyze problem etiology, compare alternative approaches, provide rationales for plans of action, and predict outcomes;

2. Listening to the reasoning of expert practitioners as they "talk through" their approaches to analyzing and solving problems;

3. Comparing data searching steps, strategies implemented, decisions made, and outcomes to that of expert practitioners who work through the same case scenario; and

4. Writing assignments that request students to analyze problems by discussing theories about causal factors, compare alternative solutions, and defend decisions about proposed actions.

Research on strategies to develop health professions students' critical thinking skills has been hindered by lack of valid assessment instruments that measure the type of reasoning skills needed during provision of health care services, in which problems are often ill structured with numerous confounding factors.[73] While many health professions educators are concerned about the lack of viable critical thinking assessment instruments, there is a long-standing tradition, especially strong in medicine, that the "collective wisdom" of the faculty is an adequate data source for assessment of a trainee's clinical acumen

and diagnostic reasoning.[27,28,36,49,62] This assumption is based on the existence of the following conditions: 1) faculty have opportunity to observe and interact with the trainee on multiple occasions over an extended period of time and across a variety of patient care situations and problems; 2) faculty can assess the depth of knowledge and underlying logic, typically via questioning, that guides the trainee's reasoning and decision making; 3) faculty have opportunities to compare their impressions of the trainee with other instructors to reach a comprehensive or global evaluation; and 4) several counterbalancing types of data are collected, including performance on "competency" patients, written examinations, problem-solving simulations, and assessment of the trainee's professionalism.[74-76] Health professions educators who have studied evaluation of learner performance in clinical settings have mixed opinions about the extent to which these conditions occur and the resulting accuracy of faculty evaluations.[77,78] For example, a recent study of dental students' perceptions of their clinical education experiences involving twenty-three U.S. and Canadian schools indicated that inconsistent and "unfair" evaluation was their primary criticism about dental school.[79] However, on the positive side, the Self-Directed Learning Readiness Scale (SDLRS) by Guglielmino has been used effectively in health professions education to measure students' SDL and to track longitudinal changes.[80,81]

Putting It All Together

Dr. Vimla Patel, director of the Decision Making and Cognition Laboratory in the Department of

Biomedical Informatics at Columbia University, has studied clinical reasoning and decision-making processes in health professions education for more than twenty-five years. Patel has reported the results of dozens of studies that investigated the thinking processes and information-seeking strategies of trainees and practicing health care professionals across a variety of medical problems and settings, including the public health arena, using sophisticated semantic and content analysis techniques employed in the disciplines of literary analysis, artificial intelligence, and cognitive science. A selected bibliography of ten of Patel's more than 100 publications in cognitive science and health professions education are indicated by references 27 and 82-91 including three studies recently published in the *Journal of Dental Education*.[27,82-91] Patel's body of research provides a reasonable best practices summary related to designing curriculum for the intertwined concepts of critical thinking and problem solving that lie between the more easily studied realms of declarative and procedural knowledge. Patel's findings can be summarized in two statements:

1. An effective process for development of the mental skills associated with clinical reasoning blends: a) initial acquisition of factual foundation knowledge (i.e., explicit, dial-up memory) in a traditional format that requires extensive reading of the literature and consistently employs in-class activity such as writing notes, analyzing problems, answering instructors' questions, and drill and practice testing, with b) case-based or issue-based seminars that allow students to clarify misconceptions and gain insight into the practical utility of foundation concepts by trying to apply them to problems. The case seminar component of a blended curriculum also allows trainees to have close contact and communication with faculty and practitioners, which provides opportunities for the modeling of expert thinking that appears to be a critical component of novice to expert maturation.

2. Trainees educated in the blended format described above do not make more accurate decisions than individuals trained in a purely classroom-based program, but they sample a wider variety of data sources, seek information from higher-quality and more desirable sources, have better understanding of the pathophysiological mechanisms (etiology) underlying diseases, and provide more sophisticated rationales and explanations for their decisions.

Conclusion

In one of his dialogues known as "Euthyphro," Plato described Socrates' method of teaching in which questions were posed to students and the students were forced to use their insight and logical reasoning to reach a conclusion, a technique that Plato described as conversational interaction.[92] Consistent with the perspectives of Socrates 2500 years ago, a review of the evidence indicates that several active learning strategies described in this article are associated with the development of the mental capacities needed for the expert practice of dentistry. These practices include:

1. In-class activity such as writing notes, analyzing problems, or reviewing cases that provide opportunities to apply the information being communicated;

2. Use of questions by instructors that require students to analyze problem etiology, compare alternative approaches, provide rationales for plans of action, and predict outcomes;

3. Frequent in-class quizzing with immediate feedback on response correctness;

4. Prospective simulations in which students perform decision making for structured and ill-structured problems;

5. Retrospective critique of cases in which decisions are reviewed to identify errors as well as exemplary performance;

6. Writing assignments that request students to analyze problems and discuss alternative theories about etiology, compare solutions, and defend decisions about proposed actions; and

7. Analyzing work products to compare how outcomes correspond to the best practice standards, including comparing the results of students' reasoning about problems to those of experts.

REFERENCES

1. Peden-McAlpine C. Expert thinking in nursing practice: implications for supporting expertise. Nurs Health Sci 1999;1:131-9.
2. Dreyfus HL, Dreyfus SE. Mind over machine: the power of human intuition and expertise in the era of the computer. New York: Free Press, 1986.
3. Olesen V. Employing competence-based education for the reform of professional practice. In: Grant G, ed. On competence: a critical analysis of competence-based reforms in higher education. Washington, DC: Jossey-Bass, 1979.
4. Hendricson WD, Kleffner JH. Curricular and instructional implications of competency-based dental education. J Dent Educ 1998;62:183-96.

5. Kahneman D, Slovic P, Terversky A, eds. Judgment under uncertainty: heuristics and biases. New York: Cambridge University Press, 1982.

6. Benner P. From novice to expert: excellence and power in clinical nursing practice. Menlo Park, CA: Addison Wesley, 1984.

7. Chi MT, Glaser R, Farr MG. The nature of expertise. Hillsdale, NJ: Lawrence Erlbaum, 1988.

8. Csikszentmihalyi M. The psychology of optimal experience. New York: Harper Perennial, 1990.

9. Ericsson KA, Kampe RT. The role of deliberate practice in the acquisition of expert performance. Psychol Rev 1993;100:363-406.

10. Ericsson KA, Charness N. Expert performance: its structure and acquisition. Am Psychol 1994;49:725-47.

11. Ericsson KA. The road to excellence: acquisition of expert performance in the arts, sciences, sports, and game. Mahwah, NJ: Erlbaum, 1996.

12. Elstein AS, Shulman LS, Sprafka SA. Medical problem solving: an analysis of clinical reasoning. Cambridge: Harvard University Press, 1978.

13. Mellers BA, Scgwartz A, Cooke ADJ. Judgment and decision making. Ann Review Psychol 1998;49:447-77.

14. Harrier RJ, Siegel BV, et al. Regional glucose metabolic changes after learning a complex visual-spatial/motor task: a positron emission tomographic study. Brain Research 1992;570:134-43.

15. Nyberg L, Persson J, Habib R, Tulving E, et al. Large scale neurocognitive networks underlying episodic memory. J Cognitive Neuroscience 2000;12:163-73.

16. Jensen E. Teaching with the brain in mind. Alexandria, VA: ASCD Press, 1998.

17. Bransford JD, Brown AL, Cocking RR, eds. How people learn: brain, mind, experience and school. Washington, DC: National Academy Press, 1999.

18. Rolls ET. Memory systems in the brain. Annu Rev Psychol 2000;51:599-630.

19. Hoffman RR. The psychology of expertise: cognitive research and empirical AI. New York: Springer-Verlag, 1991.

20. Robertson L. Memory and the brain. J Dent Educ 2002;66(1):30-42.

21. Hendricson WD, Kleffner JH. Assessing and helping challenging students: why do some students have difficulty learning? J Dent Educ 2002;66(1):43-61.

22. Horton DL, Mills CB. Human learning and memory. Annu Rev Psychol 1984;35:361-94.

23. Regehr G, Norman GR. Issues in cognitive psychology: implications for professional education. Acad Med 1996;71:988-1001.

24. Eichenbaum H, Cahill LF, Gluck MA, et al. Learning and memory: systems analysis. In: Zigmond MJ, Bloom FE, Landis SC, Roberts JL, Squire LR, eds. Fundamental neuroscience. San Diego: Academic Press, 1999.

25. Druckman D, Bjork RA, eds. In the mind's eye: enhancing human performance. Washington, DC: National Academy Press, 1991.

26. Anderson RB. Rationale and non-rational aspects of forgetting. In: Oaksford M, Chater N, eds. Rational models of cognition. Oxford: Oxford University Press, 1998: 156-64.

27. Patel VL, Groen G. Knowledge-based strategies in medical reasoning. Cognit Sci 1986;10:91-116.

28. Hunink M, Glasziou P, Siegel J, Weeks J, Pliskin J, Elstein AS. Decision making in health and medicine: integrating evidence and values. New York: Cambridge University Press, 2001.

29. Norman GR, Schmidt HG. The psychological basis of problem-based learning: a review of the evidence. Acad Med 1992;67:557-65.

30. Shiffrin R, Schneider W. Controlled and automatic human information processing: perceptual learning, automatic attending, and general theory. Psychol Rev 1977;84: 127-90.

31. Resnick LB, ed. Knowing, learning, and instruction. Hillsdale, NJ: Lawrence Erlbaum Associates, 1989.

32. Gruppen LD. Implications of cognitive research for ambulatory care education. Acad Med 1997;72:117-20.

33. Aiken E, Thomas G, Shennum W. Memory for a lecture: effects of notes, lecture rate, and information density. J Educ Psychol 1975;67:439-44.

34. Anderson J, ed. Cognitive skills and their acquisition. Hillsdale, NJ: Lawrence Erlbaum Associates, 1981.

35. Schneider W. Training high performance skills: fallacies and guidelines. Hum Factors 1985;27:285-300.

36. Kassirer JP, Kopelman RI. Learning clinical reasoning. Baltimore: Williams and Wilkins, 1991.

37. Elstein AS, Schwartz A. Clinical problem solving and diagnostic decision making: selective review of the cognitive literature. Br Med J 2002;324:729-32.

38. Maki RH, Jonas D, Kallod M. The relationship between comprehension and metacomprehension ability. Psychonomic Bull Rev 1994;1:126-9.

39. Fischman MG, Christina RW, Vercruyssen MJ. Retention and transfer of motor skills: a review for the practitioner. Quest 1982;33:181-94.

40. Hagman JD, Rose AM. Retention of military skills: a review. Hum Factors 1983;25:199-213.

41. Schendel JD, Hagman JD. On sustaining procedural skills over a prolonged retention interval. J Appl Psychol 1982;67:605-10.

42. Johnson P. The acquisition of skill. In: Smyth MM, Wing AM, eds. The psychology of human movement. London: Academic Press, 1984.

43. Kieras DE, Boviar S. The role of mental modeling in learning how to operate a devise. Cognit Sci 1984;8:255-73.

44. Loftus GR. Evaluating forgetting curves. J Exper Psychol Learn Mem Cogn 1985;11:397-406.

45. Smith E, Goodman L. Understanding instructions: the role of explanatory material. Cognition and Instruction 1984;1:359-96.

46. Schmidt RA. Summary: knowledge of results of skill acquisition—support for the guidance hypothesis. J Exper Psychol Learn Mem Cogn 1989;15:352-9.

47. Newell A, Rosenbloom PS. Mechanism of skill acquisition and the law of practice. In: Anderson JR, ed. Cognitive skills and their acquisition. Hillsdale, NJ: Lawrence Erlbaum Associates, 1981:1-55.

48. Schön DA. The reflective practitioner. New York: Basic Books, 1983.

49. Chapman GB, Sonnenberg F, eds. Decision making in health care: theory, psychology, and applications. New York: Cambridge University Press, 2000.

50. Schmidt HG, Norman GR, Boshuizen HPA. A cognitive perspective on medical expertise: theory and implications. Acad Med 1990;65:611-21.

51. Chenoweth L. Facilitating the process of critical thinking for nursing. Nurse Educ Today 1998;18:281-92.

52. Tsui L. A review of research on critical thinking. ASHE annual meeting paper. Annual meeting of the Association for the Study of Higher Education, Miami, FL, 1998. ERIC Document Reproduction Service No. ED 391 429.

53. Halpern DF. Thought and knowledge: an introduction to critical thinking. Hillsdale, NJ: Lawrence Erlbaum, 1989.

54. Kurfiss JG. Critical thinking: theory, research, practice, and possibilities. ASHE ERIC Higher Education Report, Number 2. Washington, DC: Association for the Study of Higher Education, 1988.

55. Scriven M, Paul R. Defining critical thinking. At: www.criticalthinking.org/aboutCT/defining CT.html. Accessed: April 27, 2006.

56. Bloom BS, Englehart MD, Furst EJ, Hill WH, Krathwohl DR. Taxonomy of educational objectives, handbook 1: cognitive domain. New York: Longmans, 1956.

57. Dewey J. Democracy and education: an introduction to the philosophy of education, rev. ed. New York: Free Press, 1997.

58. Walker SE. Active learning strategies to promote critical thinking. J Athletic Training 2003;38(3):263-7.

59. Facione PA, Giancarlo CA, Fancione NC, Gainen J. The disposition towards critical thinking. J Gen Educ 1995;44:1-16.

60. Williams KB, Schmidt C, Tilliss TSI, Wilkins K, Glasnapp DR. Predictive validity of critical thinking skills and disposition for the national board dental hygiene examination: a preliminary investigation. J Dent Educ 2006;70:536-44.

61. Mast TJ, Davis D. Concepts of competence. In: Mast TJ, David D, eds. The physician as learner. Chicago: American Medical Association, 1994:139-56.

62. Bordage G, Lemieux M. Semantic structures and diagnostic thinking of novices and experts. Acad Med 1991;66:S70-S72.

63. Candy PC. Self-direction for lifelong learning: a comprehensive guide to theory and practice. San Francisco: Jossey-Bass, 1991.

64. Brookfield S. Self-directed learning, political clarity, and the critical practice of adult education. Adult Educ Quarterly 1993;43:227-42.

65. Meyers C. Teaching students to think critically. San Francisco: Jossey-Bass, 1986.

66. Chafee J. Critical thinking skills: the cornerstone of development education. J Dev Educ 1992;15:2-39.

67. King PM, Kitchener KS. Developing reflective judgment: understanding and promoting intellectual growth and critical thinking in adolescents and adults. San Francisco: Jossey-Bass, 1994.

68. Adams BL. Nursing education for critical thinking: an integrative review. J Nurs Educ 1999;38(3):111-9.

69. Blumberg P. Evaluating the evidence that problem-based learners are self-directed learners: a review of the literature. In: Evensen DH, Hmelo CE, eds. Problem-based learning: a research perspective on learning interactions. Mahwah, NJ: Lawrence Erlbaum Associates, 2000: 199-226.

70. Hendricson WD, Cohen PA. Oral health in the 21st century: implications for dental and medical education. Acad Med 2001;76(12):1181-207.

71. Kassebaum D, Hendricson WD, Taft T, Haden K. The dental curriculum at North American dental institutions in 2002-03: a survey of current structure, recent innovations, and planned changes. J Dent Educ 2004;67(9):914-31.

72. Collins A, Seely-Brown J, Newman S. Cognitive apprenticeship: teaching the crafts of reading, writing, and mathematics. In: Resnick LB, ed. Knowing, learning, and instruction. Hillsdale, NJ: Lawrence Erlbaum Associates, 1989:460-76.

73. National Postsecondary Education Cooperative. The NPEC sourcebook on assessment. Volume 1: definitions and assessment methods for critical thinking, problem solving, and writing. Washington, DC: U.S. Department of Education, National Center for Education Statistics, 2000.

74. Lloyd JS, Langsley DG, eds. How to evaluate residents. Chicago: American Board of Medical Specialties, 1986.

75. McGaghie WC. Evaluating competence for professional practice. In: Curry L, Wergin JF, eds. Educating professionals. San Francisco: Jossey-Bass Publishers, 1993.

76. Chambers DW, Glassman P. A primer on competency-based evaluation. J Dent Educ 1997;61:651-66.

77. Berrong JM, Buchanan RN, Hendricson WD. Evaluation of practical clinical examinations. J Dent Educ 1983;47:656-63.

78. Hunt DD. Functional and dysfunctional characteristics of the prevailing model of clinical evaluation systems in North American medical schools. Acad Med 1996;71: S55-S63.

79. Henzi D, Jasinevicius R, Davis E, Cintron L, Isaacs M, Hendricson WD. What are dental students' perspectives about their clinical education? J Dent Educ 2006;69: 361-77.

80. McCune SK, Guglielmino LM, Garcia G. Adult self-direction in learning: a preliminary meta-analytic investigation of research using the Self Directed Learning Readiness Scale. In: Long HB, ed. Advances in self-directed learning research. Norman: Oklahoma Research Center for Continuing Professional and Higher Education, 1990: 145-56.

81. Shokar GS, Shokar NK, Romero CM, Bulik RJ. Self-directed learning: looking at outcomes with medical students. Fam Med 2002;34(3):197-200.

82. Patel VL, Cranton PA. Transfer of student learning in medical education. Acad Med 1983;58:126-35.

83. Coughlin LD, Patel VL. Processing of critical information by physicians and medical students. Acad Med 1987;62:818-28.

84. Patel VL, Groen GJ, Norman GR. Effects of conventional and problem-based medical curricula on problem solving. Acad Med 1991;66:380-9.

85. Patel VL, Groen GJ, Norman GR. Reasoning and instruction in medical curricula. Cognition and Instruction 1993;10:335-78.

86. Patel VL, Groen CJ, Patel YC. Cognitive aspects of clinical performance during patient workup: the role of medical expertise. Adv Health Sci Educ Theory Pract 1997;2: 95-114.

87. Patel VL, Glaser R, Arocha JF. Cognition and expertise: acquisition of medical competence. Clin Invest Med 2000;23:248-80.

88. Patel VL, Arocha J, Lecissi M. Impact of undergraduate medical training on housestaff problem solving performance: implications for health education in problem-based curricula. J Dent Educ 2001;65:1199-218.

89. Patel VL, Kaufman DR, Arocha JF. Emerging paradigms of cognition in medical decision making. J Biomed Inform 2002;35:52-75.

90. Patel VL, Arocha JF, Branch T, Karlin DR. Relationship between small group problem-solving activity and lectures in health science curricula. J Dent Educ 2004;68: 1058-80.

91. Patel VL, Arocha JF, Chaudhari S, Karlin DR, Briedis DJ. Knowledge integration and reasoning as a function of instruction in a hybrid medical curriculum. J Dent Educ 2005;69:1186-211.

92. Rouse WHD, trans. Great dialogues of Plato. New York: Signet, 1999.

The Dental Education Environment

ADEA Commission on Change and Innovation in Dental Education: N. Karl Haden, Ph.D.; Sandra C. Andrieu, Ph.D.; D. Gregory Chadwick, D.D.S.; Jacqueline E. Chmar, B.A.; James R. Cole, D.D.S.; Mary C. George, R.D.H., M.Ed.; Gerald N. Glickman, D.D.S., M.S.; Joel F. Glover, D.D.S.; Jerold S. Goldberg, D.D.S.; William D. Hendricson, M.A., M.S.; Cyril Meyerowitz, B.D.S., M.S.; Laura Neumann, D.D.S.; Marsha Pyle, D.D.S., M.Ed.; Lisa A. Tedesco, Ph.D.; Richard W. Valachovic, D.M.D., M.P.H.; Richard G. Weaver, D.D.S.; Ronald L. Winder, D.D.S.; Stephen K. Young, D.D.S.; Kenneth L. Kalkwarf, D.D.S., M.S.

Abstract: The second in a series of perspectives from the ADEA Commission on Change and Innovation in Dental Education (CCI), this article presents the CCI's view of the dental education environment necessary for effective change. The article states that the CCI's purpose is related to leading and building consensus in the dental community to foster a continuous process of innovative change in the education of general dentists. Principles proposed by CCI to shape the dental education environment are described; these are critical thinking, lifelong learning, humanistic environment, scientific discovery and integration of knowledge, evidence-based oral health care, assessment, faculty development, and the health care team. The article also describes influences external to the academic dental institutions that are important for change and argues that meaningful and long-lasting change must be systemic in nature. The CCI is ADEA's primary means to engage all stakeholders for the purpose of educating lifelong learners to provide evidence-based care to meet the needs of society.

Dr. Haden is President, Academy for Academic Leadership; Dr. Andrieu is Associate Dean for Academic Affairs, Louisiana State University School of Dentistry; Dr. Chadwick is Associate Vice Chancellor for Oral Health, East Carolina University; Ms. Chmar is Policy Analyst, American Dental Education Association; Dr. Cole is a member of the Commission on Dental Accreditation; Prof. George is Associate Professor, Department of Dental Ecology, University of North Carolina School of Dentistry; Dr. Glickman is Chair, Endodontics, Baylor College of Dentistry; Dr. Glover is a member of the Board of Trustees, American Dental Association; Dr. Goldberg is Dean, Case School of Dental Medicine; Mr. Hendricson is Assistant Dean, Educational and Faculty Development, University of Texas Health Science Center at San Antonio Dental School; Dr. Meyerowitz is Director, Eastman Dental Center, University of Rochester School of Medicine and Dentistry; Dr. Neumann is Associate Executive Director for Education, American Dental Association; Dr. Pyle is Associate Dean for Education, Case School of Dental Medicine; Dr. Tedesco is Vice Provost for Academic Affairs in Graduate Studies and Dean, Graduate School, Emory University; Dr. Valachovic is Executive Director, American Dental Education Association; Dr. Weaver is Acting Director, Center for Educational Policy and Research, American Dental Education Association; Dr. Winder is a former member of the Joint Commission on National Dental Examinations; Dr. Young is Dean, College of Dentistry, University of Oklahoma; and Dr. Kalkwarf is Chair of the Commission on Change and Innovation in Dental Education, President of the American Dental Education Association, and Dean of the University of Texas Health Science Center at San Antonio Dental School. Direct correspondence to Dr. Karl Haden, President, Academy for Academic Leadership, 1870 The Exchange, Suite 100, Atlanta, GA 30339; 404-350-2098 phone; khaden@academicleaders.org. Reprints of this article will not be available.

In the September 2006 *Journal of Dental Education*, the American Dental Education Association (ADEA)'s Commission on Change and Innovation in Dental Education (CCI) published a Perspectives article on "the case for change."[1] In the same issue, the CCI issued a white paper on educational strategies associated with the development of problem-solving, critical thinking, and self-directed learning.[2] In October 2006, the CCI released a draft of "Competencies for the New General Dentist," with a call for comments from ADEA members.[3] These competencies, when completed based on input from a variety of stakeholders, will serve as a benchmark for dental schools, National Boards, and accreditation standards for curriculum design, designation of knowledge and skills to be mastered by dental students, and construction of assessments to measure acquisition of entry-level general dentistry skills. In this Perspectives article, the CCI delineates its vision, its values, and the principles it considers essential to frame the kind of dental education environment of the future that will allow dental students to acquire the competency needed to serve the oral health needs of the public.

The CCI's purpose is to build consensus within the dental community by providing leadership and oversight to a systemic, collaborative, and continuous process of innovative change in the education of general dentists so that they enter the profession competent to meet the oral health needs of the public throughout the twenty-first century and to function as an important member of an efficient and effective health care team. The CCI recognizes that a variety of factors influence the curriculum at each dental school. Among these factors are expectations of the parent institution, standing or emerging research foci, strengths among specialty education programs, approaches to clinical education, and pedagogical philosophies and practices. All U.S. dental schools are fully accredited by the Commission on Dental Accreditation. The accreditation process recognizes legitimate differences among schools in the priority they place on biomedical, clinical, and behavioral sciences. While the CCI holds that diversity of curricula is a strength, the commission believes that certain principles create the best environment for change and innovation.

Principles to Shape the Dental Education Environment

Professions exist to serve the needs of society, communities, and individuals who become patients or clients in a variety of settings. The dental profession's continuing service to society is safeguarded by academic dental institutions that recruit, educate, and develop the future members of the profession: practitioners, educators, researchers, administrators, and the leaders of organized dentistry. If dental educators are to meet these purposes, change and innovation in dental education must be responsive to evolving societal needs, practice patterns, scientific developments, and economic conditions. Academic dental institutions must prepare students to enter the practice of dentistry as professionals, informed citizens, and enlightened leaders in a changing health care system.

The most serious issue facing health care today, including oral health care, is providing care for an increasing population of unserved, underserved, and uninsured patients who lack access to oral health care and face rising health care costs. At the same time, scientific advances, particularly in genetics and molecular biology, presage the emergence of new modalities of patient care. These two issues under-

score not only the importance of basic biomedical and clinical sciences in the curriculum, but also the place of economics, social sciences, and ethics. In becoming professionals, students must learn to think about a wide variety of issues to which the profession is responsible and to act for the good of society and a broad diversity of individuals who will likely become their patients. Thus, dental curricula must emphasize the acquisition of relevant knowledge, inculcate values and attitudes, and develop learning skills that will be used throughout the professional lives of its graduates. The CCI holds that the following principles should characterize the educational environment and inform dental curricula.

Critical Thinking: Cornerstone of the Dental Education Experience

Critical thinking is the one thread that weaves together the many complex educational experiences of students. Through a process of integration, reflection, and examination and analysis, students develop foundations for curiosity, an understanding of the value of science as it applies to clinical practice, and the desire and motivation for lifelong learning to contribute to the profession's place in society and its standing in the health care team.

Critical thinking is "the intellectually disciplined process of actively and skillfully conceptualizing, applying, analyzing, synthesizing, and/or evaluating information gathered from, or generated by, observation, experience, reflection, reasoning, or communication, as a guide to belief and action."[4] Because critical thinking involves a special way of gathering and considering information and responding, it is different from the mere acquisition of information or possession of a set of skills. Scriven and Paul describe the mature critical thinker as one who:

- raises vital questions and problems, formulating them clearly and precisely;
- gathers and assesses relevant information, using abstract ideas to interpret it effectively and come to well-reasoned conclusions and solutions, testing them against evidence, criteria, and standards;
- thinks with an open mind within alternative systems of thought, recognizing and assessing assumptions, implications, and consequences; and
- communicates effectively with others in determining solutions to complex problems.[4]

Critical thinking is foundational to teaching and learning any subject. An educational environment characterized by the discipline of critical thinking develops self-directed, self-disciplined, self-aware, and self-corrective learners. Dental faculty must model critical thinking not only in their pedagogy—what and how they teach—but also in their learning. With critical thinking as a guiding theme, the CCI proposes these additional principles for the continuous process of curriculum renewal in dental education.

Lifelong and Self-Directed Learning

Traditionally, dental curricula have been constructed so that students learn all current scientific and clinical content during dental school. Over time, with new discoveries and applications, students must work harder, faster, and longer if they do not want to neglect content deemed important by the faculty. Combine this situation with the reality that most students enter dental school as dependent learners, that is, dependent on the teacher to impart information while de-emphasizing the responsibility of the students to learn on their own. Traditional pedagogy in dental education focuses on the ability of students to memorize facts. These conditions result in a learning environment characterized by an overcrowded curriculum that is unevenly contemporary, one that tends to stultify, constrain, and inhibit self-directed learning.

As a corollary to critical thinking, dental curricula must help students learn how to learn. Academic dental institutions must break from the traditional teacher-centered and discipline-focused pedagogy to shift the burden of learning to the student. As the student progresses through dental school, he or she should progress from a dependent learner to an independent learner. Curricula must be contemporary, appropriately complex, and designed to encourage students to take responsibility for their learning. One might argue that attitudes and skills in learning and practice are just as important, perhaps more important, than the acquisition of technical knowledge during the four years of dental school. The explosion of scientific knowledge makes it impossible for students to comprehend and retain all the information necessary for a lifetime of practice during the four years of the dental school curriculum. Students must "learn how to learn," and faculty must serve as role models who understand and value scientific discovery.

Humanistic Environment

Academic dental institutions are societies of learners. Dental students will graduate and join a learned and, ideally, a learning society of oral health professionals. A humanistic pedagogy is one that inculcates respect, tolerance, understanding, and concern for others. When faculty and students exhibit humanistic values, there is freedom to explore, to take appropriate risks, and to learn without intimidation. A humanistic approach is characterized by close professional relationships between faculty and students, fostered by mentoring, advising, and small group interaction. Students who are respected learn to respect their patients, both present and future, as living human beings, as individuals with a diversity of backgrounds, life experiences, and values. A humanistic environment establishes a context for the development of interpersonal skills necessary for learning, for patient care, and for making meaningful contributions to the profession.

Scientific Discovery and the Integration of Knowledge

Academic dental institutions play an inexorable role in developing new knowledge, transferring that knowledge for the improvement of the oral, craniofacial, and systemic health of the public, and educating the next generations of researchers and scholars. The interrelationship among basic, behavioral, and clinical sciences is a conceptual cornerstone to clinical competence. The CCI recognizes that basic and behavioral science integrated with clinical practice is essential in the preparation of the new general dentist so that he or she can solve patients' problems and incorporate new concepts and therapies over lifetime careers. Advances in genetics and molecular biology promise to change the health care system in significant ways—probably within the lifetime of today's dental school graduates.

Learning should occur in the context of real problems rather than within singular content-specific disciplines. Learning objectives that cut across traditional disciplines and inform the expected competencies of graduates are important components to curricular design. As schools seek to decompress curricula by removing extraneous subject matter, any displacements of basic science should be counterbalanced by integrating basic science with clinical science. Beyond the acquisition of scientific knowledge at a particular point in time, the capacity to think scientifically—to apply the scientific method—is pivotal if students are to analyze and solve oral health problems, understand research, and practice evidence-based dentistry. Included in the commitment to science, scientific values, contemporary curricula, and integration of knowledge are the recognition and action needed to reconstitute and represent the social and behavioral sciences in a substantive and visible manner. The behavioral and social sciences create a true intersection for professional practice that is humanistic, scientific, and ultimately patient-centered.

Evidence-Based Oral Health Care

The American Dental Association (ADA) defines evidence-based dentistry (EBD) as an approach to oral health care that requires the judicious integration of systematic assessments of clinically relevant scientific evidence, relating to the patient's oral and medical condition and history, with the dentist's clinical expertise and the patient's treatment needs and preferences.[5] EBD is based on using thorough, unbiased reviews and critical appraisal of the best available scientific evidence in combination with clinical and patient factors to make informed decisions about appropriate health care for specific clinical circumstances. EBD relies on the role of individual professional judgment in this process. The content of dental curricula should be based on the principles of evidence-based inquiry; faculty should practice EBD and model critical appraisal for students in dental school clinics; as scholars, faculty should contribute to the body of evidence supporting oral health care strategies by conducting research to determine best practices; and students should learn and practice critical appraisal of research evidence while they are in dental school.

Assessment

The effectiveness of educational principles and pedagogical practices becomes known when student learning is assessed. Academic dental institutions should conduct regular assessments of students' learning throughout their educational experience. Such assessment should not only focus on whether the student has achieved the competencies necessary to advance professionally (summative assessment), but should also assist learners throughout their educational experience in developing the knowledge, skills, attitudes, and values considered important at their stage of learning (formative assessment). In an environment as described above, where critical thinking and humanistic values are prominent, students are encouraged to self-assess. Self-assessment is indicative of the extent to which students take responsibility for their own learning.

Successful assessment not only improves student learning; it is basic to curriculum management. As a means to improve curricula, assessment involves a dialogue between and among faculty, students, and administrators. Based on the assumption that the society of learners—faculty and students at an institution—is responsible for its outcomes, evaluation of the curriculum is a process in which both faculty and students should engage. Hence, students have roles to play on committees and in other groups that discuss, design, and modify curricula. Meaningful feedback occurs best when it is ongoing rather than a definitive evaluation at the conclusion of a course. Continuous improvement occurs only when both methods and outcomes are continuously assessed.

Faculty Development

Faculty development is not optional—it is a necessary condition for change and innovation in dental education. The environment of higher education is changing dramatically and, with it, health professions education. New dental faculty face challenges that are different from their predecessors': significant student debt and a growing gap between academic and private practice incomes; more diverse students; an explosion of knowledge and information made available through new technologies; more rapid emergence of science, such as molecular biology, which promises to change the practice of dentistry within their lifetimes; greater public accountability; more use of part-time and non-tenure track faculty; and increasing expectations that threaten to undermine the quality of faculty work-life. A subsequent CCI article will address specific issues related to faculty work-life, but among the considerations that must be considered are curricula that remain teacher-centered rather than learner-centered. As stated in a recent study of higher education, "The present educational system of courses, credits, and calendar-based systems of teaching and learning focuses by its very nature solely on how *faculty* work. As a result, all attempts to achieve efficiency and productivity within this system inevitably involve increases in faculty workload."[6] The situation in dental education has been similar.

Self-assessment is an expectation not only of students, but of faculty as well. The concepts in this document call for teachers to reexamine the relationship between what they do and what students learn, to change from the expert who imparts information to a facilitator of learning who helps the student discover new knowledge. Faculty must reexamine their teaching assumptions and practices. These concepts constitute a cultural change in dental education. For change and innovation to occur in dental education, faculty knowledge, skills, attitudes, and values must also change. As in any complex social or professional organization, people—dental faculty—will either facilitate or subvert the change process. Compelling reasons for change and innovation must be clearly stated, and the rationale for new ways of teaching and learning must be substantiated. Reward systems must recognize those who successfully make change, and administrators must align respected colleagues as champions of new ideas. Ongoing faculty development is a requirement not only to foster curricular change, but also to preserve the academic dental profession. Administrators, ADEA, and other national organizations have a responsibility to lead the way in providing programs and processes to assist faculty in implementing change and innovation in dental education.

The Health Care Team

The year 2000 report of the U.S. surgeon general on oral health in America clearly placed oral health within the context of systemic health. The surgeon general's positioning of the nation's often substandard oral health as a "silent epidemic" made a compelling case that access to oral health care is among the nation's most significant health care problems.[7] Driven by the imperative to improve access, the dental team is changing. At the 2006 ADA House of Delegates meeting, delegates accepted a workforce study that provides two new models for allied dental personnel: the Oral Preventative Assistant (OPA) and the Community Dental Health Coordinator (CDHC).[8] The American Dental Hygienists' Association continues to develop its concept of the Advanced Dental Hygiene Practitioner.[9] Considering these and other broad trends affecting the workforce, ADEA held a summit conference in 2006 on the future of allied dental education and has issued a report on unleashing the potential of the allied dental workforce.[10] As access drives a new vision of the dental team, dental school curricula must change to develop a different type of dentist, engaging dental students early in their educational experiences to work with expanded duty allied colleagues in a team environment with the dentist serving as a manager of care.

Access to oral health care and the connection of oral health to general health form a nexus that links oral health care providers to colleagues in other health professions. In 2003, a special ADEA President's Commission on access argued that family physicians, pediatricians, other primary care physicians, nurse practitioners, and physician assistants should be enlisted as part of the oral health team. Moreover, the commission maintained that dentists must become vital members of the health care team by assessing the overall health of patients through diagnosis, screening, and referral.[11] These positions are reflective of a 2001 Institute of Medicine (IOM) study that concludes: "All health care professionals should be educated to deliver patient-centered care as members of an interdisciplinary team, emphasizing evidence-based practice, quality improvement approaches, and information."[12] This vision of the health care team is clouded by the reality that students in different health professions have little interaction with each other. This situation is particularly true for dental students, who typically experience the four years of dental school in almost complete isolation from medical, nursing, pharmacy, and other students in the allied health professions and thus leave school with little sense of the overall health care system.

In a follow-up to its 2001 report, the IOM reiterated an emphasis on collaboration among nurses, pharmacists, physician assistants, and the allied health professions. Regrettably, dentistry was not represented among those who contributed to this 2003 report, and dental services were included among the allied health professions, which should be cause for reflection and concern among dental educators and practitioners.[13] A 2005 ADEA Leadership Institute study involving seven academic health centers and forty-one educational and administrative leaders indicated that, while dental schools were in favor of interprofessional activities, "there was a general impression that dental schools were isolated from the other schools at the academic health center."[14] There are significant obstacles to educating dental students to play a meaningful role on the health care team: funding; culture, including attitudes of administrators, faculty, and students; technology; reimbursement mechanisms; and perhaps the greatest obstacle, insular and overcrowded curricula. The obstacles are many, but so are the opportunities to educate dental school graduates who will assume new roles in safeguarding, promoting, and caring for the health care needs of the public.

Conclusion

The CCI proposes these principles as an environmental framework for creating the ideal dental education experience for our students and faculty. Change and innovation will occur in a variety of ways, unique to each dental school's mission. Change and innovation are also influenced by a number of organizations and stakeholders that directly affect each school's curriculum. Most of these groups operate independently of each other in adopting policies, positions, and regulations that affect dental education. Effective change must be systemic. Through ADEA, the CCI represents the one place in dental education where dental school faculty, students, administrators, and regulatory groups that affect dental education can come together with the purpose of educating lifelong learners to provide evidence-based care to meet the needs of society. CCI welcomes comments to this document and others produced by the commission through its website (www.adea.org/CCI/default.htm).

REFERENCES

1. Pyle M, Andrieu SC, Chadwick DG, Chmar JE, Cole JR, George MC, et al. The case for change in dental education. J Dent Educ 2006;70(9):921-4.
2. Hendricson WD, Andrieu SC, Chadwick DG, Chmar JE, Cole JR, George MC, et al. Educational strategies associated with development of problem-solving, critical thinking, and self-directed learning. J Dent Educ 2006;70(9):925-36.
3. Call for comments. At: www.adea.org/cci/CallforComments09292006.pdf. Accessed: October 25, 2006.
4. Scriven M, Paul R. Defining critical thinking. Foundation for Critical Thinking. At: www.criticalthinking.org. Accessed: February 22, 2006.
5. American Dental Association. At: www.ada.org/prof/resources/positions/statements/evidencebased.asp. Accessed: October 25, 2006.
6. Guskin AE, Marcy MB. Dealing with the future now. Change, July/August 2003:10-21.
7. Oral health in America: a report of the surgeon general. Rockville, MD: U.S. Department of Health and Human Services, National Institutes of Health, National Institute of Dental and Craniofacial Research, 2000.
8. American Dental Association. House Resolutions 3RC, 25RC, adopted October 19, 2006.
9. American Dental Hygienists' Association. At: www.adha.org/media/facts/adhp.htm. Accessed: October 2, 2006.
10. American Dental Education Association. Unleashing the potential of the allied dental workforce. At: www.adea.org/CEPRWeb/DEPR/Documents/Unleashing_the_Potential.pdf. Accessed: October 5, 2006.
11. Haden NK, Catalanotto FA, Alexander CJ, Bailit H, Battrell A, Broussard J Jr, et al. Improving the oral health status of all Americans: roles and responsibilities of academic dental institutions. J Dent Educ 2003;67(5):563-83.
12. Institute of Medicine. Crossing the quality chasm: a new health system for the 21st century. Washington, DC: National Academies Press, 2001.
13. Institute of Medicine. Health professions education: a bridge to quality. Washington, DC: National Academies Press, 2003.
14. Rafter ME, Pesun IJ, Herren M, Linfante JC, Mina M, Wu CD, Casada JP. A preliminary survey of interprofessional education. J Dent Educ 2006;70(4):417-26.

The Influence of "New Science" on Dental Education: Current Concepts, Trends, and Models for the Future

Anthony M. Iacopino, D.M.D., Ph.D.

Abstract: Advances in all aspects of science and discovery continue to occur at an exponential rate, leading to a wealth of new knowledge and technologies that have the potential to transform dental practice. This "new science" within the areas of cell/molecular biology, genetics, tissue engineering, nanotechnology, and informatics has been available for several years; however, the assimilation of this information into the dental curriculum has been slow. For the profession and the patients it serves to benefit fully from modern science, new knowledge and technologies must be incorporated into the mainstream of dental education. The continued evolution of the dental curriculum presents a major challenge to faculty, administrators, and external constituencies because of the high cost, overcrowded schedule, unique demands of clinical training, changing nature of teaching/assessment methods, and large scope of new material impacting all areas of the educational program. Additionally, there is a lack of personnel with adequate training/experience in both foundational and clinical sciences to support the effective application and/or integration of new science information into curriculum planning, implementation, and assessment processes. Nonetheless, the speed of this evolution must be increased if dentistry is to maintain its standing as a respected health care profession. The influence of new science on dental education and the dental curriculum is already evident in some dental schools. For example, the Marquette University School of Dentistry has developed a comprehensive model of curriculum revision that integrates foundational and clinical sciences and also provides a dedicated research/scholarly track and faculty development programming to support such a curriculum. Educational reforms at other dental schools are based on addition of new curricular elements and include innovative approaches that introduce concepts regarding new advances in science, evidence-based foundations, and translational research. To illustrate these reforms, the Marquette curriculum and initiatives at the University of Connecticut and the University of Texas Health Science Center at San Antonio dental schools are described in this article, with recognition that other dental schools may also be developing strategies to infuse new science and evidence-based critical appraisal skills into their students' educational experiences. Discussion of the rationale, goals/objectives, and outcomes within the context of dissemination of these models should help other dental schools to design approaches for integrating this new material that are appropriate to their particular circumstances and mission. For the profession to advance, every dental school must play a role in establishing a culture that attaches value to research/discovery, evidence-based practice, and the application of new knowledge/technologies to patient care.

Dr. Iacopino is Professor, Department of General Dental Sciences and Associate Dean for Research and Graduate Studies, Marquette University School of Dentistry. Direct correspondence and requests for reprints to Dr. Anthony M. Iacopino, Marquette University School of Dentistry, 1801 West Wisconsin Avenue, Milwaukee, WI 53233; 414-288-6089 phone; 414-288-3586 fax; Anthony.Iacopino@Marquette.edu.

This article is one in a series of invited contributions by members of the dental education community that have been commissioned by the ADEA Commission on Change and Innovation (CCI) in Dental Education to address the environment surrounding dental education and affecting the need for, or process of, curricular change. This article was written at the request of the ADEA CCI but does not necessarily reflect the views of ADEA, the ADEA CCI, or individual members of the CCI. The perspectives communicated here are those of the author.

Key words: dental education, dental curriculum, research, scholarship, science integration

During the twentieth century, the practice of dentistry remained relatively static. New products and technologies were introduced at a rate that allowed dentists to provide effective and efficient patient care using the procedures acquired in dental school, and they were able to complete their practice careers incorporating few if any new products, materials, techniques, and/or office equipment. The arrival of the twenty-first century has suddenly forced on dentistry a new paradigm regarding expected standards for state-of-the-art patient care. Traditional methods and procedures that have served the profession well are being questioned within the context of evidence-based rationales and emerging information/technologies. Although there are no specific data or studies to support the notion that dental graduates and established practitioners are resistant to change and incorporation of new technologies, it is generally accepted that most new practitioners use the products and technologies they were exposed to and worked with in their dental training and postgraduate residencies. For many established practitioners, any new technology that could be perceived as disrupting or interfering with customary office routines is likely to be disregarded. In a busy office, especially a solo practice, any interference with traditional patient treatment schedules is assumed to be economically unacceptable. Thus, it is likely that practitioners believe they cannot stop treating patients to adopt new technologies or learn new procedures. The problem with this mind-set is that it precludes the use of new products and technologies that would allow dentists to treat larger numbers of patients more efficiently, and perhaps more effectively, despite the time required to learn and incorporate these innovations into their practices.

New science and technologies are already making their way into all aspects of dental practice and have changed traditional approaches to diagnostics, risk assessment, prevention, and many procedures in clinical dentistry. These new science advances are primarily directed toward connective tissue biophysics/mechanics, tissue engineering, and the large areas of biotechnology (gene therapy, drug delivery, transport dynamics), molecular engineering (macromolecular structure, protein structure, and molecular therapies), informatics (patient management/record systems, data mining/management applications, and simulation/computer-assisted learning environments), and biomaterials (biocompatibility, bioengineering applications of polymers, biomimetics, implant materials, and nanotechnology of dental materials).

For example, there are now commercially available kits related to diagnosis, risk assessment, and prognosis for caries/periodontal disease based on genetic polymorphisms, biomarkers, and principles of cell biology.[1,2] In fact, the recent development of saliva as a diagnostic medium has placed dentistry at the forefront of monitoring systemic health and disease.[3] The application of genomics/proteomics to diagnostic tests and preventive measures requires that students and practitioners receive the necessary knowledge related to microbial/human genetics and the current principles of molecular medicine.[4] Given the current lack of genetics instruction in dental education, this will require significant restructuring of dental curricula and faculty development programs.[5] Within the field of restorative dentistry, the tremendous advances in biomaterials research have led to the current availability of esthetic posterior adhesive restorations, ushering the profession into the "postamalgam era."[6] It has been clearly established that this new biomimetic approach to restorative dentistry is possible through the use of composite resins/porcelains and the generation of a hard tissue bond. The development of these nanomaterials has moved nanotechnology from its theoretical foundations into mainstream practice, and there are now many examples of commercially available products demonstrating the scope of further applications of such technology.[7]

In the area of dental informatics, the application of computer and information sciences to improve dental research, education, and practice has been particularly noteworthy. Many dental schools have developed sophisticated simulation laboratories that take advantage of virtual reality technologies to teach preclinical skills, and the use of electronic teaching tools and learning environments (CD-ROM or web-based) has increased dramatically.[8,9] Although today's dental students are entering the educational program with unprecedented computer literacy, many dental faculty require significant training in order to take full advantage of current computer-aided simulation and instruction capabilities.[10,11] Most dental schools have already implemented some form of electronic paperless records, patient management systems, and digital imaging techniques. Although this technology has the ability to revolutionize patient care through rapid and efficient management of large amounts of clinical information, for it to be useful, the technology must be understood by the end users (students, faculty, and practicing clinicians). At the present time, many practitioners do not exhibit a high degree of computer literacy and are not using currently available informatics technologies to their full potential.[12]

The use of computer and imaging technology is rapidly changing the practice of orthodontics through computer-assisted appliances for tooth movement (Invisalign™ computer-generated therapy).[13] Newly available digital imaging methods that reveal minute details and enhance discrimination have added a sophisticated level of reliability/predictability to implant procedures.[14,15] Recent improvements in computer-aided design (CAD) and computer-aided manufacturing (CAM) for indirect restorations now provide for replication and digitization of the complex topography of tooth structure.[16] Over the last several years, CAD-CAM techniques have transitioned from the domain of the unreliable to mainstream practice, providing better mechanical properties, improved marginal integrity, and enhanced esthetics compared to traditional indirect techniques. Today's more reliable CAD-CAM techniques, some of which may reduce the number of patient visits, are available for the production of a wide range of ceramic restorations.

Scientific and technological advancements that generate new knowledge will continue to occur at unprecedented rates. Future advances will be made possible through emerging interdisciplinary collaborations and thought processes. Thus, significant curricular changes will be necessary to educate a new group of dental professionals who will effectively use interdisciplinary research findings to solve clinical problems and apply new technological advances to the oral health environment. In order to maintain its status as a respected scientifically based health profession, dentistry must appreciate and incorporate these advances within its education and patient care systems. The continued evolution of the dental profession will depend on the discipline's ability to translate the new science into integrated interdisciplinary services in clinical settings.[17] To ensure the continued viability of the profession, it is the responsibility of the dental education sector to facilitate the development of institutional infrastructures that are responsive to and supportive of scientific and technological advances. At the very least, faculty and students must become sophisticated consumers of research and utilize scholarly approaches to evidence-based paradigms in their clinical patient management.

Those outside of dental education may assume that such health professions education/training programs regularly transfer new knowledge and clinical applications of new technologies into their curricula; however, those within dental education realize that scientific advances usually experience a slow assimilation into the dental curriculum.[18,19] Dental education in the United States has traditionally been characterized by discipline-based, lecture-style teaching that emphasizes technical expertise,[20,21] with insufficient attention paid to the development of critical thinking/problem-solving skills and redesign of content/teaching approaches, thus resulting in a stagnant, overcrowded curriculum.[22,23] Furthermore, graduates do not have an appreciation for the application/importance of research and discovery to patient care activities and are not adequately prepared to embrace interdisciplinary technology-based education/training and informational resources critical to lifelong learning and professional growth.[24-26]

There are a variety of opinions regarding the future role of new science and research/scholarship in dental education.[25-30] Some contend that current curricula and research/scholarly training experiences maintain an adequate number of research/scholarly enterprises to develop new knowledge, disseminate new advances/technologies, and translate that information into patient care. However, recent approaches have maintained narrowly focused definitions of the perceived importance of research/scholarly activity, the purpose of research, strategies for increasing the number of future dental researchers/educators, and methods for producing graduates who incorporate evidence-based philosophies into their practices.[26,30] Furthermore, most would admit that some potentially serious problems have developed including insufficient 1) numbers of current and future research/scholarly dental faculty; 2) integration of dental research into the larger world of science; 3) application of new science to clinical practice settings; and 4) acceptance/ownership of research findings by the dental community.[25-30] To date, there are no data available to determine the degree to which the current educational system has contributed to these problems.

Historically, approaches to support new science and research/scholarship have favored accomplished investigators and established infrastructures within research-intensive institutions.[26,29,30] Dental schools designated as research non-intensive are usually associated with smaller universities, have institutional missions emphasizing teaching/service, often lack resources required for developing an infrastructure that supports elite research programs, and are unable to sustain a critical mass of experienced faculty actively engaged in research and scholarly pursuits. Within these cultures, faculty have limited time to pursue scholarly activities because a faculty-intensive teaching curriculum dominates the environment.[31] As a result, research endeavors at these schools have been largely ignored, creating a large cadre of disenfranchised faculty and students with no ability or desire to contribute to the overall agenda related to the infusion of science and discovery into the dental curriculum and patient care activities.

The present paradigm of dental education severely limits the ability to restructure the process to support infusion of new science due to an overcrowded curriculum, lack of integration of biomedical/clinical sciences, and a clinical component that operates in an environment completely removed from research/scholarly enterprises.[26,30] Within this context, new advances/technologies and the overall activity of research/scholarship become an afterthought or an arena reserved for a cloistered group of designated academic faculty. This traditional model must experience a paradigm shift, not only to increase the number of participants in science/scholarship, but also to enhance access, acceptance, and applicability of the science/scholarship. For the profession to advance, every dental school must play a role in establishing a culture that attaches value to research/discovery, evidence-based practice, and the application of new knowledge/technologies to patient care.[32]

Recent Models for Integration of New Science into the Dental Curriculum

This section reviews the curricular strategies developed by three dental schools to incorporate new science and evidence-based practice skills into students' educational experiences. These are intended to serve as models and stimulate thinking about curriculum formats that will facilitate integration of scientific advances into dental education and enhance the overall focus on research and scholarship.

Marquette University School of Dentistry

The Marquette University School of Dentistry (MUSoD) began the process of completely restructuring its dental curriculum in 1999. Over the last eight years, this process has resulted in significant changes that have produced a dynamic, nontraditional educational program that continues to evolve.[32,33] The first phase of the transition involved 1) elimination of outdated or repetitive content; 2) reduction of traditional lecture-based, discipline-specific courses; 3) integration of basic biomedical, behavioral, and clinical sciences content into appropriately sequenced four-year educational tracks; 4) implementation of case-based rounds and facilitated discussions using clinical and biomedical correlates for continuous reinforcement of key concepts; and 5) establishment of early clinical experiences and community-based experiential learning opportunities. This comprehensive effort was partially funded by the United States Department of Education through the Fund for Improvement of Post-Secondary Education (DOE FIPSE program).[33]

The second phase of the transition involved development of a dedicated curricular track providing continuous exposure to new science concepts and applications as well as student research/scholarly activity throughout all four years of dental education. This track represented mandatory hours of didactic time exposing students to topics not traditionally included in dental curricula. Additionally, students were provided with customized flexible schedules to participate in elective "hands-on" mentored research/scholarly experiences at local, national, and international sites including linkages to certificate, M.S., and Ph.D. programs. New curricular elements were designed to foster an appreciation of research/discovery, an interest in academic/research careers, and the application of new knowledge and biomedical/clinical advances to patient care. This effort was partially supported by the National Institute of Dental and Craniofacial Research (NIDCR) of the National Institutes of Health (NIH) R25 Oral Health Research Curriculum Grant.[32]

The present-day MUSoD curriculum is illustrated in Figure 1. MUSoD maintains a relatively small faculty (forty-five full-time faculty for a class size of eighty students) and is a traditional research non-intensive institution with a prominent teaching and community service mission along with a teacher-scholar faculty model. To increase the emphasis on research/scholarship, enable the application of new advances to clinical practice, and create the conditions for such a significant change to occur in the educational program, the faculty needed to be prepared and trained to support the new curriculum. Thus, it is important to note that DOE and NIDCR funding was also used to support a wide array of faculty development activities that provided skill sets required to deliver integrated biomedical/clinical content; research-oriented, evidence-based approaches to dental education; and translational case-based teaching methods emphasizing the application of new science/technologies to patient care.

The dedicated research/scholarly curriculum track was implemented by identifying areas within each semester where didactic content could be inserted. New material insertions did not add additional hours to the existing curriculum; rather, existing material was streamlined to create room for all new material. For each semester in each of the four years (D1-D4), twenty hours of time are allotted for content related to research and scholarship. These content areas provide dental students with information and perspectives not traditionally included in dental cur-

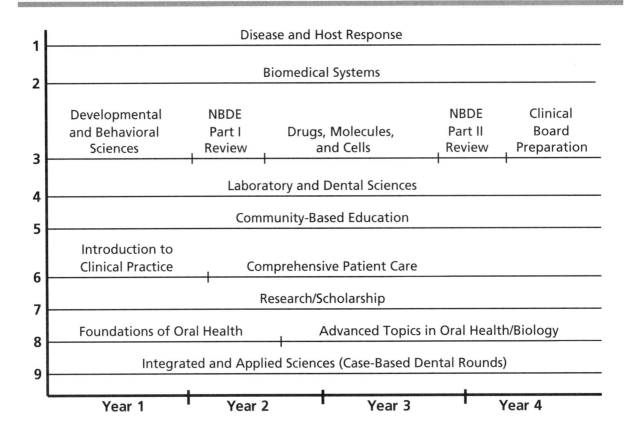

Figure 1. The new Marquette curriculum circa 2007

Note: There are nine educational tracks (1-9) that contain content from various disciplines. The tracks are structured to present material that is sequenced both vertically and horizontally to support early clinical activity and reinforce foundational concepts in clinical settings. The research/scholarly track (track 7) provides twenty contact hours of information for all students during each semester over the entire four-year curriculum (160 total contact hours). For all eligible students, time for the mentored research/scholarly experience is taken from the other tracks through customized scheduling based on student academic performance and clinical abilities (students may pursue a one-to-three-month activity in each of the four years). The case-based dental rounds (track 9) are used to integrate material from all other tracks and emphasize applications of new science to patient care.

ricula including the following: 1) careers in dental research and academia; 2) postgraduate and advanced education/training opportunities; 3) informatics and information resources; 4) evaluating scientific literature and scientific writing; 5) research design; 6) research ethics/integrity; 7) biostatistics; 8) genetic testing/risk assessment; 9) evidence-based dentistry; and 10) recent applications of biomedical/clinical science to practice. These topics, sequenced to provide a logical progression, are delivered by faculty trained through a series of formal faculty development programs described below. Teaching approaches consist primarily of presentations and facilitated discussions for the D1/D2 years and case-based rounds and structured literature reviews for the D3/D4 years. A detailed listing of the didactic content for the twenty curricular hours of each semester in the D1-D4 years is provided in Table 1.

In conjunction with the didactic portion of the dedicated research/scholarly track, MUSoD has developed a broad framework of hands-on mentored student experiences at local, national, and international sites. These experiences are defined very broadly, including traditional biomedical, clinical, and translational research as well as educational research, certificate/advanced degree programs, and topical/evidence-based reviews. The mentored research/scholarly experiences are available to all eligible students who are in good academic standing and maintaining acceptable clinical progress and

Table 1. Research/scholarly track didactic curriculum outline

Time	Content
D1 **Fall Semester** **20 Hours**	Dental Research and Academic/Research Careers • History and future of dental research • Careers in dental research and academia • Advanced education and training programs • Incentive programs attached to research/academic careers Introduction to Research/Scholarship • Types of research (descriptive/experimental/clinical/translational/applied) • Basic scientific methods • Reading and evaluating the literature • Basic descriptive and inferential statistics Evidence-Based Approaches • Searching for evidence • Using evidence • Applied evidence-based reviews Using Technology Resources Effectively • Enabling electronic sources for patient management/professional development • Role of technology in decision support, scientific inquiry, and problem solving • Use of technology resources for effective communication • Supporting lifelong learning with computer literacy and information resources (online learning systems; electronic learning environments; best practices related to guidelines for computer use, security, confidentiality, and electronic communication) Basic Computer Literacy • Basic functions and components of a computer system • Basic architecture of computer networks and use of standard/wireless networks • Select/launch applications; create/retrieve, copy, print, and save work efficiently • Using Internet for professional development with appropriate search strategies • Using digital libraries and electronic databases to retrieve pertinent information • Filter, evaluate, and reconcile information from various electronic sources software for word processing, spreadsheet, presentation, and databases
D1 **Spring Semester** **20 Hours**	Evaluation of Advertisements for Products/Materials • Levels of evidence (anecdotal, high profile endorsements without supportive data, abstracts, peer-reviewed publications) • Critique of supportive studies (authors as paid consultants, appropriate methodologies, statistics, and conclusions) Intermediate Descriptive and Inferential Statistics • Hypothesis testing • Examples from the literature Applied Biostatistics and Epidemiology • Examples from the literature • Current trends and concepts Intermediate Computer Literacy and Application Skills • Collaboration across multiple sites using various communication technologies (discussion lists, newsgroups, and teleconferencing) • Electronic oral health records • Current and emerging technologies for practice (CAD/CAM, PDAs, lasers, and digital imaging)
D2 **Fall Semester** **20 Hours**	Use of Technology for Effective Teaching • Guidelines for delivery, content, and visuals in an electronic presentation • Presentation software and graphics • Creating handouts with graphics and/or tables for case presentation or patient education • Copyright and intellectual property issues related to electronic materials • Confidentiality of private information in presentations Collecting and Working with Digital Material for Electronic Presentations • Digital cameras and scanning devices • Imaging software for basic image editing and enhancements Sophisticated Consumers of Research • Applying new knowledge and technologies to patient care • Evaluating the impact of recent advances on dental practice

(Continued)

Time	Content
D2 **Spring Semester** **20 Hours**	Molecular Medicine • Examples of biologically/genetically based diagnosis and treatment (variable patient susceptibility to disease and response to treatment; simple/complex inheritance and disease screening, risk assessment, diagnosis, and prognosis; current approaches to gene-based treatment and individualized medicine) • Perio-systemic connection (evidence-based reviews, current research findings) Research Ethics and Compliance Issues • Research ethics and integrity • Protection of animals and human subjects (IRB/IACUC, HIPAA) Leadership • Education/research • Professional (organized dentistry, societies/groups) • Community
D3/D4 **Fall/Spring Semesters** **20 Hours**	Recent Applications of Science and Technology to Patient Care • Structured literature reviews • Case-based rounds

are individually structured for each student so that students are provided with a "customized flexible schedule" that facilitates their participation without hardship or penalty. Participation in mentored experiences is designed to be part of the normal curricular time so that the overall educational program has not been lengthened. Students are permitted to access mentored experiences for up to three months each year; thus, students can complete up to one year of such experiences during their four-year educational program. Those students completing mentored research experiences are expected to participate in monthly research seminars or journal clubs, produce abstracts and posters for the annual MUSoD Student Research Day, represent MUSoD at national/international student research symposia, and present their work at the annual American Dental Education Association (ADEA), American Association for Dental Research (AADR), or International Association for Dental Research (IADR) meetings. Additionally, all students are encouraged to publish their work in peer-reviewed journals.

The highlight of this component of the curriculum track is an interinstitutional D.D.S.-Ph.D. program developed with the University of Rochester Center for Oral Biology. This unique program allows Marquette dental students to begin their Ph.D. studies with three-month research rotations each summer. During these summer rotations, students are also able to complete clinical activities, so that they maintain their class standing and complete the D.D.S. program within the normal four-year period. The entire fourth year of dental school is completed at Rochester with concurrent Ph.D. coursework, research, and clinical activity. Students graduate with their dental class and return to Rochester for an additional one to two years to complete the Ph.D. Financial incentives are provided throughout the program including $6,000 for each summer, fourth-year tuition coverage, and a $22,000 stipend for each additional Ph.D. year. The funding sources for stipends and tuition support are derived from the Marquette R25 and Rochester T32 NIH-NIDCR grant awards.

Development and implementation of a comprehensive faculty development initiative were related to critical components of the overall curriculum reform and MUSoD-designed and -delivered faculty development activities that support the new curriculum. The first phase was designed to provide programming that allowed the faculty to identify and appreciate key scientific, biomedical, behavioral, and clinical concepts that should be included in the curriculum tracks and needed to be reinforced through inclusion in case-based rounds and one-on-one teaching opportunities on the clinic floor. Introduction of the concepts involved in utilizing evidence-based decision-making strategies were included in this phase of the faculty development activities. The training was delivered interactively using group learning activities based on actual clinical dental cases; this provided an opportunity for faculty to review the biomedical and clinical science concepts that are crucial to an adequate diagnosis/treatment plan. These modules were supplemented with seminars using unique cases and interactive discussions concerning critical scientific concepts present in the cases that were influential in diagnosis/treatment planning decisions. Additionally, behavioral sciences and interdisciplinary considerations that impacted comprehensive patient management were incorporated into the cases, along with discussions of complex medical histories and treatment settings as well as use of patient scenarios featuring varying levels of debilitation/function, social/socioeconomic circumstances, and ethnic/cultural considerations.

The second phase of faculty development activities consisted of opportunities to develop instructional/teaching skills in research-oriented areas. These opportunities consisted of 1) development of skills necessary to effectively lead small group, case-based seminars involving use of an evidence-based protocol including specifically how to conduct/facilitate an effective dental rounds session; 2) use of technology in teaching and development of electronic learning environments including instruction on utilizing PowerPoint presentations, preparing and delivering courses through use of Internet tools/software packages, and using web-based information resources for instruction; 3) one-on-one teaching skills to enhance clinical learning, including appropriate questioning strategies designed to prompt students to recognize and solve patient treatment issues applying appropriate biomedical, behavioral, and clinical science concepts; and 4) development/ implementation of assessment approaches for case-based, practically applied research/scholarly curriculum track components. Thus far, this training has comprised twenty-eight formal activities consisting of self-study modules combined with seminars and workshops. A detailed listing of the faculty development activities completed during the curriculum reform process is provided in Table 2.

In addition to these institutional activities, MUSoD established a relationship with the Medical College of Wisconsin, securing two permanent training slots within its existing K30 Clinical Research Training Program. This two-year NIH-funded program supports training of clinical research scholars and is intended to increase the number of research-active MUSoD faculty who can serve as mentors for student research experiences. The program provides MUSoD faculty with an enriched academic environment to enhance development of clinical research careers through individual 1) mentoring for research and career development; 2) instruction relative to clinical research skills; and 3) assistance in identification of and access to research-related resources, research-related publications, and development of a research proposal that is submitted to an appropriate external funding agency. The K30 program uses a guided apprenticeship model and experienced faculty mentors to facilitate development of clinical research skills. The core curriculum addresses critical competencies necessary for success in clinical research such as content knowledge, methodological skills, research management skills, and socialization to the research environment. Medical College resources associated with this training program include a vigorous Clini-

---

Table 2. Faculty development activities supporting the new curriculum at Marquette University School of Dentistry

1. Integrating Biomedical and Clinical Sciences
2. Use of Technology in Teaching
3. Interdisciplinary Teams and Case-Based Teaching
4. Effective Teaching Strategies/Questioning Skills/Publishing in Education Journals
5. Leading a Problem-Based Learning Discussion
6. Using the Inquiry Method of Teaching
7. Lectures That Students Will Remember
8. Using Questions to Guide Learning in the Clinic
9. Assessment from A to Z
10. Electronic Resources for Curriculum Analysis and Evaluation
11. Utilizing PowerPoint Presentations Effectively
12. Using Blackboard for Course Management
13. Writing Effective National Board Formatted Test Items
14. Utilizing Test Management Software
15. Objective Structured Clinical Exams (OSCEs)
16. Working Productively with Challenging Students
17. Integrating Practice Management in the New Curriculum
18. Translational and Clinical Research
19. Planning a Research Study and Getting It Published
20. Evidence-Based Dentistry in the General Dentistry Setting
21. Strategic Planning: New Directions for Curriculum, Research, and Service
22. Test Development to Facilitate Higher Level Learning
23. Dedicated Research/Scholarly Curriculum Track: A Marquette Innovation
24. Impact of Diversity on Clinical Care, Education, and Scholarship
25. SMART Objectives for Grants and Proposals
26. Electronic Resources for Research and Scholarship
27. Interinstitutional Ph.D. Program: University of Rochester
28. Student Assessment: Testing and Grading

cal Research Center and highly funded investigators engaged in multidisciplinary clinical research/laboratory-based training programs.

The new MUSoD curriculum model significantly changed the culture of a research non-intensive dental school, creating a supportive environment for research/scholarship, increasing academic productivity, and altering the attitudes of faculty/students with regard to new science and its place in dental education and practice. Significant increases were demonstrated in 1) number of students participating in research/scholarship, attending national meetings, acquiring research awards, publishing manuscripts, pursuing advanced training/degrees, and expressing interest in academic/research careers; 2) number of faculty participating in development activities, publishing manuscripts, and mentoring students; and 3) institutional credibility within the university, supportive infrastructure for research/scholarship, and cultural expectations for academic excellence.

Table 3 illustrates some comparisons made using baseline data prior to the new curriculum and data collected in 2006.

University of Connecticut School of Dental Medicine

The University of Connecticut School of Dental Medicine (UConn) has developed a unique program element in "Biodontics" to introduce new science concepts related to translational research.[34] The goal of the new curricular element is to move recent discoveries and knowledge in molecular biology, biotechnology, and informatics more efficiently from scientists and inventors to dental practitioners and the patients they serve. The UConn Biodontics program applies the new science to clinical dentistry through training of dental students, dental residents, and dental school faculty in the best use of scientific and technological advances to improve patient care. The

Table 3. Student, faculty, and institutional data

Cohort	Measure	Prior to New Curriculum	After New Curriculum
Students (80/class)	• Annual participation in research/scholarship	1% (4 students/year)	15% (48 students/year)
	• Completed or pursuing certificates	0	11
	• Pursuing Ph.D. degree	0	3
	• Annual attendance at national/international meetings and symposia	1% (4 students/year)	10% (32 students/year)
	• Peer-reviewed publications	0	4
	• National research awards/fellowships	0	4
	• Summer research externships	2	13
	• National AADR SRG awards	0	3
	• Likely to pursue academic/research careers	1% (1 student/class)	10% (8 students/class)
Faculty	• Development programs attended and number of programs related to research/scholarship, evidence-based teaching, and/or mentoring skills	8/3	27/20
	• New faculty-initiated research programs	0	2
	• Completed K30 clinical research training program at Medical College of Wisconsin	0	2
	• Number of faculty mentoring students	10% (4 of 40)	50% (22 of 44)
	• Annual peer-reviewed publication rate	19/year	54/year
Institution	• Annual research budget	$25,000	$111,000
	• Regular faculty development activities targeted to research/scholarship, evidence-based teaching, and/or mentoring skills	No	Yes
	• Institutional membership in IADR	No	Yes
	• Hosts national student research conferences	No	Yes
	• Student research/scholarship graduation requirement	No	Yes
	• Ongoing invited lecture series	No	Yes
	• Monthly journal club	No	Yes
	• Emphasis on faculty research/scholarship in annual merit reviews	No	Yes

rationale for exposing dental students, residents, and faculty to this wide range of fields is to prepare them for managing dental practices that incorporate new technologies at a faster rate. This supports the overall national agenda by promoting an active, expanding profession that is adaptable and accountable to new technologies and procedures, thereby improving the general oral health of the public.

The Biodontics program promotes innovations in oral health through a specific educational program focused on the research and development of products, technologies, and equipment. At the dental student level, the material is delivered through presentations/discussions scheduled within the curriculum, along with a special eight-week elective summer course. The Biodontics material is provided by faculty, business leaders, entrepreneurs, management executives, scientists, architects, and dental manufacturers. This course is also open to dental students from other schools. At the graduate level, a structured fellowship provides opportunities for interaction with research faculty, representatives of the dental industry, entrepreneurs, and practitioners including hands-on experience with state-of-the-art technologies. As part of the program, fellows develop educational, translational research, and clinical trials programs designed to integrate basic science discoveries with clinical applications. New technologies such as probiotics, dental lasers, and electronic patient record systems were included in the program to offer a wide range of experiences.

The highest level of instruction within the Biodontics program is a formal residency that provides a certificate after two years of training, including advanced coursework in health management, public policy, integrated biological sciences (biotechnology, bioinformatics, bioethics, and genetics), methods of health research, technology transfer processes, technological innovations and technology commercialization strategies, and leadership/entrepreneurship. The goal of the Biodontics residency is to uniquely integrate basic and clinical research findings with clinical training and incorporate contemporary developments in biotechnology (molecular biology, genomics, informatics, bioengineering, and nanotechnology) with clinical dentistry.

Assessment of the impact of the UConn Biodontics program has demonstrated that incorporating new science concepts within the context of activities that can be translated to clinical practice is effective in stimulating students, residents, and faculty to use thought processes that apply new knowledge and discovery to patient care.[34] The need for educational approaches that emphasize the application of research to patient care and facilitate student entry into clinical research training programs has recently been documented.[35-38]

University of Texas Health Science Center at San Antonio Dental School

The University of Texas Health Science Center at San Antonio Dental School recently initiated a curriculum redesign project intended to infuse an appreciation of new science at all levels of the curriculum (Dr. John Rugh, personal communication). The approach involves preparation of Critically Appraised Topic summaries (CATs)[39] by students, residents, and faculty for clinical questions that arise pertinent to patient care and the development of a searchable online database (library) of high-quality, informative CATs that have been subjected to a peer review process. A CAT is a critical assessment of the available evidence that addresses a clinical question.[40-43]

The CATs database will be regularly reviewed and updated by a panel of reviewers comprised of dental school faculty and alumni practitioners under coordination of a CATs library manager and will be used to disseminate evidence-based information and promote transfer of research findings into patient care at the dental school and in the community. The CATs contain the basic foundational and evidence-based information that applies new science to clinical practice. A key component of the program is the collaborative involvement of dental students, graduate residents, faculty, and private practitioners in CATs preparation and review. This provides a mechanism to expose students, faculty, residents, and practicing dentists to recent scientific discoveries and the best clinical research on issues of high clinical relevance. Dental students write CATs in 75 percent of the clinical courses pertinent to various types of oral health problems and therapeutic approaches; residents also write CATs in six postgraduate dental education programs. The project includes a formal faculty development program on evidence-based practice emphasizing the preparation and use of CATs. The overarching goal is to promote an appreciation of new science and increase the probability that this information will be integrated into the dental curriculum and private practice settings. The searchable CATs database will be made available to all practicing dentists and ultimately to the public to help increase the rate of new science transfer to patient care.

To institutionalize the CATs curriculum component, course objectives in all four years of the curriculum have been revised to include competency in preparing CATs (asking focused questions, searching for the best evidence, critical appraisal, writing summaries, and integrating new knowledge into clinical care decisions) and other facets of evidence-based practice. The CATs curriculum component will also be coordinated with existing advanced dental student training and predental student outreach programs to enhance interest in dental research and increase the flow of students into these programs and potentially into academic careers in the oral health sciences. It is anticipated that the new curricular element will stimulate a deeper appreciation of new science, enhance skills associated with critical appraisal of the literature, promote evidence-based approaches to patient care, and foster more rapid integration of research findings into both the dental education program and private dental practice. Assessment strategies will include evaluating the impact of the project on 1) student, resident, and faculty attitudes regarding evidence-based practice; 2) student, resident, and faculty ability to utilize skills associated with CATs and implement evidence-based practice approaches; and 3) clinical instruction strategies used by faculty when working with students.

Conclusions

The three models described in this article represent curricular changes and educational approaches that support research/scholarship, evidence-based analysis, and inclusion of new science in dental education and practice. These models are intended to illustrate different methods being used to achieve the goal of infusing new science into the educational experience of dental students. It is recognized that other dental schools, not described here, may be employing similar strategies or may have developed alternative ways to achieve this goal. Incorporating learning experiences that provide students with greater exposure to research and evidence-based practice represents an emerging area of educational reform that has been negatively perceived by most dental faculty.[44] These models can be classified as disruptive innovations in dental education in that they have the potential for establishing new consumer bases for the science and technology product.[45] These approaches make the new science available to a large population of students and clinical faculty who may be motivated to apply new knowledge and technologies to patient care. As additional institutions adopt some of these approaches, this will stimulate further changes in dental education. Additionally, at the very least, this curricular approach will enlarge the cadre of individuals who can articulate the value of new science to the dental profession—a current priority of the recently created National Oral Health Advocacy Committee and National Advocacy Network of ADEA and the AADR.[46] There have been previous recommendations for cultural change within dental schools based on nontraditional, cooperative educational alliances with strong research institutions to restructure the curriculum so that it improves academic vitality, supports infusion of new science, and trains the next generation of academicians/researchers.[47,48] New curricular models will need to address the interdisciplinary integration of new science within the broad oral health environment.

The models described here also introduce a "hidden curriculum" that supports research/scholarly activity and the inclusion of new science in the daily fabric of the educational experience. It is important to note that, within these models at three U.S. dental schools, the hidden curriculum has received strong support from clinical and part-time faculty—role models who have a tremendous influence on dental students. A systematic review of the evidence related to strategies for teaching critical appraisal and evidence-based practice concepts by Coomarasamy and Khan in 2004 indicates that learner mastery of these skills occurs most effectively in the clinical context, not in the classroom, and that provider role modeling is essential.[49] The significance of the hidden curriculum on student attitudes and behaviors has been previously reported, and the influence of clinical and part-time faculty cannot be overestimated within this context.[50] Previous reports have emphasized the need for dental schools to integrate new science and research/scholarship into the curriculum so that they produce future leaders for the profession. It has been estimated that dental schools must engage 20 percent of their best and brightest students with enriched academic curricula for 20 percent of their educational program in order to accomplish this goal.[48] Since the primary mission of most dental schools is to train competent clinicians, it is important to note that the Marquette model was developed in a research non-intensive institution that has historically focused on its educational mission.

Each dental school possesses unique characteristics and has differing resources that can be focused on the broad area of curriculum reform and incorporation of new science into the educational program. However, to support a national/international agenda related to maintaining the status of the dental profession, every dental school should play a part in establishing an infrastructure that attaches value to new science, research/scholarship, evidence-based practice, and the application of new knowledge and technologies to patient care.[32] In order to accomplish this task, researchers, educators, and clinicians will have to work closely together. Thus, the true measure of success for all of these constituencies should be to continue to provide curricular models that demonstrate how all faculty can combine their efforts to address one of the most important current issues in dental education.

Acknowledgments

The Marquette curriculum redesign project was supported by DOE FIPSE grant P116B011247 and NIH NIDCR grant R25 DE015282.

REFERENCES

1. Taba M, Kinney J, Kim AS, Giannobile WV. Diagnostic biomarkers for oral and periodontal diseases. Dent Clin North Am 2005;49:551-71.
2. Kornman KS. Diagnostic and prognostic tests for oral diseases: practical applications. J Dent Educ 2005;69:498-508.
3. Wong DT. Salivary diagnostics powered by nanotechnologies, proteomics, and genomics. J Am Dent Assoc 2006;137:313-21.
4. Wright JT, Hart TC. The genome project: implications for dental practice and education. J Dent Educ 2002;66:659-71.
5. Behnke AR, Hassell TM. Need for genetics education in U.S. dental and dental hygiene programs. J Dent Educ 2004;68:819-22.
6. Magne P. Composite resins and bonded porcelain: the postamalgam era? J Calif Dent Assoc 2006;34:135-47.
7. Ure D, Harris J. Nanotechnology in dentistry: reduction to practice. Dent Update 2003;30:10-5.
8. Jasinevicius TR, Landers M, Nelson S, Urbankova A. An evaluation of two dental simulation systems: virtual reality versus contemporary non-computer-assisted. J Dent Educ 2004;68:1151-62.
9. Hillenburg KL, Cederberg RA, Gray SA, Hurst CL, Johnson GK, Potter BJ. E-learning and the future of dental education: opinions of administrators and information technology specialists. Eur J Dent Educ 2006;10:169-77.
10. Greenwood SR, Grigg PA, Stephens CD. Clinical informatics and the dental curriculum: a review of the impact of informatics in dental care and its implications for dental education. Eur J Dent Educ 1997;1:153-61.
11. Robinson MA. Issues and strategies for faculty development in technology and biomedical informatics. Adv Dent Res 2003;17:34-7.
12. Schleyer T, Spallek H. Dental informatics: a cornerstone of dental practice. J Am Dent Assoc 2001;32:605-13.
13. Lagravere MO, Flores-Mir C. The treatment effects of Invisalign orthodontic aligners: a systematic review. J Am Dent Assoc 2005;136:1724-9.
14. Du Tre F, Jacobs R, Styven S, van Steenberghe D. Development of a novel digital subtraction technique for detecting subtle changes in jawbone density. Clin Oral Invest 2006;10:235-48.
15. Swennen GR, Schutyser F. Three-dimensional cephalometry: spiral multi-slice vs cone-beam computed tomography. Am J Orthod Dentofacial Orthop 2006;130:410-6.
16. Palin W, Burke FJ. Trends in indirect dentistry: CAD/CAM technology. Dent Update 2005;32:566-72.
17. Oral health in America: a report of the surgeon general. Rockville, MD: U.S. Department of Health and Human Services, National Institute of Dental and Craniofacial Research, National Institutes of Health, 2000.
18. Tedesco LA. Issues in dental curriculum development and change. J Dent Educ 1995;59:97-147.
19. Hendricson WD, Cohen PA. Future directions in dental school curriculum, teaching, and learning. In: Haden NK, Tedesco LA, eds. Leadership for the future: the dental school in the university. Washington, DC: American Association of Dental Schools, 1999:90-5.
20. Glassman P, Meyerowitz C. Education in dentistry: preparing dental practitioners to meet the oral health needs of America in the twenty-first century. J Dent Educ 1999;63:615-25.
21. Hendricson WD, Cohen PA. Oral healthcare in the 21st century: implications for dental and medical education. Acad Med 2001;76:1181-206.
22. Tedesco LA. Curriculum change during post-IOM dental education. J Dent Educ 1996;60:827-30.
23. Boyd LD. Reflections on clinical practice by first-year dental students: a qualitative study. J Dent Educ 2002;66:710-20.
24. Baum BJ. The absence of a culture of science in dental education. Eur J Dent Educ 1997;1:2-5.
25. Bertolami CN. Rationalizing the dental curriculum in light of current disease prevalence and patient demand for treatment: form versus content. J Dent Educ 2001;65:725-35.
26. Bertolami CN. The role and importance of research and scholarship in dental education and practice. J Dent Educ 2002;66:918-24.
27. Schuler CF. Keeping the curriculum current with research and problem-based learning. J Am Coll Dent 2001;68:20-4.
28. Haden NK, Beemsterboer PL, Weaver RG, Valachovic RW. Dental school faculty shortages increase: an update on future dental school faculty. J Dent Educ 2000;64:657-73.
29. Haden NK, Valachovic RW. The ADEA-NIDCR national research conference on putting science into practice: the critical role of dental schools. J Dent Educ 2002;66:912-7.

30. Stashenko P, Niederman R, DePaola D. Basic and clinical research: issues of cost, manpower needs, and infrastructure. J Dent Educ 2002;66:927-38.

31. Dederich DN, Lloyd PM, Farmer CD, Geurink KV, Nadershahi NA, Robinson FG, et al. Perceptions of dental schools from within and outside the university. J Dent Educ 2004;68:1163-71.

32. Iacopino AM. The role of "research non-intensive" institutions within the global framework. J Dent Res 2004;83:276-7.

33. Iacopino AM, Lynch DP, Taft T. Preserving the pipeline: a model dental curriculum for research non-intensive institutions. J Dent Educ 2004;68:44-9.

34. Rossomando EF, Benitez H, Janicki BW. Developing competency in research management, entrepreneurship, and technology transfer: a workshop course. J Dent Educ 2004;68:965-9.

35. Baum BJ, Scott J, Greenspan JS, Park N, Ranney R, Schwarz E, Uoshima K. Global challenges in research and strategic planning. Eur J Dent Educ 2002;6:179-85.

36. DePaola D, Holmstrup P, Hardwick K, Lamster IB, Rifkin R. Research and the dental student. Eur J Dent Educ 2002;6:45-51.

37. Gordon SM, Heft MW, Dionne RA, Jeffcoat MA, Alfano MC, Valachovic RW, Lipton JA. Capacity for training in clinical research: status and opportunities. J Dent Educ 2003;67:622-9.

38. Murillo H, Albert RE, Snyderman R, Sung NS. Meeting the challenges facing clinical research: solutions proposed by leaders of medical specialty and clinical research societies. Acad Med 2006;81:107-12.

39. Wyer PC. The critically appraised topic: closing the evidence transfer gap. Ann Emerg Med 1997;30:639-41.

40. Taylor R, Reeves B, Ewings P, Binns S, Keast J, Mears R. A systematic review of the effectiveness of critical appraisal skills training for clinicians. Med Educ 2000;34:120-5.

41. Parkes J, Hyde C, Deeks J, Milne R. Teaching critical appraisal skills in health care settings. Cochrane Database of Systematic Reviews. 2001, Issue 3. Art. No.: CD001270. DOI: 10.1002/14651858.CD001270.

42. Werb SB, Matear DW. Implementing evidence-based practice in undergraduate teaching clinics: a systematic review and recommendations. J Dent Educ 2004;68(9): 995-1003.

43. Pluye P, Grad RM, Dunikowski LG, Stephenson R. Impact of clinical information-retrieval technology on physicians: a literature review of quantitative, qualitative and mixed methods studies. Int J Med Inform 2005;74:745-68.

44. Masella RS, Thompson TJ. Dental education and evidence-based educational best practices: bridging the great divide. J Dent Educ 2004;68:1266-71.

45. Donoff RB. It is time for a new Gies report. J Dent Educ 2006;70:809-19.

46. Bresch JE, Luke GG, McKinnon MD, Moss MJ, Pritchard D, Valachovic RW. Today's threat is tomorrow's crisis: advocating for dental education, dental and biomedical research, and oral health. J Dent Educ 2006;70:601-6.

47. Edmunds RK. Strategies for making research more accessible to dental students. J Dent Educ 2005;69:861-3.

48. Herzberg MC, Griffith LG, Doyle MJ. Driving the future of dental research. J Dent Res 2006;85:486-7.

49. Coomarasamy A, Khan KS. What is the evidence that postgraduate teaching in evidence-based medicine changes anything? A systematic review. Br Med J 2004;329:1017.

50. Masella R. The hidden curriculum: value added in dental education. J Dent Educ 2006;70:279-83.

Dentistry and Dental Education in the Context of the Evolving Health Care System

Maxwell H. Anderson, D.D.S., M.S., M.Ed.

Abstract: This article is intended to stimulate dialogue within the intertwined dental practice and dental education communities about our evolving health care system and dentistry's role within this system as it reconfigures in response to a complex interplay of influences. The changing dental disease burden in the United States is analyzed with consideration of how evolution in disease prevalence influences societal need for dental services and the resulting potential impact on the types of services provided and the education of future dental practitioners. The article concludes with discussion of a potential future scenario for practice and education in which one or both of the two health abnormalities (dental caries and periodontal diseases) most closely associated with dentistry as an area of medical specialization go away as a consequence of transformational technologies.

Dr. Anderson is Director, Anderson Dental Consulting. Direct correspondence and requests for reprints to Dr. Maxwell H. Anderson, 872 Three Crabs Road, Sequim, WA 98382; 360-683-7773 phone; 360-681-5324 fax; maxscruiser@gmail.com.

This article is one in a series of invited contributions by members of the dental and dental education community that have been commissioned by the ADEA Commission on Change and Innovation in Dental Education (CCI) to address the environment surrounding academic dentistry and affecting the need for, or process of, curricular change. This article was written at the request of the ADEA CCI, but does not necessarily reflect the views of ADEA, the ADEA CCI, or individual members of the ADEA CCI. The perspectives communicated here are those of the author.

Key words: dental care delivery, public health, health care policy, risk assessment, health care costs, evidence-based practice, dental education

As an opening qualifying statement, speculating on an evolving health care system is at best imprecise and may be wildly inaccurate. This article is written to encompass what I view as the most probable developments based on current trends and the projections of a number of health care planners, public policy formulating agencies, and emerging health care markets.

This article specifically does not consider the upcoming 2008 national elections and the potential for a universal single-payer health plan that may or may not encompass dental benefits or how such a system might be implemented. The sequence of this article is to

- examine the changing dental disease burden in the United States and hence the need for dental services;
- provide an overview of the system of dentistry since the system defines the players that may influence dental education;
- identify a number of the influencers on dental care delivery and the education system processes; and
- from these perspectives, opine on the potential impacts these influencers will have on dental education.

First and foremost, this article is meant to stimulate thoughtful discourse about our evolving health care system and dentistry's role therein. I have no lock on the truth about the future. If this perspective engenders discussion amongst dental educators regarding curriculum, staffing, facilities management, etc., it will have performed its intended purpose.

Dental Diseases and Their Distribution

Severe dental diseases were once pandemic in the U.S. population.[1] As a result, even though the average life span was significantly shorter than today,[2] edentulism was quite high, and suffering dental pain was common. Paintings of the first U.S. president with a scar on his cheek left by a fistula, reportedly of dental origin, are reminders of how far dental science has come in two hundred and thirty years.

As a pandemic, dental diseases affected virtually our entire population. This had impacts on much of our society and our health care concerns as a nation. Congress initially formed the National Institute of Dental Research, now National Institute of Dental and Craniofacial Research (NIDCR), in 1948 partially as a response to the dental condition of young men being conscripted into World War II's armed forces.[3] Many conscripts could not meet the minimum dental standard of the day of having six opposing teeth with which to "masticate a ration" and were "4-F" because of this dental condition.[4] Dental diseases were ubiquitous and crossed most socioeconomic lines.

Today we no longer face this degree of disease penetration.[5] Dentistry's two primary diseases, dental caries and periodontal diseases,[6] are no longer evenly distributed in the population. Some population segments still have epidemic disease penetration, while other sectors of society have an endemic disease distribution. In many U.S. population segments, dental diseases progress at significantly slower rates than in the past, while, in others, rapid progression is still the norm. This is not to suggest that other disease processes are not found in the orofacial structures. It is not the intent of this article to avoid those diseases and conditions. Rather, it speaks to the impacts of the two primary diseases on the work burden in daily practice and on the teaching of dental skill sets that address these areas. Treating the etiology, prevention, diagnosis, restoration, and management of these two diseases, their clinical sequela, and the cosmetic needs of patients still commands the greatest time and returns the greatest revenue within the general practice of dentistry.

The influence of this changing distribution of dental diseases on the dental health care system is that clinicians need to be not only astute diagnosticians but also must acquire significant skills in risk assessment. That is, they should have the skill sets to be able to predict who in their patient census is at higher risk for acquisition or progression of dental diseases. Unless a practitioner is treating one of the remaining highly diseased U.S. populations, it is no longer acceptable to treat all individuals in a practice as being at equal risk for disease acquisition and progression. At the same time, it is not acceptable to spend time and resources performing risk assessment in a setting where dental diseases are pandemic. A one size fits all strategy overtreats some and significantly undertreats others and may not improve health outcomes, all while consuming scarce resources. Being able to know the differences between pandemic, epidemic, and endemic distributions of diseases in our populations and which population a practice is treating is critically important. It should modulate the diagnostic, preventive, and therapeutic strategies the clinician employs. Health systems recognize this

distribution issue and are taking steps to constrain the inappropriate expenditure of resources. This will be an influence on dental practices and delivery systems and hence will impact dental education.

Both of dentistry's primary diseases are reasonably well characterized chronic biofilm-contained bacterial infections with significant influences from the patient's immune system and lifestyle. Until relatively recently, dentistry treated these infections by principally using surgical models of care. For dental caries, this surgical model is somewhat cynically described as "drill, fill, and bill." For periodontal diseases, it was scale, root planing, and surgery. When these mechanisms ran their course, extractions occurred, and fixed or removable prostheses replaced the lost teeth/tooth structure. In most cases, these models of practice represented our "best current evidence." That we have developed new models, procedures, and practices is normal and expected in a science-based profession; this development is continuously changing health care systems.

These new models emphasize more and more risk assessment and disease management often without surgical interventions. This mirrors the expectations for other health system entities. Science from within and outside our profession is making available new tools for practitioners to better recognize and predict different risk levels in our patient populations. When surgical interventions are required, many new materials and methods are available. "Minimally invasive" is not a term that originated in dentistry. It is a common term and a developing practice in medicine as well. Health systems recognize the myriad of benefits that accrue from less traumatic or atraumatic interventions.

The demographic of the U.S. population is also changing. The U.S. Census Bureau projects almost straight-line population growth with a national negative birthrate.[7] Both immigration and an aging population contribute to this growth, and both bring unique practice issues to health care systems that impact dental education.

For each of these developing areas, the health care system is adapting and evolving. Health care systems examine these emerging demographics, trends, sociopolitical influences, techniques, and technologies with the goal of providing the most efficient and effective diagnostics, preventives, and therapeutics in the populations they serve. Dentistry and dental education will need to align with these shifts.

System of Dentistry and Its Influencers

The system of dentistry includes not only health care providers like dentists and hygienists and dental schools and other entities acting as primary and tertiary treatment facilities, but also consumers (patients), payers (public, private, and patients), medical health care systems, regulatory bodies, political entities (including dental associations), manufacturers of dental products, and more. No player in the system operates independently of the others. The system of dentistry, like other parts of the health care system, represents a complex interplay of interests, influences, and influencers. To cite an example, dental education is influenced by the regulatory agencies that license dental practitioners. The regulatory body is influenced by the political winds and the emerging science of dentistry, as well as by the dental practitioner community. The practitioner community is influenced by the economy and its effect on purchasers' or patients' willingness to fund the delivery of dental services and at what level. Changes to payment coverage may be influenced by negotiated labor agreements that are also economically influenced.

This influence chain is highly branched, and this example is not intended to carve out other influences at any level. It is important to recognize that changes to one element of the health care system influence many others and that the entire symphony of players represents the health care system. Influences on the system of dentistry include the following.

Health Care Costs. The influence of total health care costs on the emerging health care system, including dentistry, is substantial. Dentistry accounts for approximately $80 billion per year in a $1.75 trillion U.S. health expenditure economy. The United States is currently spending somewhere near 15 percent of its gross domestic product on health care. This is more than most other first world nations, and the result of this spending is openly criticized and debated. This debate and its consequences are shaping the future health care system. These expenditures are from public sources like Medicaid and Medicare services, from private employer-based payment systems, and from patients themselves (whether as copayments or as self-funding activities). Surveys show that 29 percent of health care consumers skip prescribed or needed health care services because of cost. For 18 percent of Americans, health care costs are the biggest monthly expense they pay after mortgage or rent.[8] These costs influence the emerging health systems and, consequently, dental education. One of the principal influences of interest here is the cost of health care on the pricing of U.S. products in increasingly competitive world markets.

Global Economy. We are part of an emerging and continuously morphing world economy. High health care costs, at their current rates, can contribute to making U.S. products less competitive both domestically and abroad. Demanding a higher price for an equal quality product generally results in lower sales of the higher priced product, which can lead to lower corporate profits or corporate losses. In either a stagnant or a loss position, management of shareholder organizations is then likely to consider a number of cost control measures. One of the options is how it compensates its workers.

Health Care Benefits. In the United States, a major portion of our health care system evolved as an employment-based system. Health care benefits are a form of indirect employment compensation. Historically, this appears to have been at least partially the result of the wage freezes imposed on most sectors of the economy during World War II. In order to attract and retain workers in scarce labor markets in which wages were frozen, employers began using health care benefits as a way to influence workers' choice of employers.

Consumerism. Today, those employers who are purchasing health care benefits are becoming much more aggressive consumers of health care plans and services in an effort to constrain costs and keep their products competitive. These purchasers are demanding proof of value for their health care expenditures. This is the same demand on their products being requested by their customers. The choices for increasing value are either to lower prices or to increase quality. Whether an employer or a health care system, this generally leads to demand for "effective" practices. "Efficacy" is the ability to produce the desired amount of the desired effect within the system. Within health care, the principal focus of these efforts has been concentrated on medicine. But it is now being extended to dentistry, vision, pharmacy, nursing, and other allied health services. The impact on dental education will be on teaching practices that are effective in specific clinical situations. Dental education is rising to this challenge through its participation in evidence-based practices. This includes the research and publication aspect of dental education as well as the teaching and service components.

Total Health Care Costs. This search for lower total health care expenditures has helped drive the search for cause and effect between dental diseases and systemic diseases or condition and outcomes of dental interventions. Clearly, if you can perform a $70 dental prophylaxis and reduce the number of $80,000 pre-term low birthweight babies while also improving the quality of life of the child and family, you will follow that practice (assuming there are not other harms induced by the interventions). If dental interventions consistently show total health care savings, the evolving health care system will make provisions for these services. The delivery system for effective services is still being determined in health care systems. For example, if it is both health- and cost-effective to provide four periodontal maintenance visits to periodontally affected diabetic patients, health systems may co-locate hygienists in internal medicine or endocrinology clinics to provide these services.

Evidence-Based Health System Demands. There are a number of other manifestations of this consumerism. For example, the brokers and consultants for dental benefits are directing their sophisticated purchasers to demand evidence-based plan designs. They are seeing some successes with these practices in medicine and are beginning to demand similar proofs in dentistry. They are demanding to know what coverage for specific benefits gets them in improved health care outcomes for their employees and for the future costs for health services. The focus and scope of the phrase "evidence-based" used here is different from the American Dental Association's clinical definition of evidence-based decision making (EBD) that is justifiably focused on the treatment of individual patients. This "evidence" is about what is best for specific covered populations. How are diseases distributed in the population that will be "insured," and what's the most effective way to maximize the population's health while minimizing the costs? As an example, a cogent question is: if the risks for dental diseases are not evenly distributed, then why does everyone systematically get two bite-wing radiographs every year? This diagnostic practice may have made sense in 1950 when cavities and periodontal disease were pandemic, but it does not make sense now in specific populations.

Research and development in this area are ongoing by a number of interested parties including many dental schools. Development is impeded by the lack of commonly agreed on and used diagnostic codes. Such codes have the potential to significantly

improve outcomes research and are used throughout the general health care system. To the great credit of the American Dental Education Association (ADEA) and a number of the Association's constituent schools, there is real effort being expended now to remove this impediment in an open and public process.

Litigation. The U.S. culture of litigation also influences health care consumerism and the emerging health care systems. Hospital systems and health plans have been and are being sued for permitting practices that were knowingly not effective or actually harmful. One way to manage this kind of risk is to develop guidelines or practice parameters. These guidelines or practice parameters are employed to constrain practices that consistently fall outside a reasoned (evidence-based) set of options. In the case of individual practitioners, they may lose their privileges or may be dropped from payment systems if their practice is deemed to be inappropriate, ineffective, or harmful. This is a different form of risk assessment being practiced within the health care system.

Dental education may be indirectly affected by these activities. The key for most practitioners and health systems is the development of critical thinking among the system's participants. This has been an articulated goal of dental education for many years, but without much tangible emphasis in curriculum competencies (knowledge, skills, and values of dental school graduates) distributed by ADEA or the accreditation process for dental schools implemented by the Commission on Dental Accreditation. Critical thinking has a much more prominent emphasis in the revised version of curriculum competencies that ADEA is in the process of ratifying for distribution to dental schools in 2008. Whether critical thinking will become a greater focus of examining and regulatory bodies remains to be seen. This skill set is crucial for staying current in a health care industry with a rapidly changing science base. The knowledge that students and practitioners acquire today may be obsolete in the not-too-distant future. Transitioning to new practice mechanisms requires the ability to assess and think critically about that science and its sequela.

P4P (Pay for Performance). Consumers (public and private insurers, individual patients, and patient advocacy groups) are demanding proof of outcomes in medicine. They are beginning to pay differentially for those individuals and systems that perform above defined values. This includes systems where public funds are expended on health services. The Veterans Administration is one of the groups taking the lead in examining outcomes and rewarding superior per-

Making Academic Dentistry More Attractive to New Teacher-Scholars

Cathy A. Trower, Ph.D.

Abstract: This perspectives article written under the sponsorship of the Commission on Change and Innovation in Dental Education (CCI) of the American Dental Education Association (ADEA) summarizes data on the numbers of women and persons of color earning the D.D.S./D.M.D. degrees and entering the U.S. dentistry profession in the first decade of the twenty-first century and examines job factors of importance to recent graduates of doctoral programs in other academic disciplines that may have relevance for planning recruitment and retention strategies within academic dentistry. The characteristics and expectations of Generation X faculty are explored: who are they and what do they want from the academic workplace? The article describes the culture clash that often occurs when Gen Xers encounter policies and practices that were designed by and for prior generations (e.g., Traditionalists and Boomers) who filled the ranks of dental school faculty in the 1970s, 1980s, and 1990s. Recommendations for rethinking academic employment systems in ways that might make the university workplace more attractive to Generation X are described.

Dr. Trower is Co-Principal Investigator, Collaborative On Academic Careers in Higher Education (COACHE), Harvard University, Graduate School of Education. Direct correspondence and requests for reprints to her at Harvard University, Graduate School of Education, 8 Story Street, 5th Floor, Cambridge, MA 02138; 617-496-9344 phone; 617-496-9350 fax; trowerca@gse.harvard.edu.

This article is based on a presentation by the author titled "Change, Innovation, and the Quality of Faculty Work-Life" at the American Dental Education Association's 84th Annual Session, March 19, 2007, New Orleans, LA.

This article is one in a series of invited contributions by members of the dental education community that have been commissioned by the ADEA Commission on Change and Innovation (CCI) in Dental Education to address the environment surrounding dental education and affecting the need for, or process of, curricular change. This article was written at the request of the ADEA CCI but does not necessarily reflect the views of ADEA, ADEA CCI, or individual members of CCI. The perspectives communicated here are those of the author.

Key words: dental education, dental faculty, faculty development, academic careers, Gen X, diversity

The dental profession in the United States was almost exclusively male until the mid-1970s. In 1970, women were slightly less than 2 percent of the entering class; in 1984, 25 percent of the students were women. It was during this time period that openly hostile attitudes toward women were ameliorated. As described by Sinkford et al., those attitudes were the "stereotypes that characterized women as emotional, undependable, distracting, flighty, lacking in physical strength, undesirable because they are likely to get pregnant, and somehow less capable than males of practicing dentistry."[1]

Over the last three decades, the number of U.S. women dental students has steadily increased from 1.4 percent in 1970 to 40 percent in 2000. In 2000, women comprised 33 percent of advanced enrollment and 37.5 percent of dental graduates, but only 15 percent of active dentists. The number of women in full- and part-time faculty positions has also in-

creased over this period. Women were 25 percent of the full-time and 30 percent of the part-time dental faculty in 2000. Eighteen percent (ten) of dental schools now have women deans.

In contrast to the numbers of women in dentistry, the enrollment of African Americans, Hispanics, and Native Americans remains low, standing at 12 percent in 2004—lower than the percentage in 1987 through 1996. In spite of some recent increases, the percentage of underrepresented minority dental student enrollments from each group remains significantly lower than the percentage of each group in the U.S. population.[2]

At the fifty-six U.S. dental schools, between the 1990s and 2000, the number of vacant budgeted faculty positions increased over 50 percent, from 238 to 358 vacant positions.[3] Since then, there has been a downward trend to 275 in 2004-05. Importantly, a significant proportion of dental school faculty is

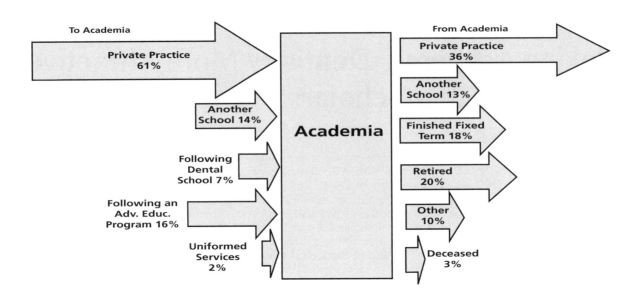

Figure 1. Movement of faculty into and out of academic positions in dental school in 2004-05

Source: Chmar JE, Weaver RG, Valachovic RW. Dental school vacant budgeted faculty positions: academic year 2004-05. J Dent Educ 2006;70:188-98.

over the age of fifty and, as observed by Schenkein and Best, departures for retirements alone are likely to deplete the ranks.[4]

Some of the shortfall is being made up by utilizing part-time faculty, redistributing teaching loads, dividing duties, and providing interdisciplinary coverage, including the use of generalists to teach in specialty areas.[3] However, "little is being done to encourage young dentists to consider academic careers."[4]

These trends are likely to continue for several reasons: the pay gap between private practice and faculty continues to grow, student debt affects postgraduate education opportunities, dental faculty retirements will likely accelerate, parent institutions will expect higher levels of scholarship, and further budget cuts may further exacerbate the situation.[2]

The dental school faculty is currently comprised of 52 percent part-time faculty, 74 percent males, 78 percent whites, with a median age of fifty-two (25 percent are over age sixty). Seventy-four percent are clinical, non-tenure track faculty. As illustrated by Figure 1, we also know where they're coming from and where they go when they leave. Most come from private practice and most leave for private practice.[5] In 2004-05, 61 percent of new faculty came directly

from private practice. Many of these new recruits are older individuals who are joining academia after a twenty-five to thirty-year private practice career; in most instances, they have had little contact with university life. In most cases, as a result, these individuals have little knowledge of the culture, structure, policies, procedures, and general expectations of the academic environment.

In short, colleges of dentistry and the American Dental Education Association (ADEA) face similar challenges to those that confront the nation's medical schools and research universities: how to recruit and retain a sustainable, diverse workforce to meet future demand. For many reasons, it has become increasingly important to know what job factors attract or repel potential faculty. The next section moves from speaking specifically about faculty issues in dental schools to speaking more broadly about young academics.

Job Factors Important for Academic Career Planning

In 2001, the Project on Faculty Appointments[6] at Harvard University conducted a study that measured the importance of nineteen job factors to recent graduates of doctoral degree programs who were planning an academic career. We learned that the top five job factors were 1) institutional support for research; 2) time for family/personal obligations; 3) quality of the department; 4) teaching load; and 5) flexibility of the work schedule. I don't know about you, but it's difficult for me to imagine my father saying he needed time for family and a flexible work schedule.

Part of the difference is not just generational but also because those receiving doctoral degrees are no longer only white males. Students of color placed significantly more importance than white students on institutional support for research, the match between one's research interests and those of others in the department, the opportunity to work with a leader in the field, and job security. Females put significantly more importance than males on the flexibility of the work schedule, time for family/personal obligations, employment opportunities for spouse/partner, teaching load, and the geographic location of the institution. Males felt that the opportunity for recognition, the quality of the department, the quality of the institution, the opportunity to work with a leader in one's field, and the quality of students were the most important considerations for academic career planning.

Ultimately, this research showed that the primary considerations of recent doctoral program graduates in choosing an academic position were finding an institution where they could do meaningful work and strike a balance between teaching and research, live comfortably (e.g., affordable housing, decent commute, good schools for children, a sense of community, safety, job opportunities for spouse/partner), and experience quality of life on the job and outside of work—that is, finding a sense of colleagueship within academia but also, and critically, a semblance of balance between work and home. These expectations for work-life represent a tall order to fill at many U.S. research universities and colleges of dentistry, but this strong desire for balance is characteristic of the so-called Generation X who in large part will become the faculty of the future in many areas of higher education including academic dentistry.

Generation X

Who are the members of this generation, and what do they want? Gen Xers were born between 1965 and 1980, and if there's one adjective that characterizes this generation, it's "skeptical." This was the latch-key generation whose parents divorced and/or whose moms worked outside the home. This makes them independent, adaptable, and resilient. They don't want anyone looking over their shoulder at work. They believe their parents suffer VDD—vacation deficit disorder. They want balance now, not when they're sixty-five. These two quotes sum up the thinking: "If they can't understand that I want a kick-ass career and a kick-ass life, I don't want to work here"; and "Why does it matter when I come and go as long as I get the work done?" Can you imagine saying that to your department chair or dean? Don't get me wrong, Gen Xers are hard workers, but they want to decide when, where, and how. This can be quite unsettling!

Table 1 demonstrates some of the key workplace factors, perceptions, and goals that distinguish

Table 1. The generations at work, according to birth year

Traditionalist 1900-45	Boomer 1946-64	Gen X 1965-80
Chain of command	Change of command	Self-command Collaborate
Build a legacy	Build a stellar career	Build a portable career
Satisfaction of a job well done	Money, title, recognition, corner office	Freedom
If we give in to demands for flexibility, who will do the work?	I can't believe the nerve of those Xers; they want it all!	I'll go where I can find the lifestyle I'm seeking.
Job changing carries a stigma.	Job changing puts you behind.	Job changing is necessary.
If I'm not yelling at you, you're doing fine.	Feedback once a year, well documented	Sorry to interrupt again, but how am I doing?

Source: Lancaster LC, Stillman D. When generations collide. New York: Harper Business, 2002.

the Traditionalist, Boomer, and Gen X generations as depicted by Lancaster and Stillman.[7]

For the most part, the Gen X faculty do not suffer silently. They bring a diverse perspective to an otherwise fairly homogeneous and entrenched faculty culture.

What does this mean for the faculty? From focus groups, interviews, and surveys conducted for the Project on Faculty Appointments at Harvard University,[6] we have discerned a conflict between the dominant perspective of senior faculty—what new scholars find—and the perspective of new faculty—what they value. There are several particularly pertinent fault lines that, taken separately and collectively, have practical implications for rethinking academic employment systems.

Senior faculty (Traditionalists and Boomers) and junior faculty (Gen Xers) live in vastly different assumptive worlds. What the former take for granted, the latter seek to reform. The changes championed by a new generation challenge the commitments and convictions of an older generation. The differences are not about right and wrong, or necessarily even about males and females or minority and majority.[8] The fundamental tension revolves around a basic, yet profound, question: "Who makes the rules?" . . . and a second question: "Who breaks the rules?"

First, there is a clash around processes. Gen X faculty want openness, equity, fairness, and transparency, but they often find a workplace where the dominant belief is that secrecy ensures quality and candor. Boomers and Traditionalists believe that the promotion and tenure process, as well as peer review of research proposals and scholarly manuscripts, must be strictly confidential in order to ensure quality control. Similarly, salaries, workload, and productivity must remain private to foster community.

In contrast, newer Gen X faculty members argue that for too long the shroud of secrecy has masked favoritism, cronyism, racism, and sexism. The tenure process has been described as "archery in the dark." Is it not possible to illuminate the target, they ask?

Second is a clash around research. Young Gen X scholars value collaboration but often find competition. They believe that the researcher is part of what he or she studies but find an assumptive world where the researcher is supposed to be completely detached. New scholars want to do multidisciplinary and problem-centered research rather than explore issues that are traditionally centered in a discipline, but unfortunately there are few multidisciplinary outlets

for publication, which is a source of frustration for the Gen X researcher.

Third, there is a clash around merit. The embedded view positions merit as being empirically determined and objectively derived. For each discipline, there are and, indeed must be, absolute standards of quality that are uniformly applied. We must treat all faculty equally. Any considerations other than merit are, by definition, extraneous. In research, merit means theoretical work organized around a discipline to advance the discipline that appears in the premier refereed journals of the discipline. The emergent view of many young scholars perceives merit as a socially constructed, subjective concept. Quality and merit are relative notions, inevitably conditioned by personal experience and tacit bias. The new generation cites, for example, studies indicating that peer assessments of identical resumes and identical research differ markedly as a function of the gender-specific name assigned to the material under review. The emergent view contends that conventional definitions of merit do not prevail when they are examined on their own merits. Instead, new Gen X scholars tend to believe that people in power valorize the norms necessary to remain in power.

Finally, there is an embedded assumption among Traditionalist and Boomer faculty that, at the end of the day, or certainly at the end of the probationary period, the quality and quantity of scholarly research matter most. Internal reviews and external markets properly place the heaviest weight on the most important and most difficult task—academic research. Scholarly output historically separated the men from the boys and now separates the most meritorious from the least. However, the emerging view of the rising Gen X faculty is that teaching, advising, and service to the campus, the community, and the profession all matter equally, along with research. The value of these activities should not be discounted because they are more nurturing, less visible, not easily documented, or disproportionately assigned to women and faculty of color. For Gen Xers, citizenship in the academic community should mean more than self-investment, self-advancement, and free agency.

There is a prevailing belief that serious, successful scholars make difficult choices and substantial sacrifices that typically place professional priorities above personal needs. Relationships, marriages, families, and recreation, at least in the short run, have to occupy a distant second place. The embedded view basically separates work and family; by and large, personal circumstances are irrelevant. In a zero-sum game, more time dedicated to family means less time devoted to career.

The emergent view, however, is that overall quality of life matters a lot and is a critical component of an individual's personal sense of satisfaction. Gen Xers recognize that it may not be possible to "have it all," but this generation seeks more than professional achievement. Gen Xers believe that home life and work life should be harmonized and not counterposed. The days of stay-at-home spouses have been replaced by dual-career families. The emergent view insists that personal life matters and that a balanced life should not be incompatible with an academic career. If academic success requires eighty-hour work weeks, then Gen Xers contend that we have misconceptualized what should constitute success. The emergent view contends that institutions should adapt to the needs of faculty, not vice versa.

The last items listed here overarch the others: how do we balance autonomy, which almost all faculty value highly, with our collective responsibility?

This cultural clash, in part, has led to a great deal of ambivalence about tenure: is it archery in the dark, or is it, as Mark Twain said of Wagner's music, "not as bad as it sounds"?

In closing, it is my belief that higher education in general and academic dentistry in particular will not be able to attract the best and brightest women and men of all races and ethnicities to the faculty if we do not pay attention to the values of new scholars, if we fail to change our tenure and promotion policies and practices to keep pace with the times and the evolving cultural expectations of our society, and, most criti-

cally, if we are unable to shed the straightjacket of past concepts about academic careers, but continue to insist that one size fits all.

I'd like to close with a quote from the *Wall Street Journal* of November 2, 1992: "The Roman Catholic Church conceded, after 359 years, that it was wrong to have condemned the Italian scientist Galileo for asserting that the Earth orbits the sun. Pope John Paul II, on Saturday, accepted the findings of a panel that studied the case." I hope we can act faster than that!

REFERENCES

1. Sinkford JC, Valachovic RW, Harrison SG. Advancement of women in dental education: trends and strategies. J Dent Educ 2003;67(1):79-83.
2. Sinkford JC, Valachovic RW, Harrison SG. Underrepresented minority dental school enrollment: continued vigilance required. J Dent Educ 2004;68(10):1112-8.
3. Haden NK, Weaver RG, Valachovic RW. Meeting the demand for future dental school faculty: trends, challenges, and responses. J Dent Educ 2002;66(9):1102-13.
4. Schenkein HA, Best HA. Factors considered by new faculty in their decision to choose careers in academic dentistry. J Dent Educ 2001;65(9):832-40.
5. Chmar JE, Weaver RG, Valachovic RW. Dental school vacant budgeted faculty positions: academic year 2004-05. J Dent Educ 2006;70(2):188-98.
6. Bleak J, Neiman H, Sternman-Rule C, Trower C. Project on Faculty Appointments. Faculty recruitment study: statistical analysis report. Cambridge, MA: Harvard Graduate School of Education, 2000.
7. Lancaster LC, Stillman D. When generations collide. New York: Harper Business, 2002.
8. Trower C, Chait R. Faculty diversity: too little for too long. Harvard Magazine 2002;104(4):33-37, 98.

Does the Dental School Work Environment Promote Successful Academic Careers?

Carroll-Ann Trotman, B.D.S., M.A., M.S.; N. Karl Haden, Ph.D.;
William Hendricson, M.S., M.A.

Abstract: A consistent theme in the national dialogue about future directions for the educational arm of dentistry is how best to cultivate a school environment that will be seen as attractive by members of the dental community who desire to serve their profession as teachers and scholars. As a first step toward stimulating broad-based reflection on the working environment within dental schools, the ADEA Commission on Change and Innovation (CCI) conducted a symposium titled "Change, Innovation, and the Quality of Faculty Work-Life" at the 2007 ADEA Annual Session in New Orleans. Aspects of this article are based on the content of this symposium, which explored research on the perceptions and concerns of dental faculty regarding the current academic workplace and provided perspectives of university faculty about university life and career growth. This article reviews the findings from two interview-based qualitative assessments of faculty perceptions of work-life in dental schools and other schools of higher education, presents a preliminary summary of the first national survey of dental school faculty regarding their impressions of the academic work environment, and makes recommendations for enhancing the dental school work environment with an emphasis on those factors that influence career growth. Results from these three studies illustrate faculty perceptions about the promotion and tenure and performance evaluation processes; workload and quality of work-life; and quality of institutional support.

Dr. Trotman is Professor of Orthodontics, and Assistant Dean for Graduate Education and Academic Development, University of North Carolina at Chapel Hill School of Dentistry; Dr. Haden is President, Academy for Academic Leadership, Atlanta, Georgia; and Mr. Hendricson is Assistant Dean, Educational and Faculty Development, University of Texas Health Science Center at San Antonio Dental School. Direct correspondence and requests for reprints to Dr. Carroll-Ann Trotman, University of North Carolina at Chapel Hill School of Dentistry, 1050 Old Dental Building, CB # 7450, Chapel Hill, NC 27599-7450; 919-966-4451 phone; carroll-ann_trotman@dentistry.unc.edu.

This article is one in a series of invited contributions by members of the dental education community that have been commissioned by the ADEA Commission on Change and Innovation (CCI) in Dental Education to address the environment surrounding dental education and affecting the need for, or process of, curricular change. This article was written at the request of the ADEA CCI but does not necessarily reflect the views of ADEA, ADEA CCI, or individual members of the CCI. The perspectives communicated here are those of the authors.

Key words: dental faculty, faculty development, mentoring, promotion and tenure, academic culture

In dental school, student success is driven by definitions, standards, and competencies; however, based on recruitment and retention patterns, conditions that promote and reinforce faculty success in the academic work environment continue to be ill-defined and are apparently applied sporadically. Consider the statistics on the dental faculty workforce in 2004-05. The American Dental Education Association (ADEA) reported that 1,039 faculty—a figure that represents 9 percent of this workforce—left dental education and 36 percent of those individuals entered private practice. Surveys of senior dental students indicated an extremely low interest (0.5 to 1.2 percent of these students) in pursuing academic careers, mainly because of financial considerations such as the burden of dental school debt and a wide disparity between academic salaries and private practice income potential.[1] These trends could be interpreted to mean that, in 2007, current dental faculty are dissatisfied with certain aspects of their academic work-life and that

maybe the work environment in dental schools does not provide a culture conducive to recruiting members of the dental community into faculty roles.

The highly publicized and well-documented faculty "brain drain" should stimulate administrative leaders in dental schools, who now find themselves with dwindling resources in terms of both faculty and finances, to assess the capacity of their institutions to foster attractive and professionally satisfying career paths for junior and mid-career faculty and to ensure continued productivity of senior faculty. As will be described in this article, areas of the academic environment that are sources of dissatisfaction for some dental school faculty also exist in the general university environment to such an extent that the challenges confronting dental education are most likely reflective of a larger set of issues that exist throughout higher education. Furthermore, recent research has shown that there is a divide throughout higher education between the perceptions of early and mid-career faculty and those of their more senior colleagues about the academic environment, and this difference in outlook encompasses both professional and personal issues.[2,3] Thus, the purposes of this article are as follows: 1) to further explore dental school faculty perceptions of their work-life and to determine the dissatisfactions, if any, that may be contributing to many early and mid-career faculty leaving academia; 2) to compare perceptions of university faculty who work outside of dental schools to those of dental faculty; 3) to present a preliminary summary of the first national survey of dental school faculty impressions of their work environment; and 4) to make recommendations for enhancing the dental school work environment with an emphasis on factors that influence career growth.

This article was sponsored by the Commission on Change and Innovation (CCI) in Dental Education, which was established by ADEA as part of the Association's overall effort to raise awareness of challenges and opportunities and promote dialogue within the academic dentistry community. The CCI was created because numerous organizations within organized dentistry and the educational community have initiated studies or proposed modifications to the process of dental education in recent years but with limited communication and coordination.[4] Thus, the fundamental mission of the CCI is to provide a central hub for communication where dental educators and representatives from organized dentistry, the dental licensure community, the Commission on Dental Accreditation, the American Dental Association's Council on Dental Education and Licensure, and the Joint Commission on National Dental Examinations can share perspectives about how to improve dental education and thereby stimulate national discussion of ideas for creating a dynamic environment for learning within dental schools. A key theme in the national discussion of future directions for the educational arm of the dental profession is how best to cultivate an attractive and intellectually stimulating "academy" that will be seen as a desirable place to work by members of the dental community who desire to serve their profession as teachers and scholars. As a first step toward stimulating broad-based reflection about the working environment within dental schools, the CCI conducted a symposium titled "Change, Innovation, and the Quality of Faculty Work-Life" at the 2007 ADEA Annual Session in New Orleans. Aspects of this article are based on the content of this symposium, which explored research on the perceptions and concerns of potential and current dental faculty regarding the current academic environment and also provided faculty perspectives about life and career growth in the university environment.

The content of the article is a summary of available and emerging research on faculty members' impressions of their work tasks and settings and the forces that influence, positively and negatively, their opportunities for career growth in the educational arm of the dental profession. This is not a methodological or formal research report; instead, our goal is to communicate findings from three distinct studies conducted across a span of seven years (2000, 2004, and 2007) that we hope will be thought-provoking and serve as a catalyst for discussion and reflection about how dental schools, individually and collectively, can build an institutional culture where individuals who desire to serve dentistry in educational and scholarly roles can be successful and satisfied both professionally and personally. Some of the information presented is based on previously published qualitative research,[5-8] as well as on selected and preliminary results from the Dental Faculty Work Environment Questionnaire, developed and administered in 2007 by the Academy for Academic Leadership for the ADEA CCI. This survey was conducted to generate quantitative data on the perceptions of tenure-track and non-tenure-track faculty members at U.S. dental schools about the work environment in academic dentistry. It was administered in February through April 2007 in an online format. Preliminary findings will be reported based on a total of 1,748 responses provided by faculty at forty-nine of fifty-six U.S. dental schools (87 percent). These data represent only highlights of certain notable outcomes. A subsequent article by Haden, targeted for winter 2007 in the CCI Perspectives Series, will provide a definitive quantitative analysis of the outcomes of the questionnaire with comparisons among categories of respondents grouped by age, gender, ethnicity, academic rank, years of experience as a faculty member, discipline/specialty, job focus, and other factors.

Methodology: 2000 and 2004 Faculty Interviews

The qualitative data were obtained from in-depth, one-on-one, telephone interviews conducted with faculty within the dental academic[5] and general university settings[6-8] in order to gauge, in as broad a manner as possible, their perspectives on issues related to faculty work-life. This type of qualitative research is used for gathering information on complex issues and offers methods for outlining these issues in rich, vivid detail.[9]

Within dentistry, ten undergraduate dental students, ten residents in dental postgraduate programs, and ten junior, untenured, full-time faculty working in various U.S. dental schools were interviewed to obtain their perceptions of the positive and negative factors associated with academic life. The individuals in each group were balanced by gender. This qualitative study was conducted in 2000 and was funded by the American Association of Orthodontists Foundation. Similar interviews were conducted in 2004 with a total of fifty untenured (junior) faculty and tenured (mid-career) faculty randomly selected from the sixteen component universities that comprise the University of North Carolina (UNC) system. The 2004 study was funded partly by the TIAA-CREF Institute and the UNC General Administration and was conducted in collaboration with Betsy E. Brown, who was formerly at the UNC General Administration and is now at North Carolina State University. The demographics of these fifty faculty interviewed in 2004 were 61 percent female and 39 percent male. White faculty made up 63 percent, while 22 percent were African American, 7 percent Asian, and 7 percent Hispanic.

The interviews were semistructured, and some of the information discussed during the interviews focused on the following issues:

- reasons for choosing an academic career;
- the institution's interest in and support for teaching, research, and public service;
- required time commitment to meet expectations;
- economic benefits and hurdles;
- benefits (health, retirement, other);
- quality of life, job location, and family support;
- tenure and promotion processes; and
- role of colleagues and senior administrators.

For a more thorough review of the dental and general university faculty perceptions, including a full discussion of all issues, a set of quotations from the individuals who were interviewed, and an in-depth description of the methodology, the reader is invited to review citations 5-8.

Methodology: 2007 Dental Faculty Work Environment Questionnaire

The research protocol for this study was reviewed and approved by the Institutional Review Board of the University of Texas Health Science Center at San Antonio (UTHSCSA) in February 2007 as exempted research. The four objectives of the study were to:

1. determine faculty members' perceptions of work-life and school environment that influence decision making about academic careers in dental education;
2. identify academic work environment factors that are sources of satisfaction to dental school faculty and identify sources of dissatisfaction;
3. elicit faculty opinions about the clarity of procedures and expectations for promotion and tenure and evaluation of job performance; and
4. determine faculty members' perceptions about the availability and value of professional development resources and activities at their dental school including mentoring, career growth planning, faculty development and continuing education programs, and administrative and peer support.

The Dental Faculty Work Environment Questionnaire was based on two sources: 1) the Faculty Job Satisfaction Survey developed for the "Study of New Scholars" at the Harvard Graduate School of Education by Trower and Chait[10]; this survey instrument has been used since 2003 in a variety of higher education institutions including professional schools; and 2) an online survey used for assessing career enhancement needs that could be addressed in faculty development programs at UTHSCSA, which was developed by William Hendricson in his capacity as Director, Educational Research and Development Division at UTHSCSA.

Design

The questionnaire was designed in an online format that employed a forced choice "menu," but included opportunities for write-in responses. The questionnaire consisted of twenty-nine questions and ninety-nine items that requested responses. Practice administrations during instrument development and pilot-testing indicated that completion time was approximately fifteen minutes. The questionnaire included eight sections: 1) background information: dental school, highest academic degree obtained, length of time as a faculty member (current position and all positions during career), current academic rank, tenure vs. non-tenure track, full-time vs. part-time, department or discipline, race/ethnicity, age, gender, total compensation, and main focus of academic appointment (teaching, research, service, administration, combination); 2) clarity of information about the promotion and tenure process, expectations, and criteria; 3) clarity of information about terms of employment in non-tenure-track positions; 4) satisfaction with day-to-day activities as a faculty member; 5) professional development support and resources including mentoring; 6) satisfaction with professional development opportunities and mentoring; 7) perceptions of the dental school environment and culture; and 8) perceptions of the dental school as a place to work.

The questionnaire was pilot-tested with a sample of forty faculty members at the UTHSCSA in January 2007. Following modifications based on pilot-test feedback, the full questionnaire was distributed electronically to faculty at fifty-six U.S. dental schools in February to April 2007. The chair of the CCI, Dr. Kenneth Kalkwarf, sent emails to the deans of each U.S. dental school informing them of the aims and methodology of the study and the uses of the data by ADEA. Deans were informed that they could elect to decline participation if they so desired. The link (URL address) to the Dental Faculty Work Environment Questionnaire and the IRB-approved information sheet (equivalent to a subject consent form for exempted education research) accompanied the message to the deans.

Subjects and Distribution

All full- and part-time dental school faculty in clinical, basic science, and behavioral departments were eligible to complete the questionnaire.

The CCI has implemented mechanisms to facilitate a national discussion of curricular issues and sharing of strategies that foster innovation in dental education. One mechanism was to establish a network of faculty who serve as CCI liaisons at U.S. dental schools. The goals of the CCI liaison network are to promote two-way communication between the schools and the commission, serve as a conduit for information exchange between the CCI and the faculty who implement the curriculum for students, and provide leadership for implementation of educational innovations. Recruitment of CCI liaisons as site coordinators for this study provided two benefits: it facilitated response by having the questionnaire come from faculty peers at each campus versus the central office of ADEA, and it provided an opportunity for the liaisons to communicate with their peers about faculty development issues and thus raise their vis-

ibility at their own schools. In February 2007, the CCI liaisons initially distributed the questionnaire to faculty at their schools via email with an embedded link to the host website and distributed it for a second time in April 2007. The liaisons received an explanatory message from the investigators that was used as the participation invitation message for their faculty peers. This message described the objectives and uses of the data by ADEA.

Response Rate and Basic Subject Demographics

Through April 15, 2007, a total of 1,748 faculty from forty-nine U.S. dental schools completed the Dental Faculty Work Environment Questionnaire; the average response rate per school was thirty-six faculty members. Overall, the subjects represent 17 percent of all U.S. full- and part-time dental school faculty and 21 percent of the faculty at the responding schools. The respondents were 34 percent female and 66 percent male, and 87 percent indicated that their "home" discipline/department was in the clinical sciences. The subjects were 81 percent Caucasian, 7 percent Asian, 7 percent Hispanic, and 3 percent African American. Distribution of subjects by academic rank was 27 percent full professors, 32 percent associate professors, 30 percent assistant professors, 6 percent instructors, lecturers, research associates, or teaching assistants, and 5 percent adjunct faculty. Approximately 78 percent of respondents were full-time, and 22 percent were part-time. By age, 28 percent reported they were sixty years and older, 37 percent were fifty to fifty-nine, 20 percent were in their forties, and 15 percent were less than forty years of age. Although the age of the respondents to the questionnaire may appear to be skewed, the age distribution is indeed representative of dental school faculty in 2007. In addition, any age-related bias in the data obtained is counterbalanced by the 2000 and 2004 interview data that were obtained primarily from junior and mid-career faculty.

The three studies conducted in 2000, 2004, and 2007 represent combined interview and questionnaire-derived data and provide faculty perspectives and insights from within academic dentistry and outside the dental school in the wider university setting. It is hoped that these data will stimulate reflection about faculty development, career planning, mentoring, and promotion and tenure processes at each academic dental institution.

Summary of Key Findings

As shown in Figure 1, key outcomes from the three studies are summarized in relation to three categories related to academic work-life (the academic evaluation process, workload and quality of work-life, and quality of institutional support). Findings from the 2000 and 2004 interviews represent the combined perceptions of the eighty interviewees: thirty dental and fifty non-dental respondents. However, in instances where dental school subjects provided uniquely different insights about academic life, their responses are described separately. Verbatim comments from transcripts of the 2000 and 2004 interviews are presented to illustrate prevailing themes. Data presented from the 2007 Dental Faculty Work Environment Questionnaire represent the opinions of only dental school faculty (n=1748). In each section, findings from the 2000 and 2004 interviews are described first, followed by corresponding data from the questionnaire.

Academic Evaluation Process

The 2000 and 2004 interviews and the 2007 Dental Faculty Work Environment Questionnaire elicited information from study participants about the promotion and tenure process, tenure expectations and criteria, and mentoring. Not surprisingly, a major theme from the interviews of faculty, including the dental faculty, was that, for those on the tenure track, the tenure and promotion process was of major importance but also a source of frustration due to lack of consistent information. Most schools have guidelines for tenure, but many faculty members perceived these guidelines as ambiguous and almost like chasing a "moving target." Many felt they had to rely on other faculty who were not related to their promotion process to obtain tangible information and insights about methods for performance evaluation and standards/expectations for achieving tenure. In addition, most respondents indicated that there was little follow-up on their progress toward obtaining tenure by their department chairs or other senior faculty. Some commented that it was important to have a head start in that it helped greatly if you came from another institution with prior or pending grant funding and publications. Others perceived a disconnect between the tenure process and other faculty work: that is, the time commitment for completing the work leading to tenure did not match the contractual work expectations. Junior dental faculty observed that they had few recently tenured role models as examples, and the dental residents who were interviewed questioned whether tenure was even a possibility.

Regarding mentoring, the importance of the department chair and other senior faculty was highlighted. Interviewed faculty felt that support from the chair in terms of protecting time in the schedule, providing feedback on progress, and being an overall advocate were critical for successful career planning and growth, although such mentoring and career guidance were only sporadically available.

Following are selected quotations[6,7] from faculty on specific topics:

[Tenure process] "It's been a situation generally that I would characterize by ambiguity.

2000 Dental Student, Resident, and Faculty Interviews	2004 Interviews with Faculty at University of North Carolina Component Schools	2007 Dental Faculty Work Environment Questionnaire by ADEA CCI
The Academic Evaluation Process		
Workload and Quality of Work-Life		
Quality of Institutional Support		

Figure 1. Structure of findings summary comprised of data sources (horizontal axis) and characteristics of academic work-life (vertical axis)

In other words, you get a message from an official and you sort of think that's right and then you'll hear someone else articulate it slightly differently."

[Tenure requirements] "The disturbing part is watching how quickly tenure requirements are changing. We have an eight-year clock here, and tenure requirements have crept up at least two or three times in the five years I've been here. . . . For the people who came in under the old rules and who are going to be scrutinized by the new rules, that's a little disturbing."

[Tenure process] "I think in this particular college there's a fairly transparent and supportive administration such that if there are issues that need to be dealt with, they seem to make you aware of them pretty quickly and then provide you the opportunity to find your way around to improve things, or if there are a series of marks that one needs to hit, they're relatively visible from the moment you get here."

[Tenure expectations] "We just had this document about teaching loads or whatever, time distribution, and it was said that you should spend 60% of your time teaching, 20% of your time on research, and 20% of your time on service. Well, that is not, if you look at the tenure package, what the university evaluates you on. And so there's a total disconnect between what I'm supposed to be doing."

Faculty who responded to the 2007 Dental Faculty Work Environment Questionnaire rated the clarity of the tenure and promotion process, performance standards and expectations, and career planning advice as minimally adequate, which is consistent with the responses obtained by interviews in 2000 and 2004. For example, less than 20 percent of not-yet-tenured faculty on tenure-track appointments said that expectations for obtaining tenure in any of the three main areas of performance (teaching, research, service) were clear. Only 14 percent of this same group of not-yet-tenured faculty reported that advice about career planning from senior faculty was clear, and more than 80 percent said that the overall process for obtaining tenure was not clear at all or could be improved. Additionally, 62 percent of ten-

ured faculty said that the process they experienced to obtain tenure was not clear or could be improved. Among dental school faculty in non-tenure-track positions, 66 percent reported that the information they received about their rights and obligations as a non-tenure appointee was either not clear or could be improved. When asked to indicate their level of satisfaction with "the mentoring I have received from senior faculty in my department," 54 percent responded ok, dissatisfied, or very dissatisfied. These data suggest that minimal progress has been made over the past seven years in clarifying the faculty evaluation process or helping faculty understand the expectations for obtaining tenure.

Workload and Quality of Work-Life

This component of the 2000 and 2004 interviews and the 2007 Dental Faculty Work Environment Questionnaire elicited information on satisfaction with day-to-day activities as a faculty member; the environment and culture; and the academic environment as a place to work. Based on the interviews, virtually all respondents, whether in dental schools or in general education settings, expressed a deep appreciation for teaching and truly appeared to value their interactions with students. Many commented on the importance of collegial dialogue and advice from department chairs and senior colleagues as having a major influence on their confidence and ability to succeed in an academic environment. Not surprisingly, work and family responsibilities clashed, and many faculty members indicated they desired information about support services to help balance these two aspects of their life. Such information included assistance with finding daycare facilities and general information on university policies and the university community. Other faculty with families whose academic work duties allowed flexibility appreciated the ability to have those flexible work schedules to assist with meeting family obligations and needs. On the negative side, some faculty expressed an awareness of competition among their colleagues and felt burdened by internal departmental politics.

Specific to dental faculty and their perceptions about academic workload, many said that they expected that academia would allow them to have more personal time than in dental practice and they would be able to maintain a predictable and standard forty-hour work week. In contrast to this expectation, many of the junior dental faculty who were interviewed reported that they actually had little control over their work schedule and overall academic life and thus saw this as a negative factor. However, junior dental faculty indicated that they liked the variety of tasks performed during an academic workday versus a private practice workday and saw this diversity of activity as a positive factor. In regard to the need to move to a different dental school for career advancement, better compensation and/or a more satisfying work environment, some junior faculty viewed relocation as a positive factor of academic life and perceived the possibility of mobility as a freedom. However, others felt that having to move to improve career prospects or working conditions was burdensome, especially when families have to be uprooted in the process.

Following are selected quotations[6,7] from faculty on specific topics:

[Work balance] "In principle I think that would be possible [i.e., to balance work and family life], but if you think about the fact that I'm on the tenure track and that you need to satisfy certain requirements, which are not very well defined, so there could be some uncertainty as to, well, am I doing enough? Am I going to make it? That makes it hard to . . . make those decisions."

[University information] "That's totally played down [university community information] and you kind of have to try and find stuff. I've been here, this is my fourth year and I still don't know anything. . . . I mean, I was not even told when graduation was or where the ceremony was."

[University policies] "To be honest I don't think I know enough about that [university policies], and I think it would be useful. The orientation for new faculty, at least when I went through it, really went through things like, well, particularly retirement plan options very, very quickly, and you know, I don't think any of us really knew what our options were, what was going on."

[Daycare] "I know the daycare director's very careful, but I mean you really need to be on it, you know, the day you get proof [of a pregnancy]. And everyone who's here knows that. So you go from the doctor to the childcare place with the letter from the doctor . . . and it's very, very expensive and it's not subsidized."

[Flexible academic work schedule] "The answer is that it's [flexibility] marvelous, but I don't think that's at all unusual. I think that all of us professors have it really good across the country when it comes to arranging our schedules, compared to most laborers in the United States."

Responses of faculty to the Dental Faculty Work Environment Questionnaire tended to support the interview results. The vast majority of faculty respondents (86 percent) enjoyed their interactions with colleagues and felt that they were treated fairly (73 percent) by their department chair. When asked to rate their department as a place to work, 73 percent responded that they were either satisfied or very satisfied, but only 62 percent rated their dental school environment as a good or excellent place to work, with more than 30 percent indicating that the environment was just "ok" and "could be better." Write-in comments submitted by dental faculty on the questionnaire indicated that multitasking was an expected and necessary aspect of their job; faculty reported that they were required to "bounce among tasks that were quite different" and "wear multiple hats such as be a clinician, educator, administrator, advisor, school citizen (serve on committees)." Faculty at both the associate and assistant professor levels reported that they were performing many of these tasks without appropriate training.

Interestingly, interviews of the dental students in 2000 revealed that while one-on-one teaching by faculty was appealing, they reported that they had few examples of full-time faculty who made academic careers look attractive. These students perceived that there were no incentives for teaching and that full-time faculty were pulled in too many directions while part-time faculty (adjuncts) were viewed as more positive role models. The old adage of academia being a fallback for failed private practice was mentioned by some of the interviewees in 2000. In addition, although many students recognized that research could enhance clinical teaching, many perceived that faculty were overburdened by research. These perceptions contributed to an overall "negative" culture in some school environments that was seen as a deterrent for entering academia.

Following are selected quotations[5] from residents on specific topics:

[On research] "I mean it's [obtaining grant funding] extremely competitive and that's pretty terrifying to be able to put in the number of years that these people have put in and then not be able to advance through the academic system."

[On success] "I haven't found very many people who are successful in doing the things I want to do, that is, being able to do research, support a lab, and also be involved clinically."

The perceptions of the students are consistent with findings from the Students' Perspective Project (SPP) conducted by Henzi et al.[11-13] In the SPP, more than 2,000 dental students from thirty-two U.S. and Canadian dental schools qualitatively evaluated the educational environment in their dental school and analyzed the strengths and weaknesses of the curriculum. From the viewpoint of the students in the SPP study, failure to create an environment conducive to keeping effective teachers was often described as a major threat to the quality of dental school. Students at virtually every school in the SPP study bemoaned the loss of high-quality faculty to the lures of private practice and provided testimonials about the impact of these losses upon their education: namely, experienced faculty with enthusiasm for teaching were replaced with individuals who had little teaching experience. Students described situations in which dentists who came directly from private practice and who had never taught were placed in charge of major courses shortly after they started work in the school. A key finding from the SPP study is that the loss of skilled instructors is diminishing the educational product delivered by dental schools in the minds of the students. Given the Generation Y students' expectations for high-quality, efficient, and cost-effective educational "service" from faculty,[14,15] will faculty retention problems ultimately drive down the perceived value of dental education in the minds of the value-conscious Gen Y learner to such an extent that prospective students will look elsewhere for a professional career? Students' concerns about the faculty "brain-drain"[13] are illustrated by these responses from SPP participants:

"Faculty shortage is the greatest threat to quality. The really good faculty consistently indicate that they are not paid enough to make the job worthwhile."

"Being able to attract quality faculty is a concern. The smart people know there's not as much money in teaching as in private practice, so it can be very difficult attracting quality full-time faculty."

"There is a shortage of quality faculty who enjoy teaching and have a positive attitude about the school and dentistry."

"One of the biggest threats is the decrease in the number of really good instructors. Many times the good ones get chased out and we the students see this."

"My classmates and I are concerned that skilled and knowledgeable faculty are becoming rare; there has been a decrease in enthusiastic, qualified instructors."

"Faculty accepting positions without having the desire to teach; there are too many older faculty and not enough younger faculty."

Junior dental faculty who were interviewed in 2000 also appreciated the importance of teaching and very much enjoyed their students' successes, but also felt that teaching was not valued by administrators, whom some viewed as untrustworthy. The following is a quote[5] from a junior faculty member that illustrates the positive perception of teaching:

[Dental faculty on teaching] "And you know teaching goes back hundreds and hundreds of years and it's a tradition, it's a wonderful tradition, it's a wonderful thing as a human being to be involved in."

Quality of Institutional Support

The 2000 and 2004 interviews and the 2007 Dental Faculty Work Environment Questionnaire elicited respondents' perceptions about support for professional development, satisfaction with compensation, and clarity of information about terms of employment. Interviewed faculty reported that support for professional development was limited. The opportunity for sabbaticals was considered very important. However, faculty reported that the availability of sabbaticals was inconsistent: they were possible in some departments, but not in others. Many faculty expressed frustration with poor pay raises and issues of salary compression, and for those faculty in the general university, many felt the need to supplement their salaries by, for example, teaching in the summer. Benefits were an issue but were state-specific. For example, some faculty in North Carolina felt that the health insurance benefits offered by the state were inadequate, but most felt that the retirement benefits were adequate. Dental students and junior dental faculty reported that faculty were given limited instructions in the how-to's of teaching, and some junior faculty felt somewhat unprepared for teaching. In addition, to accommodate a wider variety of potential faculty, some interview subjects felt that university administrators should allow greater flexibility in job requirements such as part-time, tenure-track appointments, flexible teaching schedules, etc.

Following are selected quotations[6,7] from faculty on specific topics:

[Sabbatical] "If I wanted to take a year instead of a semester, the deans have always said that would be fine, but none of my chairs have ever agreed to that because it's a small department and I'm too important and blah, blah, blah."

[Salary] "[My salary is] not even really in keeping with inflation. And I mean, you would think that, you know it's not the same job: I'm a much better teacher asset to the university now than I was 13 years ago and so I would've hoped we could've done better than an x% increase in salary."

[Salary] "My wife has a job at X University, we have no children, and I had relatively wealthy parents, you know, who paid for my college education and so forth, so I have no outstanding loans and that sort of thing. Because of this social position, I really could care less."

[Extra teaching] "The one thing that I have been able to do, which was really a sacrifice, and that was summer teaching. I have taught every summer and cannot afford not to teach in the summer. . . . I consider my summer salary as part of my yearly salary."

[Benefits] "The benefits are going down . . . almost every semester."

[Benefits] "The dental insurance, I think, is particularly upsetting because there's a cap on it."

Among respondents to the Dental Faculty Work Environment Questionnaire, 52 percent indicated that their compensation was $100,000 or less (67 percent of the individuals in this category were females, and 44 percent were males); 31 percent earned between $101,000 and $150,000; and 17 percent earned $151,000 and higher. These figures were not based solely on salary but on their total compensation package, which included salary, benefits, continuing education stipends, faculty practice reimbursements, and other compensation such as tuition and travel. Regarding satisfaction with compensation, the questionnaire results indicate that 39 percent of all respondents (e.g., all academic ranks) were equally split between being "satisfied with their compensation" and "not satisfied," with 22 percent in the "neutral" category. However, as might be expected, respondents at the assistant professor level were far more likely to report dissatisfaction with compensation. Among all assistant professors, 31 percent were satisfied with compensation, and 45 percent were not satisfied. Although less well paid at all academic ranks than their male peers, the responses of female faculty reflected the same overall response pattern: 38 percent were satisfied, 24 percent were neutral, and the remaining 38 percent were not satisfied. Regarding benefits (which were defined as number of vacation days, sick leave policies, the quality of health insurance, and retirement plan options), 73 percent of dental faculty were satisfied with the packages offered, and only 11 percent were not satisfied.

Overall, respondents to the Dental Faculty Work Environment Questionnaire provided a mixed picture about the availability of professional development resources at their schools. On the positive side, 58 percent indicated that travel funds for professional meetings were available, and more than half of the respondents indicated their schools conducted regular in-service programs, brought in outside speakers for enrichment, and conducted faculty development retreats for the whole school. On the other hand, only 20 percent of respondents reported that a formal mentoring program existed for new faculty, 25 percent reported that mentoring existed for junior faculty on tenure tracks, and 26 percent reported that their school conducted workshops on the promotion and tenure process. Overall, more than 50 percent indicated that their level of satisfaction with professional development opportunities at their school ranged from "adequate" to highly dissatisfied.

Recommendations: Enhancing the Dental School Work Environment

Much has been written on the topic of faculty recruitment and retention, specifically as it relates to the impact of work activities on faculty attitudes and perceptions. Researchers, including those in dentistry, have proposed several best practices and strategies that can be implemented to alleviate faculty concerns.[4,7,8] In this section, several recommendations are described that can be applied to academic dentistry settings. These recommendations are based on three assumptions: 1) "success" must be recognized as being different for each of the talented faculty at our institutions who are driven to teach and to foster the development of dental practitioners; 2) chairs and deans must create an environment for success that is specific to the faculty member, and this specificity should entail a process whereby a faculty member (whether newly hired, mid-career, or senior) is moved successfully through the ranks of promotion in an environment that is motivating, with supportive and challenging student interactions, collegial interactions among faculty, excitement and passion in research endeavors, expectations of fair and balanced compensation practices, and adequate time for family; and 3) as much as possible, the dental school environment must be more closely integrated into the general university environment. Only through integration can other colleges appreciate the importance of the dental school mission and the diversity of faculty necessary to support this mission. Such an appreciation can be beneficial during the promotion process for dental faculty as they move through the ranks of the university.

Our recommendations for enhancing the dental school work environment are as follows:

1. Articulate Clear Expectations of Faculty.

Clear expectations help to dispel anxiety associated with uncertainty over job performance. This is especially important for tenure guidelines. Our research suggests that junior faculty at dental schools find tenure guidelines range from being too rigid and unrealistic to unclear and vague. Obviously, some balance must be reached by administrators to have tenure guidelines that allow both flexibility and clarity. Best practices such as employing written expectations that are reviewed yearly with specific milestones of achievement can go a long way towards solving problems of trust with administrators, perceived departmental political influences, and other stresses. These milestones can be tied directly to compensation practices to ensure a measure of fairness.

2. Do Your Homework: Make Sure the Job "Fit" and Environment Are Good Ones for You.

A good resource for dental school faculty is Mary Deane Sorcinelli's "The Top Ten Things New Faculty Would Like to Hear from Colleagues."[16] Three "things" from this Top Ten can help to stabilize the academic environment for faculty, especially those taking on new academic appointments. These three are as follows: first, "figure out what matters" in their new job; second, "decide what does not matter"; and third, know that "teaching always matters." Faculty should seek advice from their mentors and senior colleagues to make these determinations, and senior administrators should provide guidance to faculty related to these three criteria for success in new academic roles. For new faculty or faculty in new roles, answering these questions about what matters to your success in your new position and what does not matter will help clarify whether the position is a good fit for both you and the department and will improve your efficiency toward meeting expectations once you are in the job.

3. Teaching Matters MOST. Make No Mistake About This!

Data from the three studies reported here and elsewhere indicate that both faculty and students greatly value the intellectual stimulation and interactions that occur during teaching. That being said, many mixed messages on teaching are perceived by faculty and students; these include being overburdened by teaching, and, yet, having no rewards or value associated with teaching activities. Some student respondents observed that some faculty were inadequately trained to teach and that training to acquire teaching skills should be offered. Hosting teaching seminars for both new and more seasoned faculty that are targeted toward teaching in the dental environment is one opportunity to help prepare new faculty for their roles and keep seasoned faculty current. Data from the Dental Faculty Work Environment Questionnaire indicate that dental schools engage in a variety of efforts to support the development of their faculty, but few schools have the resources to implement a comprehensive initiative to develop the teaching or research skills of newly hired faculty. The questionnaire responses suggest that dental school faculty perceive a need for additional professional enrichment opportunities. At the national level, as depicted in Figure 2, ADEA provides a continuum of support and enrichment that reflects the career arc of dental school faculty and consists of four inter-related components: 1) the Academic Dental Careers Fellowship Program (ADCFP) to promote and support interest in academic careers among students; 2) the Scholarship of Teaching and Learning (SoTL) online community to provide enrichment and networking opportunities for a broad segment of the ADEA membership in conjunction with ADEA's faculty development workshops at the Annual Session; 3) the Institute for Teaching and

Learning (ITL), cosponsored with the Academy for Academic Leadership (AAL), which provides an in-depth "immersion" learning experience for early career faculty or practitioners transitioning into the academic environment; and 4) the ADEA Leadership Institute for mid-career faculty who desire to attain administrative roles within their own or other institutions or enhance their effectiveness in these roles.

In the ADCFP, upper-class dental students participate in a year-long fellowship in which they teach in classrooms, labs, and the clinic, conduct research projects, interview faculty at various academic levels about academic careers, create posters and presentations to share their experience with other students at the ADEA Annual Session, write personal educational philosophy essays, and compile reflection journals to chronicle their experiences and perceptions of faculty life. The goal is to expose students to the opportunities and rewards of teaching and scholarship in dental schools. The ADEA/AAL Institute for Teaching and Learning is a national

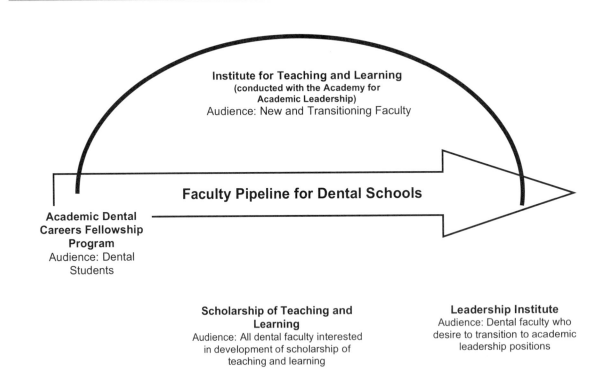

Figure 2. ADEA professional development continuum

effort to aggressively identify future faculty and provide intensive training to assist potential and new faculty to become excellent teachers, scholars, and satisfied academicians. Cohort groups of twenty-five to thirty ITL Scholars from a variety of dental schools complete a seven-day program, conducted in two phases, that addresses skills in teaching, curriculum planning, student assessment, and scholarship with "at-home" application assignments between phases, team projects, and practice teaching and peer feedback during ITL sessions. Numerous studies and comprehensive reviews of the literature indicate that the intensive, longitudinal "immersion" approaches to faculty development that involve active learning (e.g., practice teaching activities, roleplay, analysis of case scenarios, participation in simulations, self-assessment, and peer feedback) are the most likely to produce lasting modifications in behavior and retention of acquired skills.[14-27]

4. **Establish a Mentoring Structure as the Cornerstone of Faculty Development.**

Within each school, protocols for mentoring should be established to assist department chairs in monitoring faculty progress toward meeting their annual and long-term career development goals. Establishing mentoring committees for individual faculty members allows chairs to receive somewhat impartial advice in faculty progress. Timely feedback on progress should be provided to junior faculty in as collegial a manner as possible. The department chair should be an advocate for his or her faculty members and be committed to their development and mentoring, with the provision of appropriate resources when necessary for those activities that foster development. Sabbaticals should be available for mid-career and senior faculty to retool and/or enhance their academic development. The latter can be in terms of research or leadership development. As previously described, the ADEA Leadership Institute is the association's flagship career enhancement program and is specifically designed to provide dental educators with perspectives about dental education issues, insights about leadership strategies, and opportunities to acquire and practice skills associated with effective leadership. Nearly 150 dental educators who are interested in pursuing positions in academic leadership are graduates of this yearlong program. Coauthor Haden has directed the Leadership Institute for the past eight years.

5. **Create and Maintain an Atmosphere of Enthusiasm Among Faculty, Staff, and Students.**

Because faculty work-life is intimately related to our academic successes and achievements, the negativity mentioned by the dental students in terms of full-time faculty who appeared to be discontented and complaining, the negative departmental politics, and issues of distrust with administrative staff tend to weaken enthusiasm among faculty, staff, and students toward their daily activities. A major challenge, then, for dental administrators as they try to foster the recruitment of students into the academic profession is to highlight the attractiveness of an academic career and to maintain enthusiasm among faculty at a time when financial resources are dwindling. Hosting informative orientation forums for new faculty and other types of seminars focused on showcasing full-time faculty research and clinical activities may help to engage students, staff, and faculty and create a more positive atmosphere.

Acknowledgment

The authors would like to recognize the important contributions of Dr. Cathy Trower, Harvard University, Graduate School of Education, to the symposium on Dental Faculty Work Satisfaction at the 2007 ADEA Annual Session in New Orleans. Dr. Trower's research on faculty work-life in higher education was one of the sources of inspiration for the Dental Faculty Work Environment Questionnaire described in this article.

REFERENCES

1. Chmar JE, Weaver RG, Valachovic RW. Dental school vacant budgeted faculty positions: academic year 2004-05. J Dent Educ 2006;70:188-98
2. Rice RE, Sorcinelli MD, Austin AE. Heeding new voices: academic careers for a new generation. New pathways: faculty careers and employment for the 21st century. Working Paper Series, Inquiry # 7. Washington, DC: American Association of Higher Education, 2000.
3. Austin AE. Creating a bridge to the future: preparing new faculty to face changing expectations in a shifting context. Review Higher Educ 2002;26(2):119-44.
4. Kalkwarf KL, Haden NK, Valochovic RW. ADEA commission on change and innovation in dental education. J Dent Educ 2005;69(10):1085-7.
5. Trotman CA, Bennett EM, Scheffler N, Tulloch JFC. Faculty recruitment, retention, and success in dental academia. Am J Orthod 2002;122:2-8.

6. Trotman CA, Brown BE. Faculty recruitment and retention: concerns of early and mid-career faculty. TIAA-CREF Institute Research Dialogue 86. December 2005.

7. Brown BE, Trotman CA. Developing best practices: responding to the concerns of early and midcareer faculty. In: Proceedings: keeping our faculties: recruiting, retaining, and advancing faculty of color. Minneapolis: University of Minnesota, 2004:111-3.

8. Bataille GM, Brown BE. Faculty career paths: multiple routes to academic success and satisfaction. Westport, CT: ACE/Praeger Series on Higher Education, 2006.

9. Creswell J. Research design: qualitative and quantitative approaches. Thousand Oaks, CA: Sage Publications, 1994.

10. Trower CA. Making academic dentistry more attractive to new teacher-scholars. J Dent Educ 2007;71(5):601-5.

11. Henzi D, Jasinevicius R, Davis E, Hendricson W. In the students' own words: what are the strengths and weaknesses of the dental school curriculum? J Dent Educ 2007;71(5):732-48.

12. Henzi D, Jasinevicius R, Davis E, Cintron L, Isaacs M, Hendricson W. What are dental students' perspectives about their clinical education? J Dent Educ 2006;70(4):361-77.

13. Henzi D, Davis E, Jasinevicius R, Cintron L, Isaacs M, Hendricson WD. Appraisal of the dental school learning environment: a student's view. J Dent Educ 2005;69(10):1125-34.

14. Oblinger DG, Oblinger JL, eds. Educating the net generation. Boulder, CO: Educause, 2005.

15. Lancaster LC, Stillman D. When generations collide: who are they, why they clash, how to solve the generational puzzle. New York: HarperCollins, 2003.

16. Sorcinelli MD. The top ten things new faculty would like to hear from colleagues. National Teaching and Learning Forum Newsletter, March 2004.

17. Bland CJ, Stritter FT. Characteristics of effective family medicine faculty development programs. Fam Med 1988;20:15,282-8.

18. Wilkerson L, Irby DM. Strategies for improving teaching practices: a comprehensive approach to faculty development. Acad Med 1998;73(4):387-96.

19. Houston TK, Clark JM, Levine RB, Ferenchick GS, Bowen JL, Branch WT, et al. Outcomes of a national faculty development program in teaching skills; prospective follow-up of 110 medicine faculty development teams. J Gen Intern Med 2004;19(12):1220-7.

20. Cole KA, Barker LR, Kolodner K, Williamson P, Wright SM, Kern DE. Faculty development in teaching skills: an intensive longitudinal model. Acad Med 2004;79(5):469-80.

21. Davis DA, O'Brien T, Oxman AD, Haynes RB. Changing physician performance. a systematic review of the effect of continuing medical education strategies. JAMA 1995;274(9):700-5.

22. Davis D, O'Brien T, Freemantle N, Wolf FM, Mazmanian P, Taylor-Vaisey A. Impact of continuing medical education: do conferences, workshops, rounds, and other traditional continuing education activities change physician behavior or health care outcomes? JAMA 1999;282(9):867-74.

23. Hewson MG, Copeland HL. What's the use of faculty development? Program evaluation using retrospective self-assessments and independent performance ratings. Teach Learn Med 2001;13:153-60.

24. O'Brien T, Oxman AD, Davis DA, Haynes RB, Freemantle N. Audit and feedback: effects on professional practice and health care outcomes. The Cochrane Database of Systematic Reviews. 2005; Volume 3.

25. O'Brien T, Freemantle N, Oxman AD, Davis DA. Continuing education meetings and workshops: effects on professional practice and health care outcomes. The Cochrane Database of Systematic Reviews. 2005; Volume 3.

26. Skeff KM, Stratos GA, Bergen MR. Improving clinical teaching: evaluation of a national dissemination program. Arch Intern Med 1992;152:1156-61.

27. Gruppen L, Simpson D, Searle N, Robins L, Irby D, Mullan P. Medical education fellowships: common themes and overarching issues. Acad Med 2006;81(11):990-4.

Creating the Dental School Faculty of the Future: A Guide for the Perplexed

Charles N. Bertolami, D.D.S., D.Med.Sc.

Abstract: Building the faculty of the future has to be rooted in understanding the nature of future oral health delivery practices. Unfortunately, no one can reliably predict that future. Accepting any given scenario inevitably requires a leap of faith, but the cost of guessing wrong is high. In considering full-time academic careers, students are often not well prepared to make such a definitive choice. When dental educators ask dental students to consider academic life, what we are really doing is trying to induce them to make a very dramatic break with their settled career aspirations, which have already been firmly established in the minds of many of our students. The reality is that being a full-time professor of dentistry is more like being a professor in any other university discipline than it is like being a dentist in practice. Thus, the appeal of dental school to most applicants as a pathway to a practice/business career and existing admissions practices unintentionally bias the system against identifying future educators. Dental education is now engaged in a predictable blend of temporary, short-term, intermediate, and long-term approaches to finding faculty. Among these approaches are the following: cannibalizing other dental schools, collaborating with other professional schools, recruiting retired dentists, and growing our own faculty based on positive role modeling. The high cost of a dental education and the relatively low compensation of dental faculty are disincentives for some students who might otherwise consider dental education as a career option. However, the differential compensation between faculty members and owner/proprietors of dental practices may be misleading because of the business risks the latter assume. Understanding this means that dental schools might be more successful in finding future faculty by focusing on dental school applicants who fit the profile of employees rather than businesspeople because the lifetime differential in income nearly vanishes when comparisons are made between the categories of faculty member and employed dentist. At present, educators rely on a lack of self-knowledge among students in the hope that some who thought they wanted to be dentists will discover that they are ill-suited for practice and can be converted to becoming educators instead. It is not an optimal arrangement. Among practical suggestions to enhance recruitment of faculty are innovations in imprinting students early with the identity of being an educator and, in association with this concept, assisting with financing the education of future teachers. Ultimately, success in the dental educational enterprise will depend on attracting individuals who are intrinsically captivated by teaching as a moral vocation.

Dr. Bertolami is Professor of Oral and Maxillofacial Surgery and Dean of the College of Dentistry, New York University. Direct correspondence and requests for reprints to him at New York University College of Dentistry, 345 E. 24th Street, New York, NY 10010; 212-998-9898 phone; 212-995-4080 fax; Charles.bertolami@nyu.edu.

This article is one in a series of invited contributions by members of the dental and dental education community that have been commissioned by the ADEA Commission on Change and Innovation in Dental Education (CCI) to address the environment surrounding dental education and affecting the need for, or process of, curricular change. This article was written at the request of the ADEA CCI but does not necessarily reflect the views of ADEA, the ADEA CCI, or individual members of the ADEA CCI. The perspectives communicated here are those of the author.

Key words: dental education, research, scholarship, dental practice

What business are we really in? The answer to that question is important because it will determine how we go about building the dental faculty of the future to best serve the interests of the public. The corporate literature is replete with now classic examples of organizations that did not know the business they were in.[1] During the last decades of the twentieth century, the railroads thought they were in the railroad business. They were wrong. They failed to recognize that they were actually in the transportation business; not recognizing this caused them to go out of business. In contrast, the telephone company did recognize that it was not actually in the phone business; it was in the telecommunications business. As a result, the telephone companies have transformed themselves and, unlike the railroads, they have survived and often prospered. Did Eastman Kodak acknowledge in time that it could not remain in the business of manufacturing photographic film and stay in business? A 70 percent drop in its share price over the past ten years suggests that it did not. When did the Polaroid Corporation come to realize that technology would turn all cameras into instant cameras and that Polaroid would not be a player in this new world? As dental educators, knowing what business we are in and understanding the impact of social, cultural, economic, and technological advances on that business is crucial. The problem, however, is that discerning our true business is not all that easy.

Boundary Conditions and Context

Building the faculty of the future has to be rooted in understanding the nature of future oral health delivery practices. Unfortunately, no one can reliably predict that future; thus, it is impossible to know with certainty or precision what those practices will be. Accepting any given scenario inevitably requires a leap of faith, but the cost of guessing wrong is high. Thus, a certain resistance to change among practitioners is understandable, as is the difficulty some have in seeing how the world is flowing around and beyond the isolated dental office.

DePaola has described in depth the forces at play, including demographic changes, media influences, advances in science and technology, economics, public policy, corporate strategies, consumerism, and regulatory influences—which are all primary drivers of change.[2] For practitioners, things are good at the moment. The practice of dentistry is an activity that, once learned, lends itself to the feeling of effortless mastery and easy serenity.[3] The fluidity and competence with which experienced dentists negotiate their way around the oral cavity in both diagnostic and therapeutic maneuvers offer the comforting illusion that the current dentist-provider model is irreplaceable because of the highly individualized and technical aspects of care delivery. Proficiency in executing technically demanding dental procedures is so much a part of the profession's culture that it goes right to the heart of many practitioners' identities as dentists.[4] The success of the existing dental care delivery model, at least from the financial perspective of the practitioner (if not that of the public as a whole), therefore engenders reserve among both practitioners and educators for untested innovation.

The equanimity and attractiveness of dental practice are augmented by a further set of assumptions: that the dental profession will always have ultimate professional responsibility for the nation's oral health; that the public will continue to allow the profession to be self-regulating; and that the corporate sector can be relied upon to educate dentists in incremental improvements in technique and instrumentation over time.

None of these assumptions is inarguably correct; and, to the extent they are not, dental education will confront a dilemma: will it train dentists or will it educate providers of oral health care services? The difference is subtle but important because the former approach requires an increasingly unsustainable educational and economic model, while the latter implies a great increase in the diversity and qualifications of oral health care providers that the present educational system is not well suited to provide. The latter model might include not only dentists and dental hygienists, but also dental nurses, dental health aides, physicians, physician assistants, nurses, and pharmacists, as well as oral preventive assistants, community dental health coordinators, and others who will come to occupy currently vacant care delivery niches. Thus, dental educators can commiserate with Livy's first-century lament: we are able to endure neither the present condition nor its cure.[5] If we see ourselves in the dentist training business, then the kind of faculty to be built in the future will be quite different from what it will be if we see ourselves in the business of educating oral health care providers.

Who Will Be the Faculty of the Future?

In light of very substantial uncertainty over what, exactly, dental educators of the future are going to be asked to do, anybody's recommendations on the configuration of the future faculty deserve all the credibility of a wild guess. Nowhere is this more evident than in data-driven analytical studies on future adequacy of the dental workforce.[6] Despite meticulous analysis of the best available (and voluminous) data, little can be predicted with confidence beyond the admirably evasive assertion that "[if] demand for dental services grows markedly more rapidly than expected, an increase in the supply of dental care services greater than that forecast . . . may be needed to meet the increased demand. Alternatively, if demand does not grow rapidly, dental care capacity will be more than adequate and a lack of busyness among dentists could emerge."[6] Rapid and unpredictable change, uncertainty over initial assumptions, and differing objectives of the experts making the forecasts lead to at least ten different scenarios of the projected number of dentists and to twelve different forecasts of the future supply and demand for dental services—all depending on possible changes in productivity, changes in the annual output of dentists by dental schools, and different population trends.

Based upon these presently unknowable variables, supply could either outstrip demand for dental services by as much as 26 percent or, alternatively, demand could outstrip supply by almost 34 percent. The uncertainties are even greater when guessing at what the actual content of dental practice will be. Nevertheless, such analyses and their foretaste of credible outcomes are useful in sensitizing us to subtle trends as they materialize and, in theory, guiding incremental midcourse corrections aimed at titrating supply and demand.

Whatever shapes future oral health care delivery practices may assume, if the university is going to remain the vehicle for providing the requisite education, a few basic assumptions are still likely to apply. The most important of these is that either dental education will need to adapt itself to the broader realities of university life (which is evolving rapidly in its own right) or it will have to separate itself from the current university-based model of dental education. Both alternatives are plausible, and examples of each are already in evidence. Assuming the traditional university-based model of dental education, what will it take to make teaching (and the research integral to a university-based teaching model) appealing to the kinds of individuals universities will need? Can anything be learned from the current dental faculty crisis as an aid to moving forward without, at the same time, focusing obsessively on the past? A premise of this article is that there is little point to concentrating on the origin of faculty shortages of the past, regardless of whether one's viewpoint is accusatory or exculpatory, because both perspectives are moot: the people who will be needed in the future are likely to be quite different from those of the past. Also critical to designing a dental faculty for the future will be a straightforward look at impediments to careers in education such as dental graduate debt and the need to balance salary and working environment.

Moving Beyond Current Shortages

What are we going to do about the dental faculty crisis? First, let's all agree to *stop talking about it!* It is not that the numbers cited for faculty shortages are wrong; it is just that they are nothing new. The following statement comes from the 1950 *ADA Transactions, Annual Report of the Council on Dental Education:* "The Council has made a study of the number of faculty positions that are now available in

the dental schools and finds that 28 schools reported 135 vacancies."[7] Scaling this up to the current number of schools makes evident that the situation today is not much different: 245 full-time clinical faculty vacancies and seventy-seven part-time vacancies in roughly double the number of dental schools.

Further, these numbers of vacancies have to be viewed in perspective. An absolute number of just 322 for an entire nation of 300 million does not seem like all that big a problem. Maybe it actually is, in light of the smallness of the dental educational enterprise, but it just does not seem insurmountable given some ingenuity and innovative thinking; after all, we are still talking about just 322 people. For an example of a perhaps more dire situation, the nursing profession is currently seeking many thousands of new practitioners (30-40,000 by some estimates) to function in a variety of patient care and managerial roles at bachelor's, master's, and doctoral levels and also several thousand teachers for nursing schools.

Perception Becomes Reality

If "there is nothing either good or bad, but thinking makes it so,"[8] it would be interesting to know how many dozens of students have had their incipient interest in an academic career derailed by all the talk of how difficult it is to convince anyone to go into education. As a self-fulfilling prophecy, the very public and sometimes inaccurate discussion of the inadequacies of academic life may have had the unintended consequence of driving students away from teaching and research.

Appearances are important. The nature of the conversation and the attendant hand-wringing have sent students a clear message: the university is not where the action is. So where *is* the action? Astonishingly, we educators have sent students the message that a special mystique resides in the strip mall or suburban bungalow practice. For some it may, but not for all. Neil Postman has written that there is a difference between the information faculty *give* to students and the information they *give off* to students.[9] What we may have done unintentionally is to give off to students a mixed message: what we do as faculty members is not interesting, important, or fun. None of this is true. But the result is an uneasy ambiguity in the minds of even those students who have a natural inclination toward academics. That message drives out the confidence needed to try something a little different from what the majority of classmates are doing or from slavishly fulfilling the uninformed expectations of parents, family, and friends. The bottom line is this: what we as faculty members project to students is important. Students are our audience, and projecting to them that a career in education is only for the infirm, the incapable, or the otherwise deranged is wrong and perpetuates the myth that "those who can, do; those who can't, teach."

Making the Break

Educators have to understand that when it comes to making a career choice, a fifteen- or twenty-year-old might well say, "I want to be a dentist," and then follow through with this career plan, but is unlikely to say, "I want to be a dental educator" or, even more implausibly, "I want to be a junior dental scientist." The tastes of students in that critical age bracket are just not sophisticated enough to discern such a definitive choice. Therefore, what we as dental educators are really doing when we ask dental students to consider academic life is trying to induce them to make a very dramatic break with their settled career aspirations—that is, with an envisaged identity that they have had years to become comfortable with. We cannot really expect a student to make such a complete career change frivolously; yet that is precisely what is required because that is what academics really is: it is a completely different profession, though we often package it as a variant of clinical practice to make it more palatable. The reality is that being a full-time professor of dentistry is more like being a professor in any other university discipline (say law or history) than it is like being a dentist in practice. Understanding this is central to attracting students who are well suited to academic life and who, incidentally, can be entrusted to be articulate defenders of dentistry as a legitimate intellectual discipline within the university—a matter always, regrettably, open to question.

Getting a significant number of individuals to make such a dramatic break with their established career ambition is difficult for a number of reasons. First, our current target population is relatively small. Effectively, we are talking about students enrolled in dental schools, and this amounts to only about 4,500 new dental students per year. Retired dentists may be another target population; however, cultivating a robust, long-range educational enterprise cannot rely on retirees (or, for that matter, on superannuated full-time faculty members). Correspondingly, there may be a small target population of active pre-retirement dentists who are willing, for various reasons,

to give up practice and enter a full-time academic career—but, again, this population is small because of the intrinsic family and business commitments associated with giving up a dental practice, not to mention the prospect of acquiring additional education to enhance the possibility of success in academics. These entanglements are nicely described by Born and Nelson.[10] Thus, it seems credibly defensible that dental education as an intellectually alive, learned profession depends on recruiting dental students and young practitioners into full-time academic careers where they will remain and advance over their entire professional lives.

Second, the population of plausible candidates is not only small; it is already highly filtered and, to some extent, biased. All dental students have gone to college where they encountered professors. They know what academic life is all about and understand what it means to be a professor. In deciding to go to dental school, they have consciously rejected the notion of an academic career. The fixity of this idea in a student's mind—that they are going to be a dentist not a professor—generates a relatively high gradient against which dental educators have to prevail if such students are to be attracted to an academic career in spite of an explicit and antecedent decision against it.

Third, some clinical dental professors adopt, almost by tradition, a perverse attachment to a perpetual state of disaffection. Commiserating with students over the dissatisfactions of an academic career does not engender the kind of positive role modeling needed for students to consider changing their life's work from dentist to professor. For someone to change that dramatically, the action has to be interpreted as a positive and rewarding expansion of one's life goals. Some students could, under the right conditions, find themselves entranced by academic life.

Exactly what kind of student is captivated by a career in education?

Academics will be attractive to a student who is intellectually curious and who has a need to be involved in cutting-edge innovation at the interface between professional disciplines and between the profession and society in general. The academic life is for the bright student who sees universities as places where talented people work, achieve, and are recognized for their accomplishments in ways inaccessible to others in society. Such students are attracted to the higher credibility often accorded professors in professional matters because of the presumption of freedom from bias, such bias being a flaw that both academic life and the scientific method try to immunize against. It is for individuals who recognize that money does not necessarily reward excellence and so in itself may not be comprehensively satisfying. Thus, academic life will appeal to individuals who like being recognized as experts, being professionally challenged, and working within an environment that affords intellectual stimulation and growth, and who are comforted by the knowledge that, on the day before retirement, they will not be doing exactly what they were doing when they entered practice decades earlier. For the right person, academic life promotes progress and growth, and is especially appropriate for the kind of person who is attracted to self-investment, asking not what am I *getting* out of this career, but rather what am I *becoming* in this career?[11]

Born and Nelson[10] found that there is a distinct subset of dental students who might be open to alternative career options. Their findings are documented by the insightful comments from case studies of young to middle-aged dentists reported by these investigators:

"A dental education prepared a person for one career only. No options. . . . If I had it to do over I would never have chosen dentistry" (Age 35).

"Dentistry is a profession that leads to nothing else. The hardest part of a career change is that you are highly interested, motivated, and intelligent. However, nothing you have been doing lends itself to blending into other employment areas. In time you are vocationally and socially limited to a somewhat dead-end condition" (Age 40).

Solutions: Temporary, Short-Term, Intermediate, and Long-Term

Relative to producing full-time academics, the fecundity of the available recruitment pool is, at present, low. Thus, dental education is now engaged in a predictable blend of temporary, short-, intermediate-, and long-term approaches to finding faculty. Some of the options are basically a zero sum game that do nothing to advance the dental educational enterprise, while others hold long-term promise. They are represented by the letters C-C-G-G:

- *Cannibalism.* Dental schools can continue to cannibalize each other—stealing faculty from one other and counting each such recruitment an institutional success. This approach pits one institution against another, and ensures that there will be a continually changing roster of dental schools that are seen at the top of the educational pyramid in a musical chairs arrangement. Because the size of the top cohort never becomes any larger, dentistry is not enhanced as a learned profession by cannibalism; the critical mass of top-flight academic dentists remains the same—they just move from place to place.

- *Collaboration.* As both a short-term and a long-term strategy, collaboration is essential. Dentistry cannot be an isolated world whose culture and standards are both different from and lower than other health professions. If this is true for the profession as a whole, it must also be true for dental education. Dental educators need to recognize that the currency of institutions of higher learning is intellectual capital, not occupying academic real estate. Dental schools cannot afford simply to be a geographical expression, that is, a school-in-a-box. They need to be wherever the action is, and this usually means spreading out, diversifying, becoming completely intercalated with the health science center, the parent university, the community, and beyond.

It might be hard to locate such an idealized school physically because there are offices, laboratories, clinics, faculty, and students scattered all over the campus intermixed with the other health professions schools, distributed all over the city, and—through community outreach clinics and practice-based research networks—across the state and region. Such places are evolving into virtual schools; and some of our existing schools are well along this path. They occupy the tectonic interface between disciplines and professions. At their margins they resemble the tide pool: the space between land and sea—sometimes wet, sometimes dry. It is a highly creative boundary zone where life and ideas originate. As a mental image, university-based dental schools have to become miscible with other compatible and philosophically aligned professional schools to make new opportunities available, to extend the reach of the profession's official responsibilities, and to tap rich new sources of potential educators, while allowing the dental school to retain its unique identity.

The term "miscibility" is not used in the sense of two liquids becoming completely blended, but rather, as an interphase—a functionally graded interface—like two solids that blend into each other at their interface, yielding a conjoint product with properties, capacities, potentialities, and sensitivities that neither material would have alone. The unique characteristics and integrity of each component are entirely retained as one moves away from the interface toward the body of each component; yet this new composite creation, while capable of accomplishing what each of the constituents can do alone, can also do what neither can do by itself—something entirely new.

Under such conditions, other professional disciplines outside of dentistry begin to care that there is a dental school on campus. Such dental schools are more likely to be invited to participate in broad collaborative initiatives, such as the Clinical and Translational Science Award program; they become players in the National Institutes of Health (NIH) roadmap initiative and in practice-based research networks. Equally important, they begin to attract students and faculty members who feel comfortable within—and actively embrace—the new collaborative environment in which so much more becomes possible and which is requisite for success in the world today.

- *Geriatric Set.* Dental schools can continue to tap retired dentists, including retired military dentists, as a source of clinical teachers. This ample labor source plays well into the decision to locate the newest dental schools in the Sunbelt states that are havens for retired dentists. Having retirees gravitate back into dental schools after careers in practice is nothing new, but the highly successful economic model upon which the newest schools are based does require it. The problem, of course, is that what retirees can offer to educational institutions is usually somewhat limited to clinical supervision of students. With notable exceptions, they are unlikely to form a robust base for the intellectual life of the discipline. In fact, the role model of the dentist who has better things to do than to teach until reaching age fifty-five may be positively detrimental because it teaches students to delay entry into academic life. It reinforces the view that academics is just an exit strategy from professional life. Everybody wants to teach—but not full-time and certainly not now.

- *Grow Our Own.* Ultimately, growing our own is the only long-term solution to a shortage of dental faculty that will facilitate dentistry's capacity to retain its identity as both a learned profession and a caring profession. Growing our own is a solu-

tion both for individual dental schools and the profession as a whole. Some dental faculty will remain permanently at the institution where they were educated, while others will move on to other dental institutions, but in either case the strength of the dental educational enterprise is enhanced.

Although this article focuses primarily on attracting dentists into academic careers, the issues involved are not fundamentally different from what is needed to attract basic scientists into academics as well. It is easy to fall prey to the misconception that faculty shortages arise only among clinician scientists, whereas basic scientists who do not have a comparable clinical alternative as an income source can be presumed to be a reliable source of future educators. This is not true. Increasingly, Ph.D. scientists are opting for careers in the corporate sector rather than in academics. Interviewing both graduate students and postdoctoral scholars at my previous institution as chair of a search committee for the graduate school dean and also as a member of a separate site visit committee at a major university that produces a large number of Ph.D. graduates in the biomedical sciences, I posed the following question: how many are planning on careers in academics? Out of a group of perhaps forty (in total), fewer than five said that academics was the preferred option. All others were planning on entering industry—with some hoping to participate in biomedical start-up ventures stemming from graduate work, anticipating an equity position and attendant riches at an early age. One of the graduate student leaders remarked that for Ph.D. graduates it is academics, not corporate employment, that now should be considered the "alternative" career option. Evidence for this trend is not only anecdotal but is recognized as a reality.[12] Thus, growing our own has relevance not only to future clinical science faculty, but also to future basic science faculty.

How Do We Grow Our Own?

The answer is nothing new—almost a cliché, but captivating the imagination of students to consider academic careers can be achieved only through role modeling. Positive role models whom students find themselves wishing to emulate is the most powerful, perhaps the only, effective strategy to attract a new cohort of students to dental education as a viable career option.

The term "role modeling" is often used but seldom defined. What, exactly, is it? The following is proposed:[13] role modeling is a condition occurring in the mind of a student that conflates a given *action* with the *identity* of another person, a mentor whom the student respects, admires, and—ideally—feels affection toward. Expressed more simply, the student says, "This is how Dr. X would do things and I want to be just like Dr. X."

This is really the only ultimate solution to a shortage of dental faculty. It does not begin with students. It begins with faculty who are worthy of being emulated as mentors. In turn, mentor-worthiness begins as a state of mind that values all those attributes to which others might aspire. It is the opposite of disgruntlement, dissatisfaction, and victimhood. A good test for mentor-worthiness might be to take the following description and ask oneself these questions: is this me? would someone who has known me for twenty years and who knows me well describe me this way?

> Socially poised, outgoing, and cheerful, not prone to fearfulness or worried rumination? Having a capacity for commitment to people or causes, for taking responsibility, for having an ethical outlook, for being sympathetic and caring in your relationships? Comfortable with yourself, with others, and with the social universe you live in?

This description, paraphrased from the writings of Daniel Goleman,[14] defines someone with a high emotional intelligence. Goleman points out that others might use a more traditional term for the "body of skills that emotional intelligence represents: *character*."[14] Thus, the prospective mentor has to ask herself or himself, if this is not me, would I *like* it to be? It can be but it requires a decision, along with some inside information. The inside information is that none of the attributes described are intellectual in nature; they have nothing to do with IQ, physical capacities, or perceptual motor skills. They are all emotional in nature. An individual possessing these emotional traits is manifestly mentor-worthy, and is certain to attract protégés who recognize qualities that almost everyone would like to see in themselves and would be willing to work to secure.

Although mentoring starts with faculty, it does not stop there. A progression of mentor-worthiness has to be recognized and endorsed by the entire organization since certain factors, such as age, are beyond the mentor's control, yet may make someone a good mentor for one person but not for another. Kushner has pointed out that a mentor has to be a little older than the protégé, but not by too much.[15]

The student has to be able to relate to the mentor casually in a way that becomes more difficult as the age differential increases. Thus, first-year students are more likely to model themselves on fourth-year students than on senior professors. It follows that there is a mentoring opportunity for everyone within the organization, at literally every level: professors for junior faculty; junior faculty for residents and advanced students; even first-year students for applicants, college students, and high school students. Mentorship has to be talked about within an organization often and at every level. Having a mentor and being a mentor have to be understood as communal aspirations. The mentor-protégé connection can be one of the deepest and most satisfying human relationships outside of the direct family bond.[15] Mentors "even when they are gone . . . [move] us to live as, in their higher moments, they themselves wished to live."[16] The imagination of the general public has been captured by the potential depth and richness of the student-professor relationship in Albom's wildly popular book, *Tuesdays with Morrie*.[17] The bottom line is this: "connecting students to somebody or something worthwhile is everybody's business."[18] Faculty members need to appreciate the chance they have to actively cultivate protégés as one of the special gifts of academic life.

The Elephant: Finances—Academics vs. Practice

Nothing is more frustrating for educators than to encounter talented students who are committed to academic careers, especially those enrolled in D.D.S.-Ph.D. programs, being turned away from academics because of the burden of debt, the lure of high income, or both. By the time college students have gravitated to dental school as a career option, many do seem pretty materialistic—not surprising inasmuch as a profession will attract applicants in accordance with the image it projects to the lay public. Therefore, no serious effort at addressing the faculty of the future can evade the impact of debt and compensation on the choices students make—a sometimes troubling internal dialog. Interestingly, little note is made by Born and Nelson[10] of finances as being sufficiently compensatory for dentists who are otherwise dissatisfied with clinical practice. In other words, does the money make up for it all? Apparently not—and most evidently not for that subset of people whose spark of intellectual curiosity can only be ignited within a university setting.

There is no getting around that we exist in a highly materialistic mainstream culture in which economics trumps everything else. And yet, for such capitalism to work in a stable society, protected niches have always been accommodated where the rules are partially suspended to make the rest of capitalism functional. Such protected niches are like the ball bearings or the lubricant that allows an engine to function. Examples of protected niches that historically have responded to a higher calling transcending the ethos of the marketplace include medicine (until the introduction of managed care in 1995); the church and other religious and philanthropic establishments; the public service sector, including government; and academics.

But with unrestrained capitalism in the ascendant, even in the professions, and with many dislocations in how the system actually works, some of these niches are becoming less protected. In other words, it has become harder to argue on behalf of the compensating privileges of academic life inasmuch as those special privileges are no longer universally accorded high value by society.

In 1961, a report of the American Council on Education asserted that it will be "impossible to retain existing [dental school faculty] unless salaries are sufficient to provide a standard of living commensurate with at least that of the average dentist."[19] Little has changed since 1961 in terms of our understanding of how disincentivizing dental faculty salaries are for individuals contemplating academic careers. But, perhaps more optimistically, despite such a claim being made in 1961, the dental educational enterprise has somehow survived. The lesson is that the impact of finances on career choice may be more complex than a market-driven understanding of the matter admits. That compensation is an important issue no one seriously disputes; however, as observed by Nash and Brown, "greater understanding of some of the other factors at play can help planners focus on those features that are most important in career decision making."[20]

Differential Compensation

One way to address the problems stemming from income differential between dental educators and practicing dentists is to argue that these categories actually encompass three, rather than two, discrete occupations: dentist (or specialist); professor; and businessperson (understood as owner/proprietor of a practice). Different levels of work, responsibility, and risk distinguish these three jobs.

Some blend of work, responsibility, and risk are what people are actually paid for. Work is tangible labor: a product or service, including intellectual activity. It pays the least. In contrast, putting your head on the chopping block pays more: in other words, assuming personal responsibility by putting your own welfare at stake is something societies need and are quite willing to pay for. This is what corporate CEOs and university presidents do. However, what pays the most is willingness to place one's own financial assets at risk. The potential for losing personal assets has to be compensated by an equivalent potential for bringing great financial return.

Different jobs offer a different mix of these elements. How they blend goes a long way in explaining the differences in compensation between faculty members and practitioners. To the extent that students are accepted into dental schools with a higher sense of entrepreneurship and are willing, as doctors, to assume responsibility for the welfare of others (bearing the consequences of making diagnostic and therapeutic blunders) as well as being open to putting their own personal financial assets at significant risk in the building up and running of a business-based dental practice, in return for significant economic reward associated with these risks, then a strong proportion of students will find an academic career relatively unattractive.

Nash and Brown's excellent analysis of the relevant issues makes the point that anyone who is considering dentistry as an occupation—whether practice-based dentistry or academic-based dentistry—must be willing to incur significant direct educational expenses; forgo other income while in dental school; undertake grueling classwork, training, and examination; anticipate a future that begins with debt reduction; and face uncertainty about the amount and course of future earnings.[20]

For the person contemplating a career in dental academics, Nash and Brown pose the crucial question: "Are the monetary benefits from dental training large enough to repay all costs of training and yield a positive net return to the dental school faculty member?" From a strictly financial standpoint, the comparisons in Figures 1 and 2 are instructive.

Analysis of these findings reveals that a "good part of the differential between faculty compensation and owner/private practitioners can be explained as the premium that the latter receive for accepting the business risk of owning a practice. These risks include capital investment and management risk."[20] In other words, among those individuals who have a

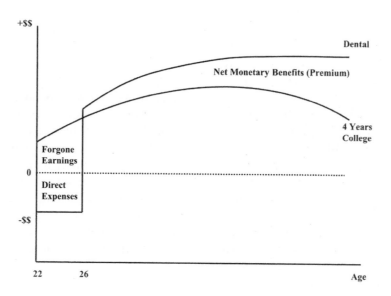

Figure 1. Model of estimating the rate of return to an investment in a dental education

Source: Nash KD, Brown LJ. Rate of return from a career as dental school faculty. In: Brown LJ, Meskin LH, eds. The economics of dental education. Chicago: American Dental Association, Health Policy Resources Center, 2004. © American Dental Association.

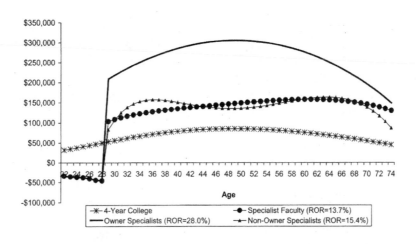

Figure 2. Average earnings of dental specialists in various careers and average earnings of four-year college graduates, by age, 2000

Source: Nash KD, Brown LJ. Rate of return from a career as dental school faculty. In: Brown LJ, Meskin LH, eds. The economics of dental education. Chicago: American Dental Association, Health Policy Resources Center, 2004. © American Dental Association.

dental (and, possibly, specialty) education, there will be some who aspire to the role of owners/proprietors and others who aspire to the role of being employed dentists. Among those dentists choosing to be employees, the lifetime differential in income between faculty members and practitioners is small. It is only when comparisons are made with owners/proprietors of dental businesses that the large differentials in income emerge.

This does not seem in any way unfair or unjust, inasmuch as "owning and equipping a dental office is expensive and not risk free. . . . Illness or accident can end a career before accrued debt is paid off . . . [and] both the capital risks and management risks must be compensated."[20] In addition, such owner/proprietors very likely initiate their businesses by first going out to secure a business loan. In contrast, neither employed dentists nor dental school faculty members are asked to make equity investments that require them to begin their careers by assuming yet more debt. Viewed this way, and by discriminating between the categories of employee/dentist versus owner/proprietor dentist as suggested by Nash and Brown, dental faculty positions can never be expected to offer salaries competitive with dentists who are proprietors of a business. In light of this, to the extent that financial comparisons are made between faculty positions and practice positions, they should be made only among the category of employed dentists: "This is the premium such individuals pay for the kinds of freedoms employees typically enjoy—including paid vacation time, possibly sick time, a lack of assets at risk, and relative ease of moving from job to job or place to place."[20]

If dental schools incorporate into their initial admissions decisions the basic qualities and personality types of the individuals being admitted, they can try to titrate probabilities of graduates opting for positions as employees versus owner/proprietors. If applicants fit the profile of those opting for positions as employees, dental schools will find themselves more competitive as a career option. Whether dental admissions processes can ever discriminate among applicants with that degree of accuracy is, of course, an open question. However, innovative testing strategies are emerging that may make such speculation more than a "quixotic venture into esoteric realms."[21] Though typical admissions evaluations rely on narrow measures of ability and achievement, especially remembered knowledge and analytical skills, other testing methods may be able to assess such elusive qualities as creativity and practical thinking—even wisdom.[21] If this is possible, perhaps ways can be devised to allow the requisite qualities for an academic career to be identified and selected early on. Doing so would almost certainly be accompanied by a drop in some of the qualities intuitively selected by dental school admissions committees today. Perhaps entrepreneurship would be one of those deprioritized qualities.

To intentionally select students who are more risk-averse and unwilling to stake their future with their own assets does sound like an attempt to make the future profession somewhat more timid in its overall outlook. This could well be true, though a similar transition has taken place in the field of pharmacy: many pharmacists once envisaged themselves as businesspeople and entrepreneurs, owners of their own pharmacies. Yet, today, almost all professionally active pharmacists are employees of large drugstore chains, hospitals, or the pharmaceutical industry. During the decades of transition, the academic standing of pharmacy within universities and hospitals grew enormously with significant new kinds of opportunities (including the Pharm.D. degree). Moreover, the large chain stores and pharmaceutical industry have become powerful political advocates on behalf of pharmacy. Admittedly, this has all occurred with significant loss of personal autonomy for pharmacists.

Is there some way the profile of the dental profession can remain entrepreneurial, not become risk-averse, and yet grow students who have an institutional or organizational perspective? If the profession of being a full-time educator is taken seriously and understood as fundamentally different from the profession of being a practicing dentist, it might be possible, provided the right kinds of people are recruited early.

Inconsistencies and Dilemmas

A clear inconsistency in the logic underlying this article (and a dilemma for dental education) is the inherent incompatibility between identifying and cultivating students for academic careers as early as possible (even during the admissions process or earlier), while recognizing that young and inexperienced students have limited capacity for making such a definitive choice. In a way, we educators rely on this lack of self-knowledge in the hope that some students who thought they wanted to be dentists will discover that they are ill-suited for practice and can be converted to becoming educators instead. This is a less than optimal strategy for building the dental school faculty of the future.

Is there a resolution to this dilemma that can be counted on to help build a future faculty that will be quantitatively and qualitatively robust? Possibly not, in which case we just continue to muddle along as we have been, hoping that enough people at critical stages in their development will guess wrong about what career suits them best, and then gravitate to academics as an alternative that allows them to salvage whatever investment they have already made in pursuing a dental education, and/or that there will continue to be a supply of retiring practitioners and military dentists in the fifty-five to sixty age range who desire to serve as clinical supervisors for a few years prior to complete retirement.

On the other hand, a slight adjustment in the thinking of key stakeholders might make a difference. Consider this thought experiment: presuming

key stakeholders to include not only dental educators and dental students, but also pre-professional college advisors, members of admissions committees, dental applicants, and practicing dentists, the construct depicted in Figure 3 categorizes dental students and dentists on the basis of their suitability for careers in practice and in education. All of the cells in the fourfold table are currently represented to varying degrees in the dental profession; the only issue is: do the cell frequencies match future needs?

Thus, within any potential applicant pool there will be those whose abilities, personalities, and interests are exceptionally well suited to either a career in practice or a career in education (Cell A). These charismatic few have all the capacities needed for assuming the risks and management responsibilities of running a business and are strongly people-oriented;

Suitability Model

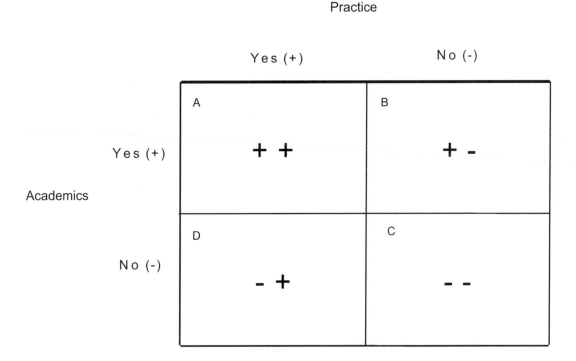

Figure 3. Generalized hypothetical categories of dental students and dentists according to their suitability to careers in education and practice

yet they also have intellects and intrinsic curiosity at levels that would serve them well as professors. These people could have chosen any profession, and we are lucky to have them in dentistry. Others (Cell B) discover themselves ill-suited to dental practice in its entirety, which means running a business as well as taking care of patients. Those represented by Cell B can do quite well in an academic environment and may, on occasion, be able to stimulate students to want to emulate them but, in general, are unlikely to do so. Cell D is where the vast majority fit, probably because this is the group we consciously select for and who are attracted to dental school in the first place: individuals well suited to practice but not to academics. And then, inevitably, there are the mistakes: Cell C, those not suited for either practice or academics.

Interestingly, some from each of these groups do eventually gravitate toward academics; the question is when? Category C individuals exploit quite early the relatively forgiving institutional culture of academic life, especially for those not pursuing promotion and tenure, but they are not positive role models for students, in fact, quite the reverse. Cell D people gravitate to academics in retirement, post-military, or when partially disabled. Their willingness to teach when other options either have been closed to them or have run their natural course does not automatically make them suitable to teach. Category A people come late, if ever, to academics—their interests and capacities being such that they are likely to migrate into many other activities, including organized dentistry, or into new initiatives apart from either dentistry or education.

Is this mental construct helpful in consciously deciding how we recruit into dental education? I think it could be, because among the four categories (and recognizing that there is a lot of blending among them) the most effective role models are the Category A individuals—but only if such people can be captured into academic careers early, recalling Kushner's[15] observation that the best role models are people who are just a bit older than the prospective protégé. The bad news is that getting Category A people to choose full-time academics early is not easy. The good news is that we do not need very many of them. The effect of even one or two such individuals in a faculty can be transformative, drawing students into academics who might otherwise not have considered it. Thus, the influence of one such individual is greatly amplified. Students may understand that they are not actually sure what they want; but they do trust the decision of someone they can relate to and who has made a similar decision, who appears to be happy with it, and who manifestly enjoys the work.

Some Practical Suggestions

Grayson Marshall[22] has advanced some ideas worth considering to capture a greater number of dental students whose temperament might suit them well for an academic career, particularly through the vehicle of the combined D.D.S.-Ph.D. program. Among these are the following:

Enhanced Recruiting. This could be achieved by the directors of conjoint degree programs working directly with D.D.S./D.M.D. admissions committees to identify candidates as early as possible. Efforts should go beyond applicants of dental schools to include predental groups touring dental schools or as part of routine outreach efforts made by visits of deans and Ph.D. program directors to undergraduate campuses. Such efforts must also include a few dynamic dental students who are engaged in combined programs and who can serve as charismatic role models for predental students.

Dental recruiters should not shy away from recruiting preprofessional health science groups, both predental and premedical. Sending faculty to undergraduate campuses could also be effective, with follow-up either by personal contact or by creating a targeted newsletter sent periodically to predental students that continues to imprint and reinforce the academic option. The pre-health professional advisors are critical in this equation.

Full-time faculty members who are scientists must be persuaded to serve on admissions committees. Their presence and influence send a message to both applicants and other members of the admissions committee.

Finances. NIH financing of D.D.S./D.M.D.-Ph.D. programs needs to be encouraged as a high educational priority. To the extent that it is fiscally feasible, dental schools need to enhance stipends for graduate students without, if possible, causing students to lose eligibility for low-interest student loans. In conjoint D.D.S./D.M.D.-Ph.D. programs when the clinical degree is awarded before the Ph.D., the NIH needs to be encouraged to permit postdoctoral stipend levels to apply during the post-D.D.S. phase (as opposed to the lower, predoctoral stipend levels).

To the extent possible, tuition waivers (or tuition supplements) need to be found to allow most or the entire burden of D.D.S./D.M.D. tuition to be covered.

Practice. It is both natural and exciting for D.D.S./D.M.D.-Ph.D. students to look forward to completing the D.D.S./D.M.D. phase of the program and then be allowed to engage in an intramural practice, deriving direct salary supplements from this source. This opportunity offers great motivation to complete the D.D.S./D.M.D. component of the program in as short a time as possible. The experience at the University of California, San Francisco (UCSF) School of Dentistry confirms that many D.D.S./D.M.D.-Ph.D. students are able, unexpectedly, to complete the D.D.S./D.M.D. component of the curriculum in just four years and that the opportunity to earn practice income provides an exhilarating strategy to cope with the financial struggles they typically encounter. Placing such students into community outreach programs as salaried personnel is also an option.

Teaching as a Moral Vocation

Whatever financial incentives can be put in place to entice students to consider academic careers are a definite bonus. However, the core question remains: what kinds of people can be sufficiently captivated by teaching that they are willing to forgo the income of a dentist-businessman or -businesswoman?

It has become a maxim of the business world that we don't invent our values, we discover them.[23] This might be a good rule of thumb summarizing why those dental students who select academic dentistry as a career choice do so. Former Cornell University president Frank Rhodes has explained this perspective through his eloquent description of teaching as a moral vocation.[24] He points out:

> A generation or two ago, a professor at a major university would have described himself as a professor or an educator; today, such an individual is likely to describe herself as an engineer, an architect, or a musicologist, and, if pressed, to say that she teaches at such-and-such university. Universities need to restore pride in the role of engineer, architect, or musicologist AS professor. A professor who is not both an expert and an enthusiastic expositor of his or her subject

is a contradiction in terms. A professor who regards his or her teaching load—note the term—only as a means of supporting a career in research [or even worse, of just making a modest income] is an impostor. Any professor worthy of the name must regard teaching as a moral vocation. It is not just courses, after all, but people who inspire, transform, and redeem. In short, professors must be not only instructors but also . . . coaches, guides to the territory, and role models.

This is a completely different job from that of being a dentist in an office, and it is one that will resonate with some but not with others. Correspondingly, the kind of person for whom a faculty position in a university holds genuine appeal will be a fundamentally different kind of person from one who sees herself or himself caring for patients hour after hour in a practice setting. The two jobs are both important and they do overlap, but they are more different than they are alike and they should be expected to attract a different subset of people. Configuring dental education in a way that exclusively favors the recruitment and education of one subset is almost guaranteed to yield a shortage of the other.

"Because of its profound impact upon both the individual student and society," according to Rhodes, "teaching can never be just a job, however demanding; not even just a career, however professional. To the best professors, teaching is a moral vocation. It is moral because it seeks to develop not only comprehension, but also commitment; it influences and shapes not only the intellect, but also the will; it involves the cultivation of not only the mind, but also the heart . . . it is a vocation because it is a calling and not simply a job."[24] This high aspiration speaks to some people and not to others.

At its best, the role of professor should resemble "a coach who encourages, trains, inspires, and prepares the student for the contest; who establishes the goals, initiates the team into both the rules and the spirit of the game, designs and calls the plays, and develops intensity, commitment, and spirit; who instills confidence in the ability and skills of his or her team; and who brings out the best in both individuals and the team, welding the differing skills and the various needs of individuals into an effective, organized whole."[24] Again, this is not better or worse than being a practicing dentist; it is just a completely different job. The key question we as dental educators have to ask ourselves is this: do we want to encourage a subset of dental school applicants with this particular aspiration? If we do, then we have to bear in mind that our job as educators is not to try to talk students into becoming professors. Rather, our job (and that of all of higher education) is to help students discover something about themselves—and a possible passion for teaching is one of those things. THAT is the business we really are in.

REFERENCES

1. Levitt T. Marketing myopia. Harvard Business Review, September/October 1975:26-48.
2. DePaola D. Scientific discovery and integration of knowledge: best practices of principles that will lead to future curriculum. ADEA 48th Annual Deans' Conference in conjunction with the Council of Sections, San Diego, CA, November 4-7, 2006.
3. Grossman L. Codex. New York: Harcourt Inc., 2005:43.
4. Bertolami CN. Rationalizing the dental curriculum in light of current disease prevalence and patient demand for treatment: form vs. content. J Dent Educ 2001;65(8):725-35.
5. Livy T. Ab urbe condita, Book 1. Foster BO, transl. Henderson J, ed. The Loeb classical library. Cambridge: Harvard University Press, 1988:7.
6. Brown LJ. Future adequacy of the dental workforce. In: Adequacy of current and future dental workforce: theory and analysis. Chicago: American Dental Association, Health Policy Resource Center, 2005:210-59.
7. Formicola A. Personal communication.
8. Shakespeare W. Hamlet, prince of Denmark, Act II, Scene II. In: Adler MJ, ed. Great books of the western world. Chicago: Encyclopaedia Brittanica, 1993:43.
9. Postman N. The disappearance of childhood. New York: Vintage Books, 1994.
10. Born DO, Nelson BJ. Male dentists at midlife: an exploration of the one life/one career imperative. Int J Aging Hum Dev 1983-84;18(3):219-35.
11. Rohn J. The art of exceptional living (audiodisc), disc 1. New York: Nightingale-Conant Corporation/Simon & Schuser, Inc., 1994.
12. Basalla M. Beyond the ivory tower: FAQ from the lecture circuit. Chronicle of Higher Education, March 23, 2007: C2.
13. Bertolami CN. Is it possible to educate students to act ethically? Global Health Nexus (New York University College of Dentistry) 2006;8(2):8-15.
14. Goleman D. Emotional intelligence. New York: Bantam Books, 1997:45.
15. Kushner H. When all you've ever wanted isn't enough: the search for a life that matters. New York: Fireside, 2002:169.
16. Gates of prayer in weekdays and at a house of mourning. Chaim Stern, ed. Central California Conference of American Rabbis, 1992. Read at Memorial Service for Lawrence H. Meskin, June 27, 2007, Santa Fe, New Mexico.
17. Albom M. Tuesdays with Morrie: an old man, a young man, and life's greatest lesson. New York: Doubleday, 1997.
18. Koh GD. How to help students achieve. Chronicle of Higher Education, June 15, 2007:B13.
19. American Council on Education, Commission on the Survey of Dentistry in the United States. The survey of dentistry: the final report. Washington, DC: American Education Council, 1961. Cited in Brown LJ, Meskin LH, eds. The economics of dental education. Chicago: American Dental Association, 2004:13.
20. Nash KD, Brown LJ. Rate of return from a career as dental school faculty. In: Brown LJ, Meskin LH, eds. The economics of dental education. Chicago: American Dental Association, 2004:41-79.
21. Sternberg RJ. Finding students who are wise, practical, and creative. Chronicle of Higher Education, July 6, 2007: B11.
22. Marshall G, director of the D.D.S.-Ph.D. program at the UCSF School of Dentistry. Personal communication.
23. Collins JC, Porras JI. Building your company's vision. Harvard Business Review, September/October 1996: 131-43.
24. Rhodes FHT. Teaching as a moral vocation. In: Rhodes FHT, ed. The creation of the future: the role of the American university. Ithaca: Cornell University Press, 2001: 58-83.

Faculty Development to Support Curriculum Change and Ensure the Future Vitality of Dental Education

Frank W. Licari, D.D.S., M.P.H., M.B.A.

Abstract: For meaningful curriculum change to occur in dental schools, faculty must go through a process of new skills development that will prepare them to teach differently and to assess students differently than they have before. Curriculum change and the faculty development process must have the support of the dental school's leadership and become a core value of the school's culture.

Dr. Licari is Executive Associate Dean for Academic Affairs, University of Illinois at Chicago College of Dentistry. Direct correspondence and requests for reprints to him at College of Dentistry, University of Illinois at Chicago, 801 South Paulina Street, Chicago, IL 60612; 312-355-3644 phone; 312-413-9050 fax; licari@uic.edu.

This article is one in a series of invited contributions by members of the dental and dental education community that have been commissioned by the ADEA Commission on Change and Innovation in Dental Education (CCI) to address the environment surrounding dental education and affecting the need for, or process of, curricular change. This article was written at the request of the ADEA CCI but does not necessarily reflect the views of ADEA, the ADEA CCI, or individual members of the ADEA CCI. The perspectives communicated here are those of the author.

Key words: faculty development, new skills, curriculum change

The American Dental Education Association's Commission on Change and Innovation in Dental Education (CCI) outlines pathways for change that include new ways to educate dental students. These proposed changes include more emphasis on self-directed learning (SDL), critical thinking development, and lifelong learning.[1] Kassebaum et al.'s survey from 2002-03 on the current state of dental education found that 80 percent of dental schools have a traditional-discipline, lecture-based, nonintegrated curriculum. However, 87 percent of dental schools surveyed felt that faculty development was needed to make curricular changes.[2]

The need for faculty development in general is not unique to dentistry. A number of studies of medical school faculty development programs found that they were effective at developing teaching skills, building colleague relationships, initiating curriculum changes, and contributing to overall academic advancement.[3-9] Unfortunately, Morahan et al.'s survey of U.S. medical schools found that no school has implemented a comprehensive faculty development system.[10]

For real curriculum change to occur, dental schools must adopt well-conceived, comprehensive, faculty development programs. Such programs must clearly define the requisite skills needed for effectiveness in an academic environment that emphasizes self-directed learning and cultivation of students' critical thinking. Faculty development programs also need to help faculty members navigate from the current steady state of a traditional curriculum through the unknown white-water rapids inevitably created by curriculum change. Moreover, the development of faculty members needs to extend beyond teaching them how to better utilize emerging technology. If the emphasis is solely on technology, it is probable that the outcome will be the creation of an e-version of current curriculum courses with very little change or integration. Rather, faculty development must focus on all of the necessary skills needed to transform the curriculum into an active-learning environment.

To be truly successful, a faculty development plan should be implemented in three stages and should allow faculty sufficient time to assimilate new knowledge and develop new skills. These stages are as follows: 1) focus on changing the culture/ understanding the need for change; 2) prepare faculty to teach in the new curriculum; and 3) prepare faculty to assess learning in the new curriculum.

Stage 1: Focus on Changing the Culture/Understanding the Need for Change

In this stage of faculty development, efforts should be directed towards understanding what it will take in the organization's culture to effectively make a curriculum change. It is logical to expect that, if dental education is to significantly change the way in which students learn, substantial efforts in faculty development are required, because nearly all of the faculty members who will be teaching in this new curriculum graduated from and have subsequently taught in a traditional curriculum. While a comprehensive faculty development program is necessary, modifying the institutional culture is an essential prerequisite to successful curriculum change.

The essence of an organization is expressed in its culture. Organizations rarely achieve significant change due to the immutability of their culture and its deeply implanted values.[11,12] An example of a corporation that succeeded in changing its culture is IBM, which in the 1990s was compelled to transform its business model to ensure its own survival. To continue to compete as a leader in an ever-evolving market, IBM had to redirect its focus from computer components and mainframe and personal computing hardware to software development, networking, and support services. It was clear that, in order to effect this change, IBM had to address the deep-seated, long-standing traditions that were expressed in its culture. Some involved traditions that may appear cosmetic but were in fact expressions of its "buttoned-down" culture—for instance, the company dress code. Gone were the long-traditional dark business suits, white shirts, and ties; in their place, employees were encouraged to adopt the business casual look of their competitors. Other changes went even deeper into the company's culture. No longer were employees guaranteed career-long employment, and for the first time in IBM's history, massive layoffs were initiated to restructure the company. Employees during this time often found themselves confused, uncomfortable, and unsure about their future, as IBM morphed into a corporation that looks nothing like the "Big Blue" that was the darling of Wall Street in the 1950s, '60s, and '70s.[13] However, the transformation was essential in positioning the company for success in today's market.

Like IBM's employees, dental educators must be prepared for a major transformation of their schools' culture. The sweeping curriculum changes necessary to put dental education on the right course for dentistry's future success will have little resemblance to the existing dental school culture and curriculum. Perhaps faculty members need to be reminded that curriculum change has been advocated since the Gies report in 1926,[14] though it has not generally been implemented. Some schools may be prevented from adopting proposed curriculum changes if they are not able to recognize that the traditional curriculum is no longer effective in preparing students for dentistry's future. However, the need for sweeping curriculum change at this point in dentistry's history must overcome any desire of individuals to remain mired in the status quo.

To be effective, a school's leadership must frequently provide faculty with justification of the need for curriculum change and remind them that their ultimate goal is to graduate better general dentists who are prepared for the future. The dental school's administrative team, led by the dean, must also commit the resources to give all faculty members the opportunity to acquire the skills necessary to participate effectively in a new curriculum. This includes the commitment by the dean to dedicate substantial protected blocks of time and finances for faculty skill development.

If meaningful curriculum change is to be achieved, all faculty members must be involved in understanding the goals of the new curriculum and must be provided with regular updates on the progress of the evolution to a new structure. An open dialogue should be developed that shares in both celebrating the successes and analyzing the failures that will occur as a new curriculum is developed and implemented.

Dental school administrators will also have to consider the development of a revised reward system for faculty members, one that will encourage new curriculum development and innovation. For example, any curriculum changes that result in the integration of the curriculum currently taught in individual discipline-based courses must provide faculty with incentives, time to plan, credit for development of interdisciplinary learning experiences and rewards, and recognition for team teaching in these new modules. Faculty members may no longer be course directors, but may instead function as part of a team of instructors, drawn from several departments/disciplines, in a course where they are only partially responsible for its development, content, and evaluation methodology. This change may require schools to alter current promotion and tenure criteria to accommodate this changing role for faculty members and correctly determine if they are worthy of promotion and/or tenure.

Stage 2: Prepare Faculty to Teach in the New Curriculum

Developing self-directed learning and critical thinking skills in students poses a major paradigm shift for most faculty members. Therefore, effectively implementing a faculty development program will depend on focusing efforts on the real challenges. Currently, most faculty members impart knowledge to students in well-organized discrete lectures designed to tell students what they need to know about the subject matter. This "spoon-feeding" approach to education does not prepare the lifelong learners that dental educators have always desired to graduate. One challenge of faculty development, therefore, is to concentrate on transforming faculty from "knowledge imparters" to "knowledge developers." In other words, faculty must evolve from those who deliver facts and information into those who guide students into becoming active learners, skilled at gathering and evaluating information. This will be no easy feat. As knowledgeable, information-laden expert faculty members observe eager novice learners struggling to discover the correct diagnosis or treatment, faculty will be constantly tempted to revert back to their traditional role of knowledge imparter. Faculty development programs should, therefore, focus on the requisite skills that faculty will need to teach in a new, active-learning curriculum. These skills include evidence-based practice strategies, small group facilitation, active lecturing, and the productive use of technology.

Every dental school will have a cadre of faculty members who will become early adopters of the initiative to change the curriculum. These individuals should be challenged to develop and pilot innovative course materials and share their successes with the rest of the faculty. In working with early adopters, it will be important to encourage them to experiment with unique teaching methodologies without fear of being blamed for failures. It is to be expected that failures or setbacks will occur when one is trying something new. Bland and Stritter's review of the literature on curriculum reform strategies and associated faculty development in medical schools found that schools undergoing a change process can expect a performance dip of two to three years' duration as the institution adopts new teaching/learning methods by trial and error.[15] Developing a culture in which innovation is encouraged and failures are accepted in the context of learning will be difficult for most dental schools, where excellence is expected and perfection is pursued.

The early adopters of the new curriculum can be utilized further as role models and mentors for other faculty members who are experiencing difficulties in adapting to change. It is often less intimidating for faculty members to seek advice on course development from their trusted peers. Early adopters who can demonstrate to other faculty members how a successful course change can be implemented will be invaluable to a dental school's success in adopting curriculum change.

Stage 3: Prepare Faculty to Assess Learning in the New Curriculum

It is impossible to have true curriculum reform and develop innovative educational methodologies without also adopting corresponding relevant and valid assessment methods for student learning. These assessment methods should also facilitate the changing roles for faculty members, as they evolve from teachers to mentors who guide students through the quest to acquire, evaluate, and assimilate knowledge.

Licari and Chambers's survey data[16] indicate that dental schools still rely heavily on the number of procedures completed and daily procedure grades to determine clinical competence and eligibility for graduation. The use of these evaluation methods indicates that dental school faculty members are still uncomfortable with adopting authentic evaluation methods that require more faculty judgment. Authentic evaluation relies on using faculty judgment to evaluate independent performance in realistic environments.

Self-directed learning and the development of critical thinking among dental students require that faculty members adopt higher order evaluation methods that assess the acquisition of these skills. These assessment methods must also be tested to make sure they are reliable and valid. Most traditional evaluation methods employed in dental schools assess students' learning according to Bloom's Knowledge and Comprehension levels.[17] These levels assess a student's ability to recall knowledge of major ideas, grasp meaning, interpret facts, and predict consequences. However, to prepare dental students to analyze, synthesize, and apply information, more sophisticated evaluation methodologies must be employed. These methodologies must include evaluations of a student's ability to problem-solve, predict patient prognosis, draw conclusions about current treatments, apply principles to other patient conditions. and relate knowledge from several sources. Faculty members will therefore need to become comfortable in the use of higher order authentic evaluation methods such as the triple-jump examination, objective structured clinical exam (OSCE), faculty ratings, and portfolios.[18,19]

Conclusion

True curriculum change designed to develop students who are active and self-directed learners will require dental schools to implement comprehensive faculty development programs that focus on changing the school's culture by having faculty develop new teaching and assessment skills. These professional development programs must reach beyond teaching faculty to utilize the latest technology. These programs should concentrate on expanding the role for faculty in learning new educational methodologies to create a new student learning environment. Dental school administrators must fully understand the need for change and make a commitment to provide the resources to facilitate this faculty development process and subsequently alter the criteria used to evaluate faculty for promotion and tenure.

REFERENCES

1. Haden NK, Andrieu SC, Chadwick DG, Chmar JE, Cole JR, George MC, et al. The dental education environment. J Dent Educ 2006;70(12):1265-70.

2. Kassebaum DK, Hendricson WD, Taft T, Haden NK. The dental curriculum at North American dental institutions in 2002-03: a survey of current structure, recent innovations, and planned changes. J Dent Educ 2004;68(9):914-31.

3. Morzinski JA, Fisher JC. A nationwide study of the influences of faculty development programs on colleague relationships. Acad Med 2002;77(5):402-6.

4. Bland CJ, Seaquist E, Pacala JT, Center B, Finstad D. One school's strategy to assess and improve the vitality of its faculty. Acad Med 2002;77(5):368-76.

5. Sachdeva AK. Faculty development and support needed to integrate the learning of prevention in the curricula of medical schools. Acad Med 2000;75(7 Suppl):S35-S42.

6. Hitchcock MA, Zoi-Helen EM. Teaching faculty to conduct problem-based learning. Teach Learn Med 2000;12(1):52-7.

7. Hewson MG, Copeland HL, Fishleder AJ. What's the use of faculty development? Program evaluation using retrospective self-assessments and independent performance ratings. Teach Learn Med 2001;13(3):153-60.

8. Rubewck RF, Witzke DB. Faculty development: a field of dreams. Acad Med 1998;73(9 Suppl):S32-S37.

9. Wilkerson L, Irby DM. Strategies for improving teaching practices: a comprehensive approach to faculty development. Acad Med 1998;73(4):387-96.

10. Morahan PS, Gold JS, Bickel J. Status of faculty affairs and faculty development offices in U.S. medical schools. Acad Med 2002;77(5):398-401.

11. Mennin SP, Krackov SK. Reflections on relevance, resistance, and reform in medical education. Acad Med 1998;73(9):S60-S64.

12. Bloom SW. The medical school as a social organization: the sources of resistance to change. Med Educ 1989;23:228-41.

13. McCune JC. Who are those people in the blue suits? Management Rev 1991;9(80):16-9.

14. Gies WJ. Dental education in the United States and Canada: a report to the Carnegie Foundation for the Advancement of Teaching. New York: Carnegie Foundation, 1926.

15. Bland CJ, Stritter FT. Characteristics of effective family medicine faculty development programs. Fam Med 1988;20:15,282-8.

16. Licari FW, Chambers DW. Some paradoxes in competency-based dental education. J Dent Educ, in press.

17. Bloom BS. Taxonomy of educational objectives. Boston: Allyn and Bacon, 1984.

18. Swing SR. Assessing the ACGME general competencies: general considerations and assessment methods. Acad Emerg Med 2002;9(11):1278-87.

19. Epstein RM, Hundert EM. Defining and assessing professional competence. JAMA 2002;287(2):226-35.

Does Faculty Development Enhance Teaching Effectiveness?

William D. Hendricson, M.A., M.S.; Eugene Anderson, Ph.D.; Sandra C. Andrieu, Ph.D.;
D. Gregory Chadwick, D.D.S.; James R. Cole, D.D.S.; Mary C. George, R.D.H., M.Ed.;
Gerald N. Glickman, D.D.S., J.D.; Joel F. Glover, D.D.S.; Jerold S. Goldberg, D.D.S.;
N. Karl Haden, Ph.D.; Kenneth L. Kalkwarf, D.D.S., M.S.; Cyril Meyerowitz, B.D.S., M.S.;
Laura M. Neumann, D.D.S.; Marsha Pyle, D.D.S., M.Ed.; Lisa A. Tedesco, Ph.D.; Richard
W. Valachovic, D.M.D., M.P.H.; Richard G. Weaver, D.D.S.; Ronald L. Winder, D.D.S.;
Stephen K. Young, D.D.S.

Abstract: Academic dentists and members of the practice community have been hearing, for more than a decade, that our educational system is in trouble and that the profession has lost its vision and may be wavering in the achievement of its goals. A core of consistently recommended reforms has framed the discussion of future directions for dental education, but as yet, most schools report little movement toward implementation of these reforms in spite of persistent advocacy. Provision of faculty development related to teaching and assessment strategies is widely perceived to be the essential ingredient in efforts to introduce new curricular approaches and modify the educational environment in academic dentistry. Analyses of the outcomes of efforts to revise health professions curricula have identified the availability and effectiveness of faculty development as a predictor of the success or failure of reform initiatives. This article will address faculty development for purposes of enhancing teaching effectiveness and preparing instructors for potential new roles associated with curriculum changes. Its overall purpose is to provide information and insights about faculty development that may be useful to dental schools in designing professional growth opportunities for their faculty. Seven questions are addressed: 1) What is faculty development? 2) How is faculty development accomplished? 3) Why is faculty development particularly important in dental education? 4) What happens when faculty development does not accompany educational reform? 5) Why are teaching attitudes and behaviors so difficult to change? 6) What outcomes can be expected from faculty development? and 7) What does the available evidence tell us about the design of faculty development programs? Evidence from systematic reviews pertaining to the teaching of evidence-based dentistry, strategies for continuing professional education, and the Best Evidence in Medical Education review of faculty development outcomes are presented to answer this question: does faculty development enhance teaching effectiveness? Characteristics consistently associated with effective faculty development are described.

All authors are members of the ADEA Commission on Change and Innovation in Dental Education. Mr. Hendricson is Assistant Dean, Educational and Faculty Development, University of Texas Health Science Center at San Antonio Dental School; Dr. Anderson is Director, Center for Educational Policy and Research, American Dental Education Association; Dr. Andrieu is Associate Dean for Academic Affairs, Louisiana State University School of Dentistry; Dr. Chadwick is Associate Vice Chancellor for Oral Health, East Carolina University; Dr. Cole is a member of the Commission on Dental Accreditation; Prof. George is Associate Professor, Department of Dental Ecology, University of North Carolina School of Dentistry; Dr. Glickman is Chair, Endodontics, Baylor College of Dentistry; Dr. Glover is a member of the Board of Trustees, American Dental Association; Dr. Goldberg is Dean, Case School of Dental Medicine; Dr. Haden is President, Academy for Academic Leadership; Dr. Kalkwarf is Chair of the Commission on Change and Innovation in Dental Education and Dean of the University of Texas Health Science Center at San Antonio Dental School; Dr. Meyerowitz is Director, Eastman Dental Center, University of Rochester School of Medicine and Dentistry; Dr. Neumann is Associate Executive Director for Education, American Dental Association; Dr. Pyle is Associate Dean for Education, Case School of Dental Medicine; Dr. Tedesco is Vice Provost for Academic Affairs in Graduate Studies and Dean, Graduate School, Emory University; Dr. Valachovic is Executive Director, American Dental Education Association; Dr. Weaver is Associate Director, Center for Educational Policy and Research, American Dental Education Association; Dr. Winder is in private practice in Tulsa, Oklahoma; and Dr. Young is Dean, College of Dentistry, University of Oklahoma. Direct correspondence to Mr. William Hendricson, University of Texas Health Science Center at San Antonio, Dental School, 7703 Floyd Curl Drive, San Antonio, TX 78229; 210-567-0436; Hendricson@uthscsa.edu. Reprints of this article will not be available.

This article is one in a series of invited contributions by members of the dental and dental education community that have been commissioned by the ADEA Commission on Change and Innovation in Dental Education (CCI) to address the environment surrounding dental education and affecting the need for, or process of, curricular change. This article is authored by the ADEA CCI but does not necessarily reflect the views of ADEA or individual members of the ADEA CCI.

Key words: teaching effectiveness, faculty development, dental education, continuing education, evidence-based practice

Ben Franklin observed that "teaching is the occupation that is the most reflected upon, cherished, praised, rejoiced, and canonized, and at our deathbeds, possibly the most remembered aside from our dear ones, yet the least rewarded, in terms of earthly goods, of all the worthwhile and necessary pursuits."[1] Franklin went on to say, "A gifted teacher is as rare as a gifted doctor, and makes far less money."[1] As evidenced by the following quotes about the goals and processes of teaching and the inspirational influence of teachers, the pedagogical arts are often associated with advances in culture and the best hopes for society ("To me the sole hope of human salvation lies in teaching."—George Bernard Shaw[2]), and there is a consistent pattern of admired attributes and strategies associated with the teaching profession:

> "You cannot teach a man anything; you can only help him find it within himself."—Galileo Galilei[2]

> "The most extraordinary thing about a really good teacher is that he or she transcends accepted educational methods."—Margaret Meade[2,3]

> "The mediocre teacher tells. The good teacher explains. The superior teacher demonstrates. The great teacher inspires."—William Arthur Ward[2,4] (One of America's most quoted writers of the twentieth century, Ward was a university administrator, college teacher, and high-level lay leader in the Methodist Church, who held administrative positions with the Red Cross and Boy Scouts, contributed regularly to *Readers' Digest, Phi Delta Kappan,* and other periodicals, and wrote a daily column that appeared in more than 200 U.S. newspapers in the 1950s and 1960s.)

> "Those who educate our youth are more honored than those who produce them; for the former only gave them life, and the latter the art of living well."—Aristotle[2,5]

> "A teacher who is attempting to teach without inspiring the pupil with a desire to learn is hammering on a cold iron."—Horace Mann[2,6] (The most famous educator in nineteenth-century America, Mann is known as the father of American public education. As secretary of education in Massachusetts in the 1830s and '40s, he established the first public school system in the United States and supervised the development of fifty school districts and the first teacher training academies. After serving as a U.S. senator, he was president of Antioch College and hired the first female faculty members at a U.S. college. His closing remarks at the 1859 Antioch commencement shortly before his death—"Be ashamed to die until you have won some victory for humanity"—became the school motto and a mainstay of commencement ceremonies.)

> "In a completely rational society, the best of us would aspire to be teachers and the rest of us would have to settle for something less, because passing civilization along from one generation to the next ought to be the highest honor and highest responsibility anyone could have."—Lee Iacocca[2,7]

> "It is in fact nothing short of a miracle that the modern methods of instruction have not yet completely strangled the holy curiosity of the inquiring mind."—Albert Einstein[2,8]

> "The most admirable of reforms cannot but fall short in practice if teachers of sufficient quality are not available in sufficient quantity. Generally speaking, the more we try to improve our schools, the heavier the teacher's task becomes; and the better our teaching methods, the more difficult they are to apply."—Jean Piaget[9]

As noted by Piaget, the success of educational reforms ultimately lies with individual instructors and their capacity, individually and collectively, to implement "new ways of doing things" during their day-to-day, hour-by-hour, moment-by-moment interactions with students. Dental educators are navigating through an era when numerous fundamental changes in curriculum format and teaching/learning methods have been proposed. Academic dentists and members of the practice community have been hearing, for more than a decade, that "our educational system is in trouble" and that the "profession has lost its vision and may be wavering in the achievement of its goals."[10] These concerns are articulated in the

2001 Future of Dentistry report by the American Dental Association. This report asserts that the dental profession's capacity to promote the oral health of the public depends on achievement of these goals: integration of emerging diagnostic, therapeutic, and communication technologies into practice; understanding and responding to evolving consumer needs and expectations; providing an adequate supply of well-trained dental educators and dental students; re-energizing and maintaining the research focus within the profession; and developing strategies to serve the needs of members of our society who do not have access to care.[11] Pyle et al., writing for the American Dental Education Association (ADEA) Commission on Change and Innovation in Dental Education, argued that "there is a compelling need for rethinking the approach to dental education in the United States" and identified three issues that frame the case for change: the financial environment within higher education that makes dental school "expensive for universities to operate and tuition-intensive for students, producing high debt levels that limit access to education and restrict career choices; the profession's apparent loss of vision for taking care of the oral health needs of all components of society and the resultant potential for marginalization of dentistry as a specialized health care service available only to the affluent; and the nature of dental school education itself, which has been described as convoluted, expensive, and often deeply dissatisfying to our consumers—the students."[12]

Figure 1 displays the dental education reform agenda, consisting of a baker's dozen list of modifications to the standard ways of doing things in U.S. dental schools that have been proposed many times in many ways by many individuals and groups.[13-15] If implemented, these reforms will require faculty to make substantial modifications in their approaches to teaching. As noted in a companion article by Licari in this issue of the *Journal of Dental Education,* provision of faculty development related to teaching and assessment strategies is widely perceived to be the essential ingredient in efforts to introduce new curricular approaches and modify the educational environment in academic dentistry.[16] Indeed, analyses of the outcomes of efforts to revise curricula in the health professions, almost always in the direction of the reform agenda in Figure 1, have identified the availability and effectiveness of faculty development as one of the key predictors of the success or failure of reform initiatives.[17-20]

Faculty development can be implemented for any of the myriad components of a modern faculty member's roles and responsibilities in health professions education including curriculum planning and management; teaching and role modeling; various facets of scholarship including mentoring other faculty; service to the institution, the community in the school's service area, or one's professional discipline/organization; and delivery of patient care services. This article will address faculty development for purposes of enhancing teaching effectiveness and preparing instructors for potential new roles associated with curriculum changes. The article is organized into seven sections addressing the following topics:

- What is faculty development?
- How is faculty development accomplished?
- Why is faculty development particularly important in dental education?
- What happens when faculty development does not accompany educational reform?
- Why are teaching attitudes and behaviors so difficult to change?
- What outcomes can be expected from faculty development?
- What does the available evidence tell us about the design of faculty development programs?

The overall purpose of this article is to provide information and insights about faculty development that may be useful to dental schools in designing professional growth opportunities for their faculty. Emphasis is placed on the critical role of faculty development in preparing teachers for taking on new roles and acquiring new instructional skills that may be needed to function effectively in implementing future dental school curricula.

What Is Faculty Development?

LuAnn Wilkerson and David Irby, two of the most published authorities on faculty development in the health professions, have written, "Academic vitality is dependent upon faculty members' interest and expertise; faculty development has a critical role to play in promoting academic excellence and innovation, and it is a tool for improving the educational vitality of our institutions through attention to the competencies needed by individual teachers and to the institutional policies required to promote academic excellence."[21]

Proposed Dental Education Reforms
1. Review the curriculum in relation to the entry-level competencies needed by general dental practitioners to eliminate outdated and peripheral material.
2. Emphasize application of the basic sciences to patient care by problem-centered learning and other integrative and active-learning methods that help students understand why they are learning this material and how it can be useful.
3. Expose students to patients and the clinical environment from the first week of the curriculum to the last week.
4. Increase emphasis on evidence-based dental practice and the processes of critical appraisal of evidence to instill a culture that values the process of scientific inquiry.
5. Organize group practice teams in the clinic to promote continuity in faculty-student interaction, and coordinate patient care and students' educational experiences.
6. Arrange for all students to receive several continuous weeks of experience providing patient care in community clinics coupled with service-learning activities such as reflection exercises, analyses of the community's health care resources and needs, and interviews with health care providers and patients in the community to create a true educational experience.
7. Arrange for senior students to provide comprehensive care for at least a semester in a general dentistry model.
8. Use the capacities of information technology to enrich and diversify students' learning experiences.
9. Organize clinical education so that patients' needs come first and students do not see patients as means to an end.
10. Eliminate the smokestack (silo) curriculum model by increasing coordination and collaboration among departments/disciplines and providing interdisciplinary teaching.
11. Implement evaluation methods for nonclinical courses that focus on students' ability to use biomedical knowledge to solve problems and measure students' capacity to explain the pathophysiology of systemic and oral diseases.
12. Focus clinical evaluation methods on students' overall performance during patient care, including assessment of patient needs, diagnosis, treatment planning, and professionalism, and not just technical skills.
13. Increase educational collaboration between dentistry and the other health professions and emphasize the interaction of dental and medical problems.

Sources:

Kassebaum DK, Hendricson WD, Taft T, Haden NK. The dental curriculum at North American dental institutions in 2002-03: a survey of current structure, recent innovations, and planned changes. J Dent Educ 2004;68(9):914-31.
Hendricson WD, Cohen PA. Oral health care in the 21st century: implications for dental and medical education. Acad Med 2001;77(12):1181-206.
DePaola DP, Slavkin HC. Reforming dental health professions education: a white paper. J Dent Educ 2004;68:1139-50.

Figure 1. Baker's dozen dental education reform agenda: commonly proposed curriculum modifications for predoctoral dental education

Faculty development has been described in various ways in the literature on cultivation of the professional skills of the academician, but consistent themes are evident. In one of the earliest works on the topic, Centra described faculty development as "the broad range of activities that institutions use to renew or assist faculty in their roles" and includes initiatives designed to improve the performance of faculty in teaching, research, and administration.[22] Bland et al. described faculty development as a "planned program to prepare institutions and faculty members for their academic roles including teaching, research, administration, writing/scholarship, and career management."[23] Bligh proposed that the goals of faculty development are to improve practice in teaching, research, and institutional service and also to "manage change by enhancing individual strengths and abilities as well as organizational capacities and the overall culture."[24] Bligh noted that faculty development programs are tangible indicators of the institutions' inner faith in their academic workforce. O'Neill and Taylor observed that extensive faculty development programs in dental education characterize campus cultures that value teaching and that "faculty development is needed at all levels of faculty life, from novice instructor through the administrator to address the various levels in the educational enterprise."[25] Hand used a panel of dental educators in a Delphi process[26] to identify the competencies necessary for three dental faculty categories: clinical teachers (who focus primarily on instructional and curricular roles), clinical scholars (classic "triple-threat" faculty who pursue teaching, research, and service), and research-intensive scholars (who primarily focus on scholarship and training of future scholars) and proposed that these "competencies for effective dental faculty" be used to structure faculty development programs that will allow individuals, especially those new to academia, to attain these essential skills.[27]

Finally, Steinart et al. proposed that it is reasonable for institutions to expect that faculty development will "result in improved teaching performance and better outcomes for students."[28] According to Steinart et al., examples of such improvements include development and use of new teaching methods and evaluation techniques, enhanced processes for analyzing, planning, and implementing curricula, new perceptions about factors that influence relationships between students and teachers, and increased commitment to educational scholarship—investigating teaching and learning processes.

How Is Faculty Development Accomplished?

Ullian and Stritter described a seven-tier hierarchy of faculty development strategies to enhance the teaching effectiveness of individual faculty and/or groups of faculty.[29] This hierarchy ranged from 1) individual, self-directed activities such as reading, reflection, and self-assessment, observation of "exemplary practice" videotapes (e.g., watching other teachers "in action" and noting techniques), evaluations of teaching effectiveness provided by students (e.g., course and instructor ratings), and analysis of "what would you do" case scenarios depicting student-teacher interactions; 2) shadowing experienced or exemplary teachers; 3) being videotaped and/or observed while teaching and receiving feedback in order to "see oneself from the students' perspective"; 4) participating in brief duration (one-hour) lectures, journal clubs, or lunch-and-learn discussion groups that expose faculty members to theoretical literature or research reports that address educational issues; 5) participating in workshops and seminars of brief duration (three to six hours) focusing on specific instructor competencies such as providing feedback, asking questions to promote critical thinking, or constructing case-based examinations; 6) participating in pedagogical skills fellowships or teaching enhancement courses of several weeks' to months' duration; and 7) various organizational strategies to promote, assess, and reward teaching effectiveness including formalized mentoring programs for new and junior faculty and sabbaticals (often intended to allow faculty to experience alternative curriculum models at other schools) and providing mechanisms, including tuition support, for faculty to participate in graduate programs in education or academic leadership.

Centra recommended that enhancement of faculty instructional skills and capacity to guide students' learning is primarily accomplished through a formalized professional development system, linked to the institution's process for making promotion and tenure and merit pay decisions, in which faculty and their chairs, with support from senior colleagues as mentors/role models, develop and continually update career growth goals and plans that are formally negotiated as a component of the faculty member's annual performance evaluation.[22] Centra's concept of formal career planning with stipulated professional growth activities is consistent with Ullian

Why Is Faculty Development Particularly Important in Dental Education?

Development of the academic skills of the faculty, with focus on instructional skills, has increasingly become a critical component of health professions education, which for decades adhered to the tradition that competence in the biological and clinical sciences naturally morphed into competence in the classroom and also allowed biomedical specialists to seamlessly switch from scientist/clinician to mentors and role models for neophyte learners in laboratories and clinics. However, as the demands on faculty continue to expand, it is now recognized that preparing health professions faculty for their teaching responsibility is a necessary function of academic institutions.

As has been widely discussed, academic dentistry is graying rapidly and continues to struggle to attract younger dental professionals into the educational arm of the profession. For the academic year 2003-04, 50 percent of dental school deans reported that faculty recruitment and retention were significant problems, and more than half of dental school deans indicated that they expected filling vacant positions to become more difficult in the future.[30] In 2004-05, 1,039 faculty (almost 10 percent of the dental faculty workforce) left dental education, with 36 percent of these departing individuals entering into private dental practice. Younger faculty members (less than forty-five years of age) of lower academic rank were predominant among those who left dental schools to enter private practice.[31] In academic dentistry, the loss of substantial numbers of junior faculty is a critical concern because the strength of educational programs rests on teachers and researchers who plan lifelong academic careers and have the time over the span of their careers to acquire the competencies and academic credentials to become valuable contributors to the overall mis-

sion of the parent institution. In 2004-05, dental schools recruited 1,150 new faculty members.[31] Over the past decade, the numbers of faculty who leave dental education have been replaced by almost equivalent numbers of individuals who are "cannibalized" (hired away) from other dental schools or are completely new to the academic environment. Many of the new recruits are older individuals in the fifty-five to sixty age range who are ending their private practice or military/public health dentistry careers. In most cases, the older, "second career" recruits into dental education have little knowledge of educational theory and teaching practices and have limited, if any, experience with policies, procedures, and general expectations of the academic environment. As described by Bertolami, dental education is more and more "hoping that there will continue to be a supply of retiring practitioners and military dentists in the fifty-five to sixty age range who desire to serve as clinical supervisors for a few years prior to complete retirement."[32]

This situation is a double-edged sword for academic dentistry. On the one hand, there is conviction among some dental educators, and increasingly from external influences (see, for example, the *New York Times* article of October 11, 2007, titled "Boom Times for U.S. Dentistry, But Not for Americans' Teeth"[33]), that the dental school curriculum needs reform; an academic culture that values the process of scientific inquiry and the scientific basis for patient care needs to be re-established; and graduates need to be instilled with a sense of social responsibility. On the other hand, the ranks of academe are increasingly populated by older but relatively inexperienced teachers moving in from the practice environment and bringing with them memories of the "way we were taught" in the 1970s and perhaps not eager to find themselves in the middle of a major upheaval in teaching methodology as they start what amounts to a transitional period between their primary career and retirement.

As Winston Churchill observed, "Any message of change must first be heard."[34] Are the demographics of dental academe in the early twenty-first century such that reform messages will be heard? Churchill also famously said, "The winds of change are blowing and we lean into them with equal measures of anticipation and dread,"[34] to reflect the conflicting emotions associated with even the *anticipation* of a future change in the way things are done.

What Happens When Faculty Development Does Not Accompany Educational Reform?

In relation to the dental education reform agenda, the Institute of Medicine report on future directions for dental education concluded, "For the most part, these reforms represent ideas advocated for many years, but only sporadically implemented. The problem in reforming dental education is not so much consensus on directions for change but difficulty in overcoming obstacles to change. Agreement on educational problems is widespread. The curriculum is crowded with redundant or marginally useful material and gives students too little time to consolidate concepts or develop critical thinking skills. Comprehensive care is more an ideal than a reality in clinical education, and instruction still focuses too heavily on procedures rather than on patient care."[35] Why is there such difficulty moving from educational ideals and goals to actual incorporation of these concepts into the routine curricular operations of dental schools?

Analysis of the adoption, or lack thereof, of four frequently advocated new ways of doing business is instructive. These four reforms, which have been extensively endorsed throughout all components of health professions education, not only dental schools, are: 1) problem-based learning (PBL); 2) applications of information technology such as web-based (online) learning and digital versions of textbooks and other educational materials collectively known as e-learning or e-curriculum; 3) creation of thematically or topically integrated curricula with courses that are team taught across traditional academic boundaries; and 4) incorporation of the principles and techniques associated with evidence-based practice, which includes emphasis on helping students acquire the intellectual skills associated with critical appraisal.

Numerous reviews of the level of adoption of these educational innovations and barriers to incorporation into routine curriculum operation point to one key determinant of the fate of these initiatives: the presence, extent, and quality of faculty development efforts.[13,16-19] For example, investigations of the effectiveness of strategies to help faculty acquire skills necessary for implementing PBL and instilling the confidence to make the leap necessary to actually use PBL in courses have demonstrated the need for active, hands-on learning with extensive practice opportunities and ample shadowing of, and mentoring by, experienced PBL facilitators.[36-39] Yet reviews of learning outcomes that can be associated with PBL and the extent of implementation of this educational model point to failures in faculty development as one of the pivotal reasons for poor outcomes, negative attitudes among both students and faculty, and even program abandonment.[40-43] Dalrymple et al. have described a longitudinal series of intensive, experiential PBL tutor training workshops that model best evidence teaching/learning strategies (as reviewed below) for faculty development and are consistent with recommendations that have emerged from the PBL literature related to development of faculty for new and different roles.[44,45]

Electronic curriculum, or e-curriculum, refers to various forms of computer-based learning including providing students with educational materials on DVD, online courses, electronic mechanisms to search the literature, email, and various applications of information technology including providing laptops to students, use of computer-based simulations in preclinical labs, podcasting, videoconferencing, use of PDAs, use of the Internet in the classroom during educational activities, and many other applications. In 2002-03, Kassebaum et al. found high levels of interest among dental educators in e-curriculum: 86 percent of North American dental schools reported that they had already expanded use of information technology (IT) in their curricula, and 82 percent of schools desired to increase IT even further during the next three years.[13] Hendricson et al. reported that virtually all U.S. and Canadian dental schools had made substantial financial investments in e-curriculum infrastructure and resources, running into millions of dollars at individual health science centers.[46] These investigators also reported that sixteen North American dental schools in academic year 2002-03 (approximately 25 percent of all dental schools) required their students to purchase or lease laptops as a matriculation requirement and a number of these schools had contracts with a commercial vendor to supply a digital version of all curriculum materials and textbooks bundled with the required laptops.[46,47]

In spite of efforts by dental schools over the past decade to provide IT resources for students and faculty, only a handful of studies have been conducted to determine the extent to which the numerous forms of e-learning have been incorporated into the curriculum by faculty and the extent to which course design and teaching/learning strategies have changed as a consequence of these initiatives. Hendricson et al. examined e-curriculum utilization in two studies published in 2004 and 2006. The first project assessed e-curriculum implementation at all U.S. and Canadian dental schools,[46] and the second analyzed perceptions of students and faculty at U.S. dental schools with high levels of investment and infrastructure for information technology.[47] The initial study of all schools revealed extensive IT advocacy, but limited incorporation of e-curriculum capacities into the mainstream, core curriculum by faculty.

A sample of 800 students, at all academic levels, at fourteen U.S. dental schools with a major IT commitment provided a mixed assessment of the value and practical utility of mandatory laptop programs, curricular support software, and web-based learning. Students reported there was minimal necessity to use laptops, associated software, or the Internet in order to perform well in their courses, and few students reported changes in study methods because most of their instructors had not modified their courses to incorporate laptop or Internet-related activities. The benefits perceived by students were primarily related to enhanced email communication with classmates and instructors, convenient access to the Internet, and the ability to receive their teachers' PowerPoints. Less than one-third of students agreed that the value of the laptop and associated software was equal to the added tuition costs. Responses by 350 faculty members at these fourteen schools revealed a similar pattern: few had made extensive use of the capacities of the laptop and bundled software, the Internet, or web-based course management systems such as Blackboard, other than as repositories for standard course materials such as the syllabus and Power-Point files and as a means to send announcements to students.[48] Academic administrators, students, and faculty all identified lack of faculty development as a significant component in the pattern of slow and hesitant adoption of information technology, a finding echoed by Andrews and Demps in a similar study of IT utilization completed by more than 1,000 course directors at North American dental schools in the same time period.[46-49]

Failure to meaningfully integrate information technology into educational programs is not unique to dental education. Zemsky and Massy, in a study titled "Thwarted Innovation: What Happened to E-Learning and Why," investigated e-learning (defined similarly to e-curriculum) at six colleges and universities that had made major investments in information technology, ranging from small liberal arts schools such as Hamilton College in New York with less than 2,000 students to major public universities such as the University of Texas at Austin and Michigan State University with many thousands of students.[50] This study explored three assumptions that have driven efforts to reform higher education through the application of information technology. Below, the investigators' conclusions about the accuracy of these assumptions follow the statement of assumption, followed by quotes from their conclusions section:

- If we build it, they will come: Not True. "Despite massive investments in both hardware and software, there has yet to emerge a viable market for e-learning products other than online course management systems such as WebCT and Blackboard and PowerPoint lectures."
- Students will take to e-learning like ducks to water: Only Partially True. "Students do want to be connected, but principally to one another; e-learning at its best is seen [by students] as a convenience and at its worst as a distraction."
- E-learning will force a change in the way we teach: Not True. "Not by a long shot; even when they use e-learning products and devices, most faculty still teach as they were taught: they stand in the front of a classroom providing lectures."

Zemsky and Massy concluded, "E-learning will only become pervasive when faculty change how they teach—not before."[50]

The creation of thematically or topically integrated curricula with courses that are team taught across traditional academic boundaries has been repeatedly advocated by curriculum reformers as one of the strategies to build a more meaningful and structurally coherent learning experience for students and also as a mechanism to promote students' capacity to blend together the various pieces of the basic, behavioral, and clinical sciences as they acquire foundational knowledge.[14,15,51-54] Yet Kassebaum et al. found that only a small percentage of North American dental schools (7 percent) followed a curriculum that could by any stretch of the definition be characterized as cross-disciplinary; instead, the vast majority of dental schools followed a traditional "smokestack" or silo curriculum, in which each department conducted its own hierarchy of courses throughout the years of dental school with little interaction with other departments.[13] The majority of participants in the Kassebaum et al. study, who were primarily academic affairs/curriculum deans, indicated that efforts had been made at their schools to establish a more integrated approach to the curriculum and remove some of the silos, but expressed frustration with both the process of trying to accomplish this reform and the outcomes: the process is "slow and difficult," "departments remain territorial," "change is a slow and humbling process," "we tried but the faculty would have nothing to do with it," and "there was much planning and debate, but ultimately, it led to no changes of any consequence."[13] Strategies proposed by curriculum specialists to overcome resistance to "breaking out of silos" focus on the need to "open faculty eyes to new ideas" and build both competence and confidence through faculty development.[55-57] The top recommendation among participants in the Kassebaum et al. study was to enhance the availability of resources and time for faculty development to help course directors learn the skills needed to implement curricular reforms that move away from the "sage on the stage" teaching model.[13]

The fourth item on the baker's dozen dental education reform agenda is evidence-based practice, which has been proposed as a mechanism to accomplish several goals, including educating dental students to provide patient care that is supported by research evidence versus the historical "in my experience" approach[58] and to instill an educational culture that values and promotes intellectual curiosity, based on the intertwined mental capacities of critical appraisal, self-directed learning, self-assessment, and reflection upon actions, decisions, and behaviors.[32,59] Teaching and learning strategies associated with the development of critical appraisal and critical thinking skills have been identified and widely communicated to the academic community over the past twenty-five years.[60-65] The philosophy and techniques of evidence-based practice (EBP) have also been extensively discussed in the literature and routinely appear in the core values and curricular philosophies of the accreditation standards of the major health professions education programs including the Commission on Dental Accreditation.[66-68] Many health professions schools report efforts to introduce concepts that are common to both EBP and the processes for critical thinking to their students,[13] yet reports have emerged that these educational experiences are not being readily transferred to the clinic or carried forth into practice after graduation.[69,70]

In 2004, for example, Coormarasamy and Khan conducted a comprehensive review of published research related to educational strategies to help medical students and residents (postgraduates) acquire critical skills associated with EBP such as question formulation, identification of information sources, literature searching, and writing critical appraisal summaries.[71] Their objective was to evaluate the effects of what the authors termed "stand-alone" (primarily classroom-based) teaching strategies (described as journal clubs, lectures, and brief thirty- to sixty-minute workshops without other supportive learning experiences) versus clinically integrated teaching (defined as case analysis simulations, bedside teaching in the clinic, case conferences in the clinic based on recent patient encounters, literature-searching assignments related to patient symptoms, case presentations using EBP principles including an appraisal of research evidence pertinent to the patient's condition, and EBP-driven chart audits to compare patient management to evidence available in the literature).

The investigators searched Medline, ERIC, the Cochrane Controlled Trials Register, the Cochrane Database of Systematic Reviews, the Database of Abstracts of Reviews (DARE), Best Evidence in Medical Education (BEME) reports, and Science Citation Index. A total of forty-two research reports were identified, but only twenty-three met standards for research design determined by the investigators. Eighteen studies measured the effects of stand-alone/classroom training, and five assessed the outcomes of clinically integrated training. Of these twenty-three studies, four were randomized trials comparing two or more EBP training methods, and the remaining nineteen were non-randomized studies. Most of the latter group employed pre- and post-testing to measure changes in knowledge, critical appraisal skills, attitudes, confidence levels, and behavior (the latter were typically measured by self-reports of EBP use). Seventeen of the twenty-three studies assessed general EBP knowledge, and all investigations, whether classroom-based or clinically integrated, found enhancements in knowledge as a consequence of training. Nine of the studies measured acquisition of specific critical appraisal skills.

The authors concluded there was weak and inconsistent evidence that the stand-alone, classroom-based studies improved critical appraisal skills, but the clinically integrated studies all reported substantial enhancements in appraisal competency. Six of the studies assessed changes in attitudes and confidence levels. None of the stand-alone studies reported changes in attitudes; however, in the clinically integrated training, all studies reported improvement in student/resident attitudes and confidence in applying EBP techniques to patient care. Fourteen studies also assessed changes in actual behaviors, usually via self-report, although two studies employed chart audits and observation/feedback by supervising clinicians. Overall, little change in behavior was found among participants in the stand-alone, classroom-oriented training groups, while all five of the clinically integrated studies reported changes in behavior in desired directions, including changes in reading habits, selection of evidence sources, and capacity to access information resources, as well as documented changes in patient management strategies and use of clinical practice guidelines.

From these data, the authors concluded that stand-alone, classroom-oriented teaching and clinically integrated learning experiences are both effective in improving the knowledge base, but it is the clinically integrated teaching of EBP, embedded with actual patient care and realistic simulations, that is most likely to produce changes in skills, attitudes, and behavior. Notably, all four of the studies that employed a randomized controlled design produced outcomes that supported the effectiveness of clinically integrated learning experiences. Coormarasamy and Khan conclude, "It is important that teachers of critical literature appraisal and evidence-based medical practice consciously find ways of integrating and incorporating the teaching of critical appraisal into routine clinical practice"—a concept supported by the outcomes of a similar review by Werb and Matear,[58] who discussed the importance of faculty development to provide instructors with the capacities to design and orchestrate clinically relevant learning experiences. In spite of the findings from systematic reviews of EBP teaching, reports persist that health professions educators still primarily restrict EBP training to classroom exercises rather than more authentic learning experiences in the context of ongoing patient care, and there have been numerous reports that the concepts and techniques of EBP are not being readily translated into clinical practice.[72-75]

In summary, all four of the core items on the education reform agenda (PBL, information technology, integrated, cross-disciplinary learning experiences, and evidence-based practice/critical appraisal skills) have struggled to find acceptance and routine use by faculty. As proposed by Coormarasamy and Khan, the barrier appears to be lack of awareness and/or lack of capacity among faculty to implement appropriate teaching/learning strategies. So, why not just "train them up" in these new techniques and "get on with it," as the old saying goes. If only it were that easy.

Why Are Teaching Attitudes and Behaviors So Difficult to Change?

The challenge facing advocates of any of the items on the baker's dozen reform agenda is how to change deeply ingrained instructional behaviors and personal philosophies about the teacher's role and relationship with students by implementing an institutional change process (transformation) that makes alternative teaching strategies attractive and desirable to faculty and importantly makes these new ways seem feasible (do-able). Based on a model of innovation transfer within complex organizations originally proposed by Szulanski,[76] Hendricson et al. described four stages in the transformation of operational methods or routines as they apply to curriculum implementation (Figure 2).[47] Transfer is defined as the process by which an organization develops and attempts to institutionalize new methods to accomplish its missions: for example, implementing teaching/learning strategies associated with acquisition of critical appraisal skills throughout the curriculum.

The four stages of the transfer process are *initiation* (conception and pre-implementation planning), *initial implementation efforts* (characterized by on-the-job, trial and error learning), *ramp-up to satisfactory performance*, and *integration with established routines*. During the initiation phase, decision makers decide to implement a new strategy or methodology to accomplish an organizational goal and then start preliminary planning that is spearheaded by a small group of inner circle advocates who support the innovation. Often the handful of individuals who comprise the inner circle are the only faculty who are in any way intellectually involved with the proposed innovation and literally the only people who are thinking about it. After a planning process behind closed doors that may span many months to several years, the new routine is ultimately unveiled for use by other individuals in the organization, who typically are not well informed about the new approach and, in fact, may be caught off guard (surprised) by the unveiling of this new approach. This stage involves resolution of problems that arise during first implementation attempts by individuals, called the outer circle, who were not involved in planning and who may not share the assumptions, enthusiasm, or skills of the inner circle and thus may experience difficulties and associated frustrations in using the

Phases During Process

Initiation	Initial Implementation Efforts		Ramp-Up to Satisfactory Performance	Integration
	Learning *before* doing	**Learning *by* doing/ trial and error**	**Improve and expand use**	**Institutionalization**
Triggers: Negative event that reflects poorly on organization Persuasive new leader Awareness of new technologies that competitors may be using **Institutional commitment** Decision is made to move ahead with a new method **Preliminary planning starts** Create inner circle group of advocates and planners	Inner circle planning meetings Experiments to test new routine under trial conditions (pilots) Decision to move ahead with formal rollout	Others within the organization (outer circle) are asked to use the new method Monitor initial use by outer circle and solve problems Identify opponents of the change effort	Improve quality by tweaking use and providing training Create successes to justify the new routine and motivate non-users to join the effort	New method is no longer perceived as being new Blends into regular operating procedures of the organization

Sources of Stickiness (Problems, Barriers)

Initiation	Initial Implementation Efforts	Ramp-Up to Satisfactory Performance	Integration
Lack of attentiveness Failure to recognize need to improve routines Failure to recognize opportunities to improve Failure to identify superior techniques that could be used	**Lack of communication and training** Poor communication between inner and outer circles Outer circle lacks motivation or does not share assumptions about value of the new method Outer circle not ready for new roles, and no training is provided No encouragement, emotional support, or rewards for outer circle	**Slow response** Failure to resolve emerging problems before they lead to discontent Flawed practice becomes institutionalized and hard to correct	**Lack of diligence** Inner circle fails to recognize problems and minimize obstacles

Figure based on: Szulanski G. The process of knowledge transfer: a diachronic analysis of success. Organizational Behav Human Decision Processes 2000;82(1):9-27.
Source: Hendricson WD, Eisenberg E, Guest G, Jones P, Panagakos F, Johnson L, Cintron L. What do dental students think about mandatory laptop programs? J Dent Educ 2006;70(5):480-99.

Figure 2. Phases during process of implementing a new operational routine and sources of problems in each phase

new routine, particularly in the absence of training. Transformation efforts that survive initial implementation evolve into a ramp-up phase, in which the organization attempts to produce successes that justify the innovation and motivate non-users to join the effort. During the integration phase, the innovation is finally absorbed into the organizational culture as a standard operating procedure and is no longer perceived to be new or different. This four-stage transfer process may take many years to complete, depending on the complexity of the innovation, the degree of resistance or apathy among the outer circle, the level of enthusiasm and persistence among the inner circle band of reformers, and the management skills of organizational leaders.[77,78]

According to Szulanski, innovations can become stuck at each of the four stages, but problems or even failure are most likely during the initial implementation stage (as highlighted in Figure 2) for the following reasons: 1) poor communication between the inner circle advocates and the outer circle, who are expected to carry the load of implementing the innovation even though they were not involved in planning; 2) lack of motivation among the outer circle and/or personal lack of confidence in their capacity to implement the new approach, which often leads to defensiveness and passive-aggressive behavior;[79] 3) failure to prepare the outer circle for new tasks and roles; and 4) failure to provide encouragement and rewards for the outer circle, especially as they struggle with the predictable and often discouraging pitfalls of early implementation.[80]

Analysis of efforts to implement the baker's dozen reforms suggests that dental schools have experienced difficulties with the hand-off from the inner circle of faculty and administrators, who are enthusiastic about these reforms, to the frontline faculty in the trenches. All four of Szulanski's points of "stickiness" are directly or indirectly issues of faculty development. For example, Hendricson and Cohen[14] identified four factors that mitigated against faculty adoption of PBL in dental schools: 1) the student-centered structure of PBL is alien to most dental school faculty, who had no experience with case-based and student-centered learning when they were in dental school; 2) department chairs have concerns about the resources needed to implement PBL and consequently are hesitant to commit their teachers to a curriculum format perceived to be faculty-intensive; 3) many dental school faculty are not comfortable with the "solve the mystery" process of PBL, which is essentially a diagnostic detective game, and have

difficulty watching students debate the merits of various patient care approaches, which faculty may see as time-consuming and inefficient; and 4) faculty repeatedly ask to be shown the evidence that PBL is a sound methodology, but often do not receive convincing answers to rectify the perception that PBL is more work for the already overworked.

Critiques of the PBL movement concluded that adoption of this educational innovation would have been enhanced by three events that largely did not occur: 1) avoid the "build it and they will come" approach by providing meaningful training to faculty *prior to implementation* of this curriculum model; 2) establish that the technique is indeed worth the extra effort by conducting research that demonstrates that assumptions about educational advantages are true; and 3) once events 1 and 2 have occurred, implement a transformational approach to ensure a comprehensive implementation of the innovation throughout the curriculum versus relegating educational innovations to the category of supplements and add-ons that can be ignored or dismissed by both students and faculty if they so desire.[37,44,81]

The take-home message from this section is that orchestrating educational reform is a complex sociological, psychological, and organizational undertaking and that faculty development lies (or should lie) at the heart of the planning and implementation of the process employed to roll out the new way of doing things.

What Outcomes Can Be Expected from Faculty Development?

Before delving into the evidence available to answer this question, three provisos are in order. First, virtually all of the evidence on the effectiveness and outcomes of faculty development is derived from studies conducted in medicine; consequently, most of the findings and conclusions presented in this section reflect the medical school or medical residency training environment. Second, there are only a handful of reports of the outcomes of faculty development in dental schools,[44,45] although there have been a number of descriptive articles in the literature that report the components and implementation of programs intended to improve instructional effectiveness. However, several recent articles in the dental education literature by Manogue et al., Chambers et al., McGrath et al., and Henzi et al.[82-86] have reported the development and use of instruments designed to assess the characteristics of effective teaching in dental school, primarily in the clinic environment, or to elicit students' impressions of teachers' effectiveness using instruments that reflect various instructional practices often associated with "good" teaching.[85,87,88] As a consequence, several instruments are now available that are unique to types of clinical teaching that occur in dental schools and which therefore can be used in future research to document outcomes of faculty development. Third, investigations of faculty development outcomes for health professions faculty are offsprings of efforts to determine the degree to which information and best practice guidelines communicated in continuing education (CE) in medicine were translated into the practice behaviors of health care providers. Review of the evidence related to the outcomes of CE, using modern methods that we now associate with the critical appraisal process in EBP, started in earnest in the 1980s, and systematic appraisal of the findings from studies of faculty development started to appear around 2000 using parallel methods. Techniques developed to study the outcomes of continuing professional education have largely been adapted to the issue of faculty development effectiveness because the focus in both arenas has evolved to assessment of which teaching/learning strategies employed in either CE or faculty development are most likely to enhance knowledge, alter attitudes and confidence, increase capacity to use skills, and change behavior either during patient care or during instructional interactions with students. Because many of the instructional techniques that are mainstays of continuing education and in-service training were adapted to the realm of professional development for faculty in academic institutions, a review of the principal findings from the evidence on CE outcomes will be presented first, in summary form, followed by a review of the evidence related to faculty development outcomes pertaining to the enhancement of teaching effectiveness.

Appraisal of the Outcomes of Continuing Education Programs for Providers

A team of investigators led by Davis and Haynes has evaluated the effects of continuing education programs on professional practice and health care outcomes for more than twenty years, producing a series of landmark reports beginning in 1984 with an article in the *Journal of the American Medical Association* (JAMA) aptly titled "A Critical Appraisal of the Efficacy of Continuing Medical Education."[89]

The second review in this series was published in 1992 in JAMA and was titled "Evidence for the Effectiveness of CME: A Review of 50 Randomized Controlled Trials."[90] The 1992 report caught the attention of the health professions education community and became one of the most widely cited educational articles of that decade. The sophisticated literature selection and appraisal techniques described in this seminal report and the analysis of the available data set the standard for subsequent reviews of outcomes evidence in health professions education. After applying rigorous criteria for research design, subject section, randomization, study implementation, and data analyses that led to the exclusion of hundreds of reports with insufficient research quality, Davis et al. identified fifty randomized controlled trials (RCTs) that assessed CE outcomes for knowledge, attitudes, skill acquisition, and changes in providers' behaviors. Davis et al. found that CE interventions that relied exclusively on lecture-based methods had the capacity to improve participants' fund of knowledge, primarily in the short term (immediately after course conclusion) as measured by pre- to post-testing, but were uniformly ineffective in promoting substantial changes in attitudes, skill levels, or confidence and rarely resulted in application of skills during actual patient care. In contrast, a subset of fourteen RCTs within the overall group of fifty studies produced different outcomes. These fourteen physician education programs employed a variety of active, learner-centered, and practice reinforcement techniques to augment lectures or were implemented largely without lectures. These techniques included completing self-assessments of practice behaviors or self-audits of patient records to identify current practice patterns and learning needs, using algorithms to solve clinical problems, applying group analysis to case scenarios, rehearsing the use of clinical practice guidelines in workshops, observing and critiquing the performance of other practitioners, receiving feedback from other providers during patient care simulations, doing problem solving to identify ways to reduce implementation barriers for practice guidelines, using debriefing exercises in which participants shared their opinions and concerns about new clinical techniques, debating the merits of practice recommendations, and distributing pocket cards, chart reminders, and posters that portrayed clinical practice recommendations. Significant changes in the desired direction in the patient care behaviors, attitudes, and confidence levels of participating physicians were found in all fourteen interventions that primarily employed active-learning strategies. Positive results for patient outcomes were also found in five of the nine studies that measured patient outcomes.[90]

In the years since this initial review of the evidence, the Davis group has periodically conducted other analyses either to update the literature as new research findings become available or to investigate other aspects of continuing education for physicians and occasionally other health care providers. Several of the principal reports appear in the references.[91-95] The findings and conclusions from these reviews have not fundamentally differed from the outcomes of the 1992 JAMA report. The group's most recent review, published in 2005 in the Cochrane Database of Systemic Reviews (Issue 3), was titled "Continuing Education Meetings and Workshops: Effects on Professional Practice and Health Care Outcomes." This analysis reviewed the findings from thirty-two studies that employed randomized trials or well-designed quasi-experimental studies with a total of 2,995 health care providers from several different disciplines. These providers participated in a variety of planned professional development activities that occurred off-site from the practice setting including meetings, lectures, workshops, symposia, and weekend courses. Ten of the studies evaluated the effects of CE programs that used active-learning strategies similar to those described for the 1992 JAMA report by the Davis team; nineteen studies addressed outcomes from CE activities that used mixed lecture and interactive strategies; and seven studies evaluated exclusively lecture-based instruction. The investigators concluded that interactive programs that employed a mixture of primarily hands-on, active-learning strategies resulted in moderately large changes in professional practice; lectures alone, they found, were unlikely to change professional practice.[95] The pattern of findings from the longitudinal series of reviews by the Davis group parallels the findings for training outcomes related to evidence-based practice by Coormarasamy and Kahn previously described.[71]

Appraisal of the Outcomes of Faculty Development Programs to Improve Teaching Effectiveness

The most comprehensive source of information about the effectiveness of faculty development initiatives to enhance teaching is the 2006 review by the Best Evidence in Medical Education Collaborative (BEME).[28] The summary report (BEME Guide No. 8) appears in the June 2006 issue of *Medical Teacher.* This report is an outstanding synopsis of the available research and also provides useful guidelines for the design of faculty development programs as well as strategies to assess outcomes. The authors also included a summary of eight studies of faculty development outcomes that received the highest ratings for quality of research design from among the entire sample of studies that were critiqued for inclusion in this systematic review. I encourage all dental educators and others who are interested in professional development techniques to place this report in their "must read" folders.

The BEME is an ad hoc international organization of health professions educators who share a mission to move the education of care providers from "opinion-based education to evidence-based education."[96] The BEME has produced a number of systematic reviews of the evidence related to various aspects of health professions education, with obviously a strong orientation to medical education, in an effort to inform, guide, and improve educational practices and also to build a culture among faculty and academic program managers that is accepting and supportive of best evidence approaches. The BEME's search for evidence considered all forms of teaching enhancement strategies described by Centra[22] and Ullian and Stritter[29] above.

The BEME group used Kirkpatrick's four-level hierarchy of educational outcomes (shown in Figure 3) as the framework for classifying and analyzing findings from studies included in the data set.[97] Kirkpatrick's model has four levels of educational outcomes: 1) the learner's *reaction* to the educational experience (opinions and perceptions); 2) indicators of *learning,* which include changes in attitudes, knowledge, and skills; 3) *behavior,* which includes changes in practice (i.e., modifications in methods); and 4) *results,* which refer to changes in the practices, policies, or infrastructure of the overall organization and/or changes in the practices/behavior of the students or colleagues of a faculty member who participated in a faculty development program.

The group conducted an electronic literature search for articles published in 1980-2002 using Medline and ERIC and supplemented by manual searches of prominent educational journals including *Academic Medicine, Advances in Health Sciences Education, Medical Education, Medical Teacher,* and *Teaching and Learning in Medicine.* Expert

Level	Type of Outcomes Evidence
Results: change among participants' students, residents, or colleagues	Evidence of improvement in student or resident learning/performance as a direct result of the educational intervention, or improvement in colleagues' performance that is attributable to the intervention.
Results: change in practices, policies, or infrastructure of a system or organization	Evidence of wider changes in the overall organization that are attributable to the educational program.
Behavior: change in behavior	Evidence that the program participant has the capacity to transfer learning into the workplace.
Learning: modification of knowledge or skills	Evidence of the acquisition of, and capacity to use, concepts, procedural/psychomotor skills, and social or communication skills.
Learning: change in attitudes	Changes in the attitudes or values among program participants toward teaching and learning issues and techniques; can also include changes in participants' intention to use a skill or confidence in using a skill.
Reaction: participants' satisfaction	Participants' views and perspectives on the learning experience: its organization, presentation, content, teaching and learning methods, and overall quality of instruction.

Source: Kirkpatrick DL. Evaluating training programs: the four levels. San Francisco, CA: Berrett-Koehler Publishers, 1997.

Figure 3. Kirkpatrick's hierarchy of educational outcomes

recommendation was also used to identify key articles, and the references for extracted articles were checked to identify additional articles that may have been published in other journals. The review process identified nearly 3,000 research reports describing various types of faculty development efforts; 303 of these were specifically related to teaching effectiveness. Review of these 303 reports eliminated 250 that provided no reports of program evaluation and instead communicated theoretical discussions of faculty development issues or presented methodological/logistical descriptions of program implementation. Of the remaining fifty-three reports that comprised the data set for the analysis, 72 percent of the studies (38/53) were conducted in the United States, and the remainder were primarily conducted in Canada and the United Kingdom. Approximately 80 percent of the studies addressed effectiveness in clinical teaching, and the remaining 20 percent addressed general teaching/learning issues and techniques that could

be applied to classroom, lab, or clinical settings. A variety of faculty development formats were used in these studies: approximately 40 percent of the studies examined the effect of workshops of varying durations ranging from one to three hours to six to eight hours; 20 percent were seminar series extending over several weeks or months (e.g., a one- to two-hour seminar once a week for six weeks or once a month for six months); 10 percent were classified as short concentrated courses comprising two to three consecutive full days; 10 percent were described as extended or longitudinal fellowship programs that included periodic activities over several months to a full year; and the remaining 20 percent included mixtures of these formats.

All of the reports described a wide range of teaching/learning methods: no programs were completely lecture-based, and all reported some type of experiential learning component including observation of practice teaching assignments followed by feedback from other program participants or course faculty. Based on evidence reviews for EBP training and continuing education, the reliance on a blend of learning experiences appears to be indicative of best practices, but the diversity of methods influenced the assessment of the BEME data, in effect, producing an appraisal of the effectiveness of faculty development programs that used experiential learning. The majority of studies (forty-seven; 89 percent) used a quasi-experimental design, and six were RCTs. Among the quasi-experimental studies, thirty-one used pre- and post-testing to measure one or more outcomes. Data collection methods to assess outcomes varied widely, and most articles reported use of several measures of effectiveness. The most frequently used techniques were participants' self-reports of post-program changes in knowledge, attitudes, and utilization of skills (fifty studies; 94 percent); end-of-program questionnaires to elicit participants' opinions about program value and quality (forty-nine studies; 92 percent); direct observation of participants' teaching performance by peers, educational specialists, or experienced faculty (sixteen studies; 30 percent); videotaping of teaching during or after the program for self-assessment and/or critique by others (fifteen studies; 28 percent); ratings of the participants' teaching by students or residents (fifteen studies; 28 percent); and comparison of pre- and post-written tests to measure changes in knowledge, confidence, and attitudes about the topic of the program (apparently fifteen studies; 28 percent, although the BEME report is not completely clear about the number of studies that used pre- and post-program testing). Other outcome measures used less frequently included expert opinion about the participant's teaching skills either during or after the program (e.g., critiques provided by educational specialists or experienced faculty), the scores of the participants' students on examinations, and patients' ratings.

The BEME report analyzed data using Kirkpatrick's four-level outcomes hierarchy according to each program format (workshops, seminar series, short concentrated course, fellowship, and mixed method). The preponderance of available evidence indicated that all of the formats produced positive outcomes for reaction, learning, and behavior to the extent that these dimensions of the hierarchy were actually measured and given the nature of the assessment strategies. Outcomes pertinent to level four (results: changes in practices, policies, or infrastructure of organization or changes in the practices of students or colleagues of faculty development

participants) were relatively sparse (nine studies reported level four outcomes), yet almost all were judged to be positive by the BEME analysts. As noted previously, all fifty-three studies employed a combination of teaching/learning methods with a decided tilt toward experiential learning, practice teaching, and self-, peer, and expert assessment. Consequently, these data reflect an assessment of the outcomes of experientially based faculty development that did not rely as heavily on lectures as the studies included in the EBP or CE reviews. In that context, the outcomes appear to be good news for those who endorse student-centered, experiential learning; however, the heavy reliance on participants' self-reports to document changes in attitudes, knowledge, and behaviors should be noted in a cautionary sense (that is, consider the source). Approximately 40 percent of the studies reported outcome measures that included direct or videotaped observation of teacher performance or students'/residents' ratings of performance. Virtually all of these assessments of actual teachers' behaviors were characterized as being positive, but many did not include a pre-training comparison to serve as a benchmark. Additionally, only eight of the fifty-three studies (the six RCTs and two of the quasi-experimental studies) employed a control group of faculty who did not undergo faculty development. If the Strength of Recommendation Taxonomy (SORT),[98] which is widely used in the EBP literature, was applied to these data, the evidence and associated practice recommendations would probably grade out at the lowest level, C, although the evidence would score high for consistency. The SORT grades appear in Figure 4.

On a more positive note, the BEME team's summary of the evidence for faculty development to enhance teaching effectiveness fundamentally answers the lead-off question for this section: what outcomes can be expected from faculty development? The BEME team concluded, despite methodological limitations, that the findings support the following outcomes:

- Overall satisfaction with faculty development programs was high. The methods used, especially those with a practical and skills-based focus, were valued by the program participants.
- Participants reported a positive change in attitudes toward faculty development and towards teaching as a result of their involvement.
- Participants reported increased knowledge of educational concepts as well as specific teaching strategies and gains in skills such as assessing

Strength of Recommendations	Characteristics of the Available Evidence
A	Consistent evidence, good-quality study design, patient/provider-oriented evidence that measures outcomes that matter to the patient or other target of the intervention such as providers or teachers. Outcome data are tangible and direct measures of patient physiology and quality of life or direct measures of provider (or teacher) behavior and performance, not indirect or surrogate measures.
B	Inconsistent evidence and/or limited quality study design that consists of indirect or surrogate measures or other methodology deficiencies.
C	Evidence consists of expert opinion, consensus opinion, usual practice heuristics, indirect or surrogate indicators, and case series data.

Good quality study design: RCT, cohort study, or systematic review that employs appropriate design. For an RCT, for example: allocation of subjects concealed, blinding if feasible, intention-to-treat analysis, adequate statistical power, adequate follow-up. For cohort study: suitable cohort design, adequate sample size, adequate spectrum of subjects, blinding, and consistent and well-defined reference standard.

Source: Ebell MK, Siwek J, Weiss BD, Woolf SH, Susman J, Ewigman B, et al. Strength of recommendation taxonomy (SORT): a patient-centered approach to grading evidence in the medical literature. Am Fam Physician 2004;69:549-57.

Figure 4. Strength of Recommendation Taxonomy (SORT) grades

learners' needs, promoting reflection, and providing feedback.
- Self-perceived changes in teaching behavior were consistently reported.
- Participants reported a greater involvement in new educational activities and establishment of new networks of colleagues.[28]

Although these are desirable outcomes, evidence in the health professions literature that faculty development unequivocally does enhance teaching effectiveness is in short supply. Well-designed studies are needed to measure the outcomes of faculty development programs that incorporate the characteristics described in the next section. Implementation of such studies represents a substantial opportunity for dental educators to advance the understanding of strategies that have the capacity to improve teaching effectiveness and also provide the necessary support for curriculum reforms.

What Does the Available Evidence Tell Us About the Design of Faculty Development Programs?

The available evidence from the EBP review by Coormarasamy and Khan, numerous reviews on continuing professional education by the Davis and Haynes group, and the BEME review indicates that certain characteristics are consistently associated with program effectiveness:
- use of experiential learning (e.g., hands-on practice of teaching skills, case or situational analysis, roleplay of student-teacher interactions);
- provision of feedback to participants about their performance;

- opportunity to apply skills within the program or soon after;
- use of peers to model exemplary teaching behaviors and share perspectives on teaching;
- programs designed to facilitate peer interaction and the building of colleague relationships;
- use of a diversity of learning experiences; and
- opportunities for post-program assessment of skills.

Final Thoughts: What About the Content of Faculty Development?

Up to this point, this review has focused primarily on the methodology of faculty development: how does the design of the program influence outcomes? Of course, it is also critical for the content of the program to be pertinent to the roles and responsibilities of the faculty who participate. Faculty development has the potential to help dental schools move forward toward implementation of the baker's dozen curricular reform agenda, but only if appropriate skills are emphasized. Several studies have demonstrated that careful needs assessment prior to conducting faculty development creates programs that are more likely to be attended, evaluated more positively, and to contain concepts and skills perceived to be transferable into the day-to-day work responsibilities of faculty.[99-105]

One of the most influential books on educational planning in the twentieth century emphasized the importance of "getting the content of training right." This book was *The Saber-Tooth Curriculum* by Abner J. Peddiwell; it was published in 1939 but still remains a required reading in schools of education and in many business schools.[106] Peddiwell tells the following story. During most of the Paleolithic era in Northern Europe, which extended from about 130,000 years ago when stone tools were developed to 10,000 years ago when agriculture was introduced, the young men of the pre-agrarian nomadic clans that roamed the continent were taught how to guard the perimeter of the camp at night with fire and noise to scare away saber-tooth tigers. According to Peddiwell's story, the training included instruction on how to make large bonfires, how to build torches that would burn for long periods of time, how to space fire-wavers around the camp perimeter for maximum effect, and how to supplement torch waving with loud noises known to frighten saber-tooth tigers. In

essence, the young men were participants in a critical professional development activity that was central to the survival of their parents and siblings and other families in the clan and which obviously addressed an important need. Due to the quality of the training, this technique for warding off saber-tooth tiger attacks worked well for several thousand years and became ingrained into the culture of the roving nomad tribes of that prehistoric era. However, over the next 10,000 years, an ice age slowly enveloped most of Europe. Saber-tooth tigers moved south to seek alternative food sources and a more hospitable climate; those that remained perished in the cold weather. Yet, among the nomadic clans, tiger scaring remained the core of the training for young men, even though there were fewer and fewer saber-tooths to scare away. Because of the traditional focus on fire-making, the elders of the clan failed to teach the younger generation more currently necessary skills such as finding alternative food sources, locating warmer places of shelter, and creating warmer clothing. The failure to transition the content of the training to cold weather survival skills had disastrous effects on these nomadic tribes.

Today, needs assessment and anticipatory planning are just as important as they were in the Paleolithic era 50,000 years ago. Let us use those tools to keep dental education relevant and effective for the future.

REFERENCES

1. Houston A, ed. Franklin: the autobiography and other writings on politics, economics, and virtue. New York: Cambridge University Press, 2004.
2. Howe R. The quotable teacher. Guilford, CT: Lyons Press, 2003.
3. Howard J. Margaret Mead: a life. New York: Simon and Schuster, 1984.
4. William WA. Brighten your corner. Dallas: Droke House, 1973.
5. Barnes J. The complete works of Aristotle. 2 vols. Princeton: Princeton University Press, 1984.
6. Cremin L. The republic and the school: Horace Mann on the education of free men. New York: Teachers College Press, 1957.
7. Iacocca L, Novak W. Iacocca: an autobiography. 2nd ed. New York: Bantam Books, 1986.
8. Hoffman B. Albert Einstein: the human side—new glimpses from his archives. Princeton: Princeton University Press, 1981.
9. Piaget J. Science of education and the psychology of the child. New York: Orion Press, 1970.
10. Roth K. Dental education: a leadership challenge for dental educators and practitioners. J Dent Educ 2007;71(8): 983-7.
11. American Dental Association. Future of dentistry. Chicago: American Dental Association, 2001.

12. Pyle M, Andrieu SC, Chadwick DG, Chmar JE, Cole JR, George MC, et al. The case for change in dental education. J Dent Educ 2006;70(9):921-4.

13. Kassebaum DK, Hendricson WD, Taft T, Haden NK. The dental curriculum at North American dental institutions in 2002-03: a survey of current structure, recent innovations, and planned changes. J Dent Educ 2004;68(9):914-31.

14. Hendricson WD, Cohen PA. Oral health care in the 21st century: implications for dental and medical education. Acad Med 2001;77(12):1181-206.

15. DePaola DP, Slavkin HC. Reforming dental health professions education: a white paper. J Dent Educ 2004;68:1139-50.

16. Licari F. Faculty development to support curriculum change and ensure the future vitality of dental education. J Dent Educ 2007;71(12):1509-12.

17. Irby DM. Faculty development and academic vitality. Acad Med 1993;68:769-73.

18. Mennin SP, Krackov SK. Reflections on relevance, resistance, and reform in medical education. Acad Med 1998;73(9 Suppl):S60-S64.

19. Bland C, Starnaman S, Wersal L, Moorhead-Rosenberg L, Zonia S, Henry R. Curricular change in medical schools: how to succeed. Acad Med 2000;75:575-94.

20. Trotman CA, Haden NK, Hendricson W. Does the dental school work environment promote successful academic careers? J Dent Educ 2007;71(6):713-25.

21. Wilkerson L, Irby DM. Strategies for improving teaching practices: a comprehensive approach to faculty development. Acad Med 1998;73(4):387-96.

22. Centra JA. Types of faculty development programs. J Higher Educ 1978;49:151-62.

23. Bland CJ, Schmitz CC, Stritter FT, Henry RC, Alusie JJ. Successful faculty in academic medicine: essential skills and how to acquire them. New York: Springer Publishing Company, 1990.

24. Bligh J. Faculty development. Med Educ 2005;39(20):120-2.

25. O'Neill PN, Taylor CD. Responding to the need for faculty development: a survey of U.S. and Canadian dental schools. J Dent Educ 2001;65(8):768-76.

26. Keeney S, Haason F, McKenna HP. A critical review of the Delphi technique as a research methodology for nursing. Int J Nurs Stud 2001;38:195-200.

27. Hand JS. Identification of competencies for effective dental faculty. J Dent Educ 2006;70(9):937-47.

28. Steinart Y, Mann K, Centeno A, Dolmans D, Spencer J, Gelula M, Prideaux D. A systematic review of faculty development initiatives designed to improve teaching effectiveness in medical education: BEME Guide No. 8. Med Teacher 2006;28(6):497-526.

29. Ullian JA, Stritter FT. Types of faculty development programs. Fam Med 1997;29:237-41.

30. Weaver RG, Chmar JE, Haden NK, Valachovic RW. Dental school vacant budgeted faculty positions: academic year 2003-04. J Dent Educ 2005;69:296-305.

31. Chmar JE, Weaver RG, Valachovic RW. Dental school vacant budgeted faculty positions: academic year 2004-05. J Dent Educ 2006;70:188-98.

32. Bertolami CN. Creating the dental school faculty of the future: a guide for the perplexed. J Dent Educ 2007;71(10):1267-80.

33. Berenson A. Boom times for U.S. dentistry, but not for Americans' teeth. The New York Times, October 11, 2007. At: http://query.nytimes.com/gst/fullpage.html?res=98 07E3DE1338F932A25753C1A9619C8B63. Accessed: October 12, 2007.

34. Blake R, Louis WR, eds. Churchill: a major new assessment of his life in peace and war. New York: W.W. Norton, 1993.

35. Field MJ, ed. Dental education at the crossroads: challenges and change. Washington, DC: National Academy Press, 1995.

36. Farmer EA. Faculty development for problem-based learning. Eur J Dent Educ 2004;8:59-66.

37. Hitchcock MA, Mylona ZE. Teaching faculty to conduct problem-based learning. Teach Learn Med 2000;12(1):52-7.

38. Irby DM. Models of faculty development for problem-based learning. Adv Health Sci Educ Theory Pract 1996;1:69-81.

39. Olmesdahl PJ, Manning DM. Impact of training on PBL facilitators. Med Educ 1999;33(10):753-5.

40. Vernon DTA, Blake RL. Does problem-based learning work? A meta-analysis of evaluative research. Acad Med 1993;68(7):550-63.

41. Albanese MA, Mitchell S. Problem-based learning: a review of the literature on its outcomes and implementation issues. Acad Med 1993;68(2):52-81.

42. Saarinen-Rahiika H, Binkley JM. Problem-based learning in physical therapy: a review of the literature. Phys Ther 1998;78:195-207.

43. Blumberg P. Evaluating the evidence that problem-based learners are self-directed learners: review of the literature. In: Evensen DH, Hmelo CE, eds. Problem-based learning: a research perspective on learning interactions. Mahwah, NJ: Lawrence Erlbaum Associates, 2000:199-226.

44. Dalrymple KR, Wuenschell C, Shuler CF. Development and implementation of a comprehensive faculty development program in PBL core skills. J Dent Educ 2006;70(9):948-55.

45. Dalrymple KR, Wuenschell C, Rosenblum A, Paine M, Crowe D, von Bergmann HC, et al. PBL core skills faculty development workshop 1: an experiential exercise with the PBL process. J Dent Educ 2007;71(2):249-59.

46. Hendricson WD, Panagakos F, Eisenberg E, McDonald J, Guest G, Jones P, et al. Electronic curriculum implementation at North American dental schools. J Dent Educ 2004;68(10):1041-57.

47. Hendricson WD, Eisenberg E, Guest G, Jones P, Panagakos F, Johnson L, Cintron L. What do dental students think about mandatory laptop programs? J Dent Educ 2006;70(5):480-99.

48. Hendricson WD, Eisenberg E, Guest G, Jones P. Implementation of electronic curriculum: where are we in 2005? Symposium presentation at American Dental Education Association Annual Session, Baltimore, MD, March 7, 2005.

49. Andrews KG, Demps EL. Distance education in the U.S. and Canadian undergraduate dental curriculum. J Dent Educ 2003;67(4):427-38.

50. Zemsky R, Massy WF. Thwarted innovation: what happened to e-learning and why: a final report for the WeatherStation Project. West Chester, PA: The Learning Alliance

for Higher Education at the University of Pennsylvania, 2004. At: www.irhe.upenn.edu/WeatherStation.html. Accessed: October 17, 2007.

51. Kuske TT, Fleming GA, Jarecky RR, Levine JH, Lewis LA. Curriculum change in the 1980s: a report of 40 southern U.S. medical schools. JAMA 1985;254:2783-6.

52. Tedesco LA. Issues in dental curriculum development and change. J Dent Educ 1995;59:97-147.

53. Pew Health Professions Commission. Critical challenges: revitalizing the health professions for the twenty-first century. San Francisco: University of California, San Francisco, Center for the Health Professions, 1995.

54. Hendricson W, Cohen P. Future directions in dental school curriculum, teaching, and learning. In: Haden K, ed. Leadership for the future: the dental school in the university. Washington, DC: Center for Educational Policy and Research, American Association of Dental Schools, 1999:37-62.

55. Bland CJ, Seaquist E, Pacala JT, Center B, Finstad D. One school's strategy to assess and improve the vitality of its faculty. Acad Med 2002;77(5):368-76.

56. Pololi L, Clay MC, Lipkin M Jr, Hewson M, Kaplan C, Frankel RM. Reflections on integrating theories of adult education into a medical school faculty development course. Med Teacher 2001;23(3):276-83.

57. Gruppen L, Simpson D, Searle N, Robins L, Irby D. Medical education fellowships: common themes and overarching issues. Acad Med 2006;81(11):990-4.

58. Werb SB, Matear DW. Implementing evidence-based practice in undergraduate teaching clinics: a systematic review and recommendations. J Dent Educ 2004;68(9):995-1003.

59. Haden NK, Andrieu SC, Chadwick DG, Chmar JE, Cole JR, George MC, et al. The dental education environment. J Dent Educ 2006;70(12):1265-70.

60. Hendricson WD, Andrieu SC, Chadwick DG, Chmar JE, Cole JR, George MC, et al. Educational strategies associated with development of problem-solving, critical thinking, and self-directed learning. J Dent Educ 2006;70(9):925-36.

61. Bransford JD, Brown AL, Cocking RR, eds. How people learn: brain, mind, experience, and school. Washington, DC: National Academy Press, 1999.

62. Regehr G, Norman GR. Issues in cognitive psychology: implications for professional education. Acad Med 1996;71:988-1001.

63. Chenoweth L. Facilitating the process of critical thinking for nursing. Nurs Educ Today 1998;18:281-92.

64. Tsui L. A review of research on critical thinking. Paper presented at the Annual Meeting of the Association for the Study of Higher Education (ASHE), Miami, FL, 1998. ERIC Document Reproduction Service No. ED 391 429.

65. Kurfiss JG. Critical thinking: theory, research, practice, and possibilities. ASHE ERIC Higher Education Report Number 2. Washington, DC: Association for the Study of Higher Education, 1988.

66. Sackett D, Richardson W, Rosenberg W, Haynes R. Evidence-based medicine: how to practice and teach EBM. London: Churchill Livingstone, 2000.

67. Richards D, Lawrence A. Evidence-based dentistry. Br Dent J 1995;179(7):270-3.

68. Sutherland SE. Evidence-based dentistry: getting started. J Can Dent Assoc 2001;67(4):204-6.

69. Norman GR, Shannon SI. Effectiveness of instruction in critical appraisal (evidence-based medicine) skills: a critical appraisal. CMAJ 1998;158:177-81.

70. Taylor R, Reeves B, Ewings P, Binns S, Keast J, Mears R. A systematic review of the effectiveness of critical appraisal skills training for clinicians. Med Educ 2000;34:120-5.

71. Coormarasamy A, Khan KS. What is the evidence that postgraduate teaching in evidence-based medicine changes anything? A systematic review. Br Med J 2004;329(October 23):1017-22.

72. Grimshaw JM, Shirran L, Thomas R. Changing provider behavior: an overview of systematic reviews of interventions. Med Care 2001;39:112-45.

73. Institute of Medicine, Committee on Quality of Health Care in America. Crossing the quality chasm: a new health care system for the 21st century. Washington, DC: National Academy Press, 2001.

74. Davis DA, Evans M, Jadah A, Perrier L. The case for knowledge translation: shortening the journey from evidence to effect. Br Med J 2003;327:33-5.

75. Pravikoff DS, Tanner AB, Pierce ST. Readiness of U.S. nurses for evidence-based practice: many don't understand or value research and have little or no training to help them find evidence on which to base their practice. Am J Nurs 2005;105:40-52.

76. Szulanski G. The process of knowledge transfer: a diachronic analysis of success. Organizational Behav Human Decision Processes 2000;82(1):9-27.

77. Tyre MJ, Orlikowski WJ. Windows of opportunity: temporal patterns of technological adaptation in organization. Organization Sci 1994;5(1):98-118.

78. Zucker LG. The role of institutionalization in cultural persistence. Am Sociol Rev 1977;42:726-43.

79. Levine A. Why innovations fail. Albany: State University of New York Press, 1980.

80. Szulanski G. Exploring internal stickiness: impediments to the transfer of best practice within the firm. Strategic Management J 1996;17:27-43.

81. Dolmans DH, De Grave W, Wolfhagen IH, van der Vleuten CP. Problem-based learning: future challenges for educational practice and research. Med Educ 2005;39(7):732-41.

82. Manogue M, Brown G, Foster H. Clinical assessment of dental students: values and practices of teachers in restorative dentistry. Med Educ 2001;35:364-70.

83. Chambers DW, Geissberger M, Leknius C. Association amongst factors thought to be important by instructors in dental education and perceived effectiveness of these instructors by students. Eur J Dent Educ 2004;8:147-51.

84. McGrath C, Wai Kit Yeung R, Comfort M, McMillan A. Development and evaluation of a questionnaire to evaluate clinical dental teachers (ECDT). Br Dent J 2005;198:45-8.

85. Henzi D, Davis E, Jasinevicius R, Hendricson W, Cintron L, Isaacs M. Appraisal of the dental school learning environment: the students' view. J Dent Educ 2005;69(10):1137-47.

86. Henzi D, Davis E, Jasinevicius R, Hendricson W. North American dental students' perspectives about their clinical education. J Dent Educ 2006;70(4):361-77.

87. Irby DM. Teaching and learning in ambulatory care settings: thematic review of the literature. Acad Med 1995;70(10):898-931.

88. Heidenreich C, Lye P, Simpson D, Lourich M. The search for effective and efficient ambulatory teaching methods through the literature. Pediatrics 2000;105(1):231-7.

89. Haynes RB, Davis DA, McKibbon A, Tugwell P. A critical appraisal of the efficacy of continuing medical education. JAMA 1984;251:61-4.

90. Davis DA, Thomson MA, Oxman AD, Haynes RB. Evidence for the effectiveness of CME: a review of 50 randomized controlled trials. JAMA 1992;268:1111-7.

91. Davis DA, O'Brien T, Oxman AD, Haynes RB. Changing physician performance: a systematic review of the effect of continuing medical education strategies. JAMA 1995;274(9):700-5.

92. Oxman AD, Thomson MA, Davis DA, Haynes RB. No magic bullets: a systematic review of 102 trials of interventions to improve professional practice. CMAJ 1995; 153(10):1423-31.

93. Davis D, O'Brien T, Freemantle N, Wolf FM. Impact of continuing medical education: do conferences, workshops, rounds, and other traditional continuing education activities change physician behavior or health care outcomes? JAMA 1999;282(9):867-74.

94. O'Brien T, Oxman AD, Davis DA, Haynes RB, Freemantle N. Audit and feedback: effects on professional practice and health care outcomes. The Cochrane Database of Systematic Reviews, 2005, Volume 3.

95. O'Brien T, Freemantle N, Oxman AD, Davis DA. Continuing education meetings and workshops: effects on professional practice and health care outcomes. The Cochrane Database of Systematic Reviews, 2005, Volume 3.

96. Harden RM, Grant J, Buckley G, Hart IR. BEME Guide No. 1: best evidence in medical education. Med Teacher 1999;21(6):553-62.

97. Kirkpatrick DL. Evaluating training programs: the four levels. San Francisco: Berrett-Koehler Publishers, 1997.

98. Ebell MK, Siwek J, Weiss BD, Woolf SH, Susman J, Ewigman B, et al. Strength of recommendation taxonomy (SORT): a patient-centered approach to grading evidence in the medical literature. Am Fam Physician 2004;69: 549-57.

99. Cole KA, Barker LR, Kolodner K, Williamson P, Wright SM, Kern DE. Faculty development in teaching skills: an intensive longitudinal model. Acad Med 2004;79(5): 469-80.

100. Hewson MG, Copeland HL. What's the use of faculty development? Program evaluation using retrospective self-assessments and independent performance ratings. Teach Learn Med 2001;13:153-1

101. Rust G, Taylor V, Morrow R, Everett J. The Morehouse faculty development program: methods and three-year outcomes. Fam Med 1998;30(3):162-7.

102. Skeff KM, Stratos GA, Bergen MR. Regional teaching improvement programs for community-based teachers. Am J Med 1999;106:76-80.

103. Skeff KM, Stratos GA, Bergen MR. Improving clinical teaching: evaluation of a national dissemination program. Arch Intern Med 1992;152:1156-61.

104. Gruppen L, Simpson D, Searle N, Robins L, Irby D, Mullan P. Educational fellowship programs: common themes and overarching issues. Acad Med 2006;81(11):990-4.

105. Searle N, Hatem C, Perkowski L, Wilkerson L. Why invest in an educational fellowship program? Acad Med 2006;81(11):936-40.

106. Peddiwell AJ. The saber-tooth curriculum. New York: McGraw-Hill, 1939.

The Quality of Dental Faculty Work-Life: Report on the 2007 Dental School Faculty Work Environment Survey

N. Karl Haden, Ph.D.; William Hendricson, M.S., M.A.; Richard R. Ranney, D.D.S., M.S.; Adriana Vargas, D.D.S.; Lina Cardenas, D.D.S., M.S., Ph.D.; William Rose, D.D.S.; Ridley Ross, D.D.S.; Edward Funk, D.D.S.

Abstract: This report is the third in a series of articles on the dental school work environment commissioned by the American Dental Education Association's Commission on Change and Innovation in Dental Education. The report is based on the most extensive research to date on faculty satisfaction in the dental school environment. The purpose of the study was to assess faculty perceptions and recommendations related to work environment, sources of job satisfaction and dissatisfaction, and professional development needs. More broadly, the study intends to provide insight into the "change readiness" of dental schools to move forward with curricular improvements and innovations. Findings are based on 1,748 responses from forty-nine U.S. dental schools obtained during the time frame of February to April 2007. The total number of respondents constituted 17 percent of all U.S. dental school faculty. The average response rate per school was thirty-six (21 percent). To elucidate the data in terms of issues related to the quality of faculty work-life based on demographics, the authors compared perceptions of various aspects of the work culture in academic dentistry among faculty with different academic ranks and academic degrees and by other variables such as age and gender, tenure versus non-tenure appointments, and full- versus part-time status. Quantitative and qualitative analyses show that the majority of faculty members described themselves as very satisfied to satisfied with their dental school overall and with their department as a place to work. Tenured associate professors expressed the greatest level of dissatisfaction. Opportunities for and support of professional development emerged as an area requiring substantially more attention from dental schools. The authors of the study suggest that dental school leaders use these findings to assess their individual dental school's work environment and to plan changes as needed.

Dr. Haden is President, Academy for Academic Leadership, Atlanta, GA; Mr. Hendricson is Assistant Dean, Educational and Faculty Development, Dental School, University of Texas Health Science Center at San Antonio, and Director of Educational Programs, Academy for Academic Leadership; Dr. Ranney is a senior consultant, Academy for Academic Leadership, and Professor Emeritus, Dental School, University of Maryland; Dr. Vargas is Assistant Professor, Department of General Dentistry, Dental School, University of Texas Health Science Center at San Antonio; Dr. Cardenas is Assistant Professor, Department of Pediatric Dentistry, Dental School, University of Texas Health Science Center at San Antonio; Dr. Rose is Assistant Professor, Department of General Dentistry, Dental School, University of Texas Health Science Center at San Antonio; Dr. Ross is Assistant Professor, Department of General Dentistry, Dental School, University of Texas Health Science Center at San Antonio; and Dr. Funk is Clinical Associate Professor, Department of General Dentistry, Dental School, University of Texas Health Science Center at San Antonio. Direct correspondence and requests for reprints to Dr. N. Karl Haden, Academy for Academic Leadership, 1870 The Exchange, Suite 100, Atlanta, GA 30339; 404-350-2098; khaden@academicleaders.org.

This article is one in a series of invited contributions by members of the dental and dental education community that have been commissioned by the ADEA Commission on Change and Innovation in Dental Education (CCI) to address the environment surrounding dental education and affecting the need for, or process of, curricular change. This article was written at the request of the ADEA CCI but does not necessarily reflect the views of ADEA, the ADEA CCI, or individual members of the ADEA CCI. The perspectives communicated here are those of the authors.

Key words: dental faculty, academic environment, quality of faculty work-life, job satisfaction, faculty development

The academic lifestyle, characterized by the unique opportunities to teach, conduct research, engage colleagues with similar interests, and work in an environment devoted to discovery and learning, is the reason that many faculty pursue academic careers. Because academicians' salaries are generally lower than similarly educated professionals working outside of higher education, monetary compensation is rarely the primary motivation for the academician.[1,2] One study of 280 new dental faculty with five years or less experience in academic dentistry indicated that eight of the top ten factors important to the decision to accept a full-time faculty position related to work environment or workload. In a list of mean ratings for factors related to the decision to accept their current full-time position, departmental working environment ranked first, while salary appears as seventh on the list.[3] In a study of 240 dental school faculty with four years or less academic experience, Schenkein and Best found that the most positive factors affecting the decision to pursue an academic career are intellectual and scientific challenges and stimulation, academic lifestyle, and interest in teaching.[4]

The quality of faculty work-life as influenced by the educational environment is a basic concern to recruitment and retention of faculty. In turn, faculty satisfaction with the work environment influences the likelihood of implementing and sustaining educational innovations. Research on efforts to enhance curricula in health professions education and incorporate educational best practices demonstrates that faculty motivation and readiness to implement innovative models of education are the primary rate-limiting factors and often constitute the most profound barriers to adoption of new techniques.[5-12] Budgeted vacant positions in U.S. dental schools have averaged over 300 annually for the past decade, with 8–11 percent of faculty of record departing each year. Lower academically ranked faculty predominate among those departing, with approximately one-third leaving dental education to enter private practice. Given these data, it is reasonable to hypothesize that low job satisfaction and poor quality of faculty work-life are challenges for the nation's dental schools.[13-16] Anecdotal observations confirm an overworked and stressed faculty, but there are few data available to reach firm conclusions about the dental school work environment.

The purpose of this study was to assess faculty perceptions and recommendations related to work environment, sources of job satisfaction and dissatisfaction, and professional development needs. More broadly, the study gives insight into the "change readiness" of dental schools to move forward with curricular improvements and innovations. The survey, conducted by the Academy for Academic Leadership on behalf of the American Dental Education Association's (ADEA) Commission on Change and Innovation in Dental Education (CCI), constitutes the most extensive national study of the dental school faculty environment to date. It is the final in a series of initiatives on dental faculty work-life sponsored by the ADEA CCI. A symposium entitled "Change,

Innovation, and the Quality of Faculty Work-Life" at the 2007 ADEA Annual Session constituted the first step. Subsequent steps included an article by Trower addressing how to make academic dentistry more attractive to new faculty, particularly those from Generation X.[17] In addition, Trotman et al. presented findings from two interview-based qualitative assessments of faculty perceptions about work-life along with preliminary findings from the 2007 Dental School Faculty Work Environment Survey.[18] In this article, we present a quantitative and qualitative analysis of the outcomes of this survey with comparisons among categories of respondents.

Dental Education in Context: The Higher Education Environment

Pyle et al. outlined a number of challenges facing dental education as a "case for change."[19] While dental education faces unique challenges, the broader higher education milieu is relevant to understanding the dental school work environment. By many accounts, higher education is in the midst of unprecedented change. Public funding of higher education has fluctuated over the past decade and is projected to trend downward in the years to come.[20,21] At the same time, policymakers, perhaps best exemplified in the recent Spellings Commission, are demanding greater accountability for educational outcomes.[22] Competition for the best students continues to grow, with universities putting substantial resources into value-added student services that have little to do with the traditional academic missions of higher education.[23,24] The globalization of higher education means that universities compete both at home and abroad for students and revenues. The methods of discovery and learning are shifting structurally, politically, and in terms of human resources. As these winds of change blow through the academy, many faculty members find themselves in an environment that is only a semblance of the one they entered years before. These changes affect the way faculty conduct their work and the quality of their faculty work-life.

In perhaps the most extensive, data-driven examination of the American faculty in more than a decade, Schuster and Finkelstein found that faculty job satisfaction has significantly eroded to the point that only about one-third of faculty characterize themselves as "satisfied" or "very satisfied," a decline from about 50 percent a generation ago.[2] American faculty are not alone. A recent study conducted on occupational stress among Canadian university faculty involving fifty-six universities and 1,470 respondents concluded that the overall level of stress was high, with 13 percent of respondents exhibiting signs of distress as reported on the general health component of the survey. Among ten different measures used in the survey, work-life balance was the most consistent stress-related measure predicting low job satisfaction and negative health symptoms.[25] These findings, indicative of high occupational stress, are similar to national surveys recently conducted in the United Kingdom and Australia.[26,27] These studies, crossing three continents, point to a common set of environmental changes currently affecting faculty work in the United States—specifically, major reductions in funding; more reliance on part-time, non-tenure-track, contract faculty; increasing workload, particularly associated with research and publication; growth in salaries that falls below that in other professions; and faculty members' perception that they have lost influence within the academic organization.

U.S. dental school faculties have not been immune to the changes encompassing their parent institutions. The environmental changes affecting U.S. higher education in general have had a similar impact on dental education. One could argue that dental education has suffered, and in most cases accommodated, more tumultuous change than the academy as a whole. Haden et al. found that dental schools have compensated for faculty shortages by utilizing part-time faculty, redistributing teaching loads, dividing duties, and providing interdisciplinary coverage, including the use of generalists to teach in specialty areas.[13] Bailit et al. observed that the difference in income between generalists who are faculty and those who are in private practice approximated $86,000 in 2000. For specialist faculty and private specialist practitioners, the difference was $170,000.[28] While these data are average salary differences across academic ranks and do not take into account income from faculty practice and benefit packages (health insurance for faculty, spouse, and family, retirement plans, paid vacation, educational stipends) available from university systems, the gap is significant and growing. This income gap combined with heavy workloads and, for some, student debt may explain why 36 percent of faculty separations in 2004–05 were departures to enter private practice.[15]

Methodology: 2007 Dental School Faculty Work Environment Survey

The research protocol for this study was reviewed and approved by the Institutional Review Board of the University of Texas Health Science Center at San Antonio (UTHSCSA) in February 2007 as exempted research (IRB Protocol #HSC20070528E). The objectives of the study were to:

1. determine faculty members' perceptions of work-life and school environment that influence their decision making about academic careers in dental education;
2. identify academic work environment factors that are sources of satisfaction to dental school faculty and those that are sources of dissatisfaction; and
3. determine faculty members' perceptions about the availability and value of professional development resources and activities at their dental school, including mentoring, career growth planning, faculty development and continuing education programs, and administrative and peer support.

The Dental School Faculty Work Environment Survey was based on two sources: the Faculty Job Satisfaction Survey developed for the Study of New Scholars at the Harvard Graduate School of Education by Trower and Chait (this survey instrument has been used since 2003 in a variety of higher education institutions including professional schools); and an online survey used for assessing career enhancement needs that could be addressed in faculty development programs at UTHSCSA that was developed by Hendricson in his capacity as director of the Educational Research and Development Division at UTHSCSA.

Design and Subjects

The questionnaire for this study was designed in an online format that employed a forced choice "menu" format, but included opportunities for write-in responses. The overall questionnaire consisted of twenty-nine questions and a total of ninety-nine items that requested responses. Practice administrations during instrument development and pilot-testing indicated that completion time was approximately twenty minutes. The questionnaire included six sections:

1. background information: dental school, highest academic degree obtained, length of time as a faculty member (current position and all positions during career), current academic rank, tenure- vs. non-tenure-track, full-time vs. part-time, department or discipline, race/ethnicity, age, gender, total compensation, and main focus of academic appointment (teaching, research, service, administration, combination);
2. satisfaction with day-to-day activities as a faculty member;
3. professional development support and resources, including mentoring;
4. satisfaction with professional development opportunities and mentoring;
5. perceptions of dental school environment and culture; and
6. perceptions of the dental school as a place to work.

The questionnaire was pilot-tested with a sample of forty-two health professions education faculty, including dental school faculty members at the UTHSCSA, in January 2007. Following modifications based on pilot-test feedback, the full questionnaire was distributed electronically to faculty at fifty-six U.S. dental schools during the time frame of February to April 2007. The chair of the ADEA CCI, Dr. Kenneth Kalkwarf, sent emails to the deans of each U.S. dental school informing them of the aims and methodology of the study and the projected uses of the data by ADEA. Deans were informed that they could elect to decline participation if they so desired. The link (URL address) to the Dental School Faculty Work Environment Survey and the IRB-approved information sheet (equivalent to a subject consent form for exempted education research) accompanied the message to the deans.

All full- and part-time dental school faculty in clinical, basic science, and behavioral departments were eligible to complete the questionnaire.

Distribution

The ADEA CCI has implemented mechanisms to facilitate a national discussion of curricular issues and sharing of strategies that foster innovation in dental education. One mechanism was to establish a network of faculty who serve as ADEA CCI liaisons at U.S. dental schools. The goals of the ADEA CCI liaison network are to promote two-way communication between the schools and the commission, serve as a conduit for information exchange between the ADEA CCI and the faculty who implement the curriculum for students, and provide leadership for implementation of educational innovations. Recruitment of ADEA CCI liaisons as site coordinators for this study provided two benefits: 1) it facilitated response by having the questionnaire come from faculty peers at each campus as opposed to the ADEA central office; and 2) it provided an opportunity for the liaisons to communicate with their peers about faculty development issues and thus raise their visibility at their schools. ADEA CCI liaisons at each dental school distributed the questionnaire by email (with an embedded link to the host website) to the faculty at their respective dental schools initially in February 2007 and for a second time in April 2007. The liaisons received an explanatory message from the investigators that was used as the participation invitation message for their faculty peers. This message described the study's objectives and projected uses of the data by ADEA.

Response Rate and Subject Demographics

Through April 15, 2007, a total of 1,748 faculty from forty-nine U.S. dental schools responded to the survey. The total number of respondents constituted 17 percent of all U.S. dental school faculty. The average response rate per school was thirty-six (21 percent). In some cases, respondents did not answer all questions or skipped items within a question, so the actual number of responses ranged from 1,621 to 1,748 on individual items. Approximately two-thirds of the respondents were male, with white/Caucasian constituting the large majority of both males and females (Table 1).

Full-time faculty, defined as those whose appointments were 80 percent time or more, comprised the majority of respondents by academic status, while

Table 1. Respondents by gender, race, and ethnicity (by percentage of total respondents)

Male	67%
Female	33%
White/Caucasian	82%
Asian/Pacific Islander	7%
Hispanic	7%
African American	3%
American Indian/Native Alaskan	0.5%
Other	0.1%

Note: Percentages may not add to 100% because of rounding.

responses by academic ranks were roughly equivalent across the three ranks of full, associate (with tenure and without tenure), and assistant professor (Table 2).

Instructors and "Other" were eliminated from analysis with academic rank as the independent variable because of too few responses for valid statistical analysis. Of 1,708 respondents, 46 percent were tenured, 49 percent were non-tenured, and 6 percent identified their status as "other."

Table 3 shows respondents by age. Although the age of respondents may appear to be decidedly skewed, the age distribution is indeed representative of dental school faculty.[15]

Data Analysis

Raw data from all responses are presented below. In addition, to elucidate the data in terms of issues related to the quality of faculty work-life based on demographics, the authors identified six variables for cross-tabulation in the data set. The authors examined these six independent variables across most of the survey items listed in the tables that follow:

- full-time versus part-time faculty;
- academic degree, considering dental only, dental plus doctorate, dental plus master's, doctorate only (e.g., Ph.D.), and master's as the highest degree;
- academic rank, considering assistant professor, associate professor with tenure, associate professor without tenure, and professor;
- tenure- versus non-tenure-track for full-time faculty;
- ethnicity; and
- gender.

Data were downloaded into a statistical software table (JMP, SAS Institute, SAS Campus Drive, Cary, NC 27513) and edited as necessary to conform to the above list of independent variables, e.g., "clinical assistant professor" was edited to "assistant professor." Distributions were produced, and contingency tables were constructed for chi-square determination to test significance of perceived differences using the JMP software. In analyses using ethnicity as the independent variable, "American Indian/Native Alaskan" and "Other" were eliminated because of too few responses for valid chi-squares, as was the case for "Instructor" and "Other" when academic rank was the independent variable. In addition, where responses were "Not applicable" or missing, those respondents were not included in the statistical analysis for that specific variable. To ensure cautious interpretation because of the multiple comparisons made, significance was set at $p<.01$.

In addition to the quantitative data, survey responses included 404 written comments to the final question on the survey: "Please comment on any aspect of faculty life in dental schools that has not been explored in this survey." Overall, approximately 23 percent of the respondents submitted answers to this question. The methodology employed for analyzing the written comments was based on recommendations for analysis of qualitative data by Denzin and Lincoln.[29]

The initial qualitative analysis of written comments identified sixteen sets of interrelated issues, hereafter described as themes. Five faculty members at the University of Texas Health Science Center at San Antonio (UTHSCSA) Dental School were each provided a portion of the narratives and were asked to independently review the responses, identify the prevailing themes from their perspectives, and rank the themes in order of frequency. These individuals were members of the Faculty Development Committee at the UTHSCSA Dental School and/or served as members of the ADEA CCI liaison team for this school. The four independent reviews were compared to each other to produce the summary that appears in the Appendix. Descriptive titles for the themes were created, and the themes were sequenced to reflect the frequency of expression by the questionnaire respondents.

Table 2. Respondents by academic status and rank (by percentage of total respondents)

Full-Time (more than 80% time)	78%
Part-Time	22%
Professor	29%
Associate Professor, with tenure	17%
Associate Professor, without tenure	19%
Assistant Professor	35%

Table 3. Respondents by age (by percentage of total respondents)

60 years or older	28%
50–59	37%
40–49	20%
Younger than 40	15%

Results

The results displayed in Tables 4–10 show the overall responses to various items in the survey. We have also highlighted areas in which statistically significant differences emerged from cross-tabulation of variables. Where there are no statistically significant differences associated with the variable, no comments are made. Data are presented based on responses to the following: satisfaction with day-to-day activities as a dental school faculty member; professional development opportunities and support; the culture of your dental school; the dental school as a place to work; and general assessment of faculty work-life, including work and life balance.

Satisfaction with Day-to-Day Activities

Table 4 shows responses on various items related to satisfaction with day-to-day activities as a dental school faculty member.

It is notable that more than 70 percent of all respondents indicated they were highly satisfied to satisfied with the overall way they spend their time as a faculty member, the nature of teaching assignments, and the intellectual challenge associated with their teaching responsibilities. By contrast, approximately one-third noted being dissatisfied to highly dissatisfied with the support and recognition for quality teaching at their schools, the amount of time provided for research, and the amount of time to write papers or prepare presentations for professional meetings.

Differences Associated with Academic Rank. Comparing day-to-day activities to demographic variables showed a significant difference ($p < .0001$) among the four professorial ranks in "the overall way I spend my time as a faculty member." More professors were highly satisfied (35 percent) than other ranks (19–26 percent), and associate professors with tenure were the most dissatisfied (11 percent compared to 4–6 percent for the other ranks). A trend emerged across a number of items: "my overall teaching workload"; "the intellectual challenge associated with my teaching responsibilities"; "the support and recognition for quality teaching"; and "the extent and nature of interaction with my faculty colleagues." Professors indicated a significantly higher level of satisfaction in all of these areas, followed by associate professors without tenure and assistant professors. For all of these items, associate professors with tenure showed significantly higher levels of dissatisfaction.

Table 4. Satisfaction with day-to-day activities as a dental school faculty member (by percentage of total respondents)

Item	Highly Satisfied to Satisfied	Adequate	Dissatisfied to Highly Dissatisfied	N/A
The overall way I spend my time as a faculty member.	71%	21%	8%	0%
The nature of my teaching assignments.	75%	18%	5%	2%
My overall teaching workload, including classrooms, labs, and clinic.	62%	21%	14%	3%
The number of students I supervise in labs and clinics.	56%	20%	12%	12%
Opportunities to work closely with students and really get to know their capabilities and needs.	62%	23%	13%	3%
The overall quality of students I teach.	68%	24%	7%	2%
The intellectual challenge associated with my teaching responsibilities.	73%	19%	7%	2%
The quality of teaching provided by my faculty colleagues.	66%	23%	9%	2%
The support and recognition for quality teaching at this school.	40%	27%	32%	1%
The extent and quality of the intramural private practice program (e.g., faculty practice).	18%	12%	25%	44%
The amount of research I am expected to do.	34%	23%	14%	29%
The type of research I am expected to do.	36%	22%	12%	30%
The amount of time I have for research.	23%	19%	31%	27%
The amount of time I have to write papers or prepare presentations for professional meetings.	24%	25%	35%	16%
The amount of time I have for service to the school, such as committee work or directing projects.	32%	34%	23%	10%
The extent and nature of interaction with my faculty colleagues.	60%	27%	13%	1%

Note: Percentages may not add to 100% because of rounding.

Differences Associated with Tenure/Non-Tenure Status. A significant difference was also evident for the item "overall way I spend my time as a faculty member" when comparing tenure- versus non-tenure-track full-time faculty (p<.01). More non-tenure-track faculty were satisfied (50 percent versus 42 percent), and fewer were dissatisfied (4 percent versus 8 percent). Likewise, among full-time faculty, non-tenure-track faculty had a greater percentage of highly satisfied responses than tenure-track faculty related to "opportunities to work closely with students and really get to know their capabilities and needs" (32 percent compared to 23 percent). Non-tenure-track faculty were more dissatisfied and highly dissatisfied (52 percent) than tenure-track faculty (37 percent) related to "the amount of time I have for research."

Differences Associated with Academic Degrees. Another area of significant difference (p<.0001) emerged from the analysis based on academic degrees. More faculty with a dental degree plus a master's (37 percent) were highly satisfied than the other groups (17 percent to 30 percent) in response to "opportunities to work closely with students and really get to know their capabilities and needs." Faculty with doctorates (e.g., Ph.D.) and dental degrees plus doctorates had the lowest percentage of highly satisfied responses (17 percent and 18 percent, respectively). More faculty with doctorates were dissatisfied with "the nature of my teaching assignments" (7 percent) than those with dental degrees only (3 percent). These findings may relate to varying expectations of the different groups by academic credential. For example, Ph.D.'s and D.D.S./Ph.D.'s may see themselves as more purely academic with different expectations than others. More dental degree plus master's degree faculty (36 percent) were highly satisfied than the other groups (19–25 percent) with "the overall quality of students I teach."

In response to "the amount of time I have for research," analysis revealed a significant difference (p<.0001) in that 26 percent of respondents holding dental degrees were highly dissatisfied, compared to other groups ranging from 9 to 21 percent. Those with dental degrees and doctorates (17 percent) and doctorates (15 percent) had more highly satisfied responses than the other groups (4–7 percent). Doctorates gave the most satisfied responses: 39 percent compared to 18–27 percent for the other groups. These findings probably reflect the demands for teaching and clinic supervision placed primarily on clinical faculty.

There were no significant differences in responses to items related to day-to-day activities based on race/ethnicity or gender.

Written Responses. The most prevalent theme in the written comments, mentioned by 28 percent of those who commented, concerned workload. Respondents described workloads as excessive and extremely varied. Written comments underscored the lack of time for professional development and other activities, with the requirement for extensive weekend and evening work to accomplish routine job functions. A number of comments indicated dissatisfaction with hiring practices that fail to recruit faculty with the necessary qualifications for job performance. In general, respondents described a high level of stress and consequent turnover due to the perception of being overworked and understaffed. The Appendix includes specific issues associated with workload.

Professional Development Opportunities

The questionnaire asked about the availability of various professional development activities, services, and resources across seventeen different items. Table 5 shows the responses to this query.

Analysis of the data indicates that a number of basic professional development activities, especially those associated with new faculty, including mentoring, new faculty orientation, and career growth planning, are not available or not done, or respondents did not know about the existence of these activities. For the item "there is a formal mentoring program for junior faculty who are not tenured," only 25 percent of respondents indicated that such support existed at their school. For the item "there is a formal mentoring program for faculty who are new to the dental school regardless of academic rank," only 20 percent of respondents indicated that such mentoring was available. In regard to "an orientation program for first-year faculty," 60 percent indicated that these orientations are not available/not conducted or responded that they were not aware of new faculty orientations at their school, while 45 percent indicated not available, not done, or do not know for the item "faculty members in my department develop career growth plans and meet with our department chair/division director/supervisor to set goals and plan professional enrichment activities." There were similar absences of professional development activity in several areas related to promotion and tenure,

Table 5. Availability of professional development activities, services, or resources at the respondent's dental school (by percentage of total respondents)

Item	Yes: Available	Not Available or Not Done	Do Not Know	N/A
There is a formal mentoring program for junior faculty who are not tenured.	25%	49%	23%	4%
There is a formal mentoring program for faculty who are new to the dental school regardless of academic rank.	20%	51%	26%	2%
There is an orientation program for first-year faculty to help them learn about the school and meet other faculty.	39%	40%	20%	1%
I meet with my department chair/division director/supervisor annually for a review of my performance in the preceding year.	77%	17%	3%	4%
I receive a written evaluation of my performance each year from my department chair/division director/supervisor.	63%	30%	5%	3%
Faculty members in my department develop career growth plans and meet with our department chair/division director/supervisor to set goals and plan professional enrichment activities.	52%	33%	12%	3%
The Promotion & Tenure Committee conducts progress reviews of tenure-track faculty during years 3–4 of the probationary period and provides feedback.	34%	20%	31%	15%
Professional assistance such as workshops or teaching observation with feedback is available to enhance teaching.	61%	25%	12%	2%
Professional assistance such as workshops, consultation, or mentoring by experienced investigators is available to enhance research skills.	50%	27%	18%	5%
Professional assistance is available to enhance writing grant proposals and manuscripts and preparing CVs.	46%	28%	21%	5%
Workshops on the promotion and tenure process are routinely conducted.	27%	44%	23%	7%
The dental school conducts an annual schoolwide faculty development day.	48%	36%	13%	2%
The dental school routinely brings in speakers and consultants to conduct faculty development on oral health topics and clinical skills.	63%	26%	9%	2%
The dental school has a regularly scheduled in-service program designed to keep the faculty abreast of new scientific developments.	49%	38%	12%	2%
Travel funds are available to support faculty participation in professional meetings.	58%	27%	13%	3%
Funding support is available for sabbaticals and fellowships.	26%	30%	37%	7%
A dedicated percentage of my weekly time is reserved for my professional development.	32%	56%	6%	7%

Note: Percentages may not add to 100% because of rounding.

or the respondents reported that they did not know if these activities occurred. In reviewing these data for the initial article that presented selected and preliminary findings from this questionnaire, Trotman et al. concluded that minimal progress has been made to clarify the faculty evaluation process or assist faculty in understanding expectations associated with promotion and tenure.[18]

Respondents were asked if, at some point in their career, a more senior faculty member effectively served as a mentor and helped in the respondent's professional development. Fifty-nine percent responded affirmatively, while 35 percent indicated that they had not received mentoring or professional guidance from a senior faculty member. Six percent did not consider the item applicable.

Whereas the items in Table 5 addressed the availability of specific professional development activities, the questionnaire also asked about the respondent's level of satisfaction with professional development support and resources at his or her dental school. Table 6 summarizes the responses across eight areas.

It is notable that one in four respondents were dissatisfied with the "mentoring I have received from senior faculty," and overall, only 42 percent of respondents indicated that they were satisfied with this aspect of professional development. Approximately 25 percent of respondents were dissatisfied with "resources available to support research," and overall, only 36 percent of respondents indicated that they were satisfied with this aspect of professional development. Twenty-two percent also expressed dissatisfaction to high dissatisfaction with the "physical environment." In general, across all the items, the level of satisfaction with professional development

Table 6. Satisfaction with the professional development support and resources at the respondent's dental school (by percentage of total respondents)

Item	Highly Satisfied to Satisfied	Adequate	Dissatisfied to Highly Dissatisfied	N/A
The commitment of my department chair/division director/supervisor to help me succeed as a faculty member.	57%	22%	18%	3%
The mentoring I have received from senior faculty in my department to assist in my professional growth.	42%	22%	25%	12%
The physical environment in which I work, including my office, computer, labs, clinics, classrooms, departmental facilities, shared common space in the dental school.	52%	26%	22%	1%
The institutional resources available to support my work (clerical support, library, information technology).	54%	27%	17%	2%
Dissemination of information about upcoming professional development programs and opportunities.	56%	28%	13%	3%
Opportunities to collaborate with other faculty on teaching, research, or service.	52%	27%	18%	3%
Resources available to support research (labs, equipment, statistical support, research coordinators, technicians, clinical research facilities).	36%	24%	25%	14%
Quality of the professional development programs I have attended at this dental school.	46%	28%	16%	10%

Note: Percentages may not add to 100% because of rounding.

support and resources was lower than for other areas examined in the survey. Across all items in Table 6, roughly one-quarter of individuals responded that their dental schools provided only adequate support in the various areas of professional development support and resources.

Differences Associated with Academic Rank. Significant differences (p<.0001) existed among the academic ranks in response to "the commitment of my department chair/division director/supervisor to help me succeed as a faculty member." Professors gave the highest percentage of highly satisfied responses (38 percent compared to 26–32 percent for other ranks), while associate professors with tenure gave the highest percentage of highly dissatisfied and dissatisfied responses (30 percent compared to 13–17 percent for other ranks). Analysis revealed similar responses about "mentoring I have received from senior faculty," "opportunities to collaborate with other faculty," and "resources available to support research." In all cases, associate professors with tenure expressed significantly higher levels of dissatisfaction than did faculty at other ranks. Professors indicated the highest levels of satisfaction for all items.

Written Comments. Comments about professional development comprised a prominent theme, mentioned by 12 percent of respondents. In general, comments indicated dissatisfaction with the amount of effort dental schools give to developing faculty skills and career guidance. Respondents mentioned

a lack of funding to support travel to meetings. Comments underscored a concern about inadequate faculty development support and career guidance for junior and minority faculty. While some respondents described mentoring experiences as uneven, a number of comments indicated that respondents experienced positive mentoring, primarily by proactive department chairs. Specific quotes about professional development are found in the Appendix.

The Culture of Dental Schools

The survey inquired about a number of items related to the overall culture—values, attitudes, behaviors, and related norms—at the respondent's dental school. Table 7 shows the responses to these items.

The large majority of respondents (87 percent) either agreed or strongly agreed that "I enjoy my interactions with faculty colleagues." Seventy-six percent feel that they "have a comfortable niche in my department." Over two-thirds of the respondents agreed or strongly agreed that their department chair/division director/supervisor "treats me fairly" in comparison to other faculty. There was strong indication that faculty and students have constructive (rather than "us against them") relationships.

One out of four respondents specified disagreement to strong disagreement that "the overall physical appearance of my dental school makes a good impression." Thirty percent did not find that "the overall culture of the dental school is characterized by openness to new ideas." In perhaps a related assessment of the "openness" of the school culture, one-third expressed dissatisfaction with reasonableness of "the decision-making process in the school about issues that face the whole faculty."

Differences Associated with Academic Rank. The trend associated with academic rank noted previously continued with responses about the culture of the dental school in that professors showed higher levels of satisfaction than other ranks. Forty-two percent of professors agreed that "faculty colleagues are eager to help" compared to other ranks, which ranged from 30–33 percent in agreement with the statement. Sixteen percent of associate professors with tenure disagreed with the item compared to 7–10 percent from other ranks. Associate professors with tenure were also most likely to disagree that "my department chair/division director/supervisor treats me fairly" when compared to other faculty, with 20 percent either disagreeing or strongly disagreeing. By comparison, other groups ranged from 6 percent to 11 percent disagreement, with 48 percent of professors agreeing with the statement about fairness of treatment. Associate professors with tenure were also more likely to strongly disagree (17 percent compared to 9–13 percent) with the overall culture being "characterized by openness to new ideas," the reasonableness of "the decision-making process in the school about issues that face the whole faculty" (22 percent compared to 9–15 percent), and satisfaction with "the diversity of the dental school faculty" (19 percent compared to 11–14 percent).

Differences Associated with Tenure/Non-Tenure Status. There was a significant difference (p<.002) between tenure and non-tenure faculty about the expectation for conformity within the department, with non-tenured faculty giving more strongly agree responses (23 percent versus 15 percent). Sixty-six percent of full-time non-tenured faculty expressed their satisfaction with the level of faculty diversity in the school by agreeing or strongly agreeing, compared to just over half of tenured faculty.

Differences Associated with Academic Degrees. Faculty who have dental plus master's degrees showed a greater likelihood of agreeing that their "faculty colleagues are eager to help me with projects," with about one-third strongly agreeing compared to 19–20 percent of other respondents.

Differences Associated with Race/Ethnicity and Gender. White/Caucasian faculty were more likely to strongly agree (30 percent) that their "contributions to the department are recognized by my colleagues" than were non-whites (20 percent). White/Caucasian faculty were also more likely to agree (41 percent compared to 38 percent of non-whites) and non-whites were more likely to strongly disagree (9 percent compared to 4 percent) about

Table 7. Perceptions of the culture of the respondent's dental school (by percentage of total respondents)

Item	Strongly Agreed to Agreed	Neutral	Disagreed to Strongly Disagreed	N/A
Overall, I enjoy my interactions with faculty colleagues.	87%	10%	3%	0.1%
I have a comfortable niche in my department in terms of a sense of belonging and being a part of the team.	76%	12%	11%	0.7%
My faculty colleagues are eager to help me with projects.	57%	27%	13%	4%
There is an expectation in my department that faculty should conform to certain views about attire/dress, personal grooming, communication style, and public behavior.	59%	27%	13%	2%
Faculty relations with students can be characterized as "us against them."	11%	19%	70%	0.8%
On the whole, my department chair/division director/supervisor treats me fairly when I compare myself to other faculty.	73%	14%	11%	3%
My contributions to the department are recognized by my colleagues.	66%	20%	13%	1%
The overall physical appearance of my dental school makes a good impression.	55%	19%	25%	1%
The overall culture in the dental school is characterized by openness to new ideas.	42%	27%	30%	1%
For the most part, the decision-making process in the school about issues that face the whole faculty is reasonable.	40%	26%	33%	2%
I am satisfied with the diversity of the dental school faculty, including age, gender, and race/ethnicity.	59%	23%	17%	1%

Note: Percentages may not add to 100% because of rounding.

satisfaction associated with diversity. Where diversity is concerned, there was also a significant difference (p<.0001) between genders, with males more likely to agree (43 percent compared to 34 percent) and females more likely to disagree (18 percent compared to 10 percent) with the statement "I am satisfied with the diversity of the dental school faculty, including age, gender, and race/ethnicity."

Written Responses. A substantial percentage (21 percent) of respondents who submitted written responses expressed concern about their dental school within the larger context and culture of the academic health center. Some indicated a sense that the dental school environment is less academic than other schools in their health science center. Comments reflected concerns about how other schools within the health science center view the dental school. In particular, issues associated with lack of research collaboration, little interaction among dental faculty and others within the health science center, lack of effort to develop community-based programs, and lack of support from central health science center and parent university administrators led some respondents to describe their dental schools as isolated. Others commented on aging and declining physical plants compared to other schools in the health science center. The Appendix includes specific issues associated with the theme of the dental school within the academic health center.

The Dental School as a Place to Work

This section of the survey addressed satisfaction related to the department as a place to work, central administration, and salary and benefits (Table 8). A large majority, 73 percent of respondents, indicated that they were very satisfied to satisfied with their place of work, "all things considered." A similar number, 73 percent, expressed satisfaction with their benefits. In contrast, 30 percent were dissatisfied to very dissatisfied with the central administration of the dental school's concern about "the work environment for the 'in the trenches' faculty," while another 20 percent were neutral. Thirty-nine percent of respondents were dissatisfied to highly dissatisfied with their total compensation package. A similar number, 38 percent, were very satisfied to satisfied.

Differences Associated with Academic Rank. When assessing the department/division/administrative unit "as a place to work," associate professors with tenure chose very dissatisfied to dissatisfied more often than did the other ranks (22 percent compared to 9–12 percent for other ranks). As expected based on the analysis described above, professors were the most likely to be very satisfied (40 percent versus 25–33 percent). Associate professors with tenure also chose "strongly disagree" more often (20 percent) than others (10–12 percent) when asked if the central administration of the dental school cares about the faculty work environment. Professors identified themselves as very satisfied to satisfied more often than other ranks (53 percent compared to 29–38 percent) relative to their level of satisfaction with their total compensation package.

Differences Associated with Academic Degrees. Faculty with doctorates (43 percent) and dental degrees plus doctorates (38 percent) agreed more often than other groups (28–32 percent) that the central administration of the dental school cares about the faculty work environment. Faculty with dental degrees only (20 percent) and master's only (20 percent) chose "disagree" more often than did

Table 8. Perceptions of the dental school as a place to work (by percentage of total respondents)

Item	Very Satisfied to Satisfied	Neutral	Dissatisfied to Very Dissatisfied	N/A
All things considered, how satisfied are you with your department/division/administrative unit as a place to work?	73%	14%	13%	0.4%
Does the central administration of the dental school (dean, associate deans, assistant deans) care about the work environment for the "in the trenches" faculty?	49%	20%	30%	1%
What is the level of your satisfaction with your total compensation package (salary and other income sources)?	38%	23%	39%	0.0%
What is the level of your satisfaction with your benefits, including the number of vacation days, sick leave policies, quality of health insurance, and retirement plan options?	73%	15%	12%	0.0%

Note: Percentages may not add to 100% because of rounding.

the others (12–13 percent). Doctorates only were most satisfied with their "total compensation package"—40 percent choosing agree compared to those with dental degrees only, 27 percent of whom chose agree. Perhaps not surprisingly, given the discrepancy between private practice and academic salaries, faculty with dental degrees only strongly disagreed most often (17 percent versus 6–10 percent).

Differences Associated with Full-Time/Part-Time Status. Full-time faculty were more likely to agree that the central administration of the dental school cares about the work environment for faculty (35 percent compared to 23 percent), and part-time faculty were more likely to be neutral (28 percent compared to 18 percent). Full-time faculty more often selected "very satisfied/satisfied" to indicate their level of satisfaction of total compensation (33 percent) than did part-time faculty (19 percent). Part-time faculty also chose "strongly disagree" with satisfaction about their compensation package more often than did full-time faculty (18 percent compared to 12 percent).

Written Comments. Most of the themes in the written comments relate in one way or another to the dental school as a place to work. Twenty-seven percent of those providing written comments expressed perceptions of a disconnect between administration and faculty, providing elucidation to responses about the central administration of the dental school shown in Table 8. Some described the relationship as adverse, while others stated that their administration does not respect faculty, involve faculty appropriately in change efforts, or accept feedback from faculty. Areas of dissatisfaction in administration-faculty relationships included those associated with curriculum change and teaching. While some respondents were specifically critical of their deans, others reported optimism related to the style, work ethic, and responsiveness of new deans. The Appendix includes specific issues associated with faculty-administration relationships.

Fifteen percent of those submitting written responses expressed concern about their level of compensation. Some noted that low salaries are a barrier to recruitment and retention of new faculty and negatively influence students' consideration of academic careers. While many comments reflect the theme of being overworked and underpaid, written comments mentioned workload issues approximately twice as often as compensation. The Appendix includes specific issues associated with compensation.

Thirteen percent of respondents made comments about promotion standards and compensation for teachers and researchers. In general, this theme included traditional concerns expressed by primarily teaching faculty about researchers receiving preferential treatment in hiring, salary, awards, and advancement. Some suggested that usual recruitment and hiring practices are bypassed to recruit researchers. Others noted that faculty with primarily teaching appointments have to teach more and engage more often in university service to compensate for researchers who do not participate actively in teaching or service. Comments indicated the perception that the reward system is not linked to performance, particularly when teaching is compared to research. Some respondents expressed dissatisfaction with the hiring of new faculty at higher salary levels than long-standing faculty. The Appendix provides further delineation of issues associated with this theme.

Analysis of written comments resulted in a number of less-mentioned themes. These themes, mentioned in less than 10 percent of all narrative comments, along with investigator commentary, are found in the Appendix.

General Assessment of Faculty Work-Life

As one means of providing an overall summary of questionnaire feedback, respondents were asked to provide a general assessment of their work-life. Table 9 shows that, considering all factors in the questionnaire, 62 percent of respondents rated their dental school as an excellent or good place to work.

Continuing a trend found in other responses in the questionnaire, a significant difference existed (p<.0001) relative to academic rank. Professors chose "excellent" more often than did other ranks (35 percent compared to 22–24 percent), with tenured associate professors selecting "fairly bad" more often

Table 9. General assessment of faculty work-life (by percentage of total respondents)

Considering all factors addressed in this questionnaire, how do you rate your dental school as a place to work?

Excellent	27%
Good	35%
Okay, but could be better	30%
Fairly bad	6%
Awful	2%

than did the other ranks (12 percent compared to 4–6 percent). Whites/Caucasians chose "excellent" more often than did other groups (28 percent compared to 20 percent), but also selected "fairly bad" more often than non-whites (7 percent compared to 3 percent). There were no significant differences in response based on gender, academic degree, or tenure/non-tenure status.

Table 10 shows that 71 percent of respondents were very satisfied to satisfied with their overall balance of work and other aspects of life. Full-time faculty chose "dissatisfied" more often (15 percent) than did part-time faculty (5 percent), and part-time faculty chose "very satisfied" more often than did full-time faculty (40 percent versus 23 percent). Associate professors with tenure chose "dissatisfied" more often than did other ranks (19 percent compared to 9–15 percent), while professors chose "satisfied" more often (49 percent compared to 37–43 percent). A significant difference (p<.0001) in response is associated with gender. Females chose "dissatisfied" more often (17 percent) than did males (13 percent). Males chose "satisfied" (47 percent versus 38 percent) and "very satisfied" (29 percent versus 24 percent) more often than did females.

Discussion

With a study this broad, it is difficult to mine all the nuances associated with statistically significant differences associated with the cross-tabulation of variables. There are, however, a number of clear messages conveyed by the data.

The assessments of dental school culture (Table 7) and the dental school as a place to work (Table 8) and the overall assessment of the work environment and work-life balance (Tables 9 and 10) convey a positive but mixed message about the dental school work environment. The message is positive because more

Table 10. Assessment of overall work and life balance (by percentage of total respondents)

How satisfied are you with the overall balance in your life, including dental school work, family, friends, spiritual, community, and recreation/hobbies?

Very satisfied	27%
Satisfied	44%
Neutral	14%
Dissatisfied	13%
Very dissatisfied	3%

Note: Percentages may not add to 100% because of rounding.

than half of the respondents gave an "excellent" or "good" overall assessment to faculty work-life (Table 9). Only 8 percent considered their faculty work-life as "fairly bad" or "awful." Seventy-three percent indicated that they were very satisfied, all things considered, with their department/division/administrative unit as a place to work. Surprisingly, given a clear message from these data and previous reports that faculty workloads are substantial and increasing, 71 percent answered that they were "very satisfied" to "satisfied" with their overall work and life balance.

The message is mixed because there are no clear benchmarks with which to compare these responses. In a survey of seventy-seven colleges and 6,773 tenure-track faculty, the Collaborative on Academic Careers in Higher Education concluded that, overall, faculty reported being "somewhat satisfied" with their department and "somewhat satisfied" with their institution as a place to work. Quantified on a scale of 1 to 5, with 5 indicating very high satisfaction and 1 signifying very low satisfaction, university respondents averaged scoring satisfaction with their department as 3.88 and with their institution as 3.65. This study also found that early career faculty rated their satisfaction with the balance between personal and professional time very low (2.8 on the 5-point scale).[30] A 2007 study of occupational stress among Canadian university faculty draws the conclusion, among many others, that 65 percent of the 1,470 faculty surveyed were satisfied in their jobs.[25] A similar study in Australia found that 58 percent were satisfied in their jobs.[27]

While notable areas of dissatisfaction and concern exist—for example, associated with professional development activities and support (Tables 5 and 6) and a perceived dichotomy between faculty and administration (Table 7)—the responses indicate that the majority of dental faculty enjoy working in their dental schools and find their jobs fulfilling. In individual interviews with dental faculty, Trotman et al. found that many junior faculty said they had little control over their work schedule and overall academic life, in contrast to the expectations that brought them to academic careers rather than private practice. Still, the junior faculty liked the variety of tasks within the academic environment and saw this diversity as a positive factor.[18]

The authors believe that faculty satisfaction in the dental school environment compares favorably with that of higher education in general. While compensation is significantly lower for dental faculty than for dentists in private practice, total compensation is generally higher than for other faculty at the university.[31,32] That the majority of dental faculty are satisfied overall with the academic culture and find many aspects of their work-life to be stimulating and fulfilling is an important message to convey to students and others who might have an interest in an academic career.

One clear trend throughout the data is that the greatest dissatisfaction with the dental school work environment is among tenured associate professors. This finding, while a concern, is not unusual. Trotman et al. described research showing a divide between the perceptions of early and mid-career faculty compared to their senior colleagues about the academic environment.[18] In a 1999 national survey of faculty, the U.S. Department of Education found that 12 percent of associate professors said they planned to leave the profession for jobs outside of academia within three years. The longer they remained at this rank, the greater the dissatisfaction. Associate professors who hold their rank for ten years or more experience greater stress and are more dissatisfied than other faculty.[33]

The findings of our study indicate that approximately 15–20 percent of associate professors with tenure who responded to the survey appear to be unfulfilled and unhappy as dental school faculty. Some of these faculty members probably entered academia when expectations for promotion and tenure were different. In many higher education institutions, including dental schools' parent universities, promotion to full professor is highly improbable without significant research and scholarship. Even while there is renewed interest in the scholarship of teaching, fostered by such national organizations as the Carnegie Foundation for the Advancement of Teaching and initiatives such as ADEA's Scholarship of Teaching and Learning community and the ADEA/Academy for Academic Leadership Institute for Teaching and Learning, the findings from this study indicate that a sense of inequity between teaching and research persists. Without the probability of promotion and corresponding pay increases, tenured associate professors may have the sense of being "stuck" in their careers. These faculty members, who are likely to have already devoted fifteen to twenty years to their academic careers, may perceive that opportunities at the dental school are limited, but that, with tenure, departure from academia to private practice is not an attractive alternative.

One message from the survey findings is that dental schools should create more or better op-

portunities for mid-career development. To make their jobs interesting and to ensure their continued contributions to the dental school, mid-career faculty also need career planning. Mid-career faculty members, unlike their junior academic colleagues, are positioned to make a transition from securing a place in the institution to assuming broader roles at the dental school and the parent institution and in the profession. Chairs can assist these faculty members through regular performance review, goal setting, and opportunities to develop new areas of competency (e.g., administration, research, new areas of teaching, and mentoring). As in any discipline, some mid-career faculty may be content to continue on a predictable, even if personally and professionally unsatisfying, path. But mid-career faculty development should become a part of every dental school's professional development activities.

Inasmuch as professional development plans need to be comprehensive and address faculty at all ranks, among the feedback that causes most concern in the survey are responses about professional development opportunities (Tables 5 and 6). The matter becomes more troublesome when faculty separations are considered. In 2004–05, ADEA reported that 36 percent of faculty departures were to enter private practice (a year earlier, nearly half of departures were to private practice). Of this number, 53 percent were at the rank of assistant professor. Based on the survey findings, assistant professors do not show particularly high levels of dissatisfaction about the work environment. Yet the exodus from dental schools each year is largely defined by departing assistant professors. There are likely a number of reasons for this phenomenon, but the survey data make clear that some dental schools are doing little for faculty to enhance early career development.

Seventy-six percent of survey respondents stated that "a formal mentoring program for faculty who are new to the dental school regardless of academic rank" was not available or they were not aware of such a program, which from our experience likely indicates that a program does not exist. Sixty percent stated that orientation programs for new faculty were either not available or they did not know of such programs. Nearly 50 percent of respondents reported that faculty did not develop career growth plans in collaboration with their chairs/division directors/supervisors or they did not know if this was done. The promotion and tenure process was unclear to many, with apparently little information provided on a formal basis. As a part of the ADEA CCI white paper initiative, Hendricson et al. delineated characteristics of effective faculty development and argued for its efficacy in improving teaching and facilitating curriculum change.[34] Based on survey responses, we conclude that many dental schools are not engaged in the basics of professional development that would assist in retention of new faculty.

There is another important message, one that is more tacit. There are a number of proxies in the data that reflect the change-readiness of dental education. Workload and time pressures are clear in both the quantitative and qualitative feedback from respondents. Dental schools are caught up by the same currents that push higher education to new places, yet the ways that higher education and dental education are provided have changed little. As Guskin and Marcy summarize the impact of these changes on faculty in a delivery system that remains relatively static: "The present educational system of courses, credits, and calendar-based systems of teaching and learning focuses by its very nature on how faculty work. As a result, all attempts to achieve efficiency and productivity within this system involve increase in faculty workload."[35]

In a survey of North American dental schools that included questions about planned curriculum changes, Kassebaum et al. found that 88 percent of the respondents (fifty-six dental schools) identified faculty development as needed to make curriculum changes. This was by far the most mentioned area of need.[36] The ADEA CCI has maintained that faculty development is a necessary condition for change and innovation in dental education. To that end, ADEA has sought to provide new opportunities for faculty to gain necessary skills to improve curricula and all aspects of teaching and learning. In a February 2008 communication, Dr. Richard W. Valachovic, ADEA executive director, described the Association's multipronged approach to encourage long and satisfying careers in academic dentistry.[37] Much remains to be done, and some of the faculty development necessary to retain faculty and equip them for lifelong academic careers can only be accomplished at the faculty member's home institution.

Conclusion

The ancient Hebrew sage Qoheleth wrote, "Be warned: the writing of many books is endless, and excessive devotion to books is wearying to the body." Qoheleth might have written the same words

about policy studies, reports, and the consequent excessive devotion to recommendations. The authors of this report make no additional recommendations for change. In the first companion article to this one, Trower provided ample guidance on making academic dentistry more attractive to Generation X faculty.[17] In the second companion article, Trotman et al. made five recommendations to enhance the dental school work environment: 1) school administration (e.g., department chairs) should articulate clear expectations of faculty; 2) faculty members should do their homework: make sure the job "fit" and environment are good for them; 3) remember that teaching matters most; 4) establish a mentoring structure as the cornerstone of faculty development; and 5) create and maintain an atmosphere of enthusiasm among faculty, staff, and students. We encourage readers to review and consider these recommendations.

One of the basic purposes of the ADEA CCI is to give members of the academic dental community concepts and tools to improve and to innovate. To that end, the ADEA CCI has provided faculty development opportunities for teams of liaisons at each dental school. The ADEA CCI has commissioned a number of white papers intended to be practical guides for schools. The authors of this report, the final of three on the dental school work environment, hope that dental school leaders will use these documents as a means of self-assessment against a national benchmark. In particular, we underscore the challenge that dental schools face to advance faculty development as a means to improve work-life satisfaction and to facilitate the changes necessary to ensure the vitality of dental education well into the future.

REFERENCES

1. Wilson R. For love, not money. Chronicle of Higher Education, September 14, 2007:36–9.
2. Schuster JH, Finkelstein MJ. The restructuring of academic work and careers: the American faculty. Baltimore: The Johns Hopkins University Press, 2006.
3. Shepherd KR, Nihill P, Botto RW, McCarthy MW. Factors influencing pursuit and satisfaction of academic dentistry careers: perceptions of new dental educators. J Dent Educ 2001;65(9):841–8.
4. Schenkein HA, Best AM. Factors considered by new faculty in their decision to choose careers in academic dentistry. J Dent Educ 2001;65(9):832–40.
5. Bland CJ, Stritter FT. Characteristics of effective family medicine faculty development programs. Fam Med 1988;20(15):282–8.
6. Bland CJ. Successful faculty in academic medicine: essential skills and how to acquire them. New York: Springer Publishing Company, 1990.

7. Wilkerson L, Irby DM. Strategies for improving teaching practices: a comprehensive approach to faculty development. Acad Med 1998;73(4):387–96.

8. Mennin SP, Krackov SK. Reflections on relevance, resistance, and reform in medical education. Acad Med 1998;73(9):S60-S64.

9. Bland CJ, Starnaman S, Wersal L, Moorhead-Rosenberg L. Curricular change in medical schools: how to succeed. Acad Med 2000;75:575–94.

10. Armstrong EG, Doyle J, Bennett NL. Transformative professional development of physicians as educators: assessment of a model. Acad Med 2004;78(7):702–8.

11. Hendricson WD, Panagakos F, Eisenberg E, McDonald J, Guest G, Jones P, et al. Electronic curriculum implementation at North American dental schools. J Dent Educ 2004;68(10):1041–57.

12. Houston TK, Clark JM, Levine RB, Ferenchick GS, Bowen JL, Branch WT, et al. Outcomes of a national faculty development program in teaching skills: prospective follow-up of 110 medicine faculty development teams. J Gen Intern Med 2004;19(12):1220–7.

13. Haden NK, Beemsterboer PL, Weaver RG, Valachovic RW. Dental school faculty shortages increase: an update on future dental school faculty. J Dent Educ 2000;64(9):657–73.

14. Haden NK, Weaver RG, Valachovic RW. Meeting the demand for future dental school faculty: trends, challenges, and responses. J Dent Educ 2002;66(9):1102–13.

15. Chmar JE, Weaver RG, Valachovic RW. Dental school vacant budgeted faculty positions: academic year 2004–05. J Dent Educ 2006;70(2):188–98.

16. Chmar JE, Weaver RG, Valachovic RW. Dental school vacant budgeted faculty positions, academic years 2005–06 and 2006–07. J Dent Educ 2008;72(3):370–85.

17. Trower CA. Making academic dentistry more attractive to new teacher-scholars. J Dent Educ 2007;71(5):601–5.

18. Trotman CA, Haden NK, Hendricson W. Does the dental school work environment promote successful academic careers? J Dent Educ 2007;71(6):713–25.

19. Pyle M, Andrieu SC, Chadwick DG, Chmar JE, Cole JR, George MC, et al. The case for change in dental education. J Dent Educ 2006;70(9):921–4.

20. Hebel S. Colleges brace for cuts as state economies take a turn for the worse. Chronicle of Higher Education, January 25, 2008. At: http://chronicle.com/weekly/v54/i20/20a01701.htm. Accessed: February 1, 2008.

21. Jones D. State shortfalls projected to continue despite economic gains: long-term prospects for higher education no brighter. Washington, DC: U.S. Department of Education, the National Center for Public Policy and Higher Education, February 2006. At: www.ed.gov/about/bdscomm/list/hiedfuture/reports/jones.pdf. Accessed: December 13, 2007.

22. A test of leadership: charting the future of U.S. higher education. Washington, DC: U.S. Department of Education, 2006.

23. Zemsky R, Wegner GR, Massy WF. Remaking the American university: market smart and mission-centered. New Brunswick: Rutgers University Press, 2006.

24. Newman F, Couturier L, Scurry J. The future of higher education: rhetoric, reality, and the risks of the market. San Francisco: Jossey-Bass, 2004.

25. Catano V, Francis L, Haines T, Kirpalani H, Shannon H, Stringer B, Lozanski L. Occupational stress among Canadian university academic staff. Canadian Association of University Teachers, 2007. At: www.caut.ca/uploads/CAUTStressStudy-EN.pdf. Accessed: January 2, 2008.

26. Tytherleigh MY, Webb C, Cooper CL, Ricketts C. Occupational stress in UK higher education institutions: a comparative study of all staff categories. Higher Educ Res Develop 2005;24:41–61.

27. Winefield AH, Gillespie N, Stough C, Dua J, Hapuararchchi J. Occupational stress in Australian universities: a national survey 2002. South Melborne, Australia: National Tertiary Education Union, 2002.

28. Bailit HL, Beazoglou TJ, Formicola AJ, Tedesco L, Brown LJ, Weaver RG. U.S. state-supported dental schools: financial projections and implications. J Dent Educ 2006;70(3):246–57.

29. Denzin NK, Lincoln YS. The Sage handbook of qualitative research. 3rd ed. Thousand Oaks, CA: Sage Publications, 2005.

30. Collaborative on Academic Careers in Higher Education (COACHE). COACHE highlights report, 2007. Cambridge: President and Fellows of Harvard College, 2007.

31. Financial inequality in higher education: the annual report on the economic status of the profession, 2006–07. Washington, DC: American Association of University Professors, 2007.

32. Faculty salary survey summary report, 2005–06. Washington, DC: American Dental Education Association, 2007.

33. National survey of postsecondary faculty. Washington, DC: U.S. Department of Education, National Center for Education Statistics, 1999.

34. Hendricson WD, Anderson E, Andrieu SC, Chadwick DG, Cole JR, George MC, et al. Does faculty development enhance teaching effectiveness? J Dent Educ 2007;71(12):1513–33.

35. Guskin AE, Marcy MB. Dealing with the future now. Change, July–August 2003:11–21.

36. Kassebaum DK, Hendricson WD, Taft T, Haden NK. The dental curriculum at North American dental institutions in 2002-03: a survey of current structure, recent innovations, and planned changes. J Dent Educ 2004;68(9):914–31.

37. Valachovic RW. Future faculty: ADEA's multipronged approach to alleviating the current crisis. Charting Progress (American Dental Education Association), February 2008.

APPENDIX

Issues Identified in Faculty Write-In Responses to 2007 Dental School Faculty Work Environment Survey

Note: Percentages add up to more than 100 percent because many respondents commented on more than one aspect of academic life.

Theme	Percentage of Respondents Who Commented on This Theme	Issues That Comprise This Theme
Workload Overworked and understaffed Hiring practices to try to cope with workload	28%	• Faculty workloads perceived to be excessive and extremely varied. • No time for professional development to learn skills needed for the job. • Extensive weekend and evening work to complete routine job functions. • Perception that academic positions are more work and higher stress than private practice. • No appreciation for teaching by administration increases faculty concern over workload. • High burnout and high turnover. • Challenge of constantly integrating new faculty into the teaching of the curriculum. • Too many faculty are not productive, which increases workload; too many "retired in place" faculty. • Difficult to be effective researcher given teaching load; administration has unrealistic expectations about how much research can be accomplished by clinical faculty in one or one-half day per week.
Faculty-administration relationships	27%	• Dental school administrators are out of touch with "in the trenches" faculty. • Adverse environment: "us" (administration) against "them" (faculty); lack of a collegial atmosphere. • Administration makes decisions that influence curriculum implementation without seeking faculty input. • Lack of faith in capacity of school leaders to solve problems facing dental schools. • Perception that administration does not respect faculty. • Perception among faculty that any feedback given to the administration is seen as complaining and griping. • Perception that deans push new plans without planning or consultation with faculty; "change for change sake." • Dean sets the environmental tone for the school, either positive or negative.
The dental school within the academic health center	21%	• Sense that dental school environment is less academic than other schools at health science centers. • Concerns about how other schools perceive dental school. • Lack of support from central administration of the HSC/parent university. • Lack of research collaboration with other schools. • Lack of effort to develop programs in the community. • No effort by dental school to establish links to other schools; perception of self-imposed isolation.

American Dental Education Association

		• Perception that dental schools lack innovation; sense of stagnation; "school is in limbo" and is not evolving to keep pace with other HSC schools.
		• Challenging environment for educational mission; too much emphasis on generating income vs. teaching.
		• Aging physical plant in comparison to other HSC schools; inadequate facilities that are not attractive to faculty candidates or prospective students.
Compensation	13%	• Perception among faculty that they are overworked and underpaid.
		• Awareness of how salary issues negatively influence students' consideration of an academic career.
		• Awareness of how salary is a barrier to recruiting quality faculty with teaching or research experience.
Unequal promotion standards and compensation for teachers and researchers	12%	• Standard recruitment and hiring practices are bypassed in order to get researchers.
		• Other faculty members have to teach more and do more university service to compensate for researchers.
		• Perception that reward system is not linked to performance.
		• Concern that new faculty are hired at higher salary than long-standing faculty, which affects morale and collegiality.
Professional development	12%	• Perception that dental schools devote inadequate effort to development of faculty skills.
		• New faculty are not well oriented to schools and parent universities; have to seek information on their own.
		• Faculty do not receive career guidance.
		• Mentoring is "hit or miss," although some proactive department chairs provide excellent mentoring.
		• Schools do not provide funding to support travel to professional meetings.

Other Themes and Associated Issues Described by 10% or Less of Respondents

Recruiting and retaining faculty for the future (10%)
- Hiring primarily addresses immediate needs and plugging gaps rather than long-term goals of the school.
- Hiring practices lean toward "buddies"; cronyism and inbreeding.
- Perception that younger faculty who graduated from different schools have difficulty getting hired.

Lack of infrastructure to maintain research program (7%)
- Lack of laboratory facilities within the dental school building for biomedical research.
- Beg, borrow, and steal approach for research staff and resources.
- Insufficient funding base to support core research equipment, statisticians, and lab technicians.

Differences in teaching philosophy among faculty (7%)
- Young faculty seen as "too soft" and "easy graders."
- Older faculty perceived to be antagonistic toward students.
- Perception that many faculty are "too set in their ways," which stifles curriculum innovation.
- Comments reflect generalist versus specialist debate about focus of the curriculum.

Faculty proactivity needed for success in academia (5%)
- Faculty have to "make it work" through their own initiatives rather than assuming that the school will help you be successful.
- Academic dentistry can be stimulating, rewarding, challenging.
- Some chairs provide effective mentoring.

Revisiting the National Board Dental Examination

Laura M. Neumann, D.D.S., M.P.H.; R. Lamont MacNeil, D.D.S., M.Dent.Sc.

Abstract: The National Board Dental Examination (NBDE) assists state boards of dentistry in determining the qualifications of dentists for initial licensure. This article explains the purpose and rationale for the policies and procedures that guide the NBDE. These examinations have been used for a number of purposes well beyond the assessment of the knowledge and abilities for entry-level dental practice. The article explores the uses and misuses of the National Boards and the relationship between dental licensure examinations and dental curricula. For National Board examinations to remain current and relevant, they must be consistent with standards and best practices for high-stakes testing, and they must focus on competencies and critical thinking skills essential for future practice. The National Board examinations have the potential to stimulate and support curricular reform through collaborative efforts of educators and practitioners who support the test development and standard-setting processes of the examinations.

Dr. Neumann is Senior Vice President, Education/Professional Affairs, American Dental Association; and Dr. MacNeil is Dean, School of Dental Medicine, University of Connecticut and a past Chair of the Joint Commission on National Dental Examinations. Direct correspondence and requests for reprints to Dr. Laura M. Neumann, American Dental Association, 211 E. Chicago Avenue, Chicago, IL 60611; 312-440-2712 phone; 312-587-4105 fax; neumannL@ada.org.

A version of this article and a companion piece were presented at the American Dental Education Association (ADEA) 47th Deans' Conference in November 2005.

Key words: National Board Dental Examination, dental education, dental curricula, dental licensure, competency, assessment

Submitted for publication 12/6/06; accepted 6/18/07

"National Boards stifle curricular innovation."[1] "National Boards force students to memorize useless facts that they never use in practice." "National Boards test outdated, irrelevant information." "National Boards should be testing knowledge for future dental practice."

Are these reasonable statements—or merely provocative assertions to enliven cocktail receptions and hallway conversation? Recent interest in curriculum reform has stimulated discussion on these and other issues related to the purpose and use of the National Board Dental Examination (NBDE). The diversity of thought and commentary on the National Board exams reveals a mixture of interest, misinformation, misunderstanding, misperception, and skepticism tempered by respect for this rite of passage from dental school to professional practice. Whether for student or dean, the results can be a welcomed affirmation of success or a nagging source of concern.

The purpose of this article is to establish a common understanding of the purpose of the NBDE along with the principles, policies, and procedures that guide development and administration of the examinations. In this context, we will explore the uses and misuses of the National Board exams and address timely questions relevant to curriculum reform. Should the dental curriculum define the content of the National Boards, or should the National Boards define the curriculum? If reform is needed, which comes first—a new curriculum or a new exam?

Purpose and History of the National Board Dental Examination

The purpose of the National Board Dental Examination is to assist state boards of dentistry in determining qualifications of dentists who seek licensure to practice dentistry.[2] There has been no change in purpose since the National Board of Dental Examiners was first established as a standing committee of the American Dental Association (ADA) in 1929 to provide and conduct examinations in the theory of the science of dentistry and to issue a certificate of qualifications to successful candidates.

The original plan was to have a three-part examination. Parts I and II would be written examinations to evaluate knowledge of the basic and dental sciences, and the third part a practical clinical examination. However, the practical examination was never given and was later eliminated to appease the state dental boards who feared that they would be unable to effectively fulfill their responsibilities to their states if they relinquished control over the entire examination process.[3] To this day, the clinical examination process continues as a function of the state boards, either individually or in conjunction with one or more independent clinical testing agencies.

Part I of the NBDE was first administered in 1933, followed by Part II in 1934. State recognition of the National Board certificate was slow at first, with participation remaining low until the mid-1950s. By 1990, all U.S. licensing jurisdictions accepted the NBDE as fulfillment of the written examination requirement for licensure.

Both the structure and name of the body overseeing the examination have changed several times over the years.[4] The dental and dental hygiene examination programs are currently administered under the direction of the Joint Commission on National Dental Examinations (JCNDE), which succeeded the Council on National Board Examinations in the early 1980s. Designation of the Joint Commission as the governing body for the National Board Dental Examination by agreement between the ADA and the American Association of Dental Examiners (AADE) resolved differing perspectives on a number of issues relating to the characteristics and control of the examination.[5,6]

Provisions of the 1980 agreement ultimately resulted in a governance structure and principles for operation of the exam program that remain in place today. These principles include the following: 1) because the National Board examination is intended for use in licensure and because licensure is solely for the protection of the public, operation of National Board programs constitutes a public trust; 2) the Joint Commission functions as an agency of the ADA for administrative purposes only; and 3) restrictions placed on the Joint Commission should be limited to those that serve to enhance public trust or are necessary to protect the ADA in its administrative role.[5]

Membership of the Joint Commission is made up of representatives from the ADA (three), AADE (six), American Dental Education Association (ADEA) (three), American Dental Hygienists' Association (one), American Student Dental Association (one), and the public (one). The ADA provides staff support to the Joint Commission through its Department of Testing Services, as well as resources and administrative services that support administration of the National Board examination. In accordance with the 1980 agreement, the Joint Commission annually conducts a meeting for representatives of the state boards, the National Dental Examiners Advisory Forum, to provide an opportunity for dialogue and sharing of information about the examination. The Joint Commission remains accountable to its member organizations with respect to its budget and overall performance and must submit a report annually to the participating organizations.

The National Board examination, in its two parts, was originally characterized as "written examinations." While the designation and intent to provide an examination on the cognitive abilities or theoretical basis for dental practice remain, the format and mode of administration are no longer limited to the paper-and-pencil format. The Joint Commission currently uses the following statement to inform candidates and others of the purpose and general content of the exams: the National Board Dental Examination assesses the ability to understand important information from basic biomedical and dental clinical sciences and the ability to apply such information in a problem-solving context.[7]

Three documents guide the operations of the Joint Commission and the NBDE: the Bylaws, the Standing Rules, and the Examination Regulations. The Bylaws specify the membership, organization, and governance of the JCNDE. The Standing Rules provide the structure and function of the committees of the Joint Commission and the process for handling examination irregularities and candidate appeals.[8] The standing committees of the Joint Commission include the Committee on Examination Development, the Committee on Administration, the Committee on Dental Hygiene, and the Committee on Research and Development. The Examination Regulations specify the details of examination operations, including fees, mechanisms for exam administration, and provisions for ensuring the validity and security of examination content.[9] Examination regulations are updated annually and published in a candidate guide or examination manual.

In addition to its own guiding documents, the Standards for Educational and Psychological Testing promulgated by the American Educational Research Association, American Psychological Association, and National Council on Measurement in Education provide guidance to the Joint Commission in defining exam content and in conducting its testing programs. These standards are considered an authoritative source of professional technical guidance for testing agencies.[10] They are intended to promote the sound and ethical use of tests and to provide a basis for evaluating the quality of testing practices.[11] The Joint Commission periodically publishes a technical report to demonstrate the validity evidence supporting the examination programs and its compliance with accepted standards.[12]

Theoretical Basis for the National Board Exams

Any discussion of National Board issues must be based on a common understanding of the theoretical underpinnings of the exams. A scientific approach to assessment recognizes that, fundamentally, assessment isn't about exam questions and scores; rather, assessment is a special kind of evidentiary argument. As Braun and Mislevy explain in their article on intuitive test theory, assessment is a process of reasoning from limited observations of student knowledge or behavior to broader inferences about what they know, have accomplished, or may do in the future.[13]

Scientific test theory is based on a link between the purpose of an assessment, conceptual perspectives on the nature of the knowledge or skills of interest, and observable manifestations of student competence, i.e., performance on an exam in the form of right and wrong answers. For the National Boards, the purpose, as previously described, is to determine whether students are qualified for entry into practice. Beliefs about their qualifications are based on statements of entry-level competence, as characterized by the ADEA Competencies for the New Dentist.[14] Probability models allow us to sample domains of students' knowledge related to these competencies, collect data, and draw conclusions about their level of competence and readiness for independent, entry-level dental practice. Matching the purpose of a test to the context in which it will be used is essential to achieving validity, i.e., confidence that the results provide relevant and appropriate information for decision making.

Validity is a fundamental consideration in the development and evaluation of examinations; it refers to the degree to which evidence and theory support the interpretations of test scores for the proposed purpose of the test. According to Fabrey, three assumptions are important for documenting the validity of a credentialing examination: 1) that there are certain critical abilities necessary for effective performance and that individuals who lack these abilities will not be able to adequately practice; 2) that individuals scoring low on the examination lack knowledge underlying these critical abilities and will not be able to practice in a safe and effective manner; and 3) that the examination can be designed to accurately identify the point at which the knowledge, skills, and abilities demonstrated on the examination are most indicative of the candidate's ability to practice in a safe and effective manner.[15] This point is most commonly known as the pass-fail point or the cut score. The relevant decision is this: does the candidate have the requisite knowledge to be granted a dental license?

Development of the National Board Examinations

Key elements of validity evidence for a licensure examination of knowledge for any profession include the content basis of the examination, as well as the role of content experts and the process for identifying and codifying examination content. The following paragraphs describe the role of these elements in the formulation of a complete examination from development of the examination blueprint to the writing and compiling of individual items according to specifications.

Content Specifications and Topics Addressed or Emphasized

The NBDE Part II provides a good framework to illustrate how a national examination is constructed. This examination consists of 500 questions organized around nine major subject areas: operative dentistry, pharmacology, prosthodontics, oral and maxillofacial surgery and pain control, orthodontics and pediatric dentistry, endodontics, periodontics, oral diagnosis, and patient management (including behavioral science, dental public health, and occupational safety).[16] The content specifications for the examination are determined using a recognized and structured psychometric process. The starting guide for selection of topic areas to be addressed in the examination is the 1997 ADEA Competencies for the New Dentist document.[14] To confirm that these competencies continue to be important and relevant, the JCNDE conducts a practice analysis survey approximately every five years. The survey asks practitioners to rate the importance of sixty-five competencies (sixty-three ADEA Competencies and two competencies taken from the Accreditation Standards for Dental Education Programs)[17] to their practice of general dentistry.

The practice analysis was last conducted in 2005 and included a randomized sample of 7,000 general dentists, stratified by licensure jurisdiction, who had been in practice for one to five years following graduation; 2,597 or 41 percent of those surveyed responded. Data from the survey are first used to confirm that each competency is still important and relevant to practice and the national examination and, second, to ultimately determine the number of test items that will be devoted to each competency and content area. The decision to retain a competency area in the examination and the number of exam items to be devoted to that competency are also influenced by comment from the profession and public as obtained through various forums, such as the JCNDE forum at the ADEA Annual Session. Using these data and input, JCNDE staff use the Rasch rating scale analysis as described by Kramer and Neumann[18] to determine the number of questions that will be devoted to discrete topic areas in the examination. For example, in the 2006 Part II examination, forty-five test items were allotted to operative dentistry, thirty test items to endodontics, forty-four items to oral diagnosis, etc. Subsequently, a panel of experts reviews and cross-links the calculated allocation of items among competencies and content areas, and may make minor adjustments in the distribution of items among content areas.

Piloting New Test Items and Role of TCCs in Exam Construction

The Joint Commission uses a specialized computer software application to manage and store National Board questions. This item bank includes questions currently in use, draft questions, and questions that have been retired from use. Each examination includes a mix of previously used items and a number of new questions created by Test Construction Committees (TCCs) in an effort to expand the item bank and to provide a supply of fresh, contemporary questions for the examination. New questions

are piloted before they are used as scored items on subsequent exams.[12] Piloted questions are analyzed statistically for difficulty and discrimination and are not included in scoring unless they fulfill JCNDE criteria. For an item to be considered effective, it must produce a difficulty index between 40 percent and 80 percent, and a corresponding discrimination index of 0.15 or higher for Part I or 0.08 or higher for Part II.[12] Questions that satisfy these criteria are retained in the test item bank and are then available for use in future examinations.

There are sixteen TCCs encompassing Part I (n=5) and Part II (n=11) related to the following subject areas: (Part I) Anatomical Sciences, Biochemistry/Physiology, Microbiology/Pathology, Dental Anatomy and Occlusion, and a multidisciplinary Testlet Development Committee; (Part II) Endodontics, Operative Dentistry, Oral and Maxillofacial Surgery-Pain Control, Oral Diagnosis, Orthodontics/Pediatric Dentistry, Patient Management, Periodontics, Pharmacology, Prosthodontics, Component B-Case Composition and Case Selection Committee, and a Consultant Review Committee.[8] The size of each TCC varies but typically consists of four to six members with approximately 80 percent of members affiliated with dental schools (full-time or part-time appointments) and approximately 20 percent from the private practice sector. Tables 1-4 list the membership for each TCC. Each year the Joint Commission asks its member organizations (AADE, ADEA, and ADA), along with other dental groups, to nominate new candidates to fill vacant positions on the TCCs. The qualifications of the candidates are reviewed by the Joint Commission before they are approved by majority vote. The standard term of a TCC member is one year, renewable for a total of five consecutive terms.

The TCCs typically meet once or twice a year at the ADA headquarters in Chicago. New test constructors receive several resource documents to provide guidance in their role: Orientation Manual for National Board Dental and Dental Hygiene Test Constructors,[19] Test Item Development Guide,[20] and Case Development Guide.[21] During their initial term of service, new members are mentored by experienced test constructors and staff with formal training and expertise in test development. The tasks of test constructors are a) to review the performance, using psychometric criteria, of recently used test items in their subject domains; b) to recommend the continuation or cessation of these items in the test item bank; and c) to propose, critique, and approve new

Table 1. Composition of NBDE Part I Test Construction Committees, 2006

Committee	Subject Matter Experts	Number of Members	Full-Time Practitioners	Total
Anatomical Sciences	Gross Anatomists	2	1	5
	Histologists	2		
Biochemistry/Physiology	Biochemists	2	1	5
	Physiologists	2		
Microbiology/Pathology	Microbiologists	2	1	5
	General Pathologists	2		
Dental Anatomy and Occlusion	Dental Anatomists	3	1	4
Testlet Development	1 Expert from Each Committee	5	4	9
Part I Totals		20	8	28

Table 2. Composition of NBDE Part II Component A Test Construction Committees, 2006

Committee	Subject Matter Experts	Number of Members	Full-Time Practitioners	Total
Operative Dentistry	Dentists	3	1	5
	Dental Materials Expert	1		
Pharmacology	Pharmacologists	3	1	4
Prosthodontics	Fixed Prosthodontists	2	1	6
	Removable Prosthodontists	2		
	Dental Materials Expert	1		
Oral and Maxillofacial Surgery	Oral and Maxillofacial Surgeons	3	1	4
Orthodontics/Pediatric Dentistry	Orthodontists	3	1	6
	Pediatric Dentists	2		
Endodontics	Endodontists	3	1	4
Periodontics	Periodontists	3	1	4
Oral Diagnosis	Oral Pathologists	2	1	6
	Dental Radiologists	2		
	Oral Diagnosis Expert	1		
Patient Management	Dental Public Health Experts	2	2	8
	Behavioral Scientists	3		
	Special Needs Expert	1		
Part II Totals		37	10	47

test items to augment the item banks for the subject area. New test items are then piloted on upcoming exams, as explained above.

Exam Construction

The role of each TCC ends when test items have been selected and assembled into a draft section for the examination. As a final step for the Part II examination, the Consultant Review Committee comprised of two experienced test constructors—a practitioner and a discipline-based dental expert—works with staff to review and refine the examination, with particular attention to case-based items. Consultant reviewers are responsible for test coherence and cohesion and for reviewing case materials for proper orientation, labeling, and linkage to test questions. At this stage, Joint Commission staff assumes primary responsibility for technical formatting, editing, and preparing the examinations for publication and administration. The Part I examination is compiled

Table 3. Composition of NBDE Part II (Component B, Case-Based) Test Construction Committees, 2006

Component B, Case Selection Committee	Subject Matter Experts	Full-Time Practitioners
Practitioners in Part II Disciplines	0	3
Dental Educator-Dentist	1	0

Component B, Case Item Committee	Subject Matter Experts	Full-Time Practitioners
General Practitioners	0	2
Restorative Dentist	0	1
Pharmacologist	0	1
Prosthodontist	1	0
Oral and Maxillofacial Surgeon	1	0
Orthodontist	0	1
Pediatric Dentist	1	0
Periodontist	1	0
Endodontist	0	1
Oral Pathologist	1	0
Dental Radiologist	1	0
Behavioral Scientist	1	0
Totals (13)	7	6

Table 4. Composition of NBDE Part II Consultant Review Committee

Part II Consultant Review Committee	Subject Matter Expert	Full-Time Practitioner
Practitioner in Part II Disciplines	0	1
Dental Educator-Dentist	1	0

independently by Commission staff from items developed and selected by the various TCCs, while the Part II examination is compiled by staff from items produced in both the discipline-based and case-based TCCs with assistance from two dentists/consultant reviewers. At any one time, as many as six comparable versions of each exam (NBDE I, NBDE II) may be active in the system.

Common Perceptions and Misperceptions About Testing and the NBDE

Dental faculty may hold a number of perceptions about the National Board examination based on their day-to-day experiences in dental education and intuitive notions about assessment and testing. The practice of making inferences from National Board scores that extend well beyond what can reasonably be supported by the purpose and principles of testing perpetuates misperceptions and misuses of the National Boards. The paragraphs that follow address a number of these assumptions from the perspective of the JCNDE.

"National Boards should test what's in the dental school curriculum."

The content of the National Board examination is outlined in a set of examination specifications that are reviewed and updated annually. The Part I and Part II exam specifications provide a blueprint for the respective examinations, delineating the major subject headings and number of items devoted to the content area, as well as the subtopics to be covered in each subject area.[16] These blueprints guide test constructors in selecting and developing test items to sample candidate knowledge across the subject areas that have been identified as important to the safe and effective practice of dentistry.

Good testing practice, as defined by the Standards for Educational and Psychological Testing, requires that the blueprint or content domain of a credentialing exam be based on a job analysis or practice analysis derived from information concerning the actual behavior of competent practitioners.[11] Joint Commission policy directs that a practice analysis be conducted every five years and that the exam specifications be based on the results of the practice analysis. The process for conducting a practice analysis has been described earlier. The Standards further advise that, in tests used for licensure, skills that may be important to success in the field but that are not directly related to the purpose of licensure should not be included.[11] As argued by Chambers in his 2004 article on initial licensure testing, content validity of an exam depends equally on knowing that tasks on the test are part of dental practice and that the tasks are critical to the safe and effective practice of dentistry.[23] Because the goals of most dental education programs emphasize the preparation of dental practitioners, there will be a substantial overlap between the content of dental curricula and the National Board exams. However, not all topics deemed appropriate for each school's mission and curriculum will be important for the purposes of demonstrating competence for safe, entry-level dental practice.

"Dental educators should determine National Board content."

Historically, the Joint Commission relied on the opinions and recommendations of subject matter experts serving on a number of discipline-based Test Construction Committees to formulate and update examination content specifications. For the most part, these individuals were dental educators nominated by their peers or personally volunteering their expertise. These test constructors were fully responsible for specifying examination content and for developing the test questions in each content area.

While the input and judgment of subject matter experts continue to play an important role in the development of individual test items, the current process for determining the overall examination blueprint, as previously explained, is confirmed by the results of the practice analysis. The Standing Rules of the Joint Commission delineate the criteria and professional credentials for selection and appointment of the subject matter experts, or consultants, to serve on Test Construction Committees.[8] Because the purpose of the exam is to determine competence for practice, each committee includes at least one full-time dental practitioner, i.e., a dentist who has practiced thirty to forty hours per week for at least ten years.

Reliance on the results of a practice analysis to provide a broad outline of the knowledge underlying contemporary, entry-level practice combined with the expertise of educators and experienced practitioners serving on Test Construction Committees offers the potential for an exam that will be valid for the intended purpose and independent of the bias of any stakeholder group. The exam blueprint and the substance of individual items must broadly sample the biomedical, behavioral, and clinical sciences underlying the new dentist competencies in a manner proportionate to the relative importance of that content to current dental practice. Joint Commission policies regarding Test Construction Committees and determination of test content are intended to guard

against turf battles and self-protectionism among committees and disciplines, as well as individual consultants who may attempt to dominate a committee or a component of an exam. Because of the significant overlap of dental curricula and exam content, it is important to have an objective process that is free of the territorialism and entrenched turfdom that have stymied curricular innovation.[24,25] Reliance on exam specifications determined by a practice analysis is intended to guard against the tendency of dental faculty to write questions on what they *are* teaching instead of what they *should be* teaching.[1] In this regard, the NBDE exam specifications set a baseline standard of the knowledge required for entry-level dental practice and can serve as an external standard or benchmark against which curriculum content and areas of emphasis can be compared.

"National Boards test minutiae and force students to memorize useless facts."

As suggested by the preceding discussion, the National Board exams sample from the vast areas of knowledge in the dental curriculum that define the competent dental practitioner. Through this sampling process, the exams will cover both critical principles and information that may be deemed by some to be of lesser importance. This approach satisfies state dental boards charged with protection of the public who believe that candidates for licensure must demonstrate that they have knowledge of basic dental terminology and sufficient foundational knowledge for use in patient care and for reading and evaluating dental research, literature, and manufacturers' product and marketing materials.

Based on a standard-setting process described below, the JCNDE identifies important criterion items and develops a pass-fail rule that relates these criterion items to a standard score scale. This process allows the National Board exams to fully sample from the breadth and depth of their content specifications while preventing individual examinees from being disadvantaged by items that may be perceived as obscure or unimportant. Also, for this reason, the raw score percentage of correct items required for a passing score may seem relatively low.

The Joint Commission agrees that the exams should stress understanding and ability to apply information in a problem-solving context and has taken a number of steps to increase the proportion of exam items that require application and analysis of information rather than rote recall. Test Construction Committees identify the cognitive level of each item, and the Joint Commission tracks the relative proportion of items at each cognitive level in each exam.[12] Table 5 provides a sample summary of the distribution of Part I items from a 2006 exam by clinical applicability and cognitive level, and Table 6 provides a sample summary of the distribution of Part II items from a 2006 exam by content category and cognitive level. Classification of items according to discipline and cognitive level is done by committees during the final phase of exam construction. All National Board items are evaluated for quality, either through pre-testing or through post-exam analyses of item statistics, such as indices of difficulty and discrimination. Items that are too easy, too difficult, or not discriminatory are eliminated from scoring and/or revised for future use.

"National Boards should test knowledge for future practice."

Discussion in the Standards indicates that the job content domain should be described in terms of worker knowledge, skills, abilities, and other personal characteristics that are clearly and operationally defined so that they can be linked to test content and for which job demands are not expected to change substantially over a specified period of time.[11] Accordingly, National Boards focus on knowledge

Table 5. Distribution of NBDE Part I test items by clinical applicability and cognitive level (# of items)

Discipline	Clinical Applicability	Understanding	Application	Reasoning
Anatomical Sciences	34	55	42	3
Biochemistry/Physiology	27	50	45	5
Microbiology/Pathology	30	52	46	2
Dental Anatomy and Occlusion	100	41	56	3

Table 6. Distribution of Part II items by content area and cognitive level, 2006 (# of items)

Part II Disciplines	Single Discipline Items	Multidisciplinary Items			Cognitive Level		
		Other Clinical Discipline	Basic Science	Behavioral Science	Under-standing	Application	Reasoning
COMPONENT A							
Operative Dentistry (45)	12	22	8	3	9	20	16
Pharmacology (34)	24	5	3	2	19	13	2
Prosthodontics (45)	35	2	5	3	7	26	12
Oral and Maxillofacial Surgery/Pain Control (43)	7	13	21	2	3	29	11
Orthodontics/Pediatric Dentistry (58)	20	20	6	12	22	24	12
Endodontics (30)	3	20	6	1	8	10	12
Periodontics (45)	8	24	12	1	13	30	2
Oral Diagnosis (44)	9	5	26	4	15	7	22
Patient Management (56)	0	28	0	28	38	12	6
Total—Component A (400 Items)	118	139	87	56	134	171	95
COMPONENT B							
(100 Items)	60	30	4	6	11	78	11
TOTALS (500)	178	169	91	62	145	249	106
Percent (100%)	35.6%	33.8%	18.2%	12.4%	29.0%	49.8%	21.2%

required for current practice—knowledge that, to the extent possible, is evidence-based. Few educators or practitioners are in a position to realistically predict future dental practice. Thus, the knowledge tested must, of necessity, focus on current practice. Shuler has noted that while it is not possible to predict the specific scientific advances that will occur in the future, the areas most likely to have impressive advances can be predicted based on the best available information.[26] Accordingly, dental curricula should cover these content areas that will serve as a foundation for understanding future scientific advances. The Part I exam has traditionally covered areas of foundational knowledge and should be reviewed to ensure that content includes growth areas of scientific understanding that would be applicable to oral health. More appropriately, the exams should test the critical thinking skills required for future practice: analysis and application of knowledge, critical evaluation and synthesis of information, and problem-solving.[27]

"National Boards are graded on a curve."

The perception that National Board exams are graded on a curve, and as a corollary that they are competitive, is both fallacious and unhealthy for candidates, education programs, and the profession. National Board exams are criterion-referenced tests.[28] That is, candidates are evaluated in relation to a standard criterion of performance. Exam results are intended to show if the candidate has met the standard, i.e., that the candidate has the minimum level of knowledge for safe, entry-level dental practice. National Board exam results are not intended to compare individuals or groups of candidates (a norm-referenced exam) or to show gradients of achievement or ability.

Terminology relating to scoring and exam results can be confusing. Official National Board scores are reported as standard scores. A raw score is simply the number or percentage of items answered correctly. A standard score is the result of the conversion of a raw score by small mathematical adjustments that make the score comparable to scores from all other test forms, past, present, and future. The conversion process equates raw scores on a common scale across multiple forms or versions of the test with a constant passing score point. This process ensures fairness and a valid interpretation of scores.

The pass-fail point is determined by a committee of distinguished content experts who make judgments to define a minimum level of acceptable performance using a formal standard-setting process.[28] Setting the performance standard involves several steps. First, the content of each item is reviewed by the content experts to determine its importance to the practice of dentistry. Items essential to success in practice are known as criterion items. Next, the content experts estimate the minimum level of knowledge of the subject matter represented in the criterion items that would be required for licensure. By means of a statistical process, candidates' performance on the criterion items is used as an index to calculate the minimum performance standard on all 400 or 500 items in a complete exam. The Joint Commission assigns the standardized score of 75 to signify the minimum performance for passing the examination and eligibility for National Board certification. The goal of the National Board scoring process is to answer this question: has the candidate passed the exam and met the standard?

"I got a 74. There was an unfair question (technical error, inaccuracy, etc.) or I would have passed. I want one point added to my score."

This plea reflects a common misperception of candidates whose scores are close, but short of the standard for passing. They perceive that the reported score is a raw score or percentage score rather than a standard score. In fact, one right or wrong answer in an exam of several hundred items generally does not equate to one point on the standard score scale.

As previously described, the Joint Commission uses a post-exam analysis process to evaluate the performance of every item on the exam with respect to difficulty, discrimination, and other characteristics. Items that do not perform appropriately or that include technical errors impacting the item may be removed from scoring. Joint Commission policy provides that up to 15 percent of items may be removed from scoring, although the number and percentage of items removed are usually quite small.

From another perspective, it is worthwhile to consider the quality of the National Board exams with respect to reliability. Over the history of the examination program, the reliability (KR_{20}) of the National Boards has consistently exceeded acceptable levels.[12,29] Accordingly, a strong likelihood exists that a candidate with a score of 74 truly lacks the minimum knowledge for safe practice and will fail to achieve a passing score on a subsequent examination without remediation or other intervention. The relatively high failure rate of repeating candidates affirms this assumption: the failure rate for repeating candidates from accredited dental schools was 26.5 percent for Part I and 25.1 percent for Part II, while the failure rate for first-time test takers was 16.3 percent for Part I and 7.7 percent for Part II in 2005.[30]

"How can I get my school into the top quintile?"

This has been a common question of dental school administrators in search of objective metrics that will serve as benchmarks to demonstrate program outcomes and satisfy university administrators' requests for accountability. The question references an annual report produced for a number of years by the Joint Commission itemizing the coded results for each school, with a breakdown of mean score in quintiles from highest to lowest mean score. The format of the report was originally intended to respond to dental schools' desire for an objective outcome measure for self-evaluation, accreditation, and reporting to higher level administration. While appearing to meet these needs, the ranking of schools by mean scores emphasized differences that were, in fact, quite small and, for the most part, practically insignificant. For example, for the reporting period May 1, 2004 through April 30, 2005, 78 percent of Part II mean scores for all schools were between 79.5 and 83.9.[31] The difference between school #6 (83.9) in the top quintile and school #14 (83.0) in the next quintile was less than one point. The difference between schools #4 and #5 (84.1) and school #34 (81.1) was only three points. The difference in mean score between the top school in the third quintile and the next highest ranked school at the bottom of the fourth quintile was one tenth of a point; the difference between the top school in the third quintile and the top school in the fourth quintile was nine-tenths of a point. The separation of schools by quintile was the result of an arbitrary mathematical computation, rather than a meaningful distinction. While it might be argued that the difference between school #1 and school #54 was significant, the more meaningful information is reflected in data relevant to the purpose of the exam—the proportion of students failing the examination.

With respect to accreditation, the outcome of interest to the Commission on Dental Accreditation (CODA) and the U.S. Department of Education (USDE) is the first-time pass rate on licensure exams.[32-34] Joint Commission scoring procedures are designed to ensure a high degree of confidence about pass-fail decisions, not about relative achievement of individual students or the effectiveness of individual faculty or educational programs based on fine distinctions among closely clustered scores at other points along the standard score continuum. In fact, the Standards for Educational and Psychological Testing indicate that tests used in credentialing may be designed to be precise only in the vicinity of the cut score; they may not be precise for those who clearly pass or clearly fail.[11]

"Competition for postgraduate programs hinges on National Board scores."

The discussion above applies equally to this statement. While National Board scores may represent objective measures of student knowledge and competence for practice, they were never intended to distinguish students by gradients of ability or achievement. Because U.S. dental schools are accredited and select students from a highly qualified and motivated pool of applicants who are cognizant of the expectations for graduation, licensure, and the demands of professional practice or advanced education, the range of scores for National Boards for students in accredited schools is narrowly clustered and skewed to the high end of the score scale.

The Joint Commission has a high level of confidence about score differences at the pass-fail point, but does not have evidence to support assumptions about comparisons at higher or lower ends of the score scale. Some studies of predictors of success in medical residencies have shown that applicants' scores on the National Board of Medical Examiners (NBME) examinations have little or no value in predicting success of residents.[35-37] A study of measures for the selection of international dental students to a U.S. D.D.S. program showed that Part II was the most significant predictor of academic performance and clinical competency in the admission process, but this use of the exam as described by the authors "to measure real-life dentistry knowledge" is more consistent with the intended purpose.[38]

Summary and Conclusions

The National Board examinations need to remain current and relevant in meeting the intended purpose of evaluating the competency of candidates for initial dental licensure. The principles and processes guiding the National Board testing program are consistent with current standards and best practices for high-stakes credentialing examinations in the health professions. Nevertheless, it is appropriate to carefully consider recommendations for change and opportunities for collaboration in improving both the quality of the examination and dental education.

As a first step, educators and practitioners should jointly review and revise the Competencies for the New Dentist. The existing competencies have served the profession well and, to a certain extent, have been validated through the Joint Commission's practice analyses. Because the competencies focus primarily on areas of knowledge and technical skill, it will be important that revisions or additions focus on competencies identified by some as lacking in both the dental curriculum and the National Board exams—skills for critical thinking and information evaluation and management.[25,26]

A companion article (following in this issue) will consider the framework for test construction activities and offer suggestions for meeting these needs. However, it is important to remember that the content and quality of items resulting from test construction activities are a reflection of the input and perspectives of individual test constructors. Reforming the exams will require the commitment and collective efforts of all who participate, the support of a dental education system that values the desired knowledge and skills, and acceptance by the state boards of dentistry.

REFERENCES

1. Alfano MC. Dental education: one dean's perspective. J Am Coll Dent 2001;68(3):8-12.
2. Joint Commission on National Dental Examinations. Joint Commission Bylaws. Chicago: American Dental Association, March 1990.
3. Teall GL. National Board of Dental Examiners. J Am Dent Assoc 1959;58:144-9.
4. Demarais DR. The history of the regional clinical examinations. J Mich Dent Assoc 1990;Nov-Dec:525-7.
5. American Dental Association. Joint report of the AADE Executive Council and the ADA Board of Trustees to the AADE General Assembly and the ADA House of Delegates on written examinations for licensure. Chicago: American Dental Association, 1980;Supplement to annual reports and resolutions 1:357-64.
6. Joint Commission on National Dental Examinations. Annual report. Chicago: American Dental Association, 1982:64-72.
7. Joint Commission on National Dental Examinations. National Board Dental Examination candidate guide, part I. Chicago: American Dental Association, 2005.
8. Joint Commission on National Dental Examinations. Standing rules. Chicago: American Dental Association, 2003.
9. Joint Commission on National Dental Examinations. Examination regulations. Chicago: American Dental Association, 2005.
10. Browning AH, Bugbee AC, Mullins MA, eds. Certification: a NOCA handbook. Washington, DC: National Organization for Competency Assurance (NOCA), 1996.
11. American Educational Research Association, American Psychological Association, and National Council on Measurement in Education. Standards for educational and psychological testing. Washington, DC: American Educational Research Association, 1999.
12. Joint Commission on National Dental Examinations. Technical report: the National Board Dental Examinations. Chicago: American Dental Association, 2004.
13. Braun HL, Mislevy R. Intuitive test theory. Phi Delta Kappan 2005;86(7):489-97.
14. American Association of Dental Schools. Proceedings of the 1997 House of Delegates. J Dent Educ 1997;61:541-51(Appendix 2),556-8.
15. Fabrey L. Basic psychometric principles. In: Browning AH, Bugbee AC, Mullins MA, eds. Certification: a NOCA handbook. Washington, DC: National Organization for Competency Assurance (NOCA), 1996.
16. Joint Commission on National Dental Examinations. National Board Dental Examinations specifications. Chicago: Joint Commission on National Dental Examinations, 2007.
17. Commission on Dental Accreditation. Accreditation standards for dental education programs. Chicago: Commission on Dental Accreditation, 2006.
18. Kramer GA, Neumann LM. Confirming the validity of Part II of the National Board Dental Examination: a practice analysis. J Dent Educ 2003;67:1286-98.
19. Joint Commission on National Dental Examinations, American Dental Association. Orientation manual for National Board dental and dental hygiene test constructors. Chicago: American Dental Association, 2007.
20. Joint Commission on National Dental Examinations, American Dental Association. Test item development guide. Chicago: American Dental Association, 2007.
21. Joint Commission on National Dental Examinations, American Dental Association. Case development guide. Chicago: American Dental Association, 2007.
22. Joint Commission on National Dental Examinations. National Board Dental Examination candidate guide, Part II. Chicago: American Dental Association, 2005.
23. Chambers DW. Portfolios for determining initial licensure competency. J Am Dent Assoc 2004;135:173-84.

24. Kassebaum DK, Hendricson WD, Taft T. The dental curriculum at North American dental institutions in 2002-03: a survey of current structure, recent innovations, and planned changes. J Dent Educ 2004;68(9):914-31.

25. Hendricson WD, Cohen PA. Oral health care in the 21st century: implications for dental and medical education. Acad Med 2001;12:1181-206.

26. Shuler CF. Emerging scientific advances: how do they enter dental curricula and the profession? J Calif Dent Assoc 2005;33(10):805-9.

27. Hupp JR. Health skepticism: the essence of critical thinking. Oral Surg Oral Med Oral Pathol 2006;102(3): 271-4.

28. Kramer GA, DeMarais DR. Setting a standard on the pilot National Board Dental Examination. J Dent Educ 1992;56(10):683-8.

29. Joint Commission on National Dental Examinations. 2006 report on the quality of recent exams. Chicago: American Dental Association, 2006.

30. Joint Commission on National Dental Examinations. Trends in numbers of candidates and failure rates. Chicago: Joint Commission on National Dental Examinations, 2005.

31. Joint Commission on National Dental Examinations. Dental school profiles: part II National Board Dental Examination, May 1, 2004-April 30, 2005. Chicago: Joint Commission on National Dental Examinations, 2005.

32. Commission on Dental Accreditation. Outcomes assessment. Chicago: American Dental Association, 2003.

33. Kershnstein K. Memorandum to Cynthia Davenport, ASPA, June 10, 2006, RE: June 2006 NACIQI Meeting.

34. Code of Federal Regulations, Title 34, Part 602—The Secretary's Recognition of Accrediting Agencies, Subpart B—The Criteria for Recognition. Federal Register, October 20, 1999.

35. Gunderman RB, Jackson VP. Are NBME examination scores useful in selecting radiology residency candidates? Acad Radiol 2000;7(8):603-6.

36. Warrick SS, Crumrine RS. Predictors of success in an anesthesiology residency. J Med Educ 1986;61(7):591-5.

37. Fine PL, Hayward RA. Do the criteria of resident selection committees predict residents' performances? Acad Med 1995;70(9):834-8.

38. Stacey DG, Whittaker JM. Predicting academic performance and clinical competency for international dental students: seeking the most efficient and effective measures. J Dent Educ 2005;69(2):270-80.

Realigning the National Board Dental Examination with Contemporary Dental Education and Practice

R. Lamont MacNeil, D.D.S., M.Dent.Sc.; Laura M. Neumann, D.D.S., M.P.H.

Abstract: Although the National Board Dental Examination (NBDE) was developed for the purpose of supporting the dental licensure process, it can have significant influence on dental school curricula. Efforts to revise and enhance dental curricula, of necessity, must engage stakeholder communities and promote an assessment process that is both valid and relevant to contemporary dental practice. The NBDE uses a systematic and objective process for test development that involves content experts from dental education and practice. This process could be enhanced by reconsidering the types of individuals who should participate in test construction, reconfiguring the groups involved in the process, augmenting training and development of test constructors, and updating the principles and documents that define the competencies and foundational knowledge required for contemporary dental practice. In addition, there is a need for ongoing research and development to explore new testing strategies that stress understanding and the ability to apply information in a problem-solving context. Finally, examinations could be enhanced with a broader array of high-quality supporting case materials through a more structured collaborative arrangement between dental schools and the National Board testing program.

Dr. MacNeil is Dean, School of Dental Medicine, University of Connecticut and a past Chair of the Joint Commission on National Dental Examinations; and Dr. Neumann is Senior Vice President, Education/Professional Affairs, American Dental Association. Direct correspondence and requests for reprints to Dr. Laura M. Neumann, American Dental Association, 211 E. Chicago Avenue, Chicago, IL 60611; 312-440-2712 phone; 312-587-4105 fax; neumannL@ada.org.

Key words: dental education, National Board Dental Examination, dental curriculum, assessment

Submitted for publication 2/6/07; accepted 6/18/07

There is perhaps no question in dental education that will elicit more debate, angst, and opinion than "what do you think about the National Board examinations?" It is a subject that invariably mixes science and emotion and juxtaposes the concepts of licensure testing (state, regional, or national), student assessment, curriculum reform, and the many pedagogical philosophies that prevail on how best to educate and examine the new dentist. In a companion article in this issue of the *Journal of Dental Education*, Neumann and MacNeil[1] review the founding and continuing principles of the National Board Dental Examination (NBDE), revisiting the history and purpose of the Joint Commission on National Dental Examinations (JCNDE) and the examinations it renders. The authors also discuss common perceptions, misconceptions, and concerns about processes used to generate and deliver examinations. This current article will build on the background provided by Neumann and MacNeil to provide additional insight into the current administrative processes underpinning dental board examinations. Suggestions are made on ways to enhance these processes with the goal of creating national examinations that are not only rigorous, valid, and discriminating but also recognized by the majority of the constituencies involved

as relevant, contemporary, and appropriately oriented to the practice of general dentistry.

National Boards and Dental School Curricula

Although it is clear that the sole purpose of the NBDE is to assist states in determining if new candidates meet minimal knowledge expectations for licensure, the NBDE has a real if unintended impact on the dental curricula of schools whose graduates pursue licensure in the United States.[2] It appears logical to predict that the content specifications of national examinations (i.e., the array of topics or knowledge areas deemed important enough by the Joint Commission to be allotted space in the examinations) will induce the curriculum committees of dental schools to include and even emphasize these areas in their educational programs. In a similar manner, the methods used within the NBDE to examine candidates in these areas might well influence the examination techniques used in courses.

The hypothesis of this article is that the NBDE influences dental school curricula content and delivery. If this hypothesis is correct, it is then reasonable for dental education institutions to encourage and strive for national examinations that will be contemporary and relevant in terms of both the knowledge base being examined and the method of assessment. Further, it is reasonable to assume that realignment in the examination process to obtain greater relevancy to the contemporary practice of general dentistry would enhance the validity of these examinations for both their intended purpose and as a more broadly applicable measure of student or new graduate competence.

Parallel Initiatives

A number of recent initiatives in organized dental education have addressed the question "do the National Boards address current, important, and relevant information?" This was a keynote topic at the American Dental Education Association (ADEA) 47th Deans' Conference in November 2005.[3] Further, it has been one of the pivotal topics addressed by the ADEA Commission on Change and Innovation in Dental Education (CCI), beginning at its inception in May 2005.[4] The CCI is an initiative supported by ADEA in conjunction with several key stakeholder organizations in dental education including the American Dental Association (ADA), the Commission on Dental Accreditation (CODA), and the JCNDE. The CCI strives to identify curriculum revision that can maximize the educational process and promote the development of dental graduates optimally prepared for the practice of dentistry over the next decades.[5] An important initial decision of the CCI was that such change could not be accomplished by dental schools working independently of organizations and groups that impact or influence dental education, including the JCNDE. A central premise of the CCI is that a large group of partners in dental education, including the major change agents like ADEA, CODA, and the JCNDE, must work in close communication and synchrony to successfully achieve change.[6]

Thus, it appears that dental education is at an opportune time to partner with other stakeholders to promote tangible curriculum revision. In the case of student assessment, a desired scenario would be for the JCNDE to understand and recognize the changing concepts emanating nationally and to promote processes whereby national examinations would, at minimum, not deter implementation of such change

in dental schools. The converse scenario—one in which national examinations might fail to recognize certain change initiatives while continuing to emphasize traditional or "pre-revision" topics or philosophies in dentistry—could significantly jeopardize the odds of achieving meaningful curriculum change. This article will explore processes that might avert such a situation, while improving examinations independent of whether national change initiatives exist or not.

Suggestions for Changes in JCNDE Processes to Improve Examinations

The current examination construction process has been in place for several decades, functions efficiently, and has produced examinations with good psychometric properties.[7] However, some limited changes, as proposed here, could further improve exam development and, in doing so, better ensure that curriculum change initiatives are appropriately recognized or reflected in national examinations.

Recommendation #1: Carefully consider the formulation of the Test Construction Committees.

It is our opinion that the most important groups or process steps in the construction of JCNDE examinations are the Test Construction Committees (TCCs).[1] While the TCCs cannot change the content specifications for the examination, except for changes in terminology or minor shifts in focus, they do determine the emphasis that will be placed on specific topics falling within each larger content domain. For example, in Operative Dentistry Content Specification 5.2.2: Indirect Restorations, emphasis might be placed on ¾ crown or porcelain jacket crown restorations rather than more contemporary CAD-CAM techniques or esthetic veneer techniques. Further, the TCCs determine those test items that will be retained in the item bank and the new test items that will be added to it. In doing so, considerable latitude is afforded to each TCC in creating and selecting test items grounded in specific topics or philosophies of dental science or therapy. While not intended, it is certainly possible that certain topics or philosophies could be stressed while others were overlooked or downplayed. This has the potential to result in a bank of examination questions for a certain content area that might not be as balanced, comprehensive, and contemporary as desired.

Additionally, each TCC has considerable flexibility in determining the type of multiple choice test item used (for example, Type I vs. Paired True-False vs. Cause-and-Effect), although there is a stated JCNDE preference for the simplest format (that being Type I multiple choice completion—a question consisting of a simple stem and one answer option amongst four possibilities).[8] More importantly, in addition to content emphasis, the TCCs have both flexibility and responsibility for the cognitive level of items, i.e., the extent of critical thinking or problem solving required for responding to an item.

Currently, most TCC members are subject matter experts in their discipline or field and either volunteer for this service or are nominated by their peers. Recently, some leaders in dental education have proposed that TCC members should not be experts but rather general dentists with acknowledged aptitude and expertise in certain subject areas, with the premise that questions emanating from a committee so comprised would tend to be more appropriate for assessing the preparation of candidates for the practice of general dentistry.[3] In light of this proposal to enhance participation by general dentists in examination development, we propose an alternative strategy to promote the formulation of examinations that are optimally referenced to the environment of general dental practice in the community.

It is our recommendation that subject matter experts continue to predominantly populate the TCCs but that the following criteria be carefully considered in their appointment: TCC members should a) possess a clear understanding of the competency level (level of knowledge, skills, and values) expected of candidates to practice *general dentistry*; b) be able to demarcate knowledge levels expected of generalists as compared to specialists, career educators, researchers, or other highly trained professionals in dentistry where there is a legitimately higher expectation of knowledge base; and c) be extremely knowledgeable in their fields while also possessing a keen grasp of and appreciation for ongoing change in the professions of dentistry and dental education. While not a simple task to identify individuals with this combination of traits, we believe that nominating groups, including dental schools, can do a better job in this area. While identifying experts is important,

we submit that it is equally important that these experts understand the practice of general dentistry and the level at which a general dentist (versus a specialist or basic scientist) must master scientific principles in order to deliver contemporary, appropriate, and safe dental care.

Recommendation #2: Require test item construction workshops.

Currently, new TCC members have the option to either attend a test item construction workshop or use reference materials provided by the JCNDE to assist them in understanding the "science and art" of formulating questions or test items.[8,9] It is our contention that formal workshops provided by experts in test item construction are critical for understanding and practicing the principles of quality test item construction. Consequently, we propose that all TCC members, upon accepting a TCC assignment, attend a formal JCNDE-sponsored workshop provided by test development experts, including those on the JCNDE staff.

In addition to the routine training of new TCC members, a national symposium and workshop of educators and testing experts should be convened to explore the application of principles of assessment to the development of item types that assess a broader range of complex cognitive behaviors, including comprehension; understanding; predicting; application and interpretation of facts, principles, and methods; analysis; and evaluation. Although there is a perception that multiple choice items are restricted to the measurement of relatively simple learning outcomes, this item type is actually quite versatile and can be useful in measuring a variety of complex learning outcomes.[10] According to Haladyna, the malady of recall and recognition from which most tests suffer is not a function of item format but limited ability to elicit higher levels of thinking in both teaching and testing.[11] With adequate training and practice, item writers can successfully write items with higher-level cognitive demand. Azer, for example, provides practical tips to help question writers create multiple choice items that test higher-level thinking and the use of information.[12] Included in his article is a useful graphic model for linking educational objectives (e.g., interpretation of key words in a scenario, problem-solving skills, integration of knowledge) with areas of knowledge (e.g., physiology, biochemistry, pathogenesis) to generate items addressing specific competencies (e.g., understand the significance of key words in a clinical scenario about a patient with diabetes and generate a hypothesis; understand the biochemical changes in the liver and muscles of patients with diabetic ketoacidosis).

Further, the administration of the NBDE in a computerized format presents an opportunity to take advantage of technology's potential for displaying graphic material, data sets, and other materials for candidate analysis and interpretation. A national symposium would offer an opportunity to review assessment principles and apply relevant dental content to formulate model item types that emphasize critical thinking skills for application in both teaching and testing. In addition to stimulating more innovative use of multiple choice items, a symposium could also encourage the development or application of new item types, such as extended matching or the *key feature* item type recently adopted for the National Board Medical Examinations,[13] and provide more experience with the testlet format recently adopted for the NBDE Part I.

Recommendation #3: Establish independent committees for examination construction design.

As stated above, test items are currently selected and formulated into complete examinations by JCNDE staff, with help from a small number of consultants with prior experience on the TCCs. We believe that the consultant review step in examination formulation is imperative and should occur for all examinations. Further, we recommend a change in the current consultant review approach such that each NBDE examination would have a dedicated Examination Formulation Committee comprised of four or five members. This select group would be nominated by major stakeholder organizations. Extreme care would be taken to identify individuals who have an optimal grasp of the demands and expectations of general dentistry along with the scientific foundation required for contemporary dental practice. These individuals need not be experts in any particular field of dentistry and indeed it may be preferable that they not be experts. While only a limited number of individuals may exist with these characteristics, it should be possible to populate a small, select committee from candidates from across the nation. Ideally, this committee should be formulated to achieve a balance among the concerns, desires, and aspirations of the following constituencies: dental academia (ADEA), examination and licensing bodies (American Association of Dental Examiners and state boards), and the practice community (ADA).

The sole purpose of the Examination Formulation Committees would be to construct "relevant and realistic" examinations using test item banks populated by items generated by the TCCs. The committee would not be permitted to change the test items provided by the TCC content experts or the test specifications. It could, however, do the following:

- Screen and select test items deemed appropriate for the assessment of candidates for competency in general dentistry.
- Determine the distribution of test items across the content specification matrix so that an appropriately broad array of topic areas important to contemporary dental practice is presented. This would reduce the possibility of an examination possessing an internal bias or a skewed emphasis on certain topics or philosophies.
- Approve the final version of each examination for distribution to candidates.
- Provide feedback to the TCCs and the JCNDE on the need for test items in certain areas or levels of understanding and on the quality and appropriateness of case materials. Ask the TCCs to provide additional test items to diversify or augment the test item bank.
- Continually refine the test item bank by deleting items of inappropriate difficulty or emphasis while endorsing test items deemed of good quality for the national examination.
- Respond to JCNDE requests as they arise.

The format described is employed in part by the National Dental Examining Board of Canada in creation of its national examinations and has proved very successful.[14] The approach has the distinct benefit of allowing the TCCs to concentrate on what they do best (i.e., create test items based on subject matter expertise), while permitting an independent committee (e.g., the Examination Formulation Committee) with a contemporary perspective on general dentistry to use these test items in design of a realistic and relevant examination oriented toward the practice of general dentistry. This approach could greatly aid in reducing the undesired possibility of examinations that may concentrate on outdated principles or concepts that are distant from those deemed critical and central to the development of competency in general dentistry.

Recommendation #4: Ensure that foundational and guiding documents used in dental education and candidate assessment truly describe and reflect the contemporary practice of general dentistry.

ADEA should continue its current initiative, under the oversight of the CCI, to define the new Competencies for the General Dentist. It is highly probable that the 1997 ADEA competencies document needs revision to keep pace with ongoing changes in dental practice and dental education, and we applaud the process by which a new document is currently being developed to reflect the current environment. This new document can then be used in future practice analysis surveys to ensure that the content specifications for future National Board examinations are as current and relevant as possible.

Recommendation #5: Research, develop, and pilot new examination and item formats.

The JCNDE should continue its current Innovative Dental Assessment Research and Development (IDEA) Small Grants Program to assist organizations, including dental schools, in developing new examinations and testing strategies for students and licensure candidates.[15] An increase in funding for projects within this program would encourage more faculty and schools to apply and would better support test instrument development. Further, dental schools and their faculty should be encouraged to become more involved in this area to not only improve examination approaches in their home institutions but to share novel or promising approaches with other schools and the JCNDE. The JCNDE has already shown willingness to pilot new examination formats (e.g., the testlet format for Part I), and it should continue to be innovative and forward-looking in this vein. Further, the JCNDE has stated that it desires to create examinations that stress candidate understanding and the ability to apply information in a problem-solving context. To do this, it appears important to migrate away from the traditional item types that focus on recall of descriptive, factual information where candidate success is probably more dependent on rote memorization than an ability to understand and think critically. A close partnership between the JCNDE and dental schools, where a wealth of educational expertise exists, would hasten the development of examinations that target the ability of candidates to synthesize information, think critically, and truly demonstrate readiness for dental practice.

Recommendation #6: Dental schools should enter into an educational collaborative with the JCNDE.

As the NBDE examinations move toward more clinically referenced exam formats, it will be essential to develop a library of contemporary case-based materials (e.g., clinical photographs, radiographs, and patient data sets) that are of excellent quality and appropriate scope. The current process of requesting TCC or ADA members to volunteer case-based materials for examinations will not accomplish this goal. We recommend that dental schools enter into a collaborative agreement with the JCNDE to provide such materials. Almost all postdoctoral advanced programs extensively document the oral condition and findings of patients under care, and many predoctoral programs do as well. The contribution of a single case by each dental school on an annual basis would provide a rich resource that could substantially expand the scope and depth of the NBDE item banks and quality of the assessment process. In exchange, schools might receive compensatory services from the JCNDE such as test item construction workshops for faculty, practice examinations, etc.

Conclusion

Overall, we submit that the NBDE examinations are of good quality and capably accomplish the task of evaluating candidates for licensure. This assessment is validated by evidence from the technical report of the JCNDE[16] and by the continued use of the exams by all licensing jurisdictions. The educators, practitioners, and other individuals who volunteer their time in JCNDE activities, along with commission staff, do an admirable job and should be commended for their commitment and service. The six recommendations provided here build on that solid base and aim to strengthen the examinations, especially as dental education morphs in response to changes in the profession, science, and society. We believe that these recommendations are timely and appropriate and, importantly, are achievable in that they can be implemented without major disruption to current processes and with limited new expense.

REFERENCES

1. Neumann LM, MacNeil RL. Revisiting the National Board Dental Examination. J Dent Educ 2007;71(10):1281-92.
2. Kassebaum DK, Hendricson WD, Taft T, Haden NK. The dental curriculum at North American dental institutions in 2002-03: a survey of current structure, recent innovations, and planned changes. J Dent Educ 2004;68(9):914-31.
3. American Dental Education Association. 47th Deans' Conference, November 2005, Ft. Lauderdale, FL.
4. What is the ADEA Commission on Change and Innovation in Dental Education? How did it get started? Bulletin of Dental Education, December 2005.
5. Pyle M, Andrieu SC, Chadwick DG, Chmar JE, Cole JR, George MC, et al. The case for change in dental education. J Dent Educ 2006;70(9):921-4.
6. Kalkwarf KL, Haden NK, Valachovic RW. ADEA Commission on Change and Innovation in Dental Education. J Dent Educ 2005;69(10):1085-7.
7. Cole JR. Legal status of dentistry and licensure. J Am Coll Dent 2002;69(2):6-12.
8. Joint Commission on National Dental Examinations. Test item development guide. Chicago: Joint Commission on National Dental Examinations, 2007.
9. Joint Commission on National Dental Examinations. Orientation manual for National Board dental and dental hygiene test constructors. Chicago: Joint Commission on National Dental Examinations, 2007.
10. Gronlund NE, Linn RL. Measurement and evaluation in teaching. New York: MacMillan, 1990.
11. Haladyna TM. Developing and validating multiple-choice test items. 3rd ed. Mahwah, NJ: Lawrence Erlbaum Associates, 2004.
12. Azer SA. Assessment in a problem-based learning course. Biochem Mol Biol Educ 2003;31:428-34.
13. Page G, Bordage G, Allen T. Developing key-feature problems and examinations to assess clinical decision-making skills. Acad Med 1995;70(3):194-201.
14. Gerrow J. Personal communication, June 5, 2006.
15. Joint Commission on National Dental Examinations. Innovative dental assessment research and development grants. Chicago: Joint Commission on National Dental Examinations, 2006.
16. Joint Commission on National Dental Examinations. Technical report. Chicago: Joint Commission on National Dental Examinations, 2006.

Assessing Dental Students' Competence: Best Practice Recommendations in the Performance Assessment Literature and Investigation of Current Practices in Predoctoral Dental Education

Judith E.N. Albino, Ph.D.; Stephen K. Young, D.D.S.; Laura M. Neumann, D.D.S., M.P.H.; Gene A. Kramer, Ph.D.; Sandra C. Andrieu, Ph.D.; Lindsey Henson, M.D.; Bruce Horn, D.D.S.; William D. Hendricson, M.S., M.A.

Abstract: In this article, the Task Force on Student Outcomes Assessment of the American Dental Education Association's Commission on Change and Innovation in Dental Education describes the current status of student outcomes assessment in U.S. dental education. This review is divided into six sections. The first summarizes the literature on assessment of dental students' performance. Section two discusses catalysts, with a focus on problem-based learning, for development of new assessment methods, while the third section presents several resources and guides that can be used to inform selection of assessment techniques for various domains of competence. The fourth section describes the methodology and results of a 2008 survey of current assessment practices in U.S. dental schools. In the fifth section, findings from this survey are discussed within the context of competency-based education, the educational model for the predoctoral curriculum endorsed by the American Dental Education Association and prescribed by the Commission on Dental Accreditation. The article concludes with a summary of assessments recommended as optimal strategies to measure three components of professional competence based on the triangulation model. The survey of assessment practices in predoctoral education was completed by 931 course directors, representing 45 percent of course directors nationwide, from fifty-three of the fifty-six U.S. dental schools. Survey findings indicate that five traditional mainstays of student performance evaluation—multiple-choice testing, lab practicals, daily grades, clinical competency exams, and procedural requirements—still comprise the primary assessment tools in dental education. The survey revealed that a group of newer assessment techniques, although frequently identified as best practices in the literature and commonly used in other areas of health professions education, are rarely employed in predoctoral dental education.

The authors are members of the Task Force on Student Outcomes Assessment of the American Dental Education Association's Commission on Change and Innovation in Dental Education. Dr. Albino is a Senior Consultant, Academy for Academic Leadership, as well as President Emerita, University of Colorado and Professor, Department of Oral and Craniofacial Biology, School of Dental Medicine and Department of Community and Behavioral Health, Colorado School of Public Health, both at the University of Colorado, Denver; Dr. Young is Dean, School of Dentistry, University of Oklahoma; Dr. Neumann is Senior Vice President, Education/Professional Affairs, American Dental Association; Dr. Kramer is Director, Department of Testing Services, American Dental Association; Dr. Andrieu is Associate Dean for Academic Affairs, School of Dentistry, Louisiana State University; Dr. Henson is Associate Dean for Academic Affairs, Medical School, University of Minnesota; Dr. Horn is with the Joint Commission on National Dental Examinations; and Prof. Hendricson is Assistant Dean for Educational and Faculty Development, Dental School, University of Texas Health Science Center at San Antonio. Direct correspondence and requests for reprints to Dr. Judith E.N. Albino, President Emerita and Professor, American Indian/Alaska Native Programs, School of Dental Medicine, Colorado School of Public Health, University of Colorado, Denver, Anschutz Medical Campus, Mail Stop F800, P.O. Box 6508, 13055 E. 17th Avenue, Aurora, CO 80045; 303-724-1467 phone; judith.albino@ucdenver.edu.

This article is one in a series of invited contributions by members of the dental and dental education community that have been commissioned by the American Dental Education Association's Commission on Change and Innovation in Dental Education (ADEA CCI) to address the environment surrounding dental education and affecting the need for, or process of, curricular change. This article was written at the request of the ADEA CCI but does not necessarily reflect the views of ADEA, the ADEA CCI, or individual members of the ADEA CCI. The perspectives communicated here are those of the authors.

Key words: dental education, dental students, competency, assessment, OSCE, triple jump exercise, critical appraisal, portfolios, competency-based education

Assessment represents a critical component of successful education in the skills, knowledge, affective processes, and professional values that define the competent practice of dentistry. In recent years, there have been reports in the dental education literature of pedagogical innovations such as problem-based or case-reinforced learning, patient simulations, web-based learning, service-learning, and other strategies designed to help students develop critical appraisal skills and gain an appreciation for the concepts of evidence-based oral health care. This movement toward a broader spectrum of teaching and learning methods in predoctoral dental education underscores the importance of utilizing appropriate assessment strategies that are consistent with the level of cognitive skills that can be developed with these new techniques. Virtually all commentaries and expert opinion on performance assessment in health professions education indicate that we must evaluate not only the recall and recognition of specific facts and the demonstration of technical skills, but also students' capacity to synthesize information within a given context and apply it in unique situations that require critical thinking and problem-solving.[1] Ultimately, the goal of assessment in health professions education is to determine students' capacity to integrate and implement the various domains of learning that collectively define competent practice, over an extended period of time, with day-to-day consistency, in a work environment that approximates the actual work setting where health care providers interact with patients.[2] Yet the literature on assessment methodologies for these purposes in dental education is relatively sparse.

Revisiting strategies employed to determine dental students' readiness to graduate and begin providing health care services to the public, or to progress to a higher level of training, is particularly critical in light of recent developments at the national level that are likely to have a dramatic effect on curriculum content and, accordingly, methods of assessment in the future. In April 2008, the American Dental Education Association (ADEA) House of Delegates approved an updated set of outcomes for predoctoral dental education, "Competencies for the New General Dentist," which define the domains of competence needed for entry-level general dentistry (see the Appendix).[3] (This document replaces the original set of predoctoral competencies approved in 1997 by ADEA.) The 2008 competencies provide a forward-looking outline of the components of general dentistry with increased emphasis on cultivating dental students' capacity for critical thinking, now the first domain in the updated document. The accreditation standards for predoctoral dental education also are undergoing a process of substantial revision, with parallel emphasis on promoting and measuring students' critical thinking capabilities and capacity for self-assessment. We hypothesize that, as the curricular implications of these revised competencies and educational standards are pondered at U.S. dental schools, there will be similar consideration of what these new directions mean for the appraisal of students' progression toward competence.

This review is divided into six sections. The first summarizes the literature on assessment of dental students' performance. Section two discusses catalysts, with a focus on problem-based learning, for development of new assessment methods, while the third section presents resources and guides that can be used to inform selection of assessment techniques for various domains of competence. The fourth section describes the methodology and results of a 2008 survey of current assessment practices in U.S. dental schools. In the fifth section, findings from this survey are discussed within the context of competency-based education, the educational model for predoctoral curriculum endorsed by ADEA and prescribed by the Commission on Dental Accreditation (CODA). The article concludes with a summary of assessments recommended as optimal strategies to measure three components of professional competence based on the triangulation model.

Literature on Assessment of Dental Students' Performance

Approximately 150 articles (not including editorials, commentaries, and brief case reports) over the past thirty years have addressed aspects of student assessment in dental school. This is a relatively small volume of literature, considering the number of dental schools worldwide. Roughly half of these articles are described below, with emphasis on the past ten to fifteen years.

Much of the literature on assessment in dental schools has focused on strategies to improve calibration among raters in preclinical laboratory courses and the clinic. Some of these articles also have addressed the technical design of rating scales used to grade students' performance on procedural tasks, including number of rating points, number of observers for clinical competence examinations, strategies for developing rating criteria, discussion of the level of detail that should be included in rating scales, and descriptions of processes for calculating students' evaluations including weighting systems but with substantial emphasis on calibration techniques to increase consistency among evaluators and making adjustments for "hawk" (hard) and "dove" (easy) raters.[4-12] These are important issues that directly influence the assessment responsibilities of clinical faculty members, but few articles have addressed the overall purposes of assessment in dental education and asked questions such as the following: what learner outcomes should be emphasized; what techniques can best measure these respective outcomes; are we evaluating acquisition of knowledge, skills, and behaviors that are meaningful for the contemporary practice of general dentistry; and do all the assessment data obtained throughout the predoctoral curriculum in classroom-based courses, labs, and clinics predict which students will be safe practitioners who add value to their communities—or do these data simply predict who can navigate the rigors of the dental school curriculum? These questions have been the subject of extensive consideration in other health professions,[13] but a similar dialogue has only begun to emerge within academic dentistry. Further, if "evaluations drive the curriculum and dictate students' study habits and priorities,"[14] what is the influence of these measurements on our students' intellectual development and attitudes about learning, and what is their influence on students' approaches to studying?

A substantial number of articles dating back to the 1960s have reported the results of studies that explored the correlation between prematriculation predictors and dental students' in-school academic performance; this has been a more substantial area of research than investigating methods for assessment of students after they matriculate.[15-24] Several studies have been conducted to explore the relationship between aspects of students' in-school academic record and National Board or licensure examination performance, with generally inconsistent results.[25-31] A small group of studies compared students' performance and clinical productivity when they function in clinical education systems that stress procurement of procedural requirements versus non-requirement-driven systems.[32-37] Several studies investigated students' impressions of assessment strategies employed by faculty with emphasis on issues of faculty consistency in clinical grading and the resulting effect on student attitudes and performance.[38-42] One investigator, David Chambers, conducted with his coauthors a series of studies to investigate approaches to measuring students' acquisition of clinical competence and other issues related to competency assessment.[43-46] Berrong et al. examined the relationship between daily grades—a mainstay of evaluation in the clinic, in which students receive a rating for each patient procedure, typically on a 0 (unacceptable) to 4 (excellent) scale—and performance on twenty-six clinical competency exams in which students work without instructor coaching.[47] These investigators found that the hundreds of daily grades that each senior student received in an academic year were poorly correlated with performance during competency exams in which students worked without instructor "rescue" unless the patient was in danger of irreversible damage. Berrong et al. concluded that daily grades were positively skewed: the average grade was in the 3.0 to 3.5 range, a solid "B," with minimal distinction between students at the high and low ends of the cumulative dental school grade point average (GPA). This study suggested that competency exams were a more reliable assessment of students' capacity to perform core skills than the traditional daily grade.

Licari and Knight, as well as Taleghani et al., described efforts by dental schools to design assessment systems for evaluating dental students' performance in ways that are consistent with the principles of competency-based education using objective structured clinical examinations (OSCEs), portfolios, and student self-assessment and emphasizing formative (nongraded) feedback.[48-50] Recently, Prihoda et al. described a technique to correct scores for student guessing on multiple-choice examinations administered in dental school.[51] Karl et al. compared dental student performance on computer-aided testing and traditional multiple-choice examinations.[52] These latter two articles are among a handful in the dental education literature over the past twenty-five years that have addressed issues and techniques related to multiple-choice testing. A few articles published in the 1970s and early 1980s addressed assessment with multiple-choice formats, but the literature has been limited since that time.[53-55]

Several authors have described the use of OSCEs and standardized patients (also known as patient-instructors or simulated patients) in dental education, and a couple of these publications reported the findings of research studies designed to assess the use of OSCEs as an evaluation tool.[56-65] Curtis et al. and

Dennehy et al. compared students' performance on OSCEs to traditional assessments.[62,64] Schoonheim-Klein et al. recently published an analysis of the reliability of a dental school OSCE and studied the number of stations needed for optimal reliability.[65]

Licari and Knight, Gadbury-Amyot et al., and Chambers have reported the use of portfolios for student assessment and discussed implementation of this technique.[48,66-68] There have been several reviews of the literature on uses of portfolios for assessment, including an excellent summary by Friedman Ben David et al.[69] Durham et al. reported use of a logbook approach for assessment of dental students' clinical competence.[70] A research team led by von Bergmann studied the relationship between problem-based learning process grades, using a triple jump assessment technique (a method to assess students' capacity to explore, appraise, and apply biomedical information to problems) and traditional content acquisition measurements (multiple-choice examinations).[71] Bondemark et al. studied dental students' use of a self-directed examination technique similar to the triple jump.[72]

Leisnert and Mattheos, Curtis et al., and Thammasitboon et al. reported the only studies we could identify on the effects of dental student self-assessment,[73-75] although the journal *Medical Teacher* has published two reviews of the literature on student self-assessment including a recent (2008) comprehensive summary by Colthart et al. in the Best Evidence in Medical Education (BEME) series published in that journal.[76,77] There have been numerous articles published in the dental education literature that describe applications of computer-aided learning (CAL), including a few that reported findings from studies investigating the influence of CAL on students' performance. The focus of most of these articles was on instruction or strategies for incorporation of CAL into the curriculum, rather than on assessment, which was often mentioned as a potential application. For this reason, we elected not to review that literature here.

In summary, our review of the available literature describing strategies for assessment of dental student performance, as well as the experiences of members of the Task Force at their own institutions, suggests that five methods have been the mainstays of dental student evaluation: multiple-choice exams, laboratory "practicals," completion of specified units (numbers) of procedural requirements, daily grades, and clinical "comps" (i.e., competency patients). The latter two involve faculty observation of students' interactions with patients and inspection of the process and outcomes of dental treatment to restore or replace tooth structure and function. Two of the purposes of the survey described below were to determine the accuracy of this perception about the predominance of the traditional data sources for student performance evaluation and to determine the extent to which a number of "new" assessment techniques, frequently described and/or employed in other areas of health professions education, are being used in predoctoral dental education. Of course, a principle mechanism for assessing dental students' progress toward graduation and certification of their readiness for graduation in the United States is the National Board Dental Examination (NBDE), Parts I and II. However, since this review focuses on assessment strategies implemented by dental schools, the NBDE will not be addressed in detail other than to acknowledge that all U.S. dental schools use Parts I and II as major indicators of students' progress.

Catalysts for New Assessment Methods in Dental Education

In dental education, alternative methods for assessment of student performance have tended to emerge as more innovative teaching methodologies have opened doors to new thinking about educational processes, including assessment. Certainly, one of the most important curricular innovations in dental education over the past forty years has been problem-based learning (PBL), in which students are engaged in working with others to structure solutions to contextualized problems and thus acquire biomedical knowledge in an inquiry-learning mode.[78] PBL is rarely employed as a primary curricular strategy in U.S. dental education, and thus the dental education literature reveals few efforts focused on assessment designed specifically for PBL.[79] Moreover, most reports evaluating PBL in both medicine[80] and dentistry[81] have relied on traditional methodologies for assessing student performance rather than evaluation techniques that are consistent with the inquiry-learning structure of PBL, which are designed to assess students' capacity for self-directed analysis and application of biomedical information.[82] In fact, some of the early criticisms of PBL were that there were no major changes in "standard performance indicators."[83] Such criticism ignored the probability that standard performance indicators such as multiple-choice tests may not measure the more sophisticated cognitive functions (application, synthesis, evaluation, critical appraisal) that PBL is intended to develop in students.

Fincham and Shuler's report on the adoption of problem-based learning in dental education[84] included a section on assessment in which they asserted the dual purposes of assessment in this context: 1) feedback for self-direction of learning and 2) assessment of abilities in the process. They pointed out that assessment methods chosen will influence what is learned and that in PBL those methods must measure "student achievement in the process of problem dissection, identification of learning objectives, and development of critical thinking skills," as well as, later on, "the application of these skills in problem-solving situations." They suggested that a variety of approaches to assessment are useful for PBL, including faculty, self-, and peer/subjective assessments, problem-solving exercises, case-based multiple-choice tests that are written to assess students' comprehension of the association between symptoms and pathophysiology, OSCEs, clinical competency assessments, and the triple jump exercise, which requires self-directed learning skills. The multimethod approach advocated by Fincham and Shuler may not be employed in many programs using PBL, but the message that assessment must be an integral part of the educational experience is now being recognized by dental educators.[85]

Resources and Guides to Inform Selection of Assessment Techniques

Decisions regarding which assessment methods to use for various purposes in dental education can be difficult in an educational environment that values and sustains traditions, operates largely in isolation from other health professions educational programs, and has not meaningfully altered teaching methods or fundamental curriculum structure for fifty years.[86-88] New techniques are emerging, many borrowed from the other health professions, though most are largely untried in dental schools by "in the trenches" faculty. Moving to alternative techniques and away from the seemingly tried-and-true comfort zone of traditional methods requires confidence that appropriate performance measurements are being

selected. Of course, the optimal assessment plan is to use the right technique for the right reasons, at the right time, and with the right group of students in order to make the right decisions about the right competencies that the student will need to function independently after graduation from dental school. Fortunately, several guides and resources exist to help faculty members make decisions about assessment methods. In a valuable review published in 1997, Chambers and Glassman described assessment techniques available to measure dental students' attainment of competence and summarized the strengths and weaknesses of these techniques.[89] The Accreditation Council for Graduate Medical Education (ACGME) produced a toolkit that recommends strategies for measuring attainment of professional competence. This toolkit is available at the ACGME website at www.acgme.org/Outcome/assess/Toolbox.pdf. Another excellent resource is the All Ireland Society for Higher Education (AISHE), which periodically publishes Case Studies of Good Practices of Assessment of Student Learning in Higher Education. The AISHE website is at www.aishe.org.

The journal *Medical Teacher* has published valuable reviews of the evidence pertaining to many aspects of health professions education in its AMEE (Association for Medical Education in Europe) series of Advancing Medical Education Guides. Recommended resources from this series include AMEE Guides No. 18, 25, and 31, which address, respectively, standard setting for student evaluation, assessment of learning outcomes for the competent and reflective physician, and workplace-based assessments.[90-92]

The Task Force on Student Outcomes Assessment of the ADEA CCI has prepared a comprehensive assessment toolkit, specifically geared to dental education, which reviews the capacity of sixteen assessment methods to measure student attainment of the new ADEA predoctoral competencies.[3] This toolkit, which was developed by Dr. Gene Kramer of the American Dental Association, will appear in the January 2009 issue of the *Journal of Dental Education*.[93] The ADEA CCI Dental Assessment Toolkit highlights the strengths and weaknesses of each technique and provides key references.

The hierarchy of cognitive skills and levels of intellectual sophistication that can be assessed is described in Figure 1, which displays Benjamin Bloom's cognitive taxonomy that has guided test developers in all areas of education since the 1950s.[94] Bloom's taxonomy can help faculty members in their efforts to plan learning experiences to help dental students achieve desired outcomes and to plan assessments that sample a range of cognitive capacities. The right column in Figure 1 provides illustrative examples of assessment tasks that students can be asked to perform at each cognitive level.

We developed Figure 2 to summarize recommendations derived from a number of reviews of performance appraisal strategies that are appropriate to assess acquisition of competencies common to many health care professions including dentistry.[1,89,91,93,95-100] The left column of Figure 2 lists ten domains of competence identified by virtually all health professions as core components of professional functioning. Seven techniques commonly described in the literature on competency assessment in the health professions ap-

Level of Cognitive Function	Student's Mental Task	Examples of Assessment Tasks
Recall (recognize)	Label a structure. Recognize a feature on a slide. Select a best response from a list.	**Identify, by labeling,** the temporal and infratemporal fossae. **From a list of options, identify** the primary cause of Wilson's disease.
Comprehension (short answer essay response or verbal response on an oral exam)	Explain etiology. Describe manifestations and characteristics.	**Explain** the pathophysiology of . . . **Describe** the symptoms of . . .
Application (solve problems)	Use information to analyze and solve problems.	**Identify** the cause of this patient's pain. **Write** a treatment plan for a patient with these symptoms and examination findings.
Analysis	Compare and contrast concepts, models, or techniques. Discern relationships between phenomena or events. Interpret information.	**Compare** the merits of approaches to providing care for this patient. **Analyze** which of the factors in this case scenario may have been related to each other and contributed to the outcome. **What are the implications** of this combination of lab findings for the patient's prognosis?
Synthesis (planning)	Develop a new plan. Identify alternative actions or responses to a situation.	**Create** a plan to remove barriers to implementation of . . . **Propose** an alternative plan for . . .
Evaluation	Judge. Assess.	**Evaluate** effectiveness of the patient's treatment. **Judge** the quality of care provided.

Source: Bloom BS, Englehart MD, Furst EJ, Hill WH, Krathwohl DR. Taxonomy of educational objectives. Handbook 1: cognitive domain. New York: Longmans, 1956.

Figure 1. Levels of learning and assessment described in Bloom's cognitive taxonomy

pear as column heads: multiple-choice tests; essays; oral (verbal) examinations; ratings based on direct observation of specific student interactions with patients; longitudinal faculty evaluations of students' overall performance across many domains of competence over an extended period of time (i.e., not based on a single encounter with a patient but on numerous encounters over several months); retrospective record review (often called chart-stimulated evaluation); and OSCEs (discussed in detail below) designed to assess students' performance in a variety of skills during one exam in which students rotate among a series of stations.[101] In medical education, variations of OSCEs are often referred to as CPEX (Clinical Performance Exam), CPX, or mini-CPX for an abbreviated version of this assessment involving an observed student interaction with a single patient in which all aspects of performance are comprehensively assessed.

The ratings shown in Figure 2 reinforce that faculty observations of students' performance during actual interactions with patients—both single encounters with one specific patient and long-term across many patient encounters—are most valued by experts in performance measurement. Both observation of single patient encounters and longitudinal assessments that reflect a student's all-around performance over two to three months can be used to measure most of the ten domains. Longitudinal evaluation across many patients may be a better data source for professional demeanor, personal attributes, and capacity to use clinic resources appropriately than are available in single encounter evaluations, which might capture "best day" or "worst day" snapshots of students that are not representative. However, single encounter assessments may be better for monitoring specific skills such as interviewing and examining patients and performing technical procedures that can be rated against criteria on checklists. In contrast to faculty observation, testing via multiple-choice questions is limited to three of the ten domains as an optimal method. Essays in which students write answers to questions with their own words in an open-ended format are considered to be a better assessment method for measuring comprehension of biomedical knowledge. On essays, for example, students can be asked to explain mechanisms and interactions that produce physiological effects or to describe how and why certain abnormalities occur. Essays are also considered optimal for problem assessment and ordering/interpreting diagnostic tests because students can be asked to provide an explanation for decisions or compare and contrast options.

Multiple-choice question (MCQ) testing is a valuable resource for certifying students' capacity to remember core principles and facts or to demonstrate recognition of fundamental associations and relationships. Such testing assesses only a limited range of the overall cognitive taxonomy depicted in Figure 1, however, and is not optimal to assess many of the competency domains considered critical for adequate professional performance. The MCQ format can be used to assess higher-level cognitive processes when case-based formats are used so that students must identify key data from a patient scenario and interpret these data in order to respond to questions written at the application level of Bloom's taxonomy.[94] For example, questions based on case scenarios can be designed to request identification of pathophysiological mechanisms that account for patient symptoms, select appropriate diagnostic tests to confirm assessments, and recognize the most suitable treatment approach from a list of options.[82,102] The National Board Dental Examination (NBDE) has adroitly incorporated case-based questions, also known as testlets or case-cluster items (in which several questions are linked to a case scenario), to stimulate students to respond at the "application" level. The Dental Assessment Toolkit developed as part of this study provides a description and examples of this assessment format.[93] When skillfully executed to assess at cognitive levels beyond sheer rote memorization, multiple-choice and other written examination formats such as short-answer essays can play a critical role in educational assessment.

The NBDE uses the multiple-choice question format with variations. The underlying content selection process for the Part I and Part II exams has become increasingly sophisticated over the past decade. The Joint Commission on National Dental Examinations has taken a thoughtful and proactive approach to populating test construction committees to obtain greater input from general dentists and, accordingly, to focus examination topics on knowledge pertinent to contemporary general dentistry.[103,104]

For clinical skills, dental educators primarily use observation with a focus on the products of technical procedures. The practice of using completion of a specified number of clinical procedures as a proxy for competence has been criticized in recent years. Dental students have identified "requirement-chasing" as a major source of anxiety and have expressed concerns about the ethical implications of using patients as educational tools.[39,42] In the traditional model of clinical education, dental stu-

| | | | | Single encounter direct observation by faculty[a] | Longitudinal assessment by faculty across many domains[b] | Record review/ chart-stimulated review[c] | |
Domains	MCQ	Essay	Oral (verbal) exam				Standardized examinations (OSCE/CPEX)
Biomedical knowledge (recall and recognition level of cognition)	●	◇	◇				◇
Problem assessment	◇ Case-based MCQ	●	●	◇	◇	●	◇
Professional behavior			◇	◇	●		◇
Personal qualities				◇	●		◇
Concern for patient's well-being				●	◇	◇	◇
Patient examination skills				●	◇		●
Patient interviewing and communication skills				●	◇		●
Ordering/interpreting diagnostic (lab) tests	◇	●	●	◇	◇	◇	●
Performing technical procedures				●	◇		● Non-invasive and reversible
Resource use and functioning within health care system					●	◇	

● Recommended
◇ Good, but may have limitations
Blank Not considered optimal

[a]Single encounter direct observation: faculty member observes and assesses student's interaction with and treatment of one patient, i.e., a single clinic appointment with one patient.

[b]Longitudinal assessment: comprehensive (summary) assessment of many aspects of performance and across several competency domains over an extended period (8–12 weeks) of observation of a student's performance by faculty members who have daily interactions with the student. Sometimes this type of assessment is called "global" or "comprehensive" evaluation to denote the focus on students' overall performance versus focus on a single patient encounter or a single procedure.

[c]Record review: faculty and students retrospectively review a student's clinical work as evidenced in the charts of patients who received treatment by that student. Record review is often called "chart-stimulated review" because the format gives faculty members an opportunity to ask students to explain and self-assess their diagnostic and treatment decisions and thus measure the students' 1) understanding of clinical principles and 2) capacity to articulate reasonable rationales for patient treatment decisions.

Figure 2. What domains of competence can be evaluated with assessment methods commonly used in health professions education?

dents are required to complete a designated number of repetitions of specified dental procedures within calendar deadlines as evidence of clinical competence (various types of amalgam, gold, and composite restorations, crowns, dentures, root canals, extractions, quadrants of periodontal scaling, etc.). In the requirement system, students' behavior in the clinic often depends on finding patients who have oral health problems that provide opportunities to perform required repetitions of the designated procedures. Some dental educators have expressed concern that overreliance on numerical requirements creates an environment in which students are encouraged to place their own training needs ahead of the patient's health needs (e.g., talking patients into procedures the student needs to perform but which the patient may not need).[87] Several studies have demonstrated that dental students operating without requirements are equally or more productive than their peers in requirement-driven systems, receive an equally diverse clinical experience, perform as well or better on indices of clinical performance, and report lower levels of stress.[32-37] Although dental faculty appeared to be moving away from the requirement system in the 1990s, anecdotal evidence and student reports suggest that this method for determining clinical competency is making a comeback.[42] One of the goals of the ADEA CCI survey of assessment practices described below was to determine the extent to which dental schools are still relying on "competency by numbers." We were also interested in the extent to which clinical faculty members continue to rely on the process of assigning one or more grades for each patient treated by a student, often at the primary faculty check-off or signature points (indicating permission to proceed), leading to the hundreds of "daily grades" that historically have been added up and averaged to provide an important data source for students' clinical evaluation.

2008 Survey of Assessment Practices in U.S. Dental Schools

Because of the limited literature on student performance measurement that is unique to predoctoral dental education, the Task Force decided that a survey of assessment practices currently being implemented within dental school curricula could provide needed additional information. The majority of the research on assessment of professional competence has occurred in other areas of health professions education; consequently, it was our aim to determine the perceptions and activities of dental school faculty with regard to student assessment strategies unique to dentistry.

Survey Methodology

The ADEA CCI online survey was conducted in the spring semester of 2008, with participation by fifty-three of fifty-six U.S. dental schools (93 percent). Course directors were asked to report how their students' competence is assessed. Nearly 1,000 faculty members responded, which comprises approximately 45 percent of U.S. dental school course directors and represents the most extensive study of dental school assessment strategies to date.

Members of the Task Force developed the initial version of the survey in the fall of 2007. The survey had three objectives. The first and primary objective was to determine what assessment strategies dental school course directors use to measure their students' progress within each of the six domains of general dentistry competence identified in the 2008 ADEA "Competencies for the New General Dentist."[3] (The domains and associated competencies appear in the Appendix.) The second objective was to determine how dental schools assess students' overall readiness for graduation and entry into unsupervised dental practice. The third objective was to determine faculty members' perceptions of several assessment issues that are unique to predoctoral dental education. The twenty-one-item online questionnaire was pilot-tested in December 2007 by eighty-nine faculty members at three U.S. dental schools who completed the survey and provided recommendations for modifications; changes suggested in wording and other clarifications were incorporated into the final survey instrument. To assess test-retest reliability of the instrument, thirty-three faculty members at one U.S. dental school also completed the survey twice at a ten-day interval. Reliability for responses for each of the six competency domains ranged from 0.78 to 0.93, and reliability for responses to the questions addressing general assessment issues was 0.84—more than acceptable levels of reliability. The survey link was emailed to dental school deans for distribution to course directors on March 17, 2008, and again on April 7. Nonresponding schools received a third email on April 21. Between May 5 and 12, personal follow-up contacts were made with the remaining nonrespondents.

Five questions in the survey elicited information about respondents' demographics. The next seven questions asked respondents to identify assessment methods their school used for the ADEA competencies from among seventeen options. Eight questions asked for information about each school's overall student assessment processes including final determination of readiness for graduation and subsequent entry into unsupervised practice. The final question was an open-ended invitation to submit written comments pertaining to dental student assessment strategies.

For the questions designed to elicit primary assessment techniques linked to each competency domain, respondents were given the name of each of the six domains listed in the "Competencies for the New General Dentist" and, for each domain, the full text of the specific competencies comprising that domain. Respondents then were asked, "Which of the methods listed below are the *most important* and *most frequently used sources of information* to assess students' competence in this domain?" Nineteen response options followed; seventeen of these options were assessment strategies shown in Figure 3. Respondents were asked to indicate all assessment techniques they use to measure students' attainment of competence, but were encouraged to designate only those methods that they routinely use. In addition to selecting one or more of the seventeen assessment techniques, respondents could also indicate that the competency is not addressed in their courses or that the competency domain is included in the curriculum but students' learning is not formally assessed.

The seventeen assessment strategies included in the survey were identified from a review of the literature, including available assessment toolkits. However, a primary source for designation of the assessments that comprised the response options was Miller's Pyramid of Professional Competence, which appears in Figure 4.[96] Miller's four-layer categorization of levels of knowing and associated assessments is probably the best-known hierarchy for describing the learning and measurement continuum in health

Assessment Method	Features Provided to Survey Respondents
Context-Free Multiple-Choice Questions (MCQ)	One-best-response questions that are not linked to a clinical context designed to assess recognition or recall of specific pieces of information, i.e., not linked to a patient care situation.
Case-Based Multiple-Choice Questions (MCQ)	Multiple-choice questions linked to scenarios describing patients' oral health and/or medical problems.
Essay	Open-ended assessment format whereby students respond in writing, with or without structural guidance, to assess their capacity to apply information to biomedical problems or to the assessment and resolution of patients' health problems.
Oral Examination	Format requiring students to respond verbally to instructors' questions, but used for similar purposes as the written essay.
Research Report and Presentation	Students investigate an assigned topic/question and prepare a report or presentation, which is graded for quality and thoroughness.
Critical Appraisal Task (also known as Critically Appraised Topic Summary or CATS)	Evidence-based format requiring generation of a research question and a review of the available literature, with critical appraisal of evidence presented in a written summary.
Computer-Based Simulation	Appraisal of students' performance on web-based simulations depicting patient care scenarios, usually involving tasks such as assessment, diagnosis, and treatment planning.

(continued)

Figure 3. Seventeen assessment strategies included in the 2008 survey of assessment practices in U.S. dental schools

Figure 3. Seventeen assessment strategies included in the 2008 survey of assessment practices in U.S. dental schools (continued)

Laboratory Exercise (Practical) Direct evaluation of students' performance of technical/procedural skills in preclinical laboratory courses and appraisal of the products of their work.

Chart-Stimulated Evaluation Review of patient care using charts (medical/dental records) as the basis for instructors' questions intended to explore students' capacity to explain rationales for treatment decisions, show comprehension of key concepts, and stimulate students' self-assessment and reflection.

Objective Structured Clinical Examination (OSCE) Students rotate from one station to another to perform specified tasks under time restrictions, such as interpreting radiographs, assembling equipment, interviewing patients, writing an assessment, conducting a head and neck examination, and measuring vital signs.

Triple Jump Exercise (TJE) In the clinical variation of the TJE included on this survey, students are observed as they interview and examine a patient (first jump); then, they write an assessment and propose a treatment plan with justifying rationale (second jump); and, finally, they explain the assessment and treatment plan and respond to faculty questions (third jump). Students receive component scores of each jump and overall scores. (Note: An alternative TJE version, often used in the preclinical years and described in the section below on CBE, was not included in this survey.)

Longitudinal Evaluation (over an extended period of time) Also called "comprehensive," "global," or "summary" evaluations, this type of assessment considers student performance in all relevant dimensions and disciplines over an extended period of time to allow assessment of reproducibility and consistency of performance, typically eight to twelve weeks in duration. Longitudinal evaluations include appraisal of students' ability to integrate knowledge and skills into relatively seamless performance that is equivalent across various disciplines that comprise a profession.

Daily Evaluation Students' performance with each patient and/or each procedure is evaluated by the supervising instructor, resulting in a "daily grade." This is similar to the single encounter evaluation shown in Figure 2.

Student Self-Assessment Critical assessment of one's own performance and reflection on ways to enhance subsequent performance.

Portfolio-Driven Assessment Students present their work over time through a variety of methods, including photographic documentation, patient charts, reports and projects, posters and abstracts, copies of evaluations, and self-comment and reflection on the learning process. Portfolios are periodically reviewed to determine extent of progress toward specified competencies.

Unit Requirements Number of procedural units performed by students or number of points awarded for completion of procedures that are used as indicators of competence.

Clinical Competency Examination Students perform designated tasks and procedures on a patient in the clinic without instructor assistance. The process of care and the products (e.g., in-mouth procedures such as an amalgam restoration) are assessed by faculty observers typically guided by a rating scale.

professions education and provides the conceptual basis for many of the prominent reviews of assessment strategies. As discussed by Wass et al., much of the research in performance assessment in the health professions over the past twenty years has been directed at determining optimal strategies to assess students' capacities at each of the four levels of this hierarchy.[98]

The base level of competence in the pyramid is "knows"—the straight factual recall or recognition of information without reference to a patient care context, typically measured by multiple-choice questions. At the subsequent "knows how" level, students are expected to demonstrate the ability to apply biomedical information to the analysis and resolution of problems presented in written cases and simulations based on real-life patient care situations (i.e., during the preclinical phase of training) and to use their accumulated knowledge to make the decisions requested in these cases/simulations. At the "knows how" level, students should also be able to explain, in their own words, how basic pathophysiological mechanisms work and how health abnormalities occur. Essays, MCQs based on scenarios, oral evaluations (questions and answers between instructor and students), and more sophisticated techniques such as the triple-jump exercise (a problem-solving simulation) are appropriate assessment tools. At the "shows how" level, students are expected to demonstrate the capacity to apply patient care skills in laboratories and simulations that approximate clinical facilities and the dynamics of provider-patient interactions. As shown in Figure 4, at this stage, more sophisticated assessment methods are used that place students in reasonably high-fidelity simulations of health care providers' actual working conditions to determine if students can apply knowledge and skills under controlled, well-supervised conditions. At the ultimate "does" level, the student is expected to execute the core tasks and responsibilities of a health care provider in "real" or very realistic working conditions with limited instructor support over an extended period of time; the aim is to determine whether the student has mastered the fundamental competencies necessary for unsupervised practice and can reproduce these skills with a consistent level of performance over several weeks to several months. Assessment techniques at this level emphasize direct observation of performance and review of representative work samples by various techniques, including the portfolio and clinical competency examinations in a variety of formats.

The Task Force used Miller's conceptualization of the Pyramid of Professional Competence to identify assessment techniques that were unique to dental education yet consistent with Miller's definitions of levels and associated measurement strategies. We dis-

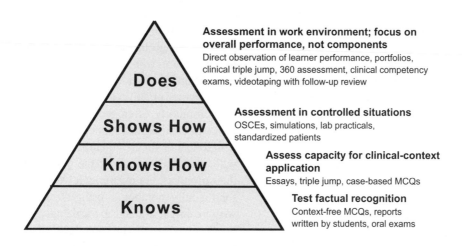

Figure 4. Miller's Pyramid of Professional Competence with examples of assessment techniques used in medical education

Source: Reproduced with permission from Miller GE. Assessment of clinical skills/competence/performance. Acad Med 1990;9:63–7.

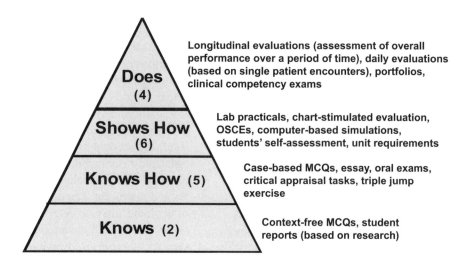

Figure 5. Distribution of seventeen assessment methods in the 2008 survey of assessment practices in U.S. dental schools among Miller's Pyramid of Professional Competence levels

tributed these techniques among Miller's hierarchical categories of knowing and doing as shown in Figure 5 to encourage respondents to consider the entire spectrum of learning as students progress toward competence. Four techniques were designated for the "does" level; six for the "shows how" level; five for the "knows how" level; and two for "knows."

To help determine the extent to which the traditional assessment techniques (MCQs, lab practicals, clinical competency exams, daily grades, and procedural unit requirements) persist as mainstays of student evaluation in relation to other potential techniques, we included several assessment strategies that are being incorporated as evaluation methods into the other health professions and are often advocated in the literature as best practices: the triple jump exercise, critical appraisal tasks (CATs), OSCEs, portfolios, chart-stimulated evaluations, and global assessment (long-term/longitudinal assessment across many components of competence).

Results of the Survey

A total of 1,025 responses from faculty members were obtained, with 931 deemed usable by virtue of completeness and acceptability of response format. Most of the responses (90 percent) were from course directors (N=841), with an additional forty-nine responses (5 percent) from academic affairs deans, all but three of whom indicated that they also serve as

course directors, and forty-one (4 percent) that were unidentifiable with respect to positions. Table 1 shows the distribution of respondents by discipline.

The dental school curriculum with a clinical training phase that is largely conducted at a school-operated clinic located within the dental school facility (unlike clinical training in other health professions) places dental school course directors in a unique position to provide perspectives about the longitudinal assessment of students' movement toward competence. In most of the other health professions, one group of faculty provide the biomedical foundations and theoretical concepts for professional practice and then another group of individuals, who are primarily practitioners in health care facilities in the community, often geographically distant, supervise students' clinical education. In contrast, many dental school faculty members are able to interact with students throughout the curriculum and track their progress. For example, it would not be unusual for a faculty member in restorative dentistry to work with freshman students in the dental anatomy course, present lectures in an entry-level operative course later in the first year or in biomaterials, teach and assess students in sophomore operative laboratory courses, and then supervise students and provide evaluations in the clinic during their junior and senior years. This is a major strength of dental education and, for purposes of this survey, allowed respondents

Table 1. Discipline/departmental affiliation of 931 respondents to the 2008 survey of assessment practices in U.S. dental schools

Discipline/Departmental Affiliation of Respondents	N	Percentage
Restorative Dentistry	158	17%
Basic Science	126	14%
Prosthodontics	80	9%
General Dentistry	77	9%
Periodontics	58	6%
Community Dentistry/Public Health	55	6%
Endodontics	54	6%
Oral Medicine/Oral Pathology	49	5%
Academic Affairs Deans	49	5%
Oral and Maxillofacial Surgery	44	5%
Diagnosis/Radiology	44	5%
Pediatric Dentistry	42	4%
Orthodontics	33	3%
Behavioral Science	31	3%
Other Disciplines	31	3%

Note: Percentages do not total 100% because of rounding.

to consider the entire pathway toward competence in many of the domains.

Almost 80 percent of the roughly 100 unusable responses were from respondents who identified themselves as basic scientists. Most of these individuals started the survey but submitted their response without selecting assessment methods for most of the competency domains. As noted subsequently in the summary of write-in comments, it appears that many of the basic science faculty perceived they did not have sufficient insight into the domains and/or did not see their component of the curriculum (the basic sciences) in these competencies and thus were reluctant to respond.

Overall, the respondents reported a total of 14,667 assessment techniques across all six domains of competency and across all seventeen evaluation methods. The average number of selected assessment methods for all six domains combined was sixteen items per respondent; thus, most of the respondents designated one to three assessment methods for each competency. Table 2 shows the overall distribution of the nearly 15,000 assessment reports from these respondents. Somewhat surprisingly to the Task Force, Critical Thinking (Domain 1) was evaluated the most frequently, with 90 percent of the respondents reporting use of various techniques to attempt appraisal of a student's capacity for critical thinking. The respondents also reported the most variety in assessment techniques for the domain of Critical Thinking, averaging nearly four different methods per respondent, suggesting some degree of experimentation in

efforts to measure students' capabilities in this area. Practice Management and Informatics, on the other hand, was the least evaluated, with only 46 percent of respondents reporting that assessment is attempted for this domain of competency. Notably, only 62 percent of course directors reported that they assess Professionalism, an area in which dental schools have experienced some well-publicized breaches in academic integrity over the past several years.

Table 3 shows the overall reported use of the seventeen assessment methods, in order of reported use from highest to lowest, across all domains of competency. Approximately 1 percent (n=126) of the 14,667 reports of assessment techniques could not be classified into one of the seventeen categories and thus are indicated as "Other" in Table 3. Two percent of the responses were "have this competency, but do not assess students' attainment at the present time." For those data representing course directors' reports of assessment strategies across all competency domains, testing by multiple-choice questions (MCQs) was far and away the most commonly used technique; 4,186 of the 14,667 (28 percent) total responses were for MCQs.

Overall, the traditional assessments in dental education (MCQs, clinical competency exams, laboratory practicals, daily grades, and procedural unit requirements) comprised 62 percent. However, only 3 percent of the respondents designated procedural requirements as an assessment technique; this was unexpected and also inconsistent with other survey data. Six new competency assessments, advocated

Table 2. Distribution of 931 U.S. dental school course directors' reports of assessment strategies among domains of the 2008 ADEA "Competencies for the New General Dentist"

ADEA Competency Domain	Total Reports of Assessment Methods	Percentage of Total Reports	Percentage of Respondents who Attempted Assessment
1. Critical Thinking	2,813	19%	90%
2. Professionalism	1,830	12%	62%
3. Communication and Interpersonal Skills	1,702	12%	59%
4. Health Promotion	1,827	12%	61%
5. Practice Management and Informatics	1,536	10%	46%
6a. Assessment, Diagnosis, and Treatment Planning	2,461	17%	79%
6b. Establishment and Maintenance of Oral Health	2,498	17%	78%

in the literature and often included in best practice reports (OSCE, CAT, portfolio, triple jump exercise, chart-stimulated evaluation, and longitudinal/global evaluation) comprised 13 percent of the respondents' reports.

Reviews of assessment techniques used for each of the domains were consistent with patterns evident in the overall data for all areas of competence. For Domain 1, Critical Thinking, the most frequently used methods were case-based and context-free MCQ (45 percent combined), and the least frequently used were chart-stimulated evaluations (4 percent), portfolios (3 percent), and triple jump (3 percent). For Domain

2, Professionalism, the most frequently used methods were daily evaluations (15 percent), case-based MCQs (14 percent), and clinical competency exams (13 percent), while portfolios (2 percent) and triple jump (1 percent) were the least used. For Domain 3, Communication and Interpersonal Skills, the most frequently used methods were daily evaluations (13 percent) and clinical competency exams (11 percent), with portfolios (2 percent) and triple jump (1 percent) used the least. For Domain 4, Health Promotion, case-based and context-free MCQs (35 percent combined) were the most frequently used, while computer simulations, chart-stimulated evaluations,

Table 3. Reported use of seventeen assessment methods by 931 U.S. dental school course directors to measure students' performance for the 2008 ADEA "Competencies for the New General Dentist"

Assessment Method	Reports	Percentage
Case-based MCQ	2,375	16%
Context-free MCQ	1,811	12%
Daily evaluation in clinic	1,758	12%
Clinical competency examination	1,628	11%
Technical skill evaluation in labs (practical)	1,166	8%
Student self-assessment	1,021	7%
Essay	559	4%
Oral (verbal) exam	557	4%
Longitudinal evaluation in clinic	537	4%
Research project and report	511	3%
Procedural unit requirements	509	3%
Computer-based simulation	439	3%
OSCE	431	3%
Have competency, but no assessment method	339	2%
Critical appraisal task (CAT)	332	2%
Chart-stimulated evaluation	291	2%
Portfolio	148	1%
Triple jump	129	1%
Other assessment methods	126	1%
Total	14,667	

Note: Percentages do not total 100% because of rounding.

and research reports (each at 3 percent), portfolios (2 percent), and triple jump (1 percent) were the least frequently used. For Domain 5, Practice Management and Informatics, the most frequently used methods were case-based and context-free MCQs, while the least frequently used were portfolios (2 percent) and triple jump (1 percent). For Domain 6a, Patient Care: Assessment, Diagnosis, and Treatment Planning, the most frequently used methods were case-based and context-free MCQs (48 percent combined), and portfolios and triple jump (2 percent each) were the least used. For Domain 6b, Patient Care: Establishment and Maintenance of Oral Health, case-based and context-free MCQs (46 percent combined) represented the most frequently used assessment method, followed by clinical competency exams (18 percent). The least used assessment methods for this domain were OSCEs and critical appraisal tasks at 4 percent each, portfolios (3 percent), and triple jump (2 percent).

Survey respondents were asked to answer a series of questions related to the overall processes by which their dental school determines the readiness of students for graduation and for entry into professional practice in the community. Responses to these questions related to overall, schoolwide assessment strategies suggest that some dental schools have begun to change their approaches to evaluating student performance and practice readiness, but many aspects of the tried and true prevail. The number of respondents indicated in the table does not equal 931 for the remaining survey items, since some course directors and/or academic affairs deans elected not to answer certain questions.

Table 4 shows responses to the question "How does your school make a comprehensive, overall assessment of students' readiness for graduation/ entry to practice?" The majority of respondents (67 percent) responded that their school employs a check-off approach whereby a student is certified as ready to graduate if he or she has passed all courses, completed all requirements and rotations, passed all comprehensive exams, completed and submitted all assignments, met the expectations of each department, and fulfilled financial obligations. Notably, 15 percent of the respondents indicated that they did not have sufficient information to answer this question.

On the question "Is your competency assessment process 'requirement-driven'?," 29 percent reported that their competency assessment process is, for the most part, "requirement-driven," and 43 percent indicated that "it's a mixture; in some departments 'yes,' and 'no' in other departments." Only 21 percent of the course directors responded, "No; competency assessment is not requirement-driven in any area." Seven percent of the respondents indicated that they did not have sufficient information to answer this question. As a crosscheck for this question, we analyzed the responses of the associate deans for academic affairs (ADAAs) who participated in this study. Approximately 73 percent of the ADAAs indicated that their competency assessment process is mostly driven by requirements or "a mixture," which is similar to the response pattern of the course directors. Responses to this question about the role of procedural requirements in the student assessment process are inconsistent with the data reported in Table 3; it could be speculated that respondents interpreted the meaning of "requirement-driven" in this particular question differently than the Task Force intended—for example, construing "requirements" to mean all expectations stipulated by courses, not just counting procedural units completed in the clinic.

Table 5 presents responses for the question "Are students assigned to clinical group practices

Table 4. Responses of 923 U.S. dental school course directors to the question "How does your school make a comprehensive, overall assessment of students' readiness for graduation/entry to practice?"

Response	Percentage
Pass all courses, complete all requirements, complete all rotations, pass all comprehensive exams, meet all expectations of individual departments, pay all bills.	67%
Complete senior year satisfactorily in group practice with a consistent core of faculty who observe student on a daily basis for an extended period of time (i.e., an in-school internship).	7%
Seniors must pass a series of competency exams that function as gatekeeper assessments (i.e., must pass in order to graduate).	7%
Departments certify students are competent in their disciplines.	4%
Do not have sufficient information to answer.	15%

and when during the curriculum?" Typically, a group practice in the dental school clinic represents an organizational structure in which a relatively small group of five to eight faculty members, often multidisciplinary but generally coordinated by a general dentist, work with a group of approximately twenty-five to thirty junior and/or senior students over an extended period of time (e.g., all year). The group structure provides some collective functions and support for both students and faculty, including screening and designation of patient families for the group, patient triage so students handle cases appropriate to their training level, case conferences and other opportunities for students and faculty to interact in small groups, and collective assessment of students' progress by the group faculty. Because of the high percentage of "don't know" answers by the course directors (20 percent), responses from the ADAAs are also shown for comparison based on the assumption that the academic deans may have a better understanding of the organizational structure of clinical education than individual faculty members. Indeed, there were differences between the responses of the course directors and the ADAAs for this question as shown in Table 5. For example, 33 percent of the ADAAs reported that their schools had clinical group practices during all four years of the curriculum, while only 12 percent of the course directors selected this option. However, 38 percent of both respondent groups reported that their school had group practices that included some combination of sophomore, junior, and senior students.

Table 6 shows the responses of the course directors and ADAAs to the question "Does your school employ gateway competency exams that students must pass to advance from year to year or to graduate?" Gateway exams are another frequently advocated assessment strategy,[1,99,100] typically designed to measure students' capacity to perform core skills prior to being certified to move ahead to a subsequent level in the curriculum or, in some cases, before being certified for graduation. Gateways are often conducted in an OSCE format. A majority of the ADAAs (57 percent) reported that their school did not use high-stakes gateway exams, although 22 percent of both the academic deans and course directors reported such use at the end of several years. A high percentage of course directors (43 percent) responded that they did not have sufficient information to answer this question.

Table 7 presents the responses of course directors and ADAAs to the question "How is your mock

Table 5. Responses of 853 U.S. dental school course directors and 48 associate deans for academic affairs (ADAAs) to the question "Are students assigned to clinical group practices and when?"

	Course Directors	ADAAs
Yes; all four years	12%	33%
Yes; sophomore, junior, and senior years	13%	19%
Yes; junior and senior years only	25%	19%
Yes; junior year only	1%	0
Yes; senior year only	8%	3%
No; don't have group practices	21%	26%
Do not have sufficient information to answer	20%	0

Table 6. Responses of 861 U.S. dental school course directors and 47 associate deans for academic affairs (ADAAs) to the question "Does your school employ gateway competency exams that students must pass to advance from year to year or to graduate?"

	Course Directors	ADAAs
Yes; end of freshman year	0	0
Yes; end of sophomore year	6%	11%
Yes; end of junior year	4%	7%
Yes; end of several years	22%	22%
No gateway exams for any year	25%	57%
Do not have sufficient information to answer	43%	3%

board used for student assessment?" Following a pattern evident in other questions about schoolwide assessment methods, a high percentage of the course directors (36 percent) indicated they did not have sufficient information to answer this question. Nearly 60 percent of the ADAAs indicated that senior students must pass the mock board to graduate. ADAAs at one-third of the responding schools reported that their mock board is either mandatory or voluntary but not formally evaluated.

The final forced-choice survey item asked respondents to answer this question: "What is your level of confidence that your school makes accurate decisions about students' readiness to function as beginning general dentists after graduation?" All of the ADAAs responded, "I have high confidence" (70 percent) or "I am somewhat confident" (30 percent), while 85 percent of the course directors selected high confidence (44 percent) or somewhat confident (41 percent). Only 5 percent of the course directors indicated they had low confidence or were not con-

Table 7. Responses of 816 U.S. dental school course directors and 46 associate deans for academic affairs (ADAAs) to the question "How is your mock board used for student assessment?"

	Course Directors	ADAAs
Mock board is mandatory but not graded; feedback is provided.	17%	21%
Mock board is voluntary and not graded; feedback is provided.	5%	12%
Mock board performance is part of senior year evaluation.	9%	4%
Seniors must pass mock board to graduate.	33%	59%
Do not have sufficient information to answer.	36%	4%

fident. None of the ADAAs indicated that they had low confidence or were not confident. Ten percent of the course directors indicated that they did not have sufficient information to answer this question. These data are notable: it can be conjectured that the longitudinal interaction of many dental school clinical faculty members with students from freshman year to senior year allows faculty members to feel confident in their appraisal of students' capacities by the time of graduation. However, there is no evidence in this survey to verify this observation, and survey respondents were not requested to identify reasons for their level of confidence.

Respondents were invited to submit write-in comments about the assessment of students' competence and readiness to graduate at their school. Ten of the twenty-one questions on the survey requested write-in comments, and the final item was an open-ended invitation for comments: "Please provide comments about assessment techniques employed or not employed at your dental school to measure students' readiness to enter general dentistry as a beginning, entry-level practitioner." Nearly 700 comments were submitted. The methodology employed for identifying major themes within these written comments was based on recommendations for qualitative data analysis by Denzin and Lincoln.[105]

Table 8 displays six prevailing themes that emerged from this analysis, in order of the frequency of expression by survey respondents. The right column provides a synopsis of the issues embedded in each theme and illustrative statements by respondents to exemplify these issues.

Concern about the "focus" of student assessment efforts (i.e., are the right skills being assessed)

was the most frequent response category (theme), with twice as many comments as the other five themes which were: what is general dentistry, pride in efforts to diversify assessments, how can holistic evaluation be accomplished, lack of awareness of the assessment methods throughout the school, and what is competency-based education. These five themes were discussed with equivalent frequency.

Overall, the results of the survey confirmed what our review of the dental literature on assessment suggested. The most frequently used assessment methods in 2008 are those that have been used in dental education for many years: multiple-choice testing, laboratory practicals, daily grades in the clinic, clinical competency exams (i.e., competency patients), and procedural unit requirements, although there was conflicting data in this survey about the extent to which student assessment is still based on requirements. While there was some indication (primarily from respondents' written comments rather than their answers to survey questions) that innovative approaches to assessment are occasionally being used, the findings of this study indicate there is no groundswell in the adoption of these new methods—even though there is evidence, and persistent advocacy by performance appraisal experts, that some mental processes and patient care skills are poorly evaluated using traditional methods.

Assessment Within Competency-Based Education

In this section, we'll consider the findings of this study in light of the principles of competency-based education (CBE), which is the designated curriculum model for dental school in the United States. As indicated in the thematic analysis of respondents' comments and research conducted recently by Licari and Chambers,[106] CBE principles, including issues and techniques of competency assessment, are not uniformly understood by dental educators.

Assessment strategies in predoctoral dental education should be implemented in a manner consistent with the philosophy of competency-based education. Two questions are especially germane to this assertion: 1) what is competency-based education? and 2) what are best practices for assessing students' readiness to provide dental care in the public domain without supervision and under their own license?

Table 8. Most frequently expressed themes among 691 written comments by 931 U.S. dental school course directors in response to the question "Please provide comments about assessment techniques employed or not employed at your dental school to measure students' readiness to enter general dentistry as a beginning, entry-level practitioner" and to requests for written comments for nine of the twenty-one survey questions

Theme	Summary and Illustrative Comments
Focus of evaluation efforts: are the right skills being assessed?	Some competencies are assessed too much and others not enough. Tendency to focus on what is most convenient to assess. For example: We tend to focus on "low hanging fruit." We ask students to play the numbers game. Too much emphasis on "line of sight" evaluation; we assess what we can see. What we evaluate we do the right way. But I'm not sure we're right in what we choose to evaluate.
What is general dentistry?	The amount of time that students and their supervising faculty spend on tasks and clinical requirements tends to shape student and faculty concepts of what constitutes general dentistry. For example: General dentistry, as an entity, has not been defined for faculty. What is the inventory of knowledge and skills that constitutes general dentistry? Faculty do not necessarily see relationship between the school's stated graduation competencies and the practice of general dentistry.
Pride in efforts to diversify assessment techniques	Perception that faculty members are "trying new things." For example: I'm basing students' grades on several assessments now; it's more work and number crunching, but it probably provides a better overall picture of their learning. Many faculty are trying to move away from rote testing in classroom courses and counting units in the clinic.
How to achieve holistic, big picture appraisal of students' overall competence	Awareness that scope of assessment should be widened to focus more on students' overall abilities instead of concentrating on the pieces. For example: Getting consensus from all departments on what to evaluate is hard. Major examinations in which many departments participate are difficult to plan and conduct. Our silos have been in place for a long time; it's hard to get cooperation across specialty and specialty-generalist boundaries.
Lack of awareness of overall assessment plan at the school	I know "my piece of the pie," but don't see the big picture. For example: Couldn't answer some of the questions about overall methods of evaluating students because I just don't know what is happening outside my own department. I imagine there is a vision somewhere of the "product" we are trying to graduate and the various evaluations to determine if this product is being produced, but most faculty are not aware of this information.
What is competency-based education? What does it mean to say that a dental student is competent?	Lack of familiarity or comfort with the concept of competency-based education and with the school's definition of competencies needed for graduation. For example: Is a competency the same as what we used to call objectives? Can a student really be called "competent" after doing a procedure once or twice? How is treatment of a comp patient different from what the student does for any patient? Does doing well on a comp make you competent? Most of us do not know who wrote the competency list for our school or when it was written and what it was based on.

What Is Competency-Based Education?

Competency-based education came into prominence in the United States during the 1950s as a post-Sputnik reaction by the educational community to demands for better outcomes in our universities—demands motivated by concern that the United States was falling behind the Soviet Union in the "space race" and in science. Four characteristics distinguish CBE: 1) trainee outcomes are based on analysis of the job responsibilities and tasks of practitioners; 2) the curriculum is focused on what students need to learn to perform these on-the-job responsibilities versus organizing the curriculum around the traditional subject matter prerogatives of disciplines; 3) hierarchically sequenced modules allow students to proceed through the curriculum at their own pace; and 4) assessment techniques measure unassisted learner performance in settings approximating real-world work environments.[2,107,108] CBE was first mentioned by the Commission on Dental Accreditation (CODA) as a philosophy for dental education in the 1995 predoctoral standards and first described as a desired curriculum model by ADEA in 1997, when the initial set of competencies was published to define the outcomes of predoctoral education.[109] The 2008 revisions of the CODA predoctoral standards, now undergoing scrutiny by dental communities of interest, and the "Competencies for the New General Dentist" adopted by the ADEA House of Delegates in April 2008 both endorse CBE as the model for the predoctoral curriculum, and both organizations now clearly identify a "general dental practitioner" as the expected outcome of dental school.

The preamble to the 2008 ADEA competencies states that a competency is "a complex behavior or ability essential for the general dentist to begin independent, unsupervised dental practice. Competency includes knowledge, experience, critical thinking and problem-solving skills, professionalism, ethical values, and technical and procedural skills. These components become an integrated whole during the delivery of patient care by the competent general dentist." The final sentence of this definition is critical for understanding competency assessment strategies in CBE.

What Assessment Methods Are Consistent with CBE?

Eleven sources and the assessment toolkits described above were primary sources for the follow-ing summary of recommendations for assessment of practice readiness.[89,91,92,98-100,110-114]

In CBE, the highest priority is determining students' readiness for practice. Appraisal of practice readiness is based on 1) assessing students' overall competence, or the capacity to "put it all together," also known as "general competence," versus focusing on individual skills, known as component competencies, which are often taught and evaluated in isolation in the disciplinary silos of the curriculum; and 2) employing multiple data sources based on the principle of triangulation.[115] In dental education, the concept of general competence was first articulated by Chambers in 2001.[116]

One of the leaders in competency-based education, Paul Pottinger, observed: "Competence cannot be meaningfully defined by endless reductions of specific skills, tasks, and actions which, in the end, fall short of real world requirements for effective performance. In fact, the more essential characteristics for success often turn out to be broad or generalized abilities which are sometimes more easily operationally defined and measured than an array of subskills that do not add up to a general competence."[117]

A key question on the survey of assessment practices in U.S. dental schools was the following: how does your school make a comprehensive assessment of students' readiness for entry into unsupervised practice? In other words, we were asking: how does your school assess Pottinger's general competence? The response options were 1) a checklist system on which students are certified for graduation if they pass all courses, meet GPA standards, complete all clinical requirements, meet all departmental expectations, complete all rotations, submit all assignments, and pay their bills; 2) an in-school internship in which a small group of faculty work with each student for several months to observe daily performance across all competency domains; 3) gatekeeper examinations to credential accomplishment of core competencies; and 4) departments certify that students are competent in areas of dentistry germane to their disciplines. As we have seen, two-thirds of the respondents selected option 1, the checklist approach. Only a handful of respondents selected options 2 and 3 (7 percent each) to comprehensively assess their seniors' readiness for general dentistry. Options 2 and 3 are the practice readiness assessments most consistent with CBE.

Figure 6 illustrates the difference between assessing component or silo competencies (the individual skills, represented by ovals inside the circle, in the general dentist's toolkit) and the new concept of general competence (the outer circle), which represents the capacity to "put it all together, consistently." Current performance measurement theory indicates that primary emphasis should be placed on assessing students' overall package of skills (the outer ring) in working conditions that approximate "authentic practice."[89,92,110] From our experience with many health professions, dental education does the best job of assessing the silo components of competence. However, as articulated by Eraut in *Professional Knowledge and Competence,* "Professional competence is more than demonstration of isolated competencies. When we see the whole, we see its parts differently than when we see them in isolation."[118]

The prevailing recommendation for measuring general competence is a pregraduation internship of at least two months' duration that resembles the work environment, tasks, and responsibilities of entry-level practitioners. During the internship, students work under daily supervision by a small group of the same faculty (for coaching consistency), who observe and assess reproducibility of component competencies, seamless transition between silo competencies during patient care, nature of the student's fund of knowledge (is it superficial or deep?), punctuality, decorum, appearance, stress management, and capacity for self-assessment and self-correction. Many dental faculty are concerned about the qualitative or subjective nature of this type of assessment, but Miller[96] asserted that "the collective wisdom of faculty who have consistent opportunities to observe and interact with the student is the essential core of performance assessment"—a perspective endorsed by virtually every review of assessment best practices in health professions education.

A fundamental principle of competency-based assessment is to measure students' practice readiness as represented by general competence (i.e., capacity to "put it all together" over an extended period of time).

Recommendations for Competency Assessment Based on Triangulation

The final section of this article describes several assessment strategies that are currently considered state of the art for measuring readiness for professional responsibilities, including in-school internships,

OSCEs, triple jump exercises, and CATS (critically appraised topic summary, known generically as critical appraisal tasks), in the context of the triangulation model of competency assessment. Readiness assessment based on multiple data sources is more likely to be accurate than single-source measures or disproportionate reliance on one measure over other potential sources of information about students' practice readiness.[115] This best practice is referred to as "triangulation" and has been recently described in the *Journal of Dental Education* by Jahangiri et al.[85] Figure 7 depicts a model of triangulation. The P in the model represents performance, including the 3 Ps: process (human factors including communication, diligence, organization, compassion, ethical behavior), product (outcomes of patient care), and procedure (technical skills necessary to provide patient care).[2] A&R represents appraisal and reflection (i.e., self-assessment and self-correction), and K represents knowledge.

In 2008, there is consensus in the literature on performance measurement about optimal assessment strategies for each leg of the triangle. For practice readiness relative to the performance leg, the pregraduation internship is considered to be an optimal approach. Internships answer this question: can senior students put it all together and function in an environment that approximates general dentistry including field experience in community clinics where they don't have three hours for one appointment, but are expected to function acceptably during four to five appointments daily? In most health professions education programs, the internship is supported by the OSCE, a technique for readiness assessment that is used for gateway examinations that students must pass in order to advance to a higher academic level, graduate, or obtain a license.[61,65] For example, the National Dental Examining Board (NDEB) of Canada implements an OSCE as a core component of the licensure process in that nation.[119]

In OSCEs, students rotate through twenty to thirty stations at timed intervals that provide a representative sampling of patient problems or clinical tasks. At action or task stations, students perform procedures under observation by trained evaluators. For instance, OSCEs typically contain several stations where students interview and examine patients trained to portray oral health problems, often with comorbidities that may influence decision making. At subsequent assessment stations, students report clinical findings to a faculty member, propose and justify a diagnosis, and compare and contrast

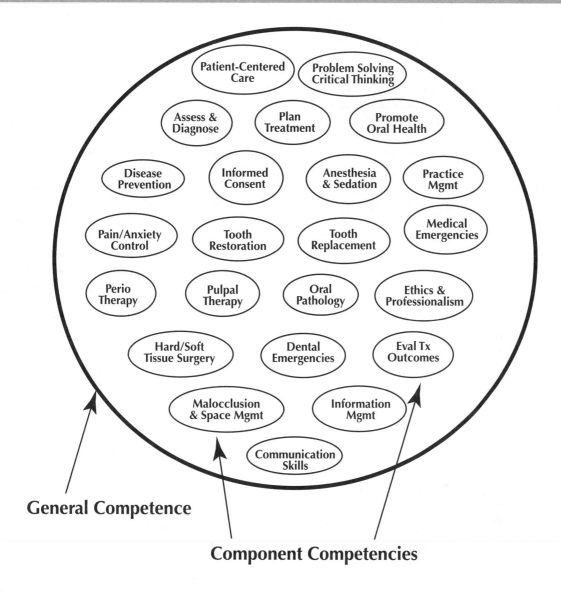

Figure 6. Component/silo competencies and general competence

therapeutic options. During OSCEs, students may be asked to demonstrate comprehension of underlying basic science principles by linking the patient's symptoms to pathophysiological mechanisms. This is accomplished by verbal questioning from a station proctor, or students may respond in writing by short answer essays or answering multiple-choice questions. At other OSCE stations, students may be asked to study case scenarios and then select answers to multiple-choice questions about diagnostic tests, assessment, and treatment planning, a format used in the OSCE administered by the NDEB of Canada.[119]

Most OSCEs contain radiographic interpretation stations as well as stations where students assess laboratory findings and measure a patient's vital signs. Students' overall scores on the OSCE are derived from their understanding of pathophysiology, use and comprehension of assessment techniques, capacity to interpret clinical findings, ability to make appropriate treatment planning decisions, performance of patient examination skills, and interpersonal skills. Trained patients known as "standardized patients" (who provide a "standard" experience for all students rotating through the station) are often used to assess patient examination skills and interpersonal skills.[56,57] The integrative nature of the OSCE, which samples a broad spectrum of competencies, is consistent with CBE assessment principles.

For the A&R leg, Self-Appraisal and Reflection, portfolios are recommended.[69] In a competency attainment portfolio, students collect evidence that demonstrates their progress toward and accomplishment of specified competencies, including longitudinal documentation of patient care, performance on competency exams, case presentations, literature reviews, reports, formative evaluations, formal performance reviews by supervising faculty, and, most importantly, students' own appraisal of their performance and reflections on needed improvements, lessons learned, and insights about dentistry or the learning process. The reflection component allows faculty members to appraise the student's level of self-awareness and capacity for reflection. Review of the portfolio content provides an opportunity for student-teacher dialogue centered on students' work products and assessment of progress. Without self-assessment and reflection, portfolios can digress to "scrapbooking." The 2006 accreditation standards for U.S. professional programs in pharmacy (developed by the American Council for Pharmaceutical Education) stipulate use of portfolios as a principal technique to measure students' attainment of competencies for the doctor of pharmacy de-

gree.[120] Many doctoral programs, in the sciences and other fields as well, now employ portfolios instead of qualifying examinations and other types of grading.

For the Knowledge leg, the triple jump exercise (TJE) is widely used in health professions education to evaluate students' capacity to access, analyze, and apply biomedical knowledge to health care problems.[121] When coupled with multiple-choice testing in the case-based "testlet" format such as now used on the NBDE (several multiple-choice questions linked to a patient scenario), triple jumps provide a mechanism for assessment of students' capacity to function at the "application" level of Bloom's cognitive taxonomy.[94] There are several variations of TJEs. Clinical TJEs[122] consist of three phases (thus, the "jumps") completed in one or two days in which students 1) interview and examine patients while observed by faculty, or are videotaped for retrospective review including student self-assessment; 2) write an assessment of the findings using the "SOAP" format (subjective data, objective data, assessment, plans) with emphasis on providing evidence from the literature to support assessment and therapeutic decisions and submit this document to the faculty member(s) who observed jump one; and 3) participate in an oral examination conducted by the observing faculty member(s) at which students are questioned about pathophysiology, diagnosis, and treatment of

Three legs of competency assessment and recommended assessment methods

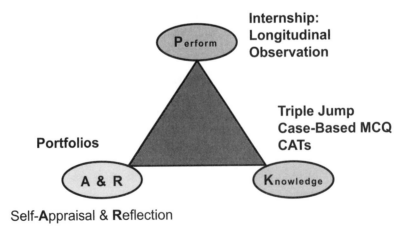

Figure 7. Triangulation model to provide multiple sources of data for three legs of competency assessment

the patient's problems and asked to review research evidence related to treatment options and outcomes. Students receive an evaluation for each jump and a cumulative score across all three jumps. TJEs implemented in the preclinical curriculum focus on students' literature-searching skills to find evidence that answers student-developed research questions pertinent to health problems. In TJEs for freshman or sophomore students, the first jump involves reading a scenario depicting a patient with an oral health problem, then identifying key issues in the case and writing a researchable question in the PICO format (patient with problem, intervention, comparison, and outcome).[123] For the second jump, students explore literature to find evidence pertinent to their question, and in the third jump, students report their findings, answer the research question, and critically appraise the quality of the evidence. As with clinical TJEs, students receive evaluations for each jump and a cumulative score across all three jumps. Both types of TJEs emphasize accessing pertinent information, application of this information to health problems, and appraisal of the quality of knowledge available to answer clinical questions.

The CATS (critically appraised topic summary) is a new technique to assess students' capacity to use biomedical knowledge to make reasoned decisions.[124-126] CATS is a cousin to the triple jump in that students start by reviewing a case scenario or an actual patient's clinical presentation, identify unknowns that need to be explored, write a researchable question in the PICO format, explore the literature to find and analyze the evidence, and then write a summary that indicates an answer to the question and recommendations based on appraisal of the research. Like the TJE and aspects of OSCEs, the CATS evaluates how students access, analyze, and apply biomedical knowledge and measures the capacity for self-directed learning.

In summary, the good news is that there are several techniques, relatively new to dental education, that can provide comprehensive assessment of several competency domains and thus are consistent with CBE emphasis on practice readiness. Because internships, OSCEs, gateways, portfolios, triple jumps, and CATS are new to academic dentistry, there are few examples to provide implementation heuristics. The findings of the survey of assessment practices in U.S. dental schools reported in this article revealed that a small percentage of dental school course directors use any of these techniques, while traditional tech-

niques such as multiple-choice testing, procedural requirements, lab practicals, clinical comps, and daily grades still comprise more than 60 percent of all assessment done in the predoctoral curriculum, and multiple-choice testing still predominates, representing almost 30 percent of all evaluations across all domains of competency. These data reveal important challenges ahead for dental educators and underscore the urgency of charting new directions in our approaches to assessment.

In embracing a competency-based model for dental education, we must also incorporate into the curriculum evaluation strategies and assessment methodologies that will ensure the achievement of our ultimate goal: the education of competent general dentists.

REFERENCES

1. Epstein RM, Hundert EM. Defining and assessing professional competence. JAMA 2002;287(2):226–35.
2. Hendricson WD, Kleffner JH. Curricular and instructional implications of competency-based dental education. J Dent Educ 1998;62(2):183–96.
3. American Dental Education Association. Competencies for the new general dentist (as approved by the 2008 ADEA House of Delegates). J Dent Educ 2008;72(7):823–6.
4. Fuller JL. The effects of training and criterion models on interjudge reliability. J Dent Educ 1972;36(4):19–22.
5. Bazan MT, Seale NS. A technique for immediate evaluation of preclinical exercises. J Dent Educ 1982;46(12):726–8.
6. del Rio CE, Dale RA, Hendricson WD. A method for training endodontic evaluators. J Dent Educ 1983;47(12): 776–8.
7. Chambers DW. Adjusting for hard and easy graders. J Dent Educ 1987;51(12):723–6.
8. Gilles JA, Hendricson WD. Environmental influences on grading. J Dent Educ 1987;51(2):111–3.
9. Courts FJ. Standardization and calibration in the evaluation of clinical performance. J Dent Educ 1997;61(12): 947–50.
10. Knight GW. Toward faculty calibration. J Dent Educ 1997;61(12):941–6.
11. Esser C, Kerschbaum T, Winkelmann V, Krage T, Faber FJ. A comparison of the visual and technical assessment of preparations made by dental students. Eur J Dent Educ 2006;10(3):157–61.
12. Licari FW, Knight GW, Guenzel PJ. Designing evaluation forms to facilitate student learning. J Dent Educ 2008;72(1):48–58.
13. Harden RM, Crosby JR, Friedman Ben-David M. AMEE guide no. 14: outcome-based education. Part 5. From competency to meta-competency: a model for the specification of learning outcomes. Med Teacher 1999;21(6):546–52.
14. Abrahamson S. Diseases of the curriculum. J Med Educ 1978;53(12):951–7.

15. Manhold JH, Manhold BS. Final report of an eight-year study of the efficacy of the dental aptitude test in predicting four-year performance in a new school. J Dent Educ 1965;29(1):41–4.

16. Dworkin SF. Dental aptitude test as performance predictor over four years of dental school: analyses and interpretations. J Dent Educ 1970;34(1):28–38.

17. Kramer GA. Predictive validity of the Dental Admission Test. J Dent Educ 1986;50(9):526–31.

18. Kramer GA, Kubiak AT, Smith RM. Construct and predictive validities of the Perceptual Ability Test. J Dent Educ 1989;53(2):119–25.

19. Gray SA, Deem LP. Predicting student performance in preclinical technique courses using the theory of ability determinants of skilled performance. J Dent Educ 2002;66(6):721–7.

20. Sandow PL, Jones AC, Peek CW, Courts FJ, Watson RE. Correlation of admission criteria with dental school performance and attrition. J Dent Educ 2002;66(3):385–92.

21. Gray SA, Deem LP, Straja SR. Are traditional cognitive tests useful in predicting clinical success? J Dent Educ 2002;66(11):1241–5.

22. Stacey DG, Whittaker JM. Predicting academic performance and clinical competency for international dental students: seeking the most efficient and effective measures. J Dent Educ 2005;69(2):270–80.

23. Bergman AV, Susarla SM, Howell TH, Karimbux NY. Dental Admission Test scores and performance on NBDE, part I, revisited. J Dent Educ 2006;70(3):258–62.

24. Park SE, Susarla SM, Massey W. Do admissions data and NBDE part I scores predict clinical performance among dental students? J Dent Educ 2006;70(5):518–24.

25. Hangorsky U. Clinical competency levels of fourth-year dental students as determined by board examiners and faculty members. J Am Dent Assoc 1981;102(1):35–7.

26. Casada JP, Cailleteau JG, Seals ML. Predicting performance on a dental board licensure examination. J Dent Educ 1996;60(9):775–7.

27. Ranney RR, Gunsolley JC, Miller LS. Comparison of National Board Part II and NERB's written examination for outcomes and redundancy. J Dent Educ 2004;68(1):29–34.

28. Ranney RR, Gunsolley JC, Miller LS, Wood M. The relationship between performance in a dental school and performance on a clinical examination for licensure. J Am Dent Assoc 2004;135(8):1146–53.

29. Stewart CM, Bates RE, Smith GE. Relationship between performance in dental school and performance on a dental licensure examination: an eight-year study. J Dent Educ 2005;69(8):864–9.

30. Chambers DW, Dugoni AA, Paisley J. The case against one-shot testing for initial dental licensure. J Calif Dent Assoc 2004;32(3):247.

31. Gadbury-Amyot CC, Bray KK, Branson BS, Holt L, Keselyak N, Mitchell TV, Williams KB. Predictive validity of dental hygiene competency assessment measures on one-shot clinical licensure examinations. J Dent Educ 2005;69(3):363–70.

32. Hicks JL, Dale RA, Hendricson WD, Lauer WR. Effects of reducing senior clinical requirements. J Dent Educ 1985;49(3):169–75.

33. Dodge WW, Dale RA, Hendricson WD. A preliminary study of the effect of eliminating requirements on clinical performance. J Dent Educ 1993;57(9):667–72.

34. Cameron CA, Phillips SL, Chasteen JE. Outcomes comparison of solo-practitioner and group practice models. J Dent Educ 1998;62(2):163–71.

35. Nowlin T, Dodge W, Hendricson WD. Results of a pilot patient-centered clinical education program. J Dent Educ 1998;62(1):106(Abstract 90).

36. Stacey MA, Morgan MV, Wright C. The effect of clinical targets on productivity and perceptions of clinical competence. J Dent Educ 1998;62(6):409–14.

37. Evangelidis-Sakellson V. Student productivity under requirement and comprehensive care systems. J Dent Educ 1999;63(5):407–13.

38. Lanning SK, Pelok SD, Williams BC, Richards PS, Sarment DP, Oh TJ, McCauley LK. Variation in periodontal diagnosis and treatment planning among clinical instructors. J Dent Educ 2005;69(3):325–37.

39. Henzi D, Davis E, Jasinevicius R, Hendricson W. North American dental students' perspectives about their clinical education. J Dent Educ 2006;70(4):361–77.

40. Haj-Ali R, Feil P. Rater reliability: short- and long-term effects of calibration training. J Dent Educ 2006;70(4):428–33.

41. Rolland S, Hobson R, Hanwell S. Clinical competency exercises: some students' perceptions. Eur J Dent Educ 2007;11(3):184–91.

42. Henzi D, Davis E, Jasinevicius R, Hendricson W. In the students' own words: what are the strengths and weaknesses of the dental school curriculum? J Dent Educ 2007;71(5):632–45.

43. Chambers DW, Geissberger M. Toward a competency analysis of operative dentistry techniques. J Dent Educ 1997;61(10):795–803.

44. Chambers DW. Faculty ratings as part of a competency-based evaluation clinic grading system. Eval Health Prof 1999;22(1):86–106.

45. Chambers DW. Do repeated clinical competency ratings stereotype students? J Dent Educ 2004;68(12):1220–7.

46. Milani JE, Chi HH, Chambers DW. Comments as part of a clinical competency rating system. J Dent Educ 2007;71(2):235–41.

47. Berrong JM, Buchanan RN, Hendricson WD. Evaluation of practical clinical examinations. J Dent Educ 1983;47(10):656–63.

48. Licari FW, Knight GW. Developing a group practice comprehensive care education curriculum. J Dent Educ 2003;67(12):1312–5.

49. Taleghani M, Soloman ES, Wathen WF. Non-graded clinical evaluation of dental students in a competency-based education program. J Dent Educ 2004;68(6):644–55.

50. Taleghani M, Soloman ES, Wathen WF. Grading dental students in a "nongraded" clinical assessment program. J Dent Educ 2006;70(5):500–10.

51. Prihoda TJ, Pinckard RN, McMahan CA, Jones AC. Correcting for guessing increases validity in multiple-choice examinations in an oral and maxillofacial pathology course. J Dent Educ 2006;70(4):378–86.

52. Karl M, Graef F, Eitner S, Beck N, Wichman M, Holst S. Comparison of computer-aided testing and traditional

multiple choice: an equivalency study. Eur J Dent Educ 2007;11(1):38–41.

53. Mayhew RB, Jacobs SS. An analysis of several responses-determined scoring techniques used to assess partial knowledge in multiple-choice testing. J Dent Educ 1975;39(10):658–65.

54. Geller LM, Shemesh M. Analysis of answer changes by dental students on multiple choice tests in pathology: attack on an educational myth. J Dent Educ 1979;43(3):159–64.

55. Kolstad R, Goaz P, Kolstad R. Nonrestricted multiple-choice examination items. J Dent Educ 1982;46(8):485–8.

56. Johnson JA, Kopp KC, Williams RG. Standardized patients for the assessment of dental students' clinical skills. J Dent Educ 1990;54(6):331–3.

57. Stilwell NA, Reisine S. Using patient-instructors to teach and evaluate interviewing skills. J Dent Educ 1992;56(2):118–22.

58. Boone WJ, McWhorter AG, Seale NS. Purposeful assessment techniques (PAT) applied to an OSCE-based measurement of competencies in a pediatric dentistry curriculum. J Dent Educ 2001;65(11):1232–7.

59. Zartman RR, McWhorter AG, Seale NS, Boone WJ. Using OSCE-based evaluation: curricular impact over time. J Dent Educ 2002;66(12):1323–30.

60. Holyfield LJ, Bolin KA, Rankin KV, Shulman JP, Jones DL, Eden BD. Use of computer technology to modify objective structured clinical examinations. J Dent Educ 2005;69(10):1133–6.

61. Schoonheim-Klein M, Habets L, Hartman AA, Van der Velden U, Hoogstraten L. Implementing an OSCE in dental education: effects on students' learning strategies. Eur J Dent Educ 2006;10(4):226–35.

62. Curtis DA, Lind SL, Brear S, Finzen FC. The correlation of student performance in preclinical and clinical prosthodontic assessments. J Dent Educ 2007;71(3):365–72.

63. Cannick GF, Horowitz AM, Garr DR, Reed SG, Neville BW, Day TA, et al. Use of the OSCE to evaluate brief communication skills training for dental students. J Dent Educ 2007;71(9):1203–9.

64. Dennehy PC, Susarla SM, Karimbux NY. Relationship between dental students' performance on standardized multiple-choice examinations and OSCEs. J Dent Educ 2008;72(5):585–92.

65. Schoonheim-Klein M, Muijtens A, Habets L, Manogue M, Van der Vleuten C, Hoogstraten L, Van der Velden U. On the reliability of a dental OSCE, using SEM: effect of different days. Eur J Dent Educ 2008;12(3):131–7.

66. Gadbury-Amyot CC, Holt LP, Overman PR, Schmidt CR. Implementation of portfolio assessment in a competency-based dental hygiene program. J Dent Educ 2000;64(5):375–80.

67. Gadbury-Amyot CC, Kim J, Palm RL, Mills GE, Noble E, Overman PR. Validity and reliability of portfolio assessment of competency in a baccalaureate dental hygiene program. J Dent Educ 2003;67(9):991–1002.

68. Chambers D. Portfolios for determining initial licensure competency. J Am Dent Assoc 2004;135:173–84.

69. Friedman Ben David M, Davis M, Harden R, Howie P, Ker J, Pippard M. AMEE medical education guide no. 24: portfolios as a method of student assessment. Med Teacher 2001;23(6):535–51.

70. Durham JA, Moore UJ, Corbett IP, Thomson PJ. Assessing competency in dentoalveolar surgery: a 3-year study of cumulative experience in the undergraduate curriculum. Eur J Dent Educ 2007;11(4):200–7.

71. von Bergmann HC, Dalrymple KR, Wong S, Shuler CF. Investigating the relationship between PBL process grades and content acquisition performance in a PBL dental program. J Dent Educ 2007;71(9):1160–70.

72. Bondemark L, Knutsson K, Brown G. A self-directed summative examination in problem-based learning in dentistry: a new approach. Med Teacher 2004;26(1):436–51.

73. Leisnert L, Mattheos N. The interactive examination in a comprehensive oral care clinic: a three-year follow up of students' self-assessment ability. Med Teacher 2006;28(6):544–8.

74. Curtis DA, Lind SL, Dellinges M, Setia G, Finzen FC. Dental students' self-assessment of preclinical examinations. J Dent Educ 2008;72(3):265–77.

75. Thammasitboon K, Sukotjo C, Howell H, Karimbux N. Problem-based learning at the Harvard School of Dental Medicine: self-assessment of performance in postdoctoral training. J Dent Educ 2007;71(8):1080–9.

76. Hols-Elders W, Bloemendaal P, Bos N, Quaak M, Sijstermans R, De Jong P. Twelve tips for computer-based assessment in medical education. Med Teacher 2008;30(7):673–8.

77. Colthart I, Bagnall G, Evans A, Allbutt H, Haig A, Illing J, McKinstry B. The effectiveness of self-assessment on the identification of learner needs, learner activity, and impact on clinical practice: BEME guide no. 10. Med Teacher 2008;30(2):124–45.

78. Susarla SM, Medina-Martinez N, Howell TH, Karimbux NY. Problem-based learning: effects on standard outcomes. J Dent Educ 2003;67(9):1003–10.

79. Kassebaum DK, Hendricson WD, Taft T, Haden NK. The dental curriculum at North American dental institutions in 2002–03: a survey of current structure, recent innovations, and planned changes. J Dent Educ 2004;68(9):914–31.

80. Albanese MA, Mitchell S. Problem-based learning: a review of the literature on its outcomes and implementation issues. Acad Med 1993;68(1):52–81.

81. Rich SK, Keim RG, Shuler CF. Problem-based learning versus a traditional educational methodology: a comparison of preclinical and clinical periodontics performance. J Dent Educ 2005;69(6):649–62.

82. Azer SA. Assessment in a problem-based learning course. Biochem Mol Biol Educ 2003;31(6):248–434.

83. Vernon DTA, Blake RL. Does problem-based learning work? A meta-analysis of evaluative research. Acad Med 1993;68:550–63.

84. Fincham AG, Shuler CF. The changing face of dental education: the impact of PBL. J Dent Educ 2001;65(5):406–21.

85. Jahangiri L, Mucciolo TW, Choi M, Spielman AI. Assessment of teaching effectiveness in U.S. dental schools and the value of triangulation. J Dent Educ 2008;72(6):707–18.

86. Tedesco LA. Issues in dental curriculum development and change. J Dent Educ 1995;59(1):97–147.

87. Hendricson WD, Cohen PA. Oral health care in the 21st century: implications for dental and medical education. Acad Med 2001;77(12):1181–206.

88. Pyle M, Andrieu SC, Chadwick DG, Chmar JE, Cole JR, George MC, et al. The case for change in dental education. J Dent Educ 2006;70(9):921–4.

89. Chambers DW, Glassman P. A primer on competency-based evaluation. J Dent Educ 1997;61(8):651–66.

90. Friedman Ben-David M. AMEE guide no. 18: standard setting in student assessment. Med Teacher 2000;22(2):120–30.

91. Shumway JM, Harden RM. AMEE guide no. 25: the assessment of learning outcomes for the competent and reflective physician. Med Teacher 2003;25(6):569–84.

92. Norcini J, Burch V. Workplace-based assessment as an educational tool: AMEE guide no. 31. Med Teacher 2007;29(9–10):855–71.

93. Kramer G, ADEA CCI Task Force on Student Outcomes Assessment. Dental assessment toolkit. J Dent Educ 2009;73(1):forthcoming.

94. Bloom BS, Englehart MD, Furst EJ, Hill WH, Krathwohl DR. Taxonomy of educational objectives. Handbook 1: cognitive domain. New York: Longmans, 1956.

95. Hoge R, Coladarci T. Teacher-based judgments of academic achievement: a review of the literature. Rev Educ Res 1989;59(3):297–313.

96. Miller GE. Assessment of clinical skills/competence/performance. Acad Med 1990;9:63–7.

97. Linn RL. Complex, performance-based assessment: expectations and validation criteria. Educ Researcher 1991;16(1):1–21.

98. Wass V, Van der Vieuten CPM, Shatzer J, Jones R. Assessment of clinical competence. Lancet 2001;357:945–9.

99. Swing SR. Assessing the ACGME general competencies: general considerations and assessment methods. Acad Emerg Med 2002;9(11):1278–87.

100. Epstein RM. Assessment in medical education. N Engl J Med 2007;356(4):387–96.

101. Carraccio C. The objective structured clinical examination: a step in the direction of competency-based evaluation. Arch Pediatr Adolesc Med 2000;154:736–41.

102. Haladyna TM. Developing and validating multiple-choice test items. 3rd ed. Mahwah, NJ: Lawrence Erlbaum Associates, 2004.

103. Neumann LM, MacNeil RL. Revisiting the National Board Dental Examination. J Dent Educ 2007;71(10):1281–92.

104. MacNeil RL, Neumann LM. Realigning the National Board Dental Examination with contemporary dental education and practice. J Dent Educ 2007;71(10):1293–8.

105. Denzin NK, Lincoln YS. The Sage handbook of qualitative research. 3rd ed. Thousand Oaks, CA: Sage Publications, 2005.

106. Licari FW, Chambers DW. Some paradoxes in competency-based dental education. J Dent Educ 2008;72(1):8–18.

107. Grant G, ed. On competence: a critical analysis of competency-based reforms in higher education. Washington, DC: Jossey-Bass, 1979.

108. Grussing PG. Curricular design: competency perspective. Am J Pharm Educ 1987;51:414–9.

109. American Dental Education Association. Competencies for the new dentist (as approved by the 1997 House of Delegates). J Dent Educ 1997;68(7):742–5.

110. Smith SR, Dollase R. AMEE guide no. 14: outcome-based education. Part 2: planning, implementing, and evaluating a competency-based curriculum. Med Teacher 1999;21:15–22.

111. Rethans J, Norcini J, Baron-Maldonado M. Relationship between competence and performance: implications for assessing practice performance. Med Educ 2002;36(10):901–9.

112. Smith SR, Dollase RH, Boss JA. Assessing students' performance in a competency-based curriculum. Acad Med 2003;78:97–107.

113. Van derVleuten CPM, Schuwirth L. Assessing professional competence: from methods to programmes. Med Educ 2005;39:309–17.

114. Van der Vieuten CPM. The assessment of professional competence: developments, research, and practical implications. Adv Health Sci Educ 1996;1:41–67.

115. Lockyer J. Multisource feedback in assessment of physician competencies. J Contin Educ Health Prof 2003;23:2–10.

116. Chambers DW. Preliminary evidence for a general competency hypothesis. J Dent Educ 2001;65(11):1243–52.

117. Pottinger PS. Comments and guidelines for research in competency identification, definition, and measurement. Syracuse, NY: Educational Policy Research Center, 1975.

118. Eraut M. Professional knowledge and competence. London: Falmer Press, 1994.

119. Gerrow JD, Murphy HJ, Boyd MA, Scott DA. Concurrent validity of written and OSCE components of the Canadian dental certification examinations. J Dent Educ 2003;67(8):896–901.

120. Accreditation Council for Pharmacy Education. Accreditation standards and guidelines for the professional program in pharmacy leading to the doctor of pharmacy degree. At: www.acpe-accredit.org/pdf/ACPE_Revised_PharmD_Standards_Adopted_Jan152006.pdf. Accessed: September 2008.

121. Feletti G, Ryan G. Triple jump exercise in inquiry-based learning: a case study. Assess Eval Higher Educ 1994;19(3):225–34.

122. Smith RM. The triple-jump examination as an assessment tool in the problem-based medical curriculum at the University of Hawaii. Acad Med 1993;13:366–72.

123. Rangachari PK. The TRIPSE: a process-oriented evaluation for problem-based learning courses in the basic sciences. Biochem Molecular Biol Educ 2002;30(1):57–60.

124. Wyer PC. The critically appraised topic: closing the evidence transfer gap. Ann Emerg Med 1997;30(5):639–41.

125. Suave R. The critically appraised topic: practical approach to learning critical appraisal. Ann R Coll Physicians Surg 1995;28:396.

126. Iacopino AM. The influence of "new science" on dental education: current concepts, trends, and models for the future. J Dent Educ 2007;71(4):450–62.

Competencies for the New General Dentist
(As approved by the 2008 ADEA House of Delegates)

Preamble

The general dentist is the primary oral health care provider, supported by dental specialists, allied dental professionals, and other health care providers. The general dentist will address health care issues beyond traditional oral health care and must be able to independently and collaboratively practice evidence-based comprehensive dentistry with the ultimate goal of improving the health of society. The general dentist must have a broad biomedical and clinical education and be able to demonstrate professional and ethical behavior as well as effective communication and interpersonal skills. In addition, he or she must have the ability to evaluate and utilize emerging technologies, continuing professional development opportunities, and problem-solving and critical thinking skills to effectively address current and future issues in health care.

As used in this document, a "competency" is a complex behavior or ability essential for the general dentist to begin independent, unsupervised dental practice. Competency includes knowledge, experience, critical thinking and problem-solving skills, professionalism, ethical values, and technical and procedural skills. These components become an integrated whole during the delivery of patient care by the competent general dentist. Competency assumes that all behaviors are performed with a degree of quality consistent with patient well-being and that the general dentist can self-evaluate treatment effectiveness. In competency-based dental education, what students learn is based upon clearly articulated competencies and further assumes that all behaviors/abilities are supported by foundation knowledge and psychomotor skills in biomedical, behavioral, ethical, clinical dental science, and informatics areas that are essential for independent and unsupervised performance as an entry-level general dentist. In creating curricula, dental faculty must consider the competencies to be developed through the educational process, the learning experiences that will lead to the development of these competencies, and ways to assess or measure the attainment of competencies.

The purpose of this document and the proposed foundation knowledge concepts are to:

- Define the competencies necessary for entry into the dental profession as a general dentist. Competencies must be relevant and important to the patient care responsibilities of the general dentist, directly linked to the oral health care needs of the public, realistic, and understandable by other health care professionals;

- Reflect (in contrast to the 1997 competencies) the 2002 Institute of Medicine core set of competencies for enhancing patient care quality and safety, and illustrate current and emerging trends in the dental practice environment; they are divided into domains, are broader and less prescriptive in nature, are fewer in number, and, most importantly, will be linked to requisite foundation knowledge and skills;

- Serve as a central resource, both nationally for the American Dental Education Association (ADEA) and locally for individual dental schools, to promote change and innovation in predoctoral dental school curricula;

- Inform and recommend to the Commission on Dental Accreditation standards for predoctoral dental education;

- Provide a framework for the change, innovation, and construction of national dental examinations, including those provided through the Joint Commission on National Dental Examinations and clinical testing agencies;

- Assist in the development of curriculum guidelines, both nationally for ADEA and locally for individual dental schools, for both foundation knowledge and clinical instruction;

- Provide methods for assessing competencies for the general dentist; and

- Through periodic review and update, serve as a document for benchmarking, best practices, and interprofessional collaboration and, additionally, as a mechanism to inform educators in other health care professions about curricular priorities of dental education and entry-level competencies of general dentists.

Domains

1. **Critical Thinking**
2. **Professionalism**
3. **Communication and Interpersonal Skills**
4. **Health Promotion**
5. **Practice Management and Informatics**
6. **Patient Care**
   A. **Assessment, Diagnosis, and Treatment Planning**
   B. **Establishment and Maintenance of Oral Health**

The statements below define the entry-level competencies for the beginning general dentist.

1. Critical Thinking

Graduates must be competent to:

1.1 Evaluate and integrate emerging trends in health care as appropriate.

1.2 Utilize critical thinking and problem-solving skills.

1.3 Evaluate and integrate best research outcomes with clinical expertise and patient values for evidence-based practice.

2. Professionalism

Graduates must be competent to:

2.1 Apply ethical and legal standards in the provision of dental care.

2.2 Practice within one's scope of competence and consult with or refer to professional colleagues when indicated.

3. Communication and Interpersonal Skills

Graduates must be competent to:

3.1 Apply appropriate interpersonal and communication skills.

3.2 Apply psychosocial and behavioral principles in patient-centered health care.

3.3 Communicate effectively with individuals from diverse populations.

4. Health Promotion

Graduates must be competent to:

4.1 Provide prevention, intervention, and educational strategies.

4.2 Participate with dental team members and other health care professionals in the management and health promotion for all patients.

4.3 Recognize and appreciate the need to contribute to the improvement of oral health beyond those served in traditional practice settings.

5. Practice Management and Informatics

Graduates must be competent to:

5.1 Evaluate and apply contemporary and emerging information including clinical and practice management technology resources.

5.2 Evaluate and manage current models of oral health care management and delivery.

5.3 Apply principles of risk management, including informed consent and appropriate record keeping in patient care.

5.4 Demonstrate effective business, financial management, and human resource skills.

5.5 Apply quality assurance, assessment, and improvement concepts.

5.6 Comply with local, state, and federal regulations including OSHA and HIPAA.

5.7 Develop a catastrophe preparedness plan for the dental practice.

6. Patient Care

A. Assessment, Diagnosis, and Treatment Planning

Graduates must be competent to:

6.1 Manage the oral health care of the infant, child, adolescent, and adult, as well as the unique needs of women, geriatric, and special needs patients.

6.2 Prevent, identify, and manage trauma, oral diseases, and other disorders.

6.3 Obtain and interpret patient/medical data, including a thorough intra/extra oral examination, and use these findings to accurately assess and manage all patients.

6.4 Select, obtain, and interpret diagnostic images for the individual patient.

6.5 Recognize the manifestations of systemic disease and how the disease and its management may affect the delivery of dental care.

6.6 Formulate a comprehensive diagnosis, treatment, and/or referral plan for the management of patients.

B. Establishment and Maintenance of Oral Health

Graduates must be competent to:

6.7 Utilize universal infection control guidelines for all clinical procedures.

6.8 Prevent, diagnose, and manage pain and anxiety in the dental patient.

6.9 Prevent, diagnose, and manage temporomandibular disorders.

6.10 Prevent, diagnose, and manage periodontal diseases.

6.11 Develop and implement strategies for the clinical assessment and management of caries.

6.12 Manage restorative procedures that preserve tooth structure, replace missing or defective tooth structure, maintain function, are esthetic, and promote soft and hard tissue health.

6.13 Diagnose and manage developmental or acquired occlusal abnormalities.

6.14 Manage the replacement of teeth for the partially or completely edentulous patient.

6.15 Diagnose, identify, and manage pulpal and periradicular diseases.

6.16 Diagnose and manage oral surgical treatment needs.

6.17 Prevent, recognize, and manage medical and dental emergencies.

6.18 Recognize and manage patient abuse and/or neglect.

6.19 Recognize and manage substance abuse.

6.20 Evaluate outcomes of comprehensive dental care.

6.21 Diagnose, identify, and manage oral mucosal and osseous diseases.

APPENDIX
Glossary of Terms

Competency: a complex behavior or ability essential for the general dentist to begin independent, unsupervised dental practice; it assumes that all behaviors and skills are performed with a degree of quality consistent with patient well-being and that the general dentist can self-evaluate treatment effectiveness.

Critical thinking: the process of assimilating and analyzing information; this encompasses an interest in finding new solutions, a curiosity with an ability to admit to a lack of understanding, a willingness to examine beliefs and assumptions and to search for evidence to support these beliefs and assumptions, and the ability to distinguish between fact and opinion.

Curriculum guidelines (content): the relevant and fundamental information that is taught for each category of foundation knowledge; these are to be used as curriculum development aids and should not be construed as recommendations for restrictive requirements.

Domain: a broad, critical category of activity for the general dentist.

Emerging technologies: current and future technologies used in patient care, including technologies for biomedical information storage and retrieval, clinical care information, and technologies for use at the point of care.

Evidence-based dentistry: an approach to oral health care that requires the judicious integration of systematic assessments of clinically relevant scientific evidence relating to the patient's oral and medical condition and history integrated with the dentist's clinical expertise and the patient's treatment needs and preferences.

Foundation knowledge and skills: the basic essential knowledge and skills linked to and necessary to support a given competency; these would serve to help guide curriculum in dental schools, assist educators in removing irrelevant, archaic information from current curricula, aid in including important new information, and help test construction committees develop examinations based upon generally accepted, contemporary information.

General dentist: the primary dental care provider for patients in all age groups who is responsible for the diagnosis, treatment, management, and overall coordination of services related to patients' oral health needs.

Health promotion: public health actions to protect or improve oral health and promote oral well-being through behavioral, educational, and enabling socioeconomic, legal, fiscal, environmental, and social measures; it involves the process of enabling individuals and communities to increase control over the determinants of health and thereby improve their health; includes education of the public to prevent chronic oral disease.

Informatics: applications associated with information and technology used in health care delivery; the data and knowledge needed for problem-solving and decision making; and the administration and management of information and technology in support of patient care, education, and research.

Interprofessional health care: the delivery of health care by a variety of health care practitioners in a cooperative, collaborative, and integrative manner to ensure care is continuous and reliable.

Management: includes all actions performed by a health care provider that are designed to alter the course of a patient's condition; such actions may include providing education, advice, treatment by the general dentist, treatment by the general dentist after consultation with another health care professional, referral of a patient to another health care professional, and monitoring the treatment provided; it may also include providing no treatment or observation.

Patient-centered care: the ability to identify, respect, and care about patients' differences, values, preferences, and expressed needs; relieve pain and suffering; coordinate continuous care; listen to, clearly inform, communicate with, and educate patients; share decision making and management; and continuously advocate disease prevention, wellness, and promotion of healthy lifestyles, including a focus on population health.

Problem-solving: the process of answering a question or achieving a goal when the path or answer is not immediately obvious, using an acceptable heuristic or strategy such as the scientific method.

Special needs care: an approach to oral health management tailored to the individual needs of people with a variety of medical conditions or physical and mental limitations that require more than routine delivery of oral care; special care encompasses preventive, diagnostic, and treatment services.

Dental Student Assessment Toolbox

Gene A. Kramer, Ph.D.; Judith E.N. Albino, Ph.D.; Sandra C. Andrieu, Ph.D.;
William D. Hendricson, M.S., M.A.; Lindsey Henson, M.D.; Bruce D. Horn, D.D.S.;
Laura M. Neumann, D.D.S., M.P.H.; Stephen K. Young, D.D.S.

The authors are members of the Task Force on Student Outcomes Assessment of the American Dental Education Association's Commission on Change and Innovation in Dental Education (ADEA CCI). Dr. Kramer is Director, Department of Testing Services, American Dental Association; Dr. Albino is a Senior Consultant, Academy for Academic Leadership, as well as President Emerita, University of Colorado and Professor, Department of Oral and Craniofacial Biology, School of Dental Medicine and Department of Community and Behavioral Health, Colorado School of Public Health, both at the University of Colorado, Denver; Dr. Andrieu is Associate Dean for Academic Affairs, School of Dentistry, Louisiana State University; Prof. Hendricson is Assistant Dean for Educational and Faculty Development, Dental School, University of Texas Health Science Center at San Antonio; Dr. Henson is Vice Dean for Education, Medical School, University of Minnesota; Dr. Horn is with the Joint Commission on National Dental Examinations; Dr. Neumann is Senior Vice President, Education/Professional Affairs, American Dental Association; and Dr. Young is Dean, School of Dentistry, University of Oklahoma, Chair of the ADEA CCI, and Chair of the ADEA CCI Task Force on Student Outcomes Assessment. Direct correspondence and requests for reprints to Dr. Gene Kramer, American Dental Association, 211 East Chicago Avenue, Suite 600, Chicago, IL 60611-2637; 312-440-7465 phone; 312-587-4105 fax; Kramerg@ada.org.

This article is one in a series of invited contributions by members of the dental education community that have been commissioned by the American Dental Education Association's Commission on Change and Innovation in Dental Education (ADEA CCI) to address the environment surrounding dental education and affecting the need for, or process of, curricular change. This article was written at the request of the ADEA CCI but does not necessarily reflect the views of ADEA, the ADEA CCI, or individual members of the ADEA CCI. The perspectives communicated here are those of the authors.

Key words: assessment, competence, dental education, dental students

Preface from the Chair of the ADEA CCI:

In 2005, the American Dental Education Association established the Commission on Change and Innovation in Dental Education (ADEA CCI) to build a consensus within the dental education community about innovative changes that are necessary in the education of general dentists to ensure that dental school graduates enter the profession fully competent to meet the oral health needs of the public.[1,2] As a part of its work, the ADEA CCI established several task forces, including the Task Force on Student Outcomes Assessment. The specific goal of this task force is to improve assessment practices in dental education. To this end, the task force, led by Dr. Gene A. Kramer, director of testing services at the American Dental Association, has created a "toolbox" designed to provide dental educators with a variety of techniques and methods for assessing the acquisition by students of competencies associated with the successful practice of dentistry. The assessment tools described range from familiar and frequently used assessment techniques such as multiple-choice and short answer essay items to newer and less familiar methods such as objective structured clinical examinations (OSCEs), portfolios, and triple jump exercises.

In the survey on competency assessment strategies used by dental schools that was reported in the December 2008 issue of the *Journal of Dental Education,*[3] it was found that the multiple-choice format is used most often by dental educators in assessing most student competencies, despite evidence to suggest that some competencies might be better assessed with other tools. The task force hopes that, by describing a range of tools and their possible applications, educators will explore ways to expand how they assess the knowledge, skills, and abilities of their students as they relate to the competencies necessary to function as beginning general dentists.

This Dental Student Assessment Toolbox is a first step in introducing alternative assessment tools and strategies into predoctoral dental education. The content of the toolbox will be honed and expanded in coming years to continue to meet the evolving needs of the dental educational community.

Stephen K. Young, D.D.S.
Chair, ADEA Commission on Change and Innovation in Dental Education
Chair, ADEA CCI Task Force on Student Outcomes Assessment

Assessment is an essential component of the educational experience. Assessment of students' progress in the dental curriculum ensures that they are acquiring the necessary knowledge, procedural/technical skills, problem-solving capacities, and critical thinking abilities. There are a variety of purposes to conducting assessment in the educational environment. The outcomes of assessment can be used to diagnose student strengths and weaknesses, to identify potential programmatic or curricular challenges, and to monitor students' progression toward, and ultimate attainment of, designated competencies that comprise the capacities of entry-level practitioners.

Assessment, however, is not a unitary concept when it comes to methodology. There are any number of methods that can be used, depending on the competencies being assessed. Using only one or two methods to assess students' attainment of the wide variety of knowledge, skills, and abilities supporting dental competencies would not be efficient or effective. Assessment methods range from simple written formats with relatively low levels of fidelity to actual demonstrations of capacity to perform skills in high fidelity situations that approximate the circumstances of general dental practice in the community. This Dental Student Assessment Toolbox was created to assist dental educators with the critical yet challenging task of determining the optimal methods for assessing students' progression toward and ultimate attainment of the competencies designated as necessary for the entry-level practice of general dentistry.

Glossary

This section provides a glossary of terms and concepts that are used in the description of the assessment methods in the toolbox.

Assessment and Assessment Tools: In the broad sense, assessment involves the gathering of information to determine the knowledge, skills, abilities, and performance levels of students or candidates for graduation, licensure, or certification. Assessment tools comprise a wide range of instruments and methodologies designed to gather this information for feedback, diagnostic purposes, and identifying successful attainment of competence.

Competency: A complex behavior or ability essential for the general dentist to begin independent, unsupervised dental practice; it assumes that all behaviors and skills are performed with a degree of quality consistent with patient well-being and that the general dentist can self-evaluate treatment effectiveness.

Fidelity: Fidelity refers to the similarity of the assessment tool to the actual competency or student performance being assessed. A high fidelity tool is one that is very similar to the actual performance.

Formative Assessment: Formative assessment involves the accumulation of evaluative information for diagnostic purposes and, in the educational context, for assessing and guiding students' development. For dental students, the findings of formative assessments are used to diagnose strengths and weaknesses for the purposes of identifying strategies to enhance student performance. For programs, the findings of formative assessments can suggest opportunities to improve the focus of the curriculum and instructional methods.

Measurement: Measurement refers to the representation of performance using the outcomes of the application of mathematical formulas to numerical data. For many years in the past, classical measurement theory was the primary system used to describe these characteristics or properties. During the last several decades, item response theory (IRT) has been the system of choice for large-scale testing. Because IRT requires large numbers of individuals, however, classical theory remains the mainstay in the academic environment.

Reliability: Reliability relates to consistency in measurement, i.e., scores derived from a reliable assessment tool are similar across assessment events. Reliability is typically reported as a value ranging from 0.0 to 1.0. Reliabilities above 0.90 are considered to be excellent. Reliabilities below 0.70 are considered suspect, and results from such an assessment tool should be interpreted with caution.

Summative Assessment: Summative assessment involves the accumulation of information. For the student, the findings of the assessments determine whether the student has accomplished programmatic goals. This form of assessment often represents the level of accomplishment, achievement, or "grade." For the program, findings determine the overall quality of the curriculum for the purposes of making decisions concerning the future of the program.

Validity: Validity refers to the accumulation of evidence gathered from a variety of sources and supporting the proposition that the assessment is, in fact, evaluating the competency of interest, or the knowledge and abilities that support the acquisition of competence. Evidence can take the form of expert opinion derived from a practice analysis, survey, or standard setting event.

Table and Descriptions of Assessment Methods

A summary table in a two-dimensional matrix is presented in the appendix. Along the vertical dimension of the table are the Competencies for the New General Dentist endorsed by the ADEA House of Delegates in April 2008;[4] sixteen assessment methodologies are presented across the horizontal dimension. Each of the sixteen assessment methods in the summary table is described in the following sections. Each intersecting cell shows the appropriate methodology for use in evaluating each competency. A "1" in the cell indicates a preferred technique, a "2" indicates an acceptable methodology, and a "3" indicates an assessment that is potentially applicable in certain circumstances. It is important to note that these indicators are suggestions. Depending on the particular competency, an alternative methodology or combination of techniques might be appropriate. Key sources that were consulted to create the summary table are cited in the general reference section of this article. The recommendations for assessment strategies that appear in the summary table are based on reviews of the performance and competency assessment literature described in the task force's prior article, published in the December 2008 JDE.[3]

The separate sections that follow describe the sixteen assessment methods that appear in the summary table. For each method, the characteristics, use, strengths, limitations, and key references are provided. As shown in Figure 1, the assessment methods are organized into six categories based on

Category	Format		
1. Written Assessment Selected and constructed response items	**Multiple-Choice Items** • Independent questions • Testlets (case-based)	**Short Answer**	**Structured Essay**
2. Faculty Assessment by Observation	**Global Ratings**	**Structured Observation** with checklists and rating scales	**Standardized Oral Exam**
3. Multisource Assessment	**Student Self-Assessment Peer Assessment**	**Patient Survey**	**Standardized Patients**
4. Simulation	**Virtual Reality** Computer-based clinical scenarios	**Models**	
5. Multi-Competency, Comprehensive Assessment	**Objective Structured Clinical Exam (OSCE)**	**Triple Jump Exercise (TJE)**	
6. Work Samples	**Portfolio**	**Record Review** Chart-stimulated review	

Figure 1. Methods for assessing dental students' attainment of competence

the nature of the assessment format and/or the type of response requested from students: 1) *selected and constructed response items (written assessment)*, in which students select a best response from a series of options or construct a response in their own words; 2) *faculty assessment by observing student performance*, in which students are observed while they perform tasks associated with professional competence by their instructors and are evaluated using checklists and rating scales to guide the appraisal process; 3) *multi-source assessment*, which refers to a group of assessment tools often used in conjunction with other methods to provide a well-rounded perspective on students' progression toward competence; 4) *simulation*, including computer-based applications and realistic models; 5) *multi-competency, comprehensive assessments*, including the objective structured clinical examination (OSCE) and triple jump exercise (TJE); and 6) *work samples*, including portfolios and record review.

REFERENCES

1. Kalkwarf KL, Haden NK, Valachovic RW. ADEA Commission on Change and Innovation in Dental Education. J Dent Educ 2005;69(10):1085–7.
2. Pyle M, Andrieu SC, Chadwick DG, Chmar JE, Cole JR, George MC, et al. The case for change in dental education. J Dent Educ 2006;70(9):921–4.
3. Albino JEN, Young SK, Neumann LM, Kramer GA, Andrieu SC, Henson L, Horn B, Hendricson WD. Assessing dental students' competence: best practice recommendations in the performance assessment literature and investigation of current practices in predoctoral dental education. J Dent Educ 2008;72(12):1405–35.
4. American Dental Education Association. Competencies for the new general dentist (as approved by the 2008 ADEA House of Delegates). J Dent Educ 2008;72(7):823–6.

Written Assessments:
Selected and Constructed Response Items

Multiple-Choice Items

Description and Characteristics

The multiple-choice item consists of two components, i.e., a stem and a series of alternatives. The stem can be an incomplete statement or a question. The dental student examinee is to select the alternative that either correctly completes the statement or provides the most appropriate response to the question.

There are two variations of importance when describing multiple-choice items. The stem is essentially a stimulus for the response. In stand-alone or independent items, the stem is the only stimulus material (Figure 2). In testlet-based or case-based multiple-choice items, additional material is provided as a stimulus (Figure 3). In the case of dental education, the additional stimulus material might consist of a dental chart or history along with a brief clinical scenario, as in a testlet. Case-based items might include radiographs, clinical photographs, and dental charting.

Uses

Notwithstanding the significant number of existing variations for this assessment method, multiple-choice items are the most frequent choice for assessing comprehension or application of theoretical knowledge. If properly constructed, they also can be used to assess problem-solving ability. Multiple-choice items also are an effective method for gathering formative and summative performance information.

Strengths and Limitations

This method is widely used because multiple-choice items can be readily developed and scored objectively and can sample widely from an extensive volume of knowledge. This item type has a relatively low level of fidelity to actual practice, however, and it is also susceptible to various measurement disturbances, such as guessing. Additional stimulus material provided in testlet or case-based items enhances the fidelity of the item type and allows for sampling more clinically relevant material from the curriculum.

Short Answer Questions

Description and Characteristics

Stimulus material is provided in a short statement or question that poses a problem requiring the dental students to respond with the solution to the problem in their own words (Figure 4).

Uses

This item type is most often used in formative assessment designed to gather information on a student's knowledge of basic information. It can also be used to assess a variety of other abilities, e.g., 1) list a differential diagnosis, 2) list steps in a procedure in order and/or priority, 3) develop a treatment plan, and 4) list etiology of disease and conditions.

Strengths and Limitations

By requiring the student to generate a response in the form of a sentence or two, this item type taps different cognitive processes than the multiple-choice item, i.e., it can be used to tap the dental student's ability to generate an original response. This item type eliminates guessing as an assessment factor; however, evaluation of the response is less objective and is subject to measurement disturbances such as the influence on the rater of spelling, handwriting, and grammatical errors. To help avoid these influences, a key is developed that focuses on the salient information to be provided in the response.

A new young adult patient presents for a routine dental examination. In reviewing the periapical radiographs, you note that the lower right second premolar appears to be congenitally missing. Which primary tooth is most likely retained in its place?

A. Canine
B. First premolar
C. Second premolar
D. First molar
E. Second molar

Figure 2. Example of an independent multiple-choice item

Age	65 years		SCENARIO
Gender	☒ Male	☐ Female	The patient presents for replacement of a filling in tooth #19. He reports that he lost the filling over a year ago, but he delayed seeking care because the tooth has not been sensitive. Upon examination, tooth #19 has a missing occlusal restoration and a fractured ML cusp.
Height	5' 9"		
Weight	240 lbs.		
B/P	170/100		
Chief Complaint	"Lost filling in back tooth"		
Medical History	Last saw his physician 2 years ago; father died of heart attack at age 52		
Current Medications	Diuretic for high blood pressure; statin for high cholesterol; low dose aspirin		
Social History	Married, grown children; retired construction foreman		

Which would be the most likely consequence of the patient's delay in having the lost restoration replaced?

A. Supra-eruption of tooth #14
B. Chewing inefficiency
C. Loss of canine disclusion
D. Mesial drift of tooth #18

Figure 3. Example of a testlet-based multiple-choice item

Q: What is the legal principle underlying the doctrine of informed consent?

A: *That a patient can only consent if adequately informed.*

Q: What are the basic elements of informed consent?

A: *A description of treatment recommendations, the benefits and risks of treatment and nontreatment, and alternative treatments.*

Figure 4. Examples of short answer questions and students' responses

Patient Scenario

An 81-year-old female presents to your office. She is 5' 4", 142 pounds, with a blood pressure reading of 122/84. She has diabetes mellitus type II and rheumatic disease with a resultant murmur; she is allergic to penicillin, photosensitive to tetracyclines, and has an atrial fibrillation. She is currently taking insulin, warfarin, and vitamin A.

The patient had rheumatic fever as a child and was diagnosed with diabetes at age 52. Lately, her appetite has been poor, and her caregiver reports frequent disorientation.

The patient had routine dental care before retirement at age 62. She has had sporadic care since then and is very frightened. She requests sedation for any "painful" treatment. Patient smoked a pack of cigarettes per day for over 50 years and quit smoking five years ago.

She is widowed with two sons who don't live in the area and is active in church and senior center activities. She resides in an assisted living facility.

She reports a chief complaint as "My back teeth hurt, and sometimes my gums bleed when I brush. My teeth seem loose and food gets caught between them."

The mandible will be treated with an interim removable partial denture, and Teeth #17, #21, #22, #27, #28, and #32 will be maintained.

Questions
- What treatment plan would most enhance the facial retention on the anterior abutments?
- Before performing any extractions on the patient, what actions should be considered? If planning intravenous conscious sedation for this patient, what is of concern to the dentist and how should it be handled?
- What is the most likely medical emergency to arise in this patient?

Figure 5. Example of a structured essay assignment based on a patient scenario

Structured Essay

Description and Characteristics

This item type is similar to the short answer item except that the response presented by the dental student is far more involved. Stimulus material is provided that poses a question or problem. The stimulus material might involve a clinical scenario. The material requires the dental student to provide a logical and detailed response to the question or problem posed (Figure 5).

Uses

The structured essay is used to evaluate the student's ability to clearly identify the salient elements of the problem and logically present a solution or resolution. This type of item addresses a full range of competencies that do not involve clinical demonstrations.

Strengths and Limitations

One of the strengths of this type of item is that it can address most competencies. In the case of competencies associated with patient care, the stimulus material provided involves some sort of clinical scenario. The evaluation of the response can be subjective, however, unless the rater is calibrated, i.e., raters have developed a clear and precise key, or set of criteria, to apply to the response.

SOURCES

Azer SA. Assessment in a problem-based learning course. Biochem Mol Biol Educ 2003;31(6):248–434.

Downing ST, Haladyna TM, eds. Handbook of test development. Mahwah, NJ: Lawrence Erlbaum, 2006.

Haladyna TM. Developing and validating multiple-choice test items. 3rd ed. Mahwah, NJ: Lawrence Erlbaum, 2004.

Haladyna TM, Downing SM. A taxonomy of multiple-choice item-writing rules. Appl Meas Educ 1989;1:37–50.

Assessment by Observation

Global Ratings

Description and Characteristics

Dental students are rated on their performance using a series of general or global rating scales following some interaction with colleagues or dental patients most often in a clinical setting (Figure 6). This form of assessment requires a clear set of performance indicators or rubrics that are judged to be important relative to the competency or competencies being evaluated. The student is rated on each indicator. The student is typically rated on a scale ranging from 1 to 5, with a 1 indicating that the competency of interest has not been successfully achieved and a 5 indicating most or all aspects of the competency have been achieved successfully. Global ratings are not restricted to a five-point scale, although more than five points tend to be confusing to the rater. For measurement purposes, it is assumed that the scale is comprised of uniformly increasing levels of success.

Uses

This is an effective form of assessment for evaluating the student on competencies related to critical thinking, communication and interpersonal skills, and professionalism, although the method is not confined to these competencies.

Strengths and Limitations

The strength of this form of assessment lies in its suitability at evaluating general behaviors in a variety of settings. The indicators of the successful acquisition of the competency must be agreed upon by raters as important or critical to the competency. The limitation of the form is the potential for subjectivity in ratings, unless only one rater is used or multiple raters are calibrated to ensure consistency.

Structured Observation with Checklists or Rating Scales

Description and Characteristics

In this type of assessment, students are exposed to a highly structured situation, most often in a clinical setting, with pre-established performance demands. Typically, students are expected to perform

It is characteristic of _____ to:						
student name						
	Agree			Disagree		
1. identify existing clinical problem and etiology successfully	5	4	3	2	1	DK
2. have sufficient information prior to beginning a procedure	5	4	3	2	1	DK
3. effectively generate ideas regarding the origin of the problem	5	4	3	2	1	DK
4. reflect on the new knowledge needed to solve a problem	5	4	3	2	1	DK
5. develop hypotheses rather than jump to conclusions	5	4	3	2	1	DK

Source: excerpted with permission from Clinical problem-solving inventory. Chicago: American Dental Association, 2003.

Figure 6. Example of a global rating scale

a specific skill, and the rating scale includes important components/attributes of that skill rather than a general set of performance parameters as are included on the previous global rating scale. The student's performance is observed by a rater or multiple raters, who use a checklist to indicate that some aspect of performance has been demonstrated or a set of rating scales to indicate the level of performance relative to the competency or competencies of interest. In the case of a checklist, the agreed upon entries address the critical aspects of the performance. As with global ratings, the student typically is rated on a scale consisting of three, four, or five points, ranging, for example, from 1 to 3, with a 1 indicating that the competency or some component of the competency has not been successfully achieved and a 3 indicating that most or all aspects of the competency have been achieved successfully (Figure 7).

Uses

As with global ratings, this is an effective form of assessment for evaluating the student on competencies related to critical thinking and communication and interpersonal skills, although the method is not confined to these competencies. The difference between global ratings and structured observations lies in the situation to which the student is exposed. With structured observation, the student is exposed to a situation that is designed to elicit specific knowledge or behaviors. It is used extensively for assessing psychomotor skills and performance of clinical procedures.

Strengths and Limitations

This assessment form is ideal for evaluating specific areas of performance, and it represents a method for evaluating competencies related to the more clinically relevant competencies. As with global ratings, however, it is susceptible to subjectivity on the part of raters.

Standardized Oral Examination

Description and Characteristics

A set of stimulus questions are developed that address critical areas of knowledge or sets of abilities related to a competency or set of competencies. All students being evaluated are exposed to the same set of questions. Students are expected to respond verbally in their own words, which allows an assessment of the student's depth of comprehension and capacity to apply knowledge and insights to different situations. Responses to the questions are assessed using a standardized rating scale or scoring system.

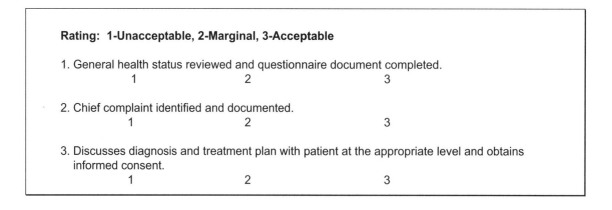

Rating: 1-Unacceptable, 2-Marginal, 3-Acceptable

1. General health status reviewed and questionnaire document completed.
        1   2   3

2. Chief complaint identified and documented.
        1   2   3

3. Discusses diagnosis and treatment plan with patient at the appropriate level and obtains informed consent.
        1   2   3

Figure 7. Example of a structured rating scale for a specific skill

Uses

This form of assessment is well suited to the evaluation of critical thinking competencies and competencies in the area of professionalism, although it can be used with other competencies exclusive of clinical demonstrations.

Strengths and Limitations

The strength of this form of assessment lies in the opportunity on the part of the rater to examine the underlying logic of the student's response, assuming that probing for further information is allowed by the design of the examination. As with other faculty assessment methods, however, structured oral examinations are susceptible to subjectivity on the part of raters.

SOURCES

Gray J. Global rating scale in residency education. Acad Med 1996;71:555–63.

Licari FW, Knight GW, Guenzel PJ. Designing evaluation forms to facilitate student learning. J Dent Educ 2008;72(1):48–58.

Ryding HA, Murphy HJ. Employing oral examinations (viva voce) in assessing dental students' clinical reasoning skills. J Dent Educ 1999;63(9):682–7.

Taleghani M, Solomon ES, Wathen WF. Non-graded clinical evaluation of dental students in a competency-based education program. J Dent Educ 2004;68(6):644–55.

Wagner J, Arteaga S, D'Ambrosio J, Hodge CE, Ioannidou E, Pfeiffer CA, et al. A patient-instructor program to promote dental students' communication skills with diverse patients. J Dent Educ 2007;71(12):1554–60.

Winckel CP, Reznick RK, Cohen R, Taylor B. Reliability and construct validity of a structured technical skills assessment form. Am J Surg 1994;167:423–7.

Multisource Assessment

This section describes several assessment tools that are often used in conjunction with other methods to provide a well-rounded perspective on students' progression toward competence.

Student Self-Assessment

Description and Characteristics

Dental students evaluate their own performance against a set of criteria related to important competencies or the knowledge, abilities, and skills underlying a competency. This approach might involve a form with rating scales associated with specific criteria. Students might also provide narratives evaluating their performance and reflecting on lessons learned and strategies for enhancement or modification of performance in the future.

Uses

This form of assessment can be applied to any competency or underlying knowledge or ability; however, it is best reserved for assessment of competencies that do not involve demonstrations of highly precise technical skills that are best evaluated by experienced clinicians. Student self-assessment can also be an important component of formative assessment. Student self-assessment has been found to be very useful in the preclinical environment.

Strengths and Limitations

Dental students are best able to assess their own performance if provided with a clearly defined set of criteria against which to make judgments and a set of standards of acceptable levels of knowledge and performance. This form is limited by students' own ability to view their knowledge or performance realistically. This approach is most effective when used in combination with or comparison to assessment by competent, experienced instructors/evaluators.

Peer Assessment

Description and Characteristics

Dental students assess each other's performance and, in some instances, knowledge. Checklists or rating scales are best incorporated into this form of assessment.

Uses

This form of assessment is well suited to evaluating the communication and interpersonal skills and health promotion competencies, although peer assessment can be useful with other competencies as well. This assumes the criteria have been clearly articulated and are relevant to essential knowledge and abilities. Peer assessment is also useful in problem-based learning and in other curricular activities in which students' contributions to group learning are important.

Strengths and Limitations

This approach to the assessment of students is limited, however, by the level of knowledge and ability of the peer group.

Patient Survey

Description and Characteristics

Patient surveys typically involve a series of rating scales or checklists designed to assess the patient's satisfaction with the performance of the student in the clinical setting. The standard survey solicits the patient's satisfaction using categories such as poor, good, and excellent, with categories in between where appropriate. Also, categories might be agree, neutral, or disagree with value judgments included on the survey.

Uses

This form of assessment is ideally suited to evaluating those competencies related to communication and interpersonal skills, as well as patient care. However, patient evaluations are not confined to assessing students' behavior. Perspectives and ratings provided by patients can be expanded to assess the quality of clinic services.

Strengths and Limitations

This form of assessment involves gathering information from patients on those aspects of care that are important to them. It should be possible to complete the assessment in a reasonable amount of time, typically ten to fifteen minutes. This involves interviewing patients and focus groups to determine the critical aspects of care that will be assessed. These aspects, in turn, are translated into a survey form. The survey can be an effective method of gathering information because it is based on the concerns of patients. Limitations include issues related to the patient's ability to understand the language on the survey, costs involved in obtaining survey information, and the challenges of obtaining a sufficient number of completed surveys to achieve reliable findings.

Standardized Patients

Description and Characteristics

Standardized patients (SPs) are trained individuals who present in a clinical situation with standardized symptoms similar to those that might be encountered with actual patients. These patients present with a full variety of symptoms that allow the dental student to develop a range of treatment plans.

Uses

Standardized patients provide essential feedback on dental student performance, often using a checklist or series of rating scales. Faculty raters also provide feedback in the form of evaluative comments. This is an effective approach to evaluating competencies related to communication and interpersonal skills and patient care.

Strengths and Limitations

This form of assessment provides the students with valuable information on their ability to think critically, their interpersonal skills in working with patients, and their ability to diagnose and develop a treatment plan. It can be subjective, however, unless patients are highly trained and calibrated.

SOURCES

Archer J. Mini-PAT (peer assessment tool): a well kept secret. J R Soc Med 2008;101:272.

Barrows HS. An overview of the uses of standardized patients for teaching and evaluating clinical skills. Acad Med 1993;68:443–51.

Butters JM, Willis DO. A comparison of patient satisfaction among current and former dental school patients. J Dent Educ 2000;64(6):409–15.

Curtis DA, Lind SL, Dellinges M, Setia G, Finzen FC. Dental students' self-assessment of preclinical examinations. J Dent Educ 2008;72(3):265–77.

Ferrell BG. Clinical performance assessment using standardized patients: a primer. Fam Med 1995;27:14–9.

Johnson JA, Kopp KC, Williams RG. Standardized patients for the assessment of dental students' clinical skills. J Dent Educ 1990;54(6):331–3.

Thammasitboon K, Sukotjo C, Howell H, Karimbux N. Problem-based learning at the Harvard School of Dental Medicine: self-assessment of performance in postdoctoral training. J Dent Educ 2007;71(8):1080–9.

Simulation

Virtual Reality (Computer-Based Clinical Scenarios)

Description and Characteristics

Computer-based clinical scenarios are designed to evaluate students' knowledge and abilities related to diagnosis and treatment planning. These scenarios can be highly sophisticated, involving and often using audio and video simulations.

Uses

Computer-based scenarios are well suited to assessing competencies associated with diagnosis and treatment planning. These scenarios tend to have high fidelity and make excellent teaching and assessment tools.

Strengths and Limitations

The strength of virtual scenarios lies in their high fidelity. Determining performance levels is difficult, however, and requires considerable research in determining salient decision points in evaluating appropriate diagnoses and treatment plans. This research involves exploring novice and expert performance with focus groups of students and expert practitioners to determine levels of acceptable performance.

Computer-based scenarios that depict actual patient care situations are time-consuming and often expensive to produce, factors reflecting common logistical limitations.

Models

Description and Characteristics

Models consist of mannequins showing various dentally related clinical challenges for the dental student to evaluate.

Uses

This form of assessment taps knowledge and problem-solving skills underlying competencies often related to diagnosis and treatment planning. Because models are standard for all students and evaluation criteria can be readily defined, evaluation can be relatively objective.

Strengths and Limitations

This form of assessment is effective largely because symptoms are easily standardized and consistent across students. Assessing performance is relatively straightforward. It is only limited if criteria are not well defined or those serving as raters are not well calibrated.

SOURCES

Buchanan JA. Use of simulation technology in dental education. J Dent Educ 2001;65(11):1225–31.

Jasinevicius TR, Landers M, Nelson S, Urbankova A. An evaluation of two dental simulation systems: virtual reality versus contemporary non-computer-assisted. J Dent Educ 2004;68(11):1151–62.

Littlefield JH, Demps EL, Keiser K, Chatterjee L, Yuan CH, Hargreaves KM. A multimedia patient simulation for teaching and assessing endodontic diagnosis. J Dent Educ 2003;67(6):669–77.

Wierinck ER, Puttemans V, Swinnen SP, van Steenberghe D. Expert performance on a virtual reality simulation system. J Dent Educ 2007;71(6):759–66.

Multi-Competency, Comprehensive Assessments

Objective Structured Clinical Examination (OSCE)

Description and Characteristics

In dental school applications, OSCEs consist of a set of work stations that involve standardized procedures for the dental student to perform. Multiple tools are used to assess students' performance on the designated tasks at these stations, which can number from ten to thirty. The time allotment at each station varies, but is usually from five to fifteen minutes.

Uses

This form of assessment provides a standardized opportunity for students to demonstrate their ability to conduct an oral examination, take comprehensive notes, and interpret the clinical situation. This is an excellent format for evaluating a full range of competencies, especially those related to diagnosis and treatment.

Strengths and Limitations

The strengths of this form of assessment are that it provides an opportunity for students to demonstrate specific clinical skills and it has high fidelity. It is also effective at evaluating competencies related to treatment. However, gathering reliable performance information can be problematic since there are a limited number of stations. It is logistically difficult and time-consuming to develop and conduct this form of assessment.

Triple Jump Exercise (TJE)

Description and Characteristics

There are two types of TJEs used in different components of the curriculum, but they involve similar techniques. A clinical TJE consists of three phases ("jumps") in which students 1) interview and examine patients while observed by faculty or, less often, are videotaped for retrospective review; 2) write an assessment of the findings from the patient assessment using the "SOAP" format (subjective data, objective data, assessment, plans), with emphasis on providing evidence from the literature to support diagnostic and therapeutic decisions and submit this document to the faculty member who observed jump one; and 3) participate in an oral examination conducted by the observing faculty member in which students are questioned about the pathophysiology, diagnosis, and treatment of the patient's problems and asked to discuss research evidence pertinent to treatment and outcomes. Students receive an evaluation for each jump and a cumulative score across all three jumps.

TJEs implemented in the preclinical curriculum focus on students' skills in searching the literature to answer health-related questions that they have developed. In a preclinical TJE, the first jump involves reading a scenario depicting a patient with an oral health problem, identifying key issues, and writing a researchable question in the PICO format (patient with problem, intervention, comparison, and outcome). During the second jump, students investigate literature to find evidence pertinent to their question, and then, in jump three, report their findings, answer the research question, and critically appraise the quality of available evidence. As with clinical TJEs, preclinical students receive evaluations for each jump and a cumulative score for the whole exercise.

Uses

The triple jump exercise is used to evaluate students' capacity to access, analyze, and apply biomedical knowledge to health care problems. When coupled with multiple-choice testing in the case-based testlet format (i.e., several multiple-choice questions linked to a patient scenario), TJEs provide a mechanism for assessment of students' capacity to function at the application level of the cognitive taxonomy. Both types of TJEs emphasize accessing pertinent information, applying this information to health problems, and appraising the quality of knowledge available to answer clinical questions.

Strengths and Limitations

The strength of this form of assessment is that it provides an opportunity for faculty to appraise the student's performance across a spectrum of skills ranging from patient assessment (conducting an interview or performing an examination) to diagnosis and treatment planning and ultimately the ability to explain the rationale for selected therapy and demonstrate understanding of the research evidence pertinent to the patient's oral health problems and therapeutic options. However, the TJE for either preclinical or clinical students is time-consuming to develop and logistically difficult to implement, requiring considerable numbers of faculty mem-

bers who need to be trained in the technique and calibrated to provide uniform assessments of each of the jumps.

SOURCES

Feletti G, Ryan G. Triple jump exercise in inquiry-based learning: a case study. Assess Eval Higher Educ 1994;19(3):225–34.

Gerrow JD, Murphy HJ, Boyd MA, Scott DA. Concurrent validity of written and OSCE components of the Canadian dental certification examinations. J Dent Educ 2003;67(8):896–901.

Rangachari PK. The TRIPSE: a process-oriented evaluation for problem-based learning courses in the basic sciences. Biochem Mol Biol Educ 2002;30(1):57–60.

Schoonhein-Klein M. The use of the objective structured clinical examination (OSCE) in dental education. Amsterdam: M.E. Schiinheim-Kleub, 2007.

Smith RM. The triple-jump examination as an assessment tool in the problem-based medical curriculum at the University of Hawaii. Acad Med 1993;13:366–72.

Work Samples

Portfolios

Description and Characteristics

Portfolios require that students gather a collection of documents demonstrating the acquisition of relevant knowledge and ability across all competencies. This form addresses both formative and summative assessment. These documents can include self-assessments, patient survey findings, and sample patient cases, including diagnosis and treatment plans. The portfolio is an opportunity for the student to show any learning product that meets certain prespecified criteria.

Uses

This is a student-centered tool, which is an effective method for evaluating a variety of competencies such as critical thinking, professionalism, and health promotion.

Strengths and Limitations

The strength of this assessment tool is that it allows for the evaluation of competencies that are not readily evaluated using other tools. However, the variability among portfolios makes consistent evaluation difficult for raters. Also, supporting students in their development of their portfolios can be time-consuming, as can evaluating the documents themselves. It has been found that, because of these limitations, portfolios can be problematic to both students and faculty raters.

Record Review (Chart-Stimulated Review)

Description and Characteristics

This methodology involves a review of the patient care records (i.e., patients' charts) developed by the student. The review consists of an evaluation of diagnostic information and an examination of findings related to treatment planning in light of standards of dental practice. Chart-stimulated review is commonly used as an assessment technique in medical education for residents and students on clerkships. The method assesses the learner's capacity to explain rationales for treatment decisions, show comprehension of key concepts, and compare and contrast alternative treatment approaches; it also is used to stimulate students' self-assessment and reflection.

Uses

Record review is effective for evaluating competencies that are not readily assessed by other tools including competencies in the domains of critical thinking, professionalism, and health promotion in the ADEA Competencies for the New General Dentist.

Strengths and Limitations

Similar to portfolios, a wide range of competencies can be evaluated with chart reviews. The variability among records can lead to subjective judgments regarding their quality, however.

SOURCES

Gadbury-Amyot CC, Holt LP, Overman PR, Schmidt CR. Implementation of portfolio assessment in a competency-based dental hygiene program. J Dent Educ 2000;64(5):375–80.

Friedman Ben David M, Davis M, Harden R, Howie P, Ker J, Pippard M. Portfolios as a method of student assessment. AMEE Medical Education Guide No. 24. Med Teacher 2001;23(6):535–51.

Logan H, Gardner T. A review of a dental record audit program within a predoctoral dental curriculum. J Dent Educ 1988;52(6):302–5.

General References on Assessment

Standards

The most authoritative source of information related to assessment standards has been developed and described in a document published by the American Educational Research Association, American Psychological Association, and National Council on Measurement in Education. This document is:

American Educational Research Association, American Psychological Association, National Council on Measurement in Education. Standards for educational and psychological testing. Washington, DC: American Educational Research Association, American Psychological Association, National Council on Measurement in Education, 1999.

The standards are currently under review, and a revised set of standards will be published in the near future.

Guides to Assessment Techniques in Health Professions Education

Joint Commission on National Dental Examinations. Case development guide: National Board Dental Examination. Chicago: American Dental Association. 2007. At: www.ada.org/prof/ed/testing/construction/nbde02_case_guide.pdf.

Joint Commission on National Dental Examinations. Case development guide: National Board Dental Hygiene Examination. Chicago: American Dental Association, 2007. At: www.ada.org/prof/ed/testing/construction/nbdhe_case_guide.pdf.

Joint Commission on National Dental Examinations. Test item development guide: National Board Dental Examination. Chicago: American Dental Association, 2007.

National Board of Medical Examiners. Subject examinations: content outlines and sample items. Philadelphia: National Board of Medical Examiners, 2003:1–38.

National Board of Medical Examiners. Section II: writing one-best-answer questions for the basic and clinical sciences. Philadelphia: National Board of Medical Examiners, 2003:33–67.

National Board of Medical Examiners. Section III: extended matching items. Philadelphia: National Board of Medical Examiners, 2003:71–103.

National Board of Medical Examiners. Appendix B. Sample item-writing templates, items, lead-ins, and option lists for the basic and clinical sciences. Philadelphia: National Board of Medical Examiners, 2003:131–80.

Textbooks and Monographs

Downing ST, Haladyna TM, eds. Handbook of test development. Mahwah, NJ: Lawrence Erlbaum, 2006.

Fortune JC, Cromack TR. Developing and using clinical examinations. In: Impara JC, ed. Licensure testing: purposes, procedures, and practices. Lincoln, NE: Buros Institute of Mental Measurements, 1995:149–65.

Haladyna TM. Developing and validating multiple-choice test items. 3rd ed. Mahwah, NJ: Lawrence Erlbaum, 2004.

Irvine SH, Kyllonen PC, eds. Item generation for test development. Mahwah, NJ: Lawrence Erlbaum, 2002.

LaDuca A, Downing SM, Henzel TR. Systematic item writing and test construction. In: Impara JC, ed. Licensure testing: purposes, procedures, and practices. Lincoln, NE: Buros Institute of Mental Measurements, 1995:117–48.

Middle States Commission on Higher Education. Student learning assessment: options and resources. Philadelphia: Middle States Commission on Higher Education, 2003.

Schmeiser CB, Welch CJ. Test development. In: Brennan RL, ed. Educational measurement. 4th ed. Washington, DC: American Council on Education and Praeger Publishers, 2006:307–54.

Journal Articles: Summaries of Assessment Best Practices

Azer SA. Assessment in a problem-based learning course. Biochem Mol Biol Educ 2003;31(6):248–434.

Chambers DW, Glassman P. A primer on competency-based evaluation. J Dent Educ 1997;61(8):651–66.

Epstein RM. Assessment in medical education. N Engl J Med 2007;356(4):387–96.

Epstein RM, Hundert EM. Defining and assessing professional competence. JAMA 2002;287(2):226–35.

Friedman Ben David M, Davis M, Harden R, Howie P, Ker J, Pippard M. Portfolios as a method of student assessment. AMEE medical education guide no. 24. Med Teacher 2001;23(6):535–51.

Hoge R, Coladarci T. Teacher-based judgments of academic achievement: a review of the literature. Rev Educ Res 1989;59(3):297–313.

Linn RL. Complex, performance-based assessment: expectations and validation criteria. Educ Researcher 1991;16(1):1–21.

Miller GE. Assessment of clinical skills/competence/performance. Acad Med 1990;9:63–7.

Norcini J, Burch V. Workplace-based assessment as an educational tool. AMEE guide no. 31. Med Teacher 2007;29(9 & 10):855–71.

Shumway JM, Harden RM. The assessment of learning outcomes for the competent and reflective physician. AMEE guide no. 25. Med Teacher 2003;25(6):569–84.

Smith SR, Dollase RH, Boss JA. Assessing students' performance in a competency-based curriculum. Acad Med 2003;78:97–107.

Swing SR. Assessing the ACGME general competencies: general considerations and assessment methods. Acad Emerg Med 2002;9(11):1278–87.

Van der Vieuten CPM. The assessment of professional competence: developments, research, and practical implications. Adv Health Sci Educ 1996;1:41–67.

Van der Vieuten CPM, Schuwirth L. Assessing professional competence: from methods to programmes. Med Educ 2005;39:309–17.

Wass V, Van der Vieuten CPM, Shatzer J, Jones R. Assessment of clinical competence. Lancet 2001;357(March 24):945–9.

Other Resources

Paul R, Nosich GM. A model for the national assessment of higher order thinking, section four. Critical thinking community, 1993. At: www.criticalthinking.org/assessment/a-model-nal-assessment-hot.cfm.

The assessment toolkit developed by the Accreditation Council for Graduate Medical Education can be accessed at www.acgme.org/Outcome/assess/Toolbox.pdf.

Organizations Involving Assessment

American Dental Education Association, Washington, DC. At: www.adea.org.

American Educational Research Association, Washington, DC. At: www.aera.net.

American Psychological Association, Washington, DC. At: www.apa.org.

Association for Psychological Science, Washington, DC. At: www.psychologicalscience.org.

National Council on Measurement in Education, Washington, DC. At: www.ncme.org.

APPENDIX

Summary Table of Assement Techniques to Measure Dental Students' Attainment of the 2008 ADEA Competencies for the New General Dentist

Along the vertical dimension of the table are the Competencies for the New General Dentist endorsed by the ADEA House of Delegates in April 2008; sixteen assessment methodologies are presented across the horizontal dimension. Each intersecting cell shows the appropriate methodology for use in evaluating each competency. A "1" in the cell indicates a preferred technique, a "2" indicates an acceptable methodology, and a "3" indicates an assessment that is potentially applicable in certain circumstances. It is important to note that these indicators are suggestions. Depending on the particular competency, an alternative methodology or combination of techniques might be appropriate.

Toolbox of assessment techniques to measure dental students' attainment of the 2008 ADEA Competencies for the New General Dentist (1: Preferred; 2: Acceptable; 3: Potentially Applicable)

Competencies for the New General Dentist	Written Assessment			Faculty Observation		
	Multiple-Choice	Short Answer	Structured Essay	Global Ratings	Structured Observation	Standardized Oral Exam
Critical Thinking						
Graduates must be competent to:						
1.1 Evaluate and integrate emerging trends in health care as appropriate.	3	2	1			
1.2 Utilize critical thinking and problem-solving skills.			1		2	
1.3 Evaluate and integrate best research outcomes with clinical expertise and patient values for evidence-based practice.			2		1	
Professionalism						
Graduates must be competent to:						
2.1 Apply ethical and legal standards in the provision of dental care.			1			3
2.2 Practice within one's scope of competence and consult with or refer to professional colleagues when indicated.					1	
Communication and Interpersonal Skills						
Graduates must be competent to:						
3.1 Apply appropriate interpersonal and communication skills.					1	
3.2 Apply psychosocial and behavioral principles in patient-centered health care.					3	
3.3 Communicate effectively with individuals from diverse populations.					1	

Multisource Assessment				Simulation		MCA		Work Samples	
Self Assess-ment	Peer Assess-ment	Patient Survey	Standar-dized Patients	Virtual Reality	Models	OSCE	TJE	Portfolio	Record Review
				3					
								3	
									2
						2			3
	3	2							
		2	1						
		2	3						

(Continued)

Toolbox of assessment techniques to measure dental students' attainment of the 2008 ADEA Competencies for the New General Dentist *(continued)*

	Written Assessment			Faculty Observation		
	Multiple-Choice	Short Answer	Struc-tured Essay	Global Ratings	Struc-tured Obser-vation	Standar-dized Oral Exam
Health Promotion						
Graduates must be competent to:						
4.1 Provide prevention, intervention, and educational strategies.	3					2
4.2 Participate with dental team members and other health care professionals in the management and health promotion for all patients.			3			
4.3 Recognize and appreciate the need to contribute to the improvement of oral health beyond those served in traditional practice settings.			3			
Practice Management and Informatics						
Graduates must be competent to:						
5.1 Evaluate and apply contemporary and emerging information including clinical and practice management technology resources.						
5.2 Evaluate and manage current models of oral health care management and delivery.		2	1			
5.3 Apply principles of risk management, including informed consent and appropriate record keeping in patient care.						2
5.4 Demonstrate effective business, financial management, and human resource skills.						
5.5 Apply quality assurance, assessment, and improvement concepts.						
5.6 Comply with local, state, and federal regulations, including OSHA and HIPAA.	2	3				
5.7 Develop a catastrophe preparedness plan for the dental practice.			1			3
Patient Care: Assessment, Diagnosis, and Treatment Planning						
Graduates must be competent to:						
6.1 Manage the oral health care of the infant, child, adolescent, and adult, as well as the unique needs of women, geriatric, and special needs patients.				2	1	
6.2 Prevent, identify, and manage trauma, oral diseases, and other disorders.				2	3	
6.3 Obtain and interpret patient/medical data, including a thorough intra/extra oral examination, and use these findings to accurately assess and manage all patients.	3	2				
6.4 Select, obtain, and interpret diagnostic images for the individual patient.	3				1	
6.5 Recognize the manifestations of systemic disease and how the disease and its management may affect the delivery of dental care.	1					
6.6 Formulate a comprehensive diagnosis, treatment, and/or referral plan for the management of patients.			1			

| Multisource Assessment | | | | Simulation | | MCA | | Work Samples | |
Self Assess-ment	Peer Assess-ment	Patient Survey	Standar-dized Patients	Virtual Reality	Models	OSCE	TJE	Portfolio	Record Review
								1	
							2	1	2
2							2	1	
				3				1	2
						3			
		3							1
2		1						3	
1								2	3
									1
								2	
			3						
				1		2			
							2	2	1
				2			2		
				2		3			
				3			2		2

(Continued)

Toolbox of assessment techniques to measure dental students' attainment of the 2008 ADEA Competencies for the New General Dentist *(continued)*

	Written Assessment			Faculty Observation		
	Multiple-Choice	Short Answer	Structured Essay	Global Ratings	Structured Observation	Standardized Oral Exam
Patient Care: Establishment and Maintenance of Oral Health						
Graduates must be competent to:						
6.7 Utilize universal infection control guidelines for all clinical procedures.	2				1	
6.8 Prevent, diagnose, and manage pain and anxiety in the dental patient.	2				1	
6.9 Prevent, diagnose, and manage temporomandibular disorders.	2				1	
6.10 Prevent, diagnose, and manage periodontal diseases.	2				1	
6.11 Develop and implement strategies for the clinical assessment and management of caries.			3			
6.12 Manage restorative procedures that preserve tooth structure, replace missing or defective tooth structure, maintain function, are esthetic, and promote soft and hard tissue health.	2				1	
6.13 Diagnose and manage developmental or acquired occlusal abnormalities.	2				1	
6.14 Manage the replacement of teeth for the partially or completely edentulous patient.	3					
6.15 Diagnose, identify, and manage pulpal and periradicular diseases.	2				1	
6.16 Diagnose and manage oral surgical treatment needs.	2				1	
6.17 Prevent, recognize, and manage medical and dental emergencies.					1	
6.18 Recognize and manage patient abuse and/or neglect.	1					
6.19 Recognize and manage substance abuse.	1					
6.20 Evaluate outcomes of comprehensive dental care.				1		2
6.21 Diagnose, identify, and manage oral mucosal and osseous diseases.	1					

Multisource Assessment				Simulation		MCA		Work Samples	
Self Assess-ment	Peer Assess-ment	Patient Survey	Standar-dized Patients	Virtual Reality	Models	OSCE	TJE	Portfolio	Record Review
						3			
			2	3					
				3					
				3					
				2				1	
					2	3			
								3	
					2	1			
				3			3		
				3					
			2			3			
				2					3
				2					3
								3	1
				2		3			

Dental Education: A Leadership Challenge for Dental Educators and Practitioners

Kathleen Roth, D.D.S.

Abstract: By all outward signs, the dental profession is prospering. However, signs of a looming crisis in dental education threaten the future effectiveness of the profession. Transforming dental education through the application of principles espoused by the ADEA Commission on Change and Innovation in Dental Education (CCI) is essential for securing the future of the profession. To meet the future oral health needs of the public, dental schools must retain their research mission and prepare students for evidence-based practice. To accomplish this, both the curricular content and the environment and approach to dental education must change. Besides the knowledge and abilities needed to care for a more diverse and aging population, future practitioners must possess tools needed to thrive in the world of small business and have the ethical foundation to conduct themselves as responsible professionals. Ensuring the future of the profession is a leadership challenge to be shared by both dental educators and practitioners.

Dr. Roth is President, American Dental Association. Direct correspondence and requests for reprints to Dr. Laura M. Neumann, Senior Vice President, Education/Professional Affairs, American Dental Association, 211 East Chicago Avenue, Chicago, IL 60611; 312-440-2712 phone; 312-587-4105 fax; neumannL@ada.org.

This article is one in a series of invited contributions by members of the dental and dental education community that have been commissioned by the ADEA Commission on Change and Innovation in Dental Education (CCI) to address the environment surrounding dental education and affecting the need for, or process of, curricular change. This article was written at the request of the ADEA CCI but does not necessarily reflect the views of ADEA, the ADEA CCI, or individual members of the ADEA CCI. The perspectives communicated here are those of the author.

Key words: dental education, curriculum, dental practice

The American Dental Association's (ADA) 2001 future of dentistry report presented a vision of improved health and quality of life for all through optimal oral health, and challenged the profession to take a leadership role in achieving that vision.[1] The report asserts that dentistry's future ability to promote the oral health of the nation will depend on its capacity to integrate new, better technologies into practice, to respond to changing consumer needs, to ensure a sufficient supply of well-trained dental educators and dental students, to maintain a strong research focus, and, all the while, to address the needs of those people who do not have access to care. While the report makes it clear that a strong educational system is critical to the future vision, there have been signs that our education system is in trouble. In making the case for the need to transform dental education through wide-ranging systemic change, the American Dental Education Association (ADEA) Commission on Change and Innovation in Dental Education (CCI) suggests that the profession has lost its vision and may be wavering in achieving its goals.[2] How do we get back on track? How does the profession secure the future it envisions?

By all outward signs, our profession is in great shape. Dentist incomes continue to rise, exceeding those of primary care physicians.[3,4] Professional journals advertise numerous practice and employ-ment opportunities, and approximately 97 percent of dental graduates are employed or otherwise professionally active in dentistry at one year after graduation.[5] Anecdotally, dentists are very positive about the profession and, to date, feel somewhat insulated from the ills of a broken health care system that plagues other health professions.

Symptoms of a looming crisis in dental education suggest that the status quo cannot be sustained unless significant steps are taken to address the challenges facing dental education.[6] Pyle et al. have described these challenges: declining financial support in the face of high, escalating costs; high student debt; faculty shortages; an outdated, irrelevant curriculum; and a frustrating environment for learning and patient care, among others.[2] From the viewpoint of practitioners, there have been additional signs: the perceived commercialization of dental education,[7] the opening of new dental schools in non-research-oriented institutions,[8] and recent dental school cheating scandals.[9-12] Finally, despite the evidence that many Americans enjoy very good oral health, there are constant reminders of the changing demographics and health status of our society and the significant number of individuals who continue to lack access to care.[13]

The ADEA CCI's strategy to involve stakeholders, including representatives from the ADA, offers an ideal opportunity for the practice community to become engaged in a process for securing our vision for the future.[14] Practitioners and leaders in organized dentistry care deeply about the profession and want to have a voice in the education of their future colleagues. Opportunities for collaboration in this endeavor are important to ensure support rather than obstruction of evolving change by alumni and local dental communities. A partnership between dental education and dental practice will ensure that the proposed changes in dental education result in new graduate competencies that are realistic and relevant. The principles proposed by the ADEA CCI to shape the dental education environment represent critical concerns of the profession and important points of leverage in transforming the dental curriculum and ultimately new graduates.

A critical focus for change must be the culture and environment of dental education. With few exceptions, the current generation of dental practitioners remember their own dental education experiences as highly frustrating. What were the sources of student disdain? Course content or assignments that were irrelevant or never put in context. A perception that some techniques and procedures were outdated or not relevant to contemporary dental practice. A mismatch between what was published as curricular requirements and what was really required to survive and succeed, sometimes referred to as the "hidden curriculum." Intimidating methods of clinical and preclinical instruction. Faculty who didn't seem to know how to teach or test. An inefficient, complex, and convoluted patient care system that compromised patient welfare and dignity. Recent studies confirm persistent concerns and support the need for a humanistic environment that fosters collegial, professional interactions and promotes learning as a positive growth experience.[15,16] Providing an appropriate emotional climate beginning in the freshman year and doing more to show faculty and administrative support for students and nurturance during their clinical years are areas that may need more attention. Students need to be treated with the respect of professional colleagues from the time they enter dental school and understand the associated obligations of ethical conduct and professional responsibility.

The current generation of student looks at work-life issues very differently from the way mature practitioners do, and faculty must account for these differences in their approach to working with students and preparing them for their professional obligations. The demands of dental practice, the economic environment, and societal expectations will present tremendous challenges to students. Dental school is an important and appropriate setting for students to learn, understand, and adopt the concept of professionalism. This is the time for students to understand their responsibilities for competence, integrity, and respect and compassion for patients; to understand their obligations to society and the profession; and to develop a commitment to excellence and lifelong learning. Although dental schools may consider professionalism to be integral or inherent to the dental curriculum, more emphasis is needed in this area. The Accreditation Council for Graduate Medical Education (ACGME) Outcome Project provides an excellent example of how teaching and assessment of professionalism can be more systematically incorporated into the curriculum.[17]

A second overriding concern of the practice community relates to a changing perception of the mission of the dental school and its role and relationship to its parent institution. Observations of directions taken by new dental schools and existing schools impacted by diminishing financial support raise concerns about the potential for dental schools to maintain a strong research mission. Despite the important contributions to dentistry by pioneers of the profession, we can no longer count on the opinions of experts as the basis for oral health care. Dentistry must be evidence-based. The profession needs to be able to depend on a cadre of academic dentists and their colleagues to conduct university-based research, free of commercial influence, that will generate new knowledge and technology to support future dental practice. It is a concern to see so few dentists participating in dentist-scientist programs or choosing an academic career that includes full engagement in research and scholarship. Dental schools must find a way to take full advantage of funding opportunities to support the development of research-capable academicians and ensure that these individuals receive the mentoring and sustained support to assume leadership roles in dental research.

By the same token, dental faculty who engage in research must be able to share their findings and support the translation of research into practice. The instruction of dental students should not be isolated from the research function of the dental school, and students should benefit from the opportunity to understand and adopt the critical thinking and problem-solving processes that are the foundation of research activity. Regardless of whether students have opportunities to participate in original dental research, all should have the experience and ability to critically appraise clinical research and interpret the validity of findings. This exposure should enhance their awareness of the areas of new knowledge and developing technology that could potentially impact the direction of future practice. Instead of relying on the set of knowledge and techniques acquired from their dental curriculum to support their entire careers, students should be prepared to anticipate, evaluate, and adopt new information and technology. Many practitioners take the cookbook approach to practice and rely on the wisdom of experts from the lecture circuit and throw-away journals because they were conditioned in dental school to emulate sage clinicians rather than to understand, analyze, and work through a problem using appropriate resources and problem-solving skills.

From the perspectives of both students and practitioners, dental curricula do not appear to be cutting edge, and dental schools are often the last places that practitioners consider when looking for continuing education. Why is this? Are dental schools wisely skeptical of the latest new gadget or technique that is likely unproven in superiority or effectiveness? Is there a lack of curiosity, creativity, and entrepreneurial initiative to support clinical trials of new products and techniques? Is it a lack of resources to purchase the latest equipment and materials? Is the curriculum too crowded with traditional areas of knowledge and techniques that are irrelevant, outdated, or no longer important or consistent with patient oral health conditions and needs? Even if students are too inexperienced to master multiple techniques or approaches to clinical problems, they need to be exposed to emerging areas of science and treatment modalities in an environment that includes a process for quality assessment and control so that they will be prepared to evaluate and implement new approaches in their own practices without undue hesitation or harm to patients. Recent news of significant partnerships between dental schools and industry offer a sign of hope that availability of equipment and materials will be less of a limitation.[18] However, these relationships carry the burden of additional vigilance in managing commercial influence and bias in evaluating clinical effectiveness. Community-based clinical experiences, such as those promulgated by the Robert Wood Johnson Foundation's Pipeline, Profession, and Practice Program and the Macy Study, may offer exposure to a greater variety of clinical practices, materials, and techniques in addition to achieving other objectives.[19,20]

Many dental practitioners wonder if they could pass Part I of the National Board Dental Examination today, let alone a final examination from a current dental school course. This calls into question the idea that a circumscribed set of facts or knowledge can serve the needs of a dental practitioner throughout his or her career. When considered in conjunction with previous thoughts, it appears that the dental curriculum could benefit from some aggressive pruning as well as a review of the methods of assessment. Although a small set of basic principles and associated technical vocabulary may be needed as a foundation for learning, more emphasis must be placed on critical thinking and self-directed learning as recommended by the CCI. Instead of passively sitting through hours of lecture, students need to be engaged in learning in a way that requires them to learn in context and be able to access the knowledge that is pertinent to the situation. Understanding basic biomedical sciences will continue to be a necessity for comprehension of clinical sciences and emerging advances in areas such as molecular biology and genetics that may ultimately change the approach to oral health care, but schools should continue to evaluate the level of detail, as well as the appropriate time and source of instruction, e.g., predental versus predoctoral. Many schools, for example, have reconsidered the amount of time devoted to various topics and laboratory assignments in areas such as gross anatomy and histology, freeing up time for other purposes.

In considering what courses or content to include in the curriculum, dental schools should be encouraged to use a more evidence-based approach, instead of relying on internal discussion and recommendations of faculty who may naturally tend to promote the importance of their own content areas. Important sources of data that should inform curricular decisions include information on research topic areas sponsored or conducted by the National Institute of Dental and Craniofacial Research, the ADA Research Agenda, surveys on dental services rendered, data from the National Health and Nutrition Examination Surveys (NHANES) and other epidemiologic studies, and individual state oral health needs assessments. Shuler's article on the adoption of emerging scientific advances identifies sources of information that can contribute to decision making about directions for curricular change.[21] For public schools, focus groups of dental practitioners within the state can provide more locally relevant guidance on decisions about whether there is a need to change the amount of time and/or competencies for such topics as complete dentures. Engaging other health professionals may also prove valuable. The ADA, for example, has learned through discussion with the American Academy of Pediatrics of the need for general dentists who are fully capable of providing services for children in the very young age group from birth to three years. This information is also consistent with data on oral health disparities.[22,23] Data on the trends in distribution of dental services show significant changes in proportion of services in different categories, with dentists delivering almost twice as many diagnostic and preventive services in 1999 as in 1959.[24,25] This suggests that significantly more curricular attention should be devoted to developing the diagnostic capabilities of dental graduates. This direction is further supported by data on the demographic and medical characteristics of dental patients—an aging population with complex medical histories. In addition, changing scopes of practice for allied dental personnel suggest that the role of the dentist may continue to evolve with greater emphasis on diagnosis and overall patient management than on routine preventive and basic restorative services.

It has become evident that mastery of basic biomedical, behavioral, and clinical sciences is not sufficient for ensuring a successful dental practice. Today's practitioner must be able to effectively operate and manage a small business in a highly competitive economic environment. Whether practice owner, associate, or employee, today's dentist's success depends on substantial understanding and competence in basic business principles: accounting, marketing, insurance and reimbursement mechanisms, and human resources management, for example. In addition, he or she must have a working knowledge of basic legal principles, recordkeeping, and the legislative and regulatory requirements that impact health care practice. Students should not be expected to learn these principles and best practices by trial and error or by osmosis during a period of association with a mature practitioner. While some dental educators may consider courses in these areas to lack substance in comparison to the basic biomedical sciences, these business topics are the foundation for undergraduate and graduate programs in business administration and provide the know-how that allows other small business leaders to compete for the public's spending dollar and to achieve success in the community business environment.

In addition to didactic learning experiences that provide a foundation in these topics, practical learning experiences within the dental school or a community-based clinical setting are essential. Again, the concepts of ethical professional conduct must be an integral part of this instruction. It is as important for students to be confronted with challenging business decisions in a guided learning environment as it is for them to receive feedback to guide self-assessment on the quality of a restoration. Our future practitioners must have the critical thinking and clinical skills necessary to provide quality oral health care for the public and must graduate with a clear understanding of the tools needed to thrive in the world of small business as well.

Several examples and suggestions in this article have advanced the importance of community-based learning activities for dental students. Community-based programs serve important purposes, not only for the student, but for the dental school, the profession, and the public. ADEA's 2003 policy statement, "Improving the Oral Health Status of All Americans: Roles and Responsibilities of Academic Dental Institutions," clearly describes the role of the dental school in preparing students to meet their professional and social responsibilities of providing competent care for a diverse population and improving the oral health of all groups of society with special attention to those who are vulnerable and underserved.[26] Student assignments to off-site clinics can provide needed care to the underserved; teach students about their professional obligation to serve the public good; help students better understand the complex needs of the underserved and develop the skills for delivering culturally competent care; and provide opportunities for interaction with other health care providers and community leaders. Community-based clinical experiences should include exposure to private dental practices. Such arrangements could provide important opportunities for collaboration with the practicing community. Developing closer relationships among students, community practitioner mentors, and dental schools allows dentists in the practicing community to learn from students about advances in science, technology, and clinical techniques, as well as the critical thinking approach to practice, and diminishes the potential for a future profession at odds with itself because of diverging approaches to patient care. Engaging members of the practice community in various roles, such as mentor to students, adjunct faculty, or advisory committee members, can help to keep dental education well grounded and facilitate the growth of the profession through the integration of new ideas into practice and the adoption of evidence-based dentistry. Further, such relationships can help with the daunting challenge of ensuring that students graduate with the breadth and depth of technical competence necessary to meet the current oral health needs of the public while preparing both students and practitioners for a much different, but unknown, future. As the dental education curriculum is transformed, it would be valuable to allow community dentists to have access to current course materials. New technology and the use of electronic teaching materials and methods should make access to components of the dental curriculum feasible and could expand lifelong learning opportunities for practitioners.

Today's students are not only tomorrow's practitioners but the leaders of the profession. Ensuring the future of the profession is a leadership challenge that must be shared by both dental educators and the practice community. The process of becoming a dentist is much akin to that of a leader—an arduous journey of continuous learning and self-development. The last and most important leadership test is sharing what you have learned with the next generation.[27]

REFERENCES

1. American Dental Association. Future of dentistry. Chicago: American Dental Association, 2001.
2. Pyle M, Andrieu SC, Chadwick DG, Chmar JE, Cole JR, George MC, et al. The case for change in dental education. J Dent Educ 2006;70(9):921-4.
3. Maremont M. Why dentists are smiling. Wall Street Journal, January 10, 2005.
4. Mertz E, O'Neil E. The growing challenge of providing oral health care services to all Americans. Health Aff 2002;21(5):65-77.
5. American Dental Association. The 2005 survey of dental graduates. Chicago: American Dental Association, September 2006.
6. DePaola D, Slavkin H. Reforming dental health professions education. J Dent Educ 2004;68:1139-50.
7. Spalding PM, Bradley RE. Commercialization of dental education: have we gone too far? J Am Coll Dent 2006;73:30-5.
8. Bailit H, Beazoglou T, Formicola AJ, Tedesco L, Brown J, Weaver RG. U.S. state-supported dental schools: financial projections and implications. J Dent Educ 2006;70(3):246-57.
9. Sherman T, Margolin J. Cheating scam rocks UMDNJ dental school. Newark Star-Ledger, May 16, 2006.
10. UNLV cheaters still get diplomas (editorial). Las Vegas Review Journal, June 14, 2006.
11. Rudavsky S. Cheating scandal snares nearly half of IU dental class. The Indianapolis Star, May 8, 2007.
12. Felsenfeld AL. An ethical perspective. J Calif Dent Assoc 2006;34(9):693-4.
13. Guay AH. Access to dental care: solving the problem for underserved populations. J Am Dent Assoc 2004; 135:1599-605.
14. Kalkwarf KL, Haden NK, Valachovic RL. ADEA Commission on Change and Innovation in Dental Education. J Dent Educ 2005;69(10):1085-7.
15. Henzi D, Davis E, Jasinevicius R, Hendricson W. In the students' own words: what are the strengths and weaknesses of the dental school curriculum. J Dent Educ 2007; 71(5):632-45.
16. Henzi D, Davis E, Jasinevicius R, Hendricson W, Cintron L, Isaacs M. Appraisal of the dental school learning environment: the students' view. J Dent Educ 2005; 60(10):1137-47.
17. Accreditation Council for Graduate Medical Education. Advancing medical professionalism: an educational resource from the ACGME Outcome Project. Chicago: ACGME, 2004.
18. American Dental Education Association. Nobel Biocare forms partnership with two dental schools. Bulletin of Dental Education, June 2007.
19. Bailit H, Formicola A, Herbert K, Stavisky J, Zamora G. The origins and design of the dental pipeline program. J Dent Educ 2005;69(2):232-8.
20. Bailit HL, Beazoglou TJ, Formicola AJ, Tedesco L. Financing clinical dental education. J Dent Educ 2007;71(3): 322-30.
21. Shuler CF. Emerging scientific advances: how do they enter dental curricula and the profession? J Calif Dent Assoc 2005;33(10):805-9.
22. Beltran-Aguilar ED, Barker LK, Canto MT, Dye BA, Gooch BA, et al. Surveillance for dental caries, dental sealants, tooth retention, edentulism, and enamel fluorosis—United States, 1988-1994 and 1999-2002. MMWR 2005;54(03):1-44.
23. Oral health U.S., 2002. Bethesda, MD: Dental, Oral, and Craniofacial Data Resource Center, 2002.
24. American Dental Association. The 1990 survey of dental services rendered. Chicago: American Dental Association, 1994.
25. American Dental Association. The 1999 survey of dental services rendered. Chicago: American Dental Association, 2002.
26. Haden NK, Catalanotto FA, Alexander CJ, Bailit H, Battrell A, Broussard J, et al. Improving the oral health status of all Americans: roles and responsibilities of academic dental institutions. J Dent Educ 2003;67:563-83.
27. Moyer D. The final test. Harvard Business Rev 2007; 85(1):128.

Managing Change in Dental Education: Is There a Method to the Madness?

Geralyn Crain, D.D.S.

Abstract: The literature surrounding dental education in the United States is replete with calls for change in the way that dental students are being educated. These calls are being echoed with curriculum models and examples of best practices, but what is missing is specific information about how to implement a desired change—that is, discussion of the change process itself. Knowledge of the organizational change process in other settings, particularly in higher education and professional education, may be of interest to academic program managers in dental schools who are planning or are engaged in change. Historical and theoretical perspectives on organizations and change are presented in this article as groundwork for more detailed discussion about management of change. Seventeen research-based principles of change in higher education and factors in dental education that influence change processes and outcomes are presented and synthesized into guidelines for a hypothetical model for change in a dental school environment. Issues pertinent to the practical management of change are presented, including reframing organizational complexity, change leadership, values/competence/commitment, and organizational learning. An appreciation for change as an ongoing and manageable process will enhance a dental school's viability in a rapidly changing world and ultimately benefit dental graduates and the communities they serve.

Dr. Crain is Clinical and Research Assistant Professor, School of Dentistry, University of Missouri–Kansas City (UMKC) and an Interdisciplinary Ph.D. Candidate in the School of Dentistry's Department of Oral Biology and the UMKC Henry W. Bloch School of Business and Public Administration's Department of Public Affairs. Direct correspondence and requests for reprints to her at University of Missouri–Kansas City, School of Dentistry, Department of Oral Biology, Room 3156, 650 East 25th Street, Kansas City, MO 64108; 816-235-5419 phone; 816-235-5524 fax; gdkmq3@umkc.edu.

This article is one in a series of invited contributions by members of the dental education community that have been commissioned by the ADEA Commission on Change and Innovation in Dental Education (CCI) to address the environment surrounding dental education and affecting the need for, or process of, curricular change. This article was written at the request of the ADEA CCI but does not necessarily reflect the views of ADEA, the ADEA CCI, or individual members of the CCI. The perspectives communicated here are those of the author.

Key words: organizational change, change management, dental education, curriculum reform

> **"The art of progress is to preserve order amid change and to preserve change amid order."**
> —*Alfred North Whitehead*

To meet the changing needs of society, there have been many calls for change in the way that dental students are educated. International and national attention has focused on the need for curriculum reform in health care education, including dental education, in order to address existing inadequacies, such as an increasing focus on high tech procedures to the detriment of a more humanistic, holistic, and evidence-based approach to health care. If an individual dental school chooses to engage in change, regardless of the magnitude, in addition to focusing on *what* to change, focusing on managing the process—*how* to change—will enhance success in achieving change that is comprehensive and sustainable.

The current dental education literature contains multiple presentations of the rationale for curricular reform.[1-4] Recommendations for curriculum content and educational strategies have been published as curriculum models, pedagogical techniques, and examples of best practices.[5-11] But despite the articulation of compelling rationales and substantive recommendations for educational reform, there are relatively few studies of the change process itself in dental education. Kassebaum et al. conducted a survey that resulted in a cross-sectional view of predoctoral curricula and curriculum evaluation strategies, as well as recently implemented and planned changes in North American dental schools.[12] Although that study did not address the change process itself, a method for managing curriculum revision was described that involved an ideal curriculum committee comprised of faculty who could be counted upon to take a "wide view" and focus on the best interests of the entire school versus parochially defending departmental/disciplinary turf. With regard to the curriculum change process itself, Kassebaum et al. summarized the responses to survey questions about process as "the tortuous and emotionally laden path to educational reform." Currently, a targeted inquiry into dental schools that have recently planned or implemented changes, with emphasis on process issues during the initiation phase of the planning, is under development (a proposed project of Dr. Karen Novak, 2008 ADEA/William J. Gies Foundation Education Fellow). A transformational change in the curriculum at a private Midwest school of dental medicine, with particular emphasis on the architecture of the change process, has recently been reported,[13] and a theoretical analysis of the organizational change process in one public U.S. dental school that has recently undergone significant curriculum and clinic changes is also under way ("Qualitative Analysis of the Organization Change Process in Dental Education: A Case Study," my dissertation project). Two articles in the December 2007 issue of the *Journal of Dental Education* highlighted the importance of faculty development to successful change and emphasized issues germane to the process of implementing curriculum reforms.[14,15] Finally, Dharamsi et al. studied the curricular change process at the University of British Columbia School of Dentistry by exploring its social constructs.[16] These examples demonstrate that whereas many schools are involved with changes, relatively few authors have chosen to bring focus to particular aspects of the change process itself or have published their experiences in the dental education literature.

In contrast, beyond dental education, there is a great deal written about the change process in organizations in general[17,18] and in educational institutions in particular, especially in higher education.[19-23] These and other studies investigated the organizational and educational reform processes in various settings and reached the conclusion that change initiatives are as likely to be derailed over disagreements about process as they are about substance. Further, it was found that when individuals paid attention to and were personally comfortable with the process/procedural aspects of the reform effort, greater success resulted.

This article was invited by the American Dental Education Association (ADEA) Commission on Change and Innovation in Dental Education (CCI) in order to present information about the organizational change process with a focus on factors that may be unique to the academic environment. Utilizing established knowledge about change and innovation in other educational and non-educational organizations as a framework, the purpose of this article is to raise awareness of these processes and, in particular, to espouse the perspective that change and innovation are processes that can and should be managed systematically to ensure success. It should be acknowledged that all dental schools, as with all organizations, experience ongoing changes of various magnitudes, sometimes as a consequence of calculated, purposeful planning to achieve targeted modifications and sometimes as a result of reactive and spontaneous response to unexpected events and undesired outcomes ("firefighting"). Many dental schools have probably experienced impressive change and innovation in both content (*what* was changed) and process (*how* the change was accomplished) without reporting these outcomes and strategies in the literature. Still, a cursory review of salient features that emerge from the organizational change literature, particularly in that of higher education and in professional education, may be of interest to those who are in the midst of or in the planning or reflective stages of change.

The type of change being called for in dental education (change that cultivates critical thinking, evidence-based practice, and lifelong learning, for example) is deemed "transformational" and is to be distinguished from 1) "unplanned" change that arises in response to some unforeseen situation and 2) "superficial" change that reflects a new way of doing the same old thing. Rather, transformational change is systemic (deeper), is pervasive (more widespread), and may involve the altering of the beliefs and understandings held by individuals within the organization. The American Council on Education (ACE) conducted the Project on Leadership and Institutional Transformation, which included a six-year study on change in higher education involving twenty-six universities.[19-23] (A synopsis of the report is posted on the ADEA CCI website at www.adea.org/adeacci/Documents/SynopsisACE.pdf.) The authors of this landmark study defined the characteristics of transformational change in the following ways: 1) it alters the culture of the institution by changing select underlying assumptions and institutional behaviors, processes, and products; 2) it is deep and pervasive, affecting the whole institution; 3) it is intentional; and 4) it occurs over time. These authors defined "successful" change not only in terms of outcomes, but as a modification that is sustained without reversion to a previous state even though the details of reform may indeed be modified over a period of time as the new way of doing business is merged into the culture of the institution.

The "process" of change refers to *how* and *why* a change is initiated, implemented, evaluated, and sustained. "Innovation" in organizations refers to the initiation and adoption of new ideas and practices and is often considered concomitant with change. Although change and innovation are separate processes, unless otherwise noted, innovation will be implied within the organizational change process in this article.

To apply what is known about organizational change to dental education, it is useful to begin with a perspective that views organizations as entities that exist within unique external and internal environments. Although this perspective is seemingly intuitive, this was not always the case as will be described in the next section. A brief historical overview of formal thought about organizations is presented to provide a foundation for further discussion of factors that influence organizational change. Knowledge about the broader organizational framework, in addition to a focus on individual member behavior, increases the likelihood that successful change will occur.

Organizations: A Historical Perspective

The definition of an organization today differs significantly from that of the past. Early models of organization were based on the localization of power over subordinates, such as in military settings, where the notion of "control" was inseparable from that of "organization." By the nineteenth century, increased growth and complexity in this country gave rise to more political means to organize and control. In the late 1880s, Woodrow Wilson, who was a professor of political science at the time, was one of the first to focus on the organization as an entity and to propose theories about such issues as personnel and management.[24] What emerged over the next five decades was a fixation on the strict management of people and organizations in systematic and predictable ways.[24,25] By the 1930s, a countermovement to this obsession with bureaucracy and efficiency evolved. Perhaps the most significant contribution during this time came from Nobel laureate Herbert Simon, who introduced the concept of "bounded rationality" to call into question the strict rational decision making

found in scientific management thought.[26] Simon and others argued that there is not a one-size-fits-all model of administration and that attention needs to be paid to the unique and complex environments influencing each organization and to the behaviors of the individuals who constitute it.

In the 1940s, sociologists such as Kurt Lewin began taking an interest in research on organizations as social entities. Lewin, a social scientist at MIT, is considered to have pioneered the thinking about organizational change. His model of "unfreezing— movement—and refreezing" individual behavior that collectively results in organizational change is considered foundational.[27] Among Lewin's other fundamental contributions is the now obvious notion that motivation for change must first occur in order for a change effort to be successful. He also championed action research, a type of reflection performed by the participants of an organization themselves, as a meaningful way to manage a change process.

After World War II, the traditional management school was firmly replaced by the human relations school with a focus on topics that included leadership, roles, values, goals, motivation, collaboration, and shared decision making. The decades since have cultivated a deeper construct of the complexity within organizations that brings to light such variables as the organizational culture, the adoption of innovations, social network analysis, and other elements that contribute to the complexity that defines the word "organization" today. Organizational learning, both inwardly focused and in response to the external environment, is one concept that has since dominated the change literature and will be discussed in further detail below.

To summarize, formal thought about organizations and change has evolved over the past 125 years from a mechanistic view in which institutions, including those in the academic arena, were perceived to function most effectively as top-down, hierarchically arranged entities requiring strict management, toward attention since World War II to the human side of organizations and the unique environments within and external to an organization that profoundly affect its operations. Change as handed down in a linear fashion from a controlling upper-level management has been replaced with an understanding that meaningful and lasting change occurs within the dynamic interplay of a complexity of variables. Awareness of the evolution in thought about organizations creates a richer context within which change can be further considered. The next section reviews contemporary theories that provide the foundation for organizational change processes.

Organizations: A Theoretical Perspective

Although every organization is unique, all organizations share some common elements—social, psychological, and behavioral structures—making the application of principles across organizational settings possible.[28] What is known about change in non-dental school environments, such as in higher education and in other professional education, can be useful and timely to dental education as it faces calls for change.

There are numerous individual theories or models of change reported in the literature, which authors have attempted to group according to similarities.[29,30] Although each model adopts a unique perspective on change, all address questions of *why* a change occurs, *how* it unfolds, the *timing* of when it occurs and how long it takes, and what its *outcomes* are. A summary of six main categories of change theories, primarily based on the work of Kezar, is presented in Table 1.

Each of the six categories of theory underlies a different perspective on why organizations change. It should be noted, however, that these distinctions represent a theoretical dissection for the purpose of analysis and that, in reality, an organization may exhibit an overlap of more than one approach to change for any given situation. Those who are armed with a better understanding of why a change is being contemplated can then tackle issues related to managing the change process by utilizing the best approach.

Change Models in Higher Education

Most of the research findings related to change in educational settings come from studies in higher education, although literature exists in which principles from change research in higher education have been examined in professional education settings, for example, in schools of medicine, nursing, pharmacy, occupational therapy, social work, and education.[31-36] A more in-depth exploration of the principles of change in higher education follows and will be discussed within the context of dental education in the following section.

A meta-analysis conducted by Kezar of thirty years of organizational change research in higher education revealed that, due to the unique culture found in academic settings, change in higher education can best be explained through three of the six change models listed in Table 1: the political, social-cognitive, and cultural models.[30] The political model for creating change emphasizes the importance in academic settings of such things as interest groups and power in influencing change, the significance of informal processes such as behind-the-scenes communication, and the effectiveness of persistence—that is, that those who persist in bringing up an idea for change and who provide strategies were the most likely to make the change occur. The social-cognitive model of change views a school's internal environment to be more influential on change than the external environment. Such things as discussion, debate, reframing, and sense-making (helping faculty and students comprehend the key concepts underlying the change proposal) are inherent processes in university environments and are important elements in the change process according the social-cogni-

Table 1. Six categories of organizational change models

Change Model	Major Features
Evolutionary	Change is the result of adaptation to a changing environment.
Teleological	Change is intentional and managed by leaders, change agents, and others.
Life Cycle	Change occurs during stages of organizational growth, maturity, and decline.
Dialectical (Political)	Change is the resolution of conflicting states of being: the current state and a desired state. Change is often negotiated through political channels.
Social-Cognitive	Change is tied to learning and sense-making and is inherent in the need to change one's behavior.
Cultural	Change is related to alteration of values, beliefs, and rituals.

Source: Adapted from Kezar AJ. Understanding and facilitating change in higher education in the 21st century: recent research and conceptualizations. ASHE-ERIC Education Report 28(4). San Francisco: Jossey-Bass, 2001.

tive model of change.[17] Finally, the cultural model focuses on the importance of campus history and tradition and of symbolic events and activities, such as a well-attended town hall meeting or kick-off event to fuel the momentum for change. As a result of this meta-analysis, seventeen research-based principles of change in higher education were described by Kezar[30] and appear in Table 2.

These principles of change could be adapted for use in a dental education environment as the first building blocks of a change model that individual dental schools may find useful. Although theoretical or actual assessments of the institutional environment and the application of various change processes in dental education are not yet available in the literature, a number of authors have speculated about the dental education environment and its responsiveness to change. These observations, which are outlined in the next section, together with the seventeen research-based principles of change in higher education outlined in Table 2 will be incorporated into a hypothetical model for change in a dental school setting.

Table 2. Seventeen principles of change in higher education and implications for management of the change process

Research-Based Principle of Change	Description and Implications for Change
1. Promote organizational self-discovery.	Existing structure and internal environment (history, habits, and norms that shape institutional practice and philosophies) profoundly influence change. Mechanisms that draw people together to talk, relate, and understand issues will enhance change efforts.
2. Realize that the culture of the institution (and institutional type) affects change.	The unique culture found in each academic institution shapes the way a change emerges, the process of change, and the outcomes. Institutions should assess their culture and tailor a change strategy accordingly.
3. Be aware of politics.	Given the political nature of organizations and institutions of higher education in particular, advocates for change must develop an understanding of alliances, coalitions, people of influence, how informal processes can be used, what conflicts exist, and what motivations underlie the change and those resistant to it.
4. Lay groundwork.	Planning processes should begin with groundwork that includes self-assessment, institutional audits, and an analysis of the change proposal for institutional compatibility.
5. Focus on adaptability.	Deep, pervasive change (transformational) is difficult to achieve across an entire academic setting. Rather, initiating incremental changes and creating an environment that supports innovation will result in more lasting change.
6. Facilitate interaction to develop new mental models and sense-making.	In academic settings, explanation and rationale are powerful tools for managing change. All those involved should be brought together through strategic planning, committee work, staff and faculty development, and events in order to help them develop understanding, new mental models, and new language about the changes.
7. Balance external forces with the internal environment.	In academic settings, the environment within the institution has a greater effect on change than outside influences. Leaders should directly respond to external forces only when there is a clear indication that an external factor will adversely influence school operations or policy. When change to external forces is indicated, leaders should ensure widespread dialogue and decision making within the school.
8. Help people understand a logical progression to the end results.	The use of metaphors, stories, and symbolism should be combined with establishing a vision, planning, and assessment, in order to make the change initiative understandable.

(continued)

Change in Dental Education

Many authors have offered observations about the dental education environment and how those elements might effect change.[1,2,4,8,9,11,14,15,37,38] Some of those observations are grouped according to themes and presented in Table 3.

These various observations reveal the perceptions that dental education, for the most part, is dominated by traditional curricula and teaching models; is plagued by a continued disconnect between the biomedical and dental sciences and among the dental disciplines; and is challenged by a workforce composition that includes full-time/part-time faculty, tenure/non-tenure-track appointments, and research/clinical/discipline-specific faculty, resulting in little opportunity to integrate curricula or practice. In addition, many retiring practitioners who are the main source of new faculty for many dental schools are generally not enthusiastic about working in a chaotic environment where change is happening and may have little personal energy for, or commitment to, a change process, given the fact that they largely

Table 2, continued

9. Realize that change is a disorderly process.	Forced orderly approaches to change often fail in academic institutions. Being open to ambiguity and to nonlinear processes is important for institutional leaders and change agents to understand.
10. Promote shared governance or collective decision making.	Higher education is characterized by a culture of shared governance. Joint activities of administrators and faculty are needed to ensure success in collaborative change efforts.
11. Articulate and maintain core characteristics.	Academic institutions often have strong cultures, traditions, and history. In addition to focusing on what and why things need to change, it is important to communicate core values, continuity, and the things the institution wants to preserve and why.
12. Be aware of image.	Higher education institutions are concerned with institutional image and are influenced by other "leading" institutions and by national organizations; therefore, appealing to institutional image and emulation can be used as a lever for positive change.
13. Connect the change process to individual and institutional identity.	Identity (deeply entrenched beliefs, habits, and norms) is important to the change process in higher education. Discussions related to the mission and other methods are needed to achieve the goal of engaging both institutional- and individual-level identities.
14. Create a culture of risk, and help people to change belief systems.	In order to achieve stability and efficiency, people need to feel comfortable making different choices under new conditions. Create an environment that is supportive of risk and allows change without blame or reprimand.
15. Use multiple perspectives when viewing a change, and realize that various aspects of the organization will need different change models.	Each part of the organization has specific characteristics and needs, making a multiple perspectives approach to change necessary. A combination of political, cultural, and other approaches should guide the management of change in individual areas and in the institution as a whole.
16. Vary the change strategy by change initiative.	Each change initiative has a unique nature, necessitating alignment with an appropriate change strategy. Institutions need to evaluate the change initiative (is it more procedural, cultural, political, etc.?) and design a change strategy accordingly.
17. Combine models or approaches to change.	Different strategies and models of change should be combined in order to customize an approach that is suitable for an individual school.

Source: Adapted from Kezar AJ. Understanding and facilitating change in higher education in the 21st century: recent research and conceptualizations. ASHE-ERIC Education Report 28(4). San Francisco: Jossey-Bass, 2001.

see themselves as five- to ten-year employees transitioning from their practice or military careers into retirement.[15,39]

As seen in Table 3, other factors influencing change in dental education are the strong influences of its internal and external environments. Internally, dental schools, for the most part, have not traditionally cultivated a culture or reward system that values teaching excellence, evidence-based educational methodology, or scholarship that might otherwise predispose the faculty to openness to change and innovation. Faculty members often work autonomously, contributing further to the challenge of integration and change. From the external environment, some assert that the most powerful constraints to change in dental education arise from national board, licensure, accreditation, and reimbursement issues—all of which occur in the milieu of dwindling financial and workforce resources. With these aspects of dental education in mind, taken together with the research-based principles of change in higher education mentioned previously, some guidelines to develop a model for change in dental education could be pondered:

1. Be aware of the distinctive characteristics of dental education.
2. Develop a process for systematic and systemic internal and external environmental assessment.
3. Realize the need to develop individual school context-based models of change.
4. Design methods to overcome structural, political, and cultural elements that may hinder change and innovation.

Table 3. Aspects of dental education that influence change, as described in the literature

Entrenched curriculum design
- Little evidence of the universal urgency to incorporate twenty-first century science into the curriculum and thus to patient care.
- Disconnect between biomedical and dental disciplines.
- Comfort in a more vocational rather than academic direction to dental education.
- The need to convert clinical education to a general practice-based, comprehensive care model without an adequate number of faculty.
- Reliance on expert clinicians to teach without an institutional educational philosophy, resulting in factionalism and parochialism.
- Lack of alternative curricular models in dental education (most schools operate very similar educational programs).

Traditional teaching models
- Existing teaching models that emphasize teaching rather than learning.
- Deeply ingrained instructional behaviors and personal philosophies about a teacher's roles and relationship with students.
- Teaching and learning techniques that emphasize passive acquisition of information rather than active, student (self)-directed learning that promotes development of critical thinking skills.
- Information presented in unfocused contexts without planned coordination among courses and topics.
- Fully synchronized curriculum that does not allow faster learners to move on or slower learners to take more time.
- Tradition of anecdotal vs. evidence-based clinical practice.
- Remnants of requirements-based clinical education blended with comprehensive care patient-centered model, resulting in tensions between what is intended to be taught and what students learn.

Traditional structure and culture
- Strong tradition of departmental autonomy and faculty allegiance to disciplines rather than to the dental school as a whole.
- Departmentalization that contributes to parochialism and resistance to change.
- Lack of a learning culture that values teaching excellence, evidence-based educational methodology, faculty scholarship, and leadership.
- Prevailing personality of dental faculty (conservative, cautious, risk averse).
- Reluctance of faculty members to be critical of colleagues.
- Lack of faculty mobility among dental schools and high levels of inbred recruiting of own graduates, which encourages narrowness of vision.

(continued)

5. Be cognizant of the human aspects of change. Work with individuals to enhance skills and confidence related to new behaviors and then reward desired behavior.
6. Foster creativity, adaptability, and sense-making during change.
7. Plan strategies to overcome traditional teaching and curriculum practices.
8. Balance change with maintaining valued traditions.
9. Find creative ways to engage the broader dental and health care communities in an effort to integrate dental practice and education.
10. Adopt a long-term perspective on change in order to keep pace with an ongoing and rapidly changing environment.

Organizational Change Management: A Practical Perspective

It is clear from anecdotal evidence (e.g., hallway talk at professional meetings) as well as findings from the Kassebaum et al. study[12] that many dental schools have ongoing experience with managing change. However, the relationship between methods employed by these institutions to achieve structural or programmatic modifications and well-documented practices in change management may not be clear. This section summarizes change management themes

Table 3, continued

External influencing factors
- National boards, licensure, accreditation, and reimbursement issues perceived to be barriers to innovation and creativity.
- Interdependence of oral health profession with other health professions (hard to change one without changing another).
- Cottage industry mentality of the dental profession (tradition of "splendid isolation" from remainder of health care system).
- Lack of an umbilicus connecting dental school and practice to the broader health care system, which hinders implementing an integrated model of dental education and patient care.
- Relatively isolationist practice of dental specialties in practice and education settings.
- Practice independence, which fosters rugged individualism and infrequent peer input—traits that predominate among the many boomer-age practitioners who are currently the main source of new faculty.
- Political nature of organized dentistry and dental education.
- Lack of transformational leadership in organized and academic dentistry.

Financial and workforce constraints
- Perceived discrepancy in salary between careers in dental academic and private practice settings.
- Overall satisfaction with professional work-life, but dissatisfaction with professional development and support.
- Narrow financial margins, making it difficult to absorb costs associated with change (so the status quo or mere tweaking of the status quo prevails).
- Faculty manpower and economics: limited resources to recruit, develop, and retain talented dental faculty who advance the profession through teaching and research.
- Unique composition of full-time and part-time faculty, tenure- and non-tenure-track appointments, biomedical and clinical faculty, and discipline-specific faculty—making it difficult to obtain consensus among competing interests.

Sources: Crawford JM, Adami G, Johnson BR, Knight GW, Knoernschild K, Obrez A, et al. Curriculum restructuring at a North American dental school: rationale for change. J Dent Educ 2007;71(4):524–31; DePaola DP. The revitalization of U.S. dental education. J Dent Educ 2008;72(2 Suppl):28–42; Formicola AJ, Bailit HL, Beazoglou TJ, Tedesco LA. The Macy study: a framework for consensus. J Dent Educ 2008;72(2 Suppl):95–7; Geissberger MJ, Jain P, Kluemper GT, Paquette DW, Roeder LB, Scarfe WC, Potter BJ. Realigning biomedical science instruction in predoctoral curricula: a proposal for change. J Dent Educ 2008;72(2):135–41; Faggion CM Jr, Tu YK. Evidence-based dentistry: a model for clinical practice. J Dent Educ 2007;71(6): 825–31; Masella RS, Thompson TJ. Dental education and evidence-based educational best practices: bridging the great divide. J Dent Educ 2004;68(12):1266–71; Licari FW. Faculty development to support curriculum change and ensure the future vitality of dental education. J Dent Educ 2007;71(12):1509–12; Hendricson WD, Anderson E, Andrieu SC, Chadwick DG, Cole JR, George MC, et al. Does faculty development enhance teaching effectiveness? J Dent Educ 2007;71(12):1513–33; Bertolami CN. Rationalizing the dental curriculum. J Dent Educ 2001;65(8):725–35; Haden NK, Hendricson W, Ranney RR, Vargas A, Cardenas L, Rose W, et al. The quality of dental faculty work-life: report on the 2007 dental school faculty work environment survey. J Dent Educ 2008;72(5):514–31.

that have particular relevance to change in dental schools, in hopes that they might inform or validate change efforts already under way or contemplated for the near future. The themes are reframing organizational complexity; change leadership; values, competence, and commitment among employees; and organizational learning. These are followed by a brief look at resistance to change.

Reframing Organizational Complexity

A widely used practical guide for reframing the complexities within an organization is Bolman and Deal's framework, which visualizes the organization through four main perspectives or lenses: the structural, human resource, political, and symbolic.[40] The first lens gives focus to organizational structures that support an organization's goals; these structures might include work roles, tasks, technology, and the environment. Effective organizational structure exhibits a clear division of labor and appropriate mechanisms to integrate individual, group, and organizational efforts. The human resource lens brings into focus issues related to individual and organizational needs (e.g., training, motivation, and rewards) and suggests that a healthy human relations environment is one in which the reciprocal needs of the organization and the individual are met. For example, humans have a need to express their talents and skills; organizations need human contributions to operate. When there is a good fit between these individual and organizational needs, both benefit.[41] The political lens focuses on the issues of power, coalitions, negotiation, and conflict management. Due to the diversity of such factors as values, behaviors, skills, and interests, especially within an environment of limited resources, management of political influences is key. Finally, Bolman and Deal refer to a symbolic frame through which organizations are viewed as social and cultural entities, in which emphasis on meaning, purpose, and values is important. Because culture reflects shared values and beliefs, creating a common vision and excitement through ceremonies, rituals, and symbols is an important aspect of an organization.

When applied to managing a planned change, the Bolman and Deal framework can be a useful tool to systematically evaluate each of these four aspects of an organization and to proactively anticipate within which area an organization's strengths and potential barriers to change may exist.[41] A more detailed list of issues related to each frame is outlined in Table 4. The practical implications of the Bolman and Deal framework are indicated in the right column.

Change Leadership

The importance of the leadership role in managing change has been unequivocally demonstrated. Although the literature on leadership is immense, making it difficult to select representative material germane to academic dentistry, a logical choice for the discussion of leadership in academic settings is the previously described ACE initiative on change in higher education. The findings of this national study of many institutions demonstrate that the effect of leadership on organizational culture and the change process is profound.[19-23] Some of the conclusions about effective change leadership from the ACE study are the following:

- Change leaders display attitudes and approaches that facilitate change by 1) anchoring the change in academic values; 2) creating a culture of trust; and 3) adopting a long-term perspective on change.
- Change leaders help people develop new ways of thinking in addition to different practices, structures, and policies.
- Change leaders foster new thinking by allowing the questioning of the status quo and by encouraging faculty to explore how and why current mechanisms have become insufficient; change leaders also question assumptions and encourage others to do so; they create and communicate new ideas, develop new language, and attach new meanings to familiar language and concepts.
- Change leaders understand that people respond differently to the same information, react to different stimuli, and are motivated differently, necessitating a variety of approaches to communicate a common message.
- Change leaders frame a positive change agenda that is persistently and clearly communicated.
- Change leaders are cognizant of the change process and adjust their actions in response to what they learn from stakeholders and dissenters.
- Change leaders are sensitive to the balance among speed, deliberation, and persistence; they intentionally regulate the intensity of the change effort.
- Change leaders find ways to negotiate and to resolve conflicts (or at least to hear all parties) and then keep moving.

Table 4. A frame approach to understanding organizations and change

Frame	Issues	Path to Organizational Effectiveness
Structural	Rules, regulations, goals, policies, roles, tasks, job designs, job descriptions, technology, environment, chain of command, vertical and horizontal coordinating mechanisms, assessment and reward systems, standard operating procedures, authority spans and structures, spans of control, specialization and division of labor, information systems, formal feedback loops, boundary scanning, and management processes.	Develop and implement a clear division of labor for accomplishing the tasks necessary to move the change process forward. Create appropriate mechanisms to integrate individual, group, and unit efforts. Provide effective and diligent overall management of the change process.
Human resource	Needs, skills, relationships, norms, perceptions and attitudes, morale, motivation, training and development, interpersonal and group dynamics, supervision, teams, job satisfaction, participation and involvement, informal organization, support, respect for diversity, and formal and informal leadership.	Tailor the organization to meet individual needs. Train the individual in relevant skills to meet new organizational needs.
Political	Key stakeholders, divergent interests, scarce resources, areas of uncertainty, individual and group agendas, sources and bases of power, power distributions, formal and informal resource allocation systems and processes, influence, conflict, competition, politicking, coalitions, formal and informal alliances and networks, interdependence, control of rewards and punishment, and informal communication channels.	Identify and engage, both formally and informally, key individuals with influence. Bargain, negotiate, build coalitions, set agendas, and manage conflict.
Symbolic	Culture, rituals, ceremonies, stories, myths, symbols, metaphors, meaning, spirituality, values, vision, charisma, passions, and commitments.	Create a common vision. Devise relevant rituals, ceremonies, and symbols. Manage meaning. Infuse the culture with passion, creativity, and soul.

Source: Adapted from Gallos JV. Reframing complexity: a four-dimensional approach to organizational diagnosis, development, and change. In: Gallos JV, ed. Organization development. San Francisco: Jossey-Bass, 2006:347,352.

Values, Competence, and Commitment

The importance of basing organizational goals on shared values appears throughout change literature and cannot be underestimated. Successful leaders are described as being able to communicate how the goals of an organization relate to individual values and desires and how the success of the organization inspires individual gains.[42] Impressive momentum for a change can come about if individuals share a view of what can and should be and, in particular, if that vision fits with individual and collective values and goals.

But what if the prevailing wind is "if it ain't broke, don't fix it"? How does a leader or change agent effect change when the majority believes the status quo seems perfectly fine or is, at least, acceptable? A possible tactic is to reframe the issue using facts. Inside-the-box definitions most likely result in inside-the-box solutions (or non-action and resistance if people believe there is no need to change). Instead, by using hard data as a foundation (a method that appeals to most educators and researchers), a problem could be reframed by not only describing it, but by emphasizing a pivotal issue in a compelling way that leads to the inevitable questioning of the status quo. In other words, the answer to the question "if it ain't broke, why fix it?" lies in one's narrow interpretation of the word "broke." One method for reframing an issue in this way has been described as taking three steps.[43] First, discuss the conventional interpretation of a situation so that everyone begins with a common understanding. Second, point out exceptions to the norm that are working especially well either in the workplace or in other settings. Finally, reframe the problem focusing on the exceptions and cultivate home-grown solutions through widespread participation in a safe and supportive environment. The bottom line: change leaders in a resistant or apathetic environment must nurture ownership, not buy-in. It is far more effective to induce a change (through new ways of thinking about a problem) than to impose a change.[31]

Of course, the notion of effective leadership predicates the existence of competent and committed employees. Dave Ulrich, in his 1998 article titled "Intellectual Capital = Competence x Commitment,"[44] suggests ways to increase competence within an organization: "buy, build, borrow, bounce, and bind." "Buy" talent through hiring of competent individuals; "build" talent through training and development; "borrow" talent through partnerships outside the organization; "bounce" individuals with low or sub-par performance; and "bind" or retain good talent. This scenario is not unlike Jim Collins's 2001 *Good to Great* analogy "First you have to get the right people on the bus (and the wrong people off the bus), and then figure out where to drive it."[45] Many leaders of organizations ponder "just how do you ensure committed employees?" Creating a sense of community, clarifying the mission, guaranteeing organizational justice, supporting employee development, and, most important, valuing individual organizational members is one reportedly effective combination to cultivate employee commitment.[46] The following statement by Pfeffer and Veiga[47] effectively summarizes the issues of employee commitment and competence:

Simply put, people work harder because of the increased involvement and commitment that come from having more control and say in their work; people work smarter because they are encouraged to build skills and competence; and people work more responsibly because more responsibility is placed in hands of employees farther down in the organization. These practices work not because of some mystical process, but because they are grounded in sound social science principles that have been shown to be effective by a great deal of evidence. And they make sense.

Organizational Learning

A theme that has dominated change literature in recent decades, and has particular relevance to change in dental education, is individual and organizational learning in which personal and institutional maturation occurs through self-reflection and by means of open and effective communication. In an article titled "Teaching Smart People How to Learn," Chris Argyris asserts that most people in the workplace confuse "learning" with "problem-solving" and that they instead need to reflect critically on their own behavior and how it might be contributing to the organization's problem.[48] Argyris and Schon coined the terms "single-loop" and "double-loop" learning to distinguish between the two processes of learning and problem-solving.[49] In single-loop learning, only a superficial treatment of a problem occurs, resulting in a quick fix or a new way of doing the same old thing. Double-loop learning reflects a deeper analysis of the underlying issues that, when addressed, can result in more meaningful problem-solving and change. The problem is that there is often a discrepancy between what people say they do (espoused theory) and what they actually do (theory in practice). Argyris and Schon encourage a "reflective practice" to realign the two and say it is especially necessary to do so when contemplating organizational change. With regard to teaching smart people how to learn, Argyris[48] says:

Highly skilled professionals are frequently very good at single-loop learning. After all, they have spent much of their lives acquiring academic credentials, mastering one or a number of intellectual disciplines, and applying those disciplines to solve real-world problems. But ironically, this very fact helps explain why professionals are often so bad at double-loop learning.

Put simply, because many professionals are almost always successful at what they do, they rarely experience failure. And because they have rarely failed, they have never learned how to learn from failure. So whenever their single-loop learning strategies go wrong, they [often] react defensively. In short, their ability to learn shuts down precisely at the moment they need it the most. . . . Teaching people how to reason about their behavior in new and more effective ways breaks down the defenses that block learning.

The first step in beginning to infuse double-loop learning in an organization is for leaders and managers to begin using it themselves by critically evaluating their own espoused theories and theories in practice. Next, the key to teaching others how to reason productively is to show how it can make a difference in their own performance and in that of the organization. There is much literature (both theoretical and lay) that addresses effective communication and conflict management. Although it is not always comfortable practicing open and honest communication, the rewards that come from addressing underlying issues and developing effective solutions result in a collective satisfaction and momentum that can fuel further change. If practiced at the organizational level, open communication and reflection can result in an organization's increased capacity to examine its internal and external environments and to adapt accordingly in a rapidly changing world.

Resistance to Change

No discussion about change would be complete without addressing the issue of its resistance. Interestingly, the change literature both acknowledges and discounts the notion of resistance. Most theorists believe that people do not resist change per se. Resistance to change is often more accurately described as resistance to ambiguity.[50] In order to feel more comfortable, people need a sense of understanding why a change is proposed and, more important, how it is going to affect them and their work. They need proper resources and training to perform new tasks; from transformational leadership, we know that they need help and support in learning how to think in new ways and understanding they will not be penalized in the process. With needs met, ambiguity diminishes, as should the resistance to change. The practical techniques described here—such as Bolman and Deal's framework for scanning the organization for potential change barriers; effective communication practices including negotiation and conflict management; and relating the change to individual values, competence, and commitment—are effective mechanisms to address resistance to change and necessary components of any organizational change toolkit.

Conclusions

This article presents only a taste of the vast information available regarding the organizational change process and its management. In this context, my goal is to stimulate further discussion about the relevance and application of organizational change theory, research, and heuristics to dental education. Further research is needed to better understand factors associated with successful and unsuccessful change in this as-of-yet little explored professional education setting. Future work needs to be done to identify unique elements of dental education environments before existing change theory can be validated or new theory about change in dental education can be generated. Ultimately, it would be beneficial if individual dental schools could assess their own readiness for change by being able to identify factors that enhance and detract from change initiatives upon which they choose to embark. What is clear is that any attempt at subsequent application of change theory in dental education will grind to a halt if schools continue to adhere to traditional models and environments that are riddled with barriers to change.

The biomedical information explosion that is pouring new information into the practice of the profession at an alarming rate has outpaced the current capacity for dental curricula to absorb. Recommendations for curricula content and new pedagogy are being introduced at an increasingly fervent pace, making concurrent guidance through the change process extremely beneficial. Similar to student competencies, one could imagine organizational competencies—in particular, those that induce desirable behaviors related to change and its management. Just as we face the calls for evidence-based practice and evidence-based education, we could include evidence-based change as the driver that underlies reform of any type. However, a call for balance when considering change must be made. It would be a mistake for schools to "change for change's sake" in response to the current environment. Academic institutions, dental schools notwithstanding, are built on a foundation of long-standing tradition. Positive aspects of that tradition may not need to change and can serve as a durable foundation when reforms are considered that have the potential to enhance the academic, scholarly, and service outcomes of the overall institution. In other words, the old adage "don't throw out the baby with the bathwater" certainly holds true for change in dental education as well.

Following discussion of the management of change up to this point, a few comments about complexity and chaos are in order. As we know, change is anything but orderly. Organizations can be thought of as dynamic nonlinear systems whose challenge is to keep operating amid seeming chaos. We can not possibly fully control, manage, or predict the world. Instead, change upon change should be anticipated. A dental school that is capable of continually scanning its environment and changing accordingly will prevail. Better yet, a school that adopts a "change as usual" modus operandi will better absorb external and internal pressures for change and may even inspire creative thinking about what might be coming on the horizon. The change process itself should be a learning experience. Any attempt at change (whether failed or successful) should, upon careful reflection, provide insight into the process that can inform future change efforts. In other words, an individual change initiative should not be measured in terms of its success or failure, but rather thought of as an experiment that provides invaluable information for future efforts. In sum, promising potential exists for those in dental education to view change as not the result of serendipity, but as a process that can and should be managed. A dental school could adopt the attitude that change is not something to be endured: it is a way of being. Ultimately, a society that is served by graduates from such an institution would benefit.

Acknowledgments

The author would like to thank Drs. Cynthia Gadbury-Amyot and Joan Gallos for their helpful comments on this article.

REFERENCES

1. Crawford JM, Adami G, Johnson BR, Knight GW, Knoernschild K, Obrez A, et al. Curriculum restructuring at a North American dental school: rationale for change. J Dent Educ 2007;71(4):524–31.
2. DePaola DP. The revitalization of U.S. dental education. J Dent Educ 2008;72(2 Suppl):28–42.
3. Pyle M, Andrieu SC, Chadwick DG, Chmar JE, Cole JR, George MC, et al. The case for change in dental education. J Dent Educ 2006;70(9):921–4.
4. Formicola AJ, Bailit HL, Beazoglou TJ, Tedesco LA. The Macy study: a framework for consensus. J Dent Educ 2008;72(2 Suppl):95–7.
5. Holmes DC, Boston DW, Budenz AW, Licari FW. Predoctoral clinical curriculum models at U.S. and Canadian dental schools. J Dent Educ 2003;67(12):1302–11.
6. Iacopino AM. The influence of "new science" on dental education: current concepts, trends, and models for the future. J Dent Educ 2007;71(4):450–62.
7. Brown JP. A new curriculum framework for clinical prevention and population health, with a review of clinical caries prevention teaching in U.S. and Canadian dental schools. J Dent Educ 2007;71(5):572–8.
8. Geissberger MJ, Jain P, Kluemper GT, Paquette DW, Roeder LB, Scarfe WC, Potter BJ. Realigning biomedical science instruction in predoctoral curricula: a proposal for change. J Dent Educ 2008;72(2):135–41.
9. Faggion CM Jr, Tu YK. Evidence-based dentistry: a model for clinical practice. J Dent Educ 2007;71(6):825–31.
10. Hendricson WD, Andrieu SC, Chadwick DG, Chmar JE, Cole JR, George MC, et al. Educational strategies associated with development of problem-solving, critical thinking, and self-directed learning. J Dent Educ 2006;70(9):925–36.
11. Masella RS, Thompson TJ. Dental education and evidence-based educational best practices: bridging the great divide. J Dent Educ 2004;68(12):1266–71.
12. Kassebaum DK, Hendricson WD, Taft T, Haden NK. The dental curriculum at North American dental institutions in 2002–03: a survey of current structure, recent innovations, and planned changes. J Dent Educ 2004;68(9):914–31.
13. Pyle MA, Goldberg JS. Engineering curriculum change at a private Midwest school of dental medicine: a faculty innovation. J Dent Educ 2008;72(3):288–98.
14. Licari FW. Faculty development to support curriculum change and ensure the future vitality of dental education. J Dent Educ 2007;71(12):1509–12.
15. Hendricson WD, Anderson E, Andrieu SC, Chadwick DG, Cole JR, George MC, et al. Does faculty development enhance teaching effectiveness? J Dent Educ 2007;71(12):1513–33.
16. Dharamsi S, Clark DC, Boyd MA, Pratt DD, Craig B. Social constructs of curricular change. J Dent Educ 2000;64(8):603–9.
17. Weick K, Quinn RE. Organizational change and development. Annu Rev Psychol 1999;50(1):361–86.
18. Austin J, Bartunek J. Theories and practices of organization development. In: Gallos J, ed. Organization development. San Francisco: Jossey-Bass, 2006.
19. Eckel P, Hill B, Green M. On change I: en route to transformation. Washington, DC: American Council on Education, 1998.
20. Eckel P, Hill B, Green M, Mallon W. On change II: reports from the road. Washington, DC: American Council on Education, 1999.
21. Eckel P, Hill B, Green M, Mallon W. On change III: taking charge of change. Washington, DC: American Council on Education, 1999.
22. Hill B, Green M, Eckel P. On change IV: what governing boards need to know and do about institutional change. Washington, DC: American Council on Education, 2001.
23. Eckel P, Green M, Hill B. On change V: riding the waves of change. Washington, DC: American Council on Education, 2001.
24. Shafritz JM, Hyde AC, Parkes SJ. Classics of public administration. Belmont, CA: Thomson, 2004.
25. Taylor FW. Shop management (1903). The principles of scientific management (1911). Testimony before the Special House Committee (1912). In: Taylor FW. Scientific management. New York: Routledge, 2003.
26. Simon HA. Models of bounded rationality. Cambridge, MA: MIT Press, 1982.
27. Mirvis P. Revolutions in OD. In: Gallos JV, ed. Organization development. San Francisco: Jossey-Bass, 2006.
28. Scott R. Organizations: rational, natural, and open systems. Englewood Cliffs, NJ: Prentice Hall, 1992.
29. Van de Ven AH, Pool MS. Explaining development and change in organizations. Acad Management Rev 1995;20:510–40.
30. Kezar AJ. Understanding and facilitating change in higher education in the 21st century: recent research and conceptualizations. ASHE-ERIC Education Report 28(4). San Francisco: Jossey-Bass, 2001.
31. Bland CJ, Starnaman S, Wersal L, Moorhead-Rosenberg L, Zonia S, Henry R. Curricular change in medical schools: how to succeed. Acad Med 2000;75:575–94.

32. Kramer NA. Capturing the curriculum: a curriculum maturation and transformation process. Nurse Educator 2005;30(2):80–4.

33. Watson MC, Bond CM, Grimshaw JM, Mollison J, Ludbrook A, Walker AE. Educational strategies to promote evidence-based community pharmacy practice: a cluster randomized controlled trial (RCT). Fam Pract 2002;19(5):529–36.

34. Provident IM. Mentoring: a role to facilitate academic change. Internet J Allied Health Sci Pract 2005;3(2):1–16.

35. Green R, Dezendorf P, Lyman S, Lyman S. Infusing gerontological content into curricula: effective change strategies. Educ Gerontology 2005;31(2):103–21.

36. Dean C. Curricular change process: a case study (learning organizations, problem-based learning, total quality management). Dissertation Abstracts Int 2005;58-05(Section A):1512.

37. Bertolami CN. Rationalizing the dental curriculum in light of current disease prevalence and patient demand for treatment: form vs. content. J Dent Educ 2001;65(8):725–35.

38. Haden NK, Hendricson W, Ranney RR, Vargas A, Cardenas L, Rose W, et al. The quality of dental faculty work-life: report on the 2007 dental school faculty work environment survey. J Dent Educ 2008;72(5):514–31.

39. Bertolami CN. Creating the dental school faculty of the future: a guide for the perplexed. J Dent Educ 2007;71(10):1267–80.

40. Bolman L, Deal T. Reframing organizations: artistry, choice, and leadership. San Francisco: Jossey-Bass, 2003.

41. Gallos JV. Reframing complexity: a four-dimensional approach to organizational diagnosis, development, and change. In: Gallos JV, ed. Organization development. San Francisco: Jossey-Bass, 2006.

42. Lawler E. Business strategy: creating the winning formula. In: Gallos JV, ed. Organization development. San Francisco: Jossey-Bass, 2006.

43. Pascale RT, Sternin J. Your company's secret change agents. Harvard Business Review, May 2005.

44. Ulrich D. Intellectual capital = competence x commitment. In: Osland JS, Kolb DA, Rubin IM, eds. The organizational behavior reader. 7th ed. Upper Saddle River, NJ: Prentice-Hall, 2001:484–96.

45. Collins J. Good to great: why some companies make the leap . . . and others don't. New York: HarperBusiness, 2001.

46. Dessler G. How to earn your employees' commitment. Acad Management Exec 1999;13(2):58–67.

47. Pfeffer J, Veiga J. Putting people first for organizational success. Acad Management Exec 1999;13(2):37–48.

48. Argyris C. Teaching smart people how to learn. In: Gallos JV, ed. Organization development. San Francisco: Jossey-Bass, 2006.

49. Argyris C, Schon DA. Theory in practice: increasing professional effectiveness. San Francisco: Jossey-Bass, 1974.

50. Weiss A. What constitutes an effective internal consultant? In: Gallos JV, ed. Organization development. San Francisco: Jossey-Bass, 2006.

Willing, Ready, and Able? How We Must Exercise Leadership for Needed Change in Dental Education

Peter A. Cohen, Ph.D.; Lisa A. Tedesco, Ph.D.

Abstract: For over twenty-five years, dental education has had the benefit of environmental analyses and institutional planning for change. Strong programs for leadership development have emerged to give direction to these efforts. Leading and thriving, not merely surviving, are universal aspirations, yet we remain vexed by finances, structures, and traditions. This article takes a look at change and examines the difference between technical frameworks for leadership and adaptive leadership. Leadership for change is viewed as an activity, not as a position of formal authority. The skills necessary to address the beliefs, attitudes, and culture that place limiting boundaries on adaptive leadership are described. Using the work of Heifetz and Linsky, the relationship between authority and adaptive leadership is defined. Resistance to change is presented as reaction to loss, which needs to be addressed in a fundamental way, through leadership activity and engagement. If change and innovation are to be sustained, leadership must be less accidental, less technical, and more adaptive.

Dr. Cohen is Professor and Dean, College of Health Professions, Wichita State University; Dr. Tedesco is Vice Provost for Academic Affairs–Graduate Studies, Dean of the Graduate School, and Professor in the Rollins School of Public Health, Emory University. Direct correspondence and requests for reprints to Dr. Peter A. Cohen, Dean, College of Health Professions, Wichita State University, 1845 Fairmount, Wichita, KS 67260-0043; 316-978-3600 phone; 316-978-3025 fax; Peter.Cohen@wichita.edu.

This article is one in a series of invited contributions by members of the dental education community that have been commissioned by the American Dental Education Association's Commission on Change and Innovation in Dental Education (ADEA CCI) to address the environment surrounding dental education and affecting the need for, or process of, curricular change. This article was written at the request of the ADEA CCI but does not necessarily reflect the views of ADEA, the ADEA CCI, or individual members of the ADEA CCI. The perspectives communicated here are those of the authors.

Key words: leadership, change, dental education

For nearly twenty-five years, individuals and groups have inveighed dental education to pay attention to environmental pressures and seek the change that would continue to produce strong lines of oral health professionals and researchers. Researchers and educators, in groups and as individuals, have encouraged, guided, and exhorted academic dentistry to examine the scientific, educational, economic, and sociocultural environment surrounding our schools so that we would lead and thrive, not merely survive.[1-6]

Most recently, two national projects, both highly visible, have provided a breadth and depth of guidance for needed change in dental education. Pyle et al., members of the American Dental Education Association's Commission on Change and Innovation in Dental Education (ADEA CCI), argued that "there is a compelling need for rethinking the approach to dental education in the United States."[5] In a series of twenty-one articles published in the *Journal of Dental Education* from 2006 to 2008, the ADEA CCI has called attention to problems that on their face continue to vex dental educators at every level. Pyle et al. state that these problems are "1) the challenging financial environment of higher education, making dental schools very expensive and tuition-intensive for universities to operate and producing high debt levels for students that limit access to education and restrict career choices; 2) the profession's apparent loss of vision for taking care of the oral health needs of all components of society and the resultant potential for marginalization of dentistry as a specialized health care service available only to the affluent; and 3) the nature of dental school education itself, which has been described as convoluted, expensive, and often deeply dissatisfying to its students."[5]

The Macy Study,[6] the other national project, has shown through compelling examination of historical trend data, review of archival narratives and records, and policy analyses that new models of dental education are needed to address the financial and educational challenges of dental education. Dental schools have increasing difficulty meeting their education, research, clinical care, and service missions. The cost of clinical education is out of balance with the other segments of dental education's mission, threatening the institutional vitality of dental schools. Resources continue to decline for research, curriculum innovation, faculty recruitment and retention, and faculty development because of the high cost of school-based clinical education. Contributors to the Macy Study National Convocation observed that the current responses of schools to these economic challenges have not been adequate and that the most promising solutions require new models of clinical dental education—models that are organizationally and systemically sensitive to "financial viability and institutional vitality" through attention to patient-centered care, cost, and efficiency, as called for in the 1995 Institute of Medicine report on dental education.[2]

With all this in mind, how must we exercise leadership for needed change? We write this article to provide a view of change in dental education that places leadership in the context of adaptation.

Current Status of Leadership in Dental Education

Even with the careful study and wise guidance of the projects cited above, the movement toward changes being implemented simply to prevent further erosion of programs appears to be proceeding at a slow pace.[7] And it appears that the problems described in the ADEA CCI articles and the Macy Study report are not new—which comes as no surprise to any of us in dental education. In fact, in 1983 the American Dental Association's report on the future of dentistry[8] warned of the close of several dental schools if the negative financial trends weren't addressed. By the late 1990s, seven dental schools had closed.

To be sure, our goal in this article is not to focus on the challenges facing dental schools per se. Rather, it is our intention to link these ongoing, persistent issues to misconceptions of leadership and a new understanding of what it will take to move us forward to productive solutions.

First, we must ask several questions: How do we shape our understanding of the problems? Are our current practices of leadership providing us with an understanding of what is hanging in the balance? How are we working to understand whether the cultures for education, pedagogy, and clinical care are changing? How must we proceed to ensure that the right degree of attention and persistence is applied to the questions of change? Is change mindful and adaptive or more or less accidental and technical? More importantly, how is the responsibility for leadership diffused throughout the dental school and its stakeholders? Our read of the past and current conditions within and around dental education suggests that leadership is more accidental and technically understood and less adaptive to address sustainable change and innovation.

The Challenges Facing Dental Education Are Adaptive in Nature

The challenges and questions described above cannot be met by applying our current thinking and leadership approaches. We have been oriented to view leadership through a *technical* lens: here is the problem; this is what we need to do about it. Technical problems can be solved through the knowledge of experts and senior authorities. We are accustomed, indeed well trained, to define or diagnose a case that solves the problem presented. We also would like to be able to "fix" the challenges/problems facing dental education through the application of our existing knowledge and expertise. But for many of the systemic challenges facing dental education, no clear solutions exist; they do not lend themselves to technical, "quick-fix" answers. These are problems we can't solve through application of our traditional conceptions of leadership; instead, contemporary challenges facing dental education are *adaptive* in nature. The parameters and magnitude of these challenges are ill defined and evolving, and they involve our willingness and ability to confront existing values, beliefs, and ways of being. We must develop new competencies to effectively exercise leadership in this adaptive environment. The challenges we face cannot be addressed solely by applying the knowledge of experts or through the repetition of previous responses to emerging challenges.

In writing this article, we were strongly influenced by the leadership model developed by Ron Heifetz and Marty Linsky of Harvard University's John F. Kennedy School of Government and Cambridge Leadership Associates (www.cambridge-leadership.com/index.php4),[9] especially in regard to their work with Ed O'Malley, president and CEO of the Kansas Leadership Center (www.kansasleader shipcenter.org/index.html).[10] We strongly believe that their model of adaptive leadership provides the best guidance and hope for dental education.

Adaptive challenges bring to light the gap between our aspirations and current reality. The seven principles underlying educational reform articulated by the Macy Study[6] describe our collective aspirations for dental education (Figure 1).

How will we bridge the gap between the current state of dental education and these aspirations? It is quite unsettling to think that there might be a shortcoming in our leadership competence. Thinking adaptively, we must consider these interrelated questions: what can we keep that is valuable, what can we let go of, and what do we need to change? Deciding what to keep, what to give up, and in what ways we need to innovate cannot be approached technically. Rather, these decisions tap into deeply held values, beliefs, and ways of being. When we decide to promote change, we must also recognize and acknowledge that what seems to be a good idea for us can imply great loss for others. Heifetz and Linsky are fond of saying, "People don't resist change. People resist loss."

Leadership Is an Activity, Not a Position

We see leadership in dental education as mobilizing others to make progress on difficult (adaptive) issues[9] and, therefore, take the position expressed by the Kansas Leadership Center that "individuals do not become leaders, but that individuals choose to exercise leadership."[10] Because leadership is an activity not a position, it can be achieved by anyone, but no one does it all the time. Leadership can be fleeting, in-the-moment interventions that bridge competing factions and serve to mobilize others to move forward an adaptive challenge.

In the exercise of leadership, then, it becomes important to clarify the role of authority and distinguish authority from leadership. From the perspective of Heifetz and Linsky, authority is viewed as a delivery of services in exchange for power. People in positions of authority (for example, deans and department chairs) are rewarded for meeting others' expectations and acting within their scope of authority. We want those in authority to be consistent and predictable. However, adaptive challenges often require improvisational thinking and action.

---

1. Dentistry is a learned, self-regulating profession that is comparable to but organizationally separate from medicine.

2. Every dental school must be an integral part of a university, and the majority must be based at research-extensive universities (Carnegie Foundation definition), where faculty scholars advance the sciences underlying the practice of dentistry and pass the knowledge on to students, residents, and others.

3. Dental schools must have the resources needed to

   • recruit and retain adequate numbers of well-qualified faculty;

   • provide faculty with sufficient income, space, equipment, time, and administrative support to pursue their scholarly activities;

   • recruit and maintain a diverse student body and faculty;

   • maintain their physical plants; and

   • invest in new educational technologies and learning resources.

4. The teaching, research, and service programs of all dental schools must contribute to reducing oral health disparities.

5. Dental students need the same basic understanding of human biology and behavior as medical students and advanced knowledge of the basic, social, and clinical sciences relevant to the diagnosis, prevention, and treatment of oral diseases/conditions in healthy and medically compromised patients.

6. Clinical training should include adequate time in community-based, patient-centered delivery sites, providing evidence-based care to diverse groups of patients, efficiently.

7. The curriculum should prepare graduates to enter practice; however, in the future, this could shift to preparing students to enter general or specialty residency programs.

Source: Formicola AJ, Bailit HL, Beazoglou TJ, Tedesco LA. Introduction to the Macy Study report. J Dent Educ 2008;72(2 Suppl):6.

Figure 1. Macy Study principles underlying educational reform in dental education

---

Consistency and predictability may actually work against the exercise of leadership in real time. Some people who are comfortable in the role of authority are not good at exercising leadership beyond this role. Through this view, deans and department chairs are authorized to deliver specific services for their constituents, but not authorized to exercise leadership. Otherwise, we might actually be tackling these tough, adaptive issues.

Adaptive leadership requires going beyond a title-bound authorization no matter what one's position. Thus, anyone (administrator, faculty, staff, student) can choose to exercise leadership beyond his or her authority. But what are the consequences of doing this? It is dangerous to question values, beliefs, and ingrained ways of operating. Leading beyond one's authority typically results in resistance. One person's ideas for progress are often viewed by others as loss. That is why adaptive leadership is so difficult, and so rare, in dental education.

Competencies for the Exercise of Leadership

Our position is that the exercise of leadership occurs as an action in *real time* and *over time*. Leadership is not a set of traits, characteristics, and dispositions. Most contemporary models conceptualize leadership through a series of practices. For example, Kouzes and Posner[11] propose five distinct practices: modeling the way, inspiring a shared vision, challenging the process, enabling others to act, and encouraging the heart. Kotter suggests an eight-stage process for leading change.[12] These approaches are appropriate for building a leadership skill set; we view them as important and necessary, indeed fundamental, but not sufficient for the full exercise of leadership.

The Kansas Leadership Center, in its work to promote civic leadership throughout the state of Kansas and in consultation with Cambridge Leadership Associates, has articulated four competencies for the exercise of leadership: diagnosing the situation, managing self, facilitating interventions, and energizing others. To us, this framework for understanding and exercising leadership makes sense for dental education. Let's take a look at each of these competencies.

Diagnosing the Situation

The key to this competency is determining what is going on in the moment, in the current situation, or in the larger organizational context, so we can figure out how to intervene within the system to mobilize others to make progress. Fundamentally, this competency requires us to be able to observe and interpret what is going on within a group, an organization, or a system. Heifetz and Linsky apply the metaphor of getting on the balcony to observe what is happening on the dance floor. Adaptive leadership requires us to move fluidly between being in the midst of the action (the dance floor) and stepping back to observe what is actually happening in the moment as well as to interpret what it means (the balcony). Interpretation can be a contentious and tricky activity. Heifetz and Linsky argue that we tend to interpret events as technical problems rather than recognizing the adaptive elements of these challenges, or to reduce problems to tangible, technical aspects so they can be addressed with technical solutions; we tend to focus on what is happening among individuals rather than viewing what is happening at the system level; and we tend to accept comfortable explanations rather than acknowledging that competing values are embedded in the situation and in potential responses to the situation.

When diagnosing the situation, the following types of questions may help:
- What are the formal relationships among the dental school's stakeholders? Where are the informal alliances?
- Where do senior authorities (e.g., dean, department chairs) stand on the issue?
- What factions exist in the dental school?
- What are the primary hidden issues in the dental school?
- What has been done so far to work the problem? What have people decided not to do?
- What is at stake for individuals in the dental school? What do individuals stand to lose?
- What issues or values are represented in the dental school? What would observing the dental school operations and relationships over a period of time tell you about the school's values?
- How is the situation viewed by the key players? What stories are they telling themselves?
- What has each individual contributed to the problem?
- What options are off the table for the dental school and individuals in the dental school, and why?

- What possible interpretations has the dental school been understandably unwilling to consider?
- What would success look like to all stakeholders?

Managing Self

The key to this competency is how we manage ourselves when played or pressed to do what people *want* us to do rather than what people *need* us to do. When in positions of authority, we are faced with a huge range of expectations, and we are under tremendous pressure to satisfy as many of these expectations as possible. Heifetz and Linsky are fond of saying, "Leadership is disappointing your own people at a rate they can absorb." To accomplish this, we must be cognizant of our true values to ensure that these values align with the leadership work we promote. More important than formal authority, our degree of informal authority (our ability to influence change) will be based largely on what we do rather than what we say. We must consider how our typical ways of problem-solving, what Heifetz and Linsky refer to as "default settings," inhibit progress on difficult issues. For example, when things get heated, do we work to make the group more comfortable, or do we prefer to stir things up? We need to recognize when our default settings are helpful and when they are not helpful. If these default settings cover a relatively small range of behaviors, can we expand our operational range of behaviors so that we are more effective in a greater variety of situations? Going back to the previous example, if our default setting is to make a situation more comfortable, can we get ourselves to "turn up the heat" when that is what would be required for progress to be made?

Another critical aspect of managing self is to separate the role we play in an organization or system from our true selves. Most of us have experienced being attacked because of our stance on an issue, so this can serve as a live example of the need to separate role from self. If we take the attack personally, then we, in effect, displace the focus from the adaptive issue and, instead, we become the issue. By making the issue personal (about our self), we remove ourselves from the role of effectively exercising leadership. Keeping a steadfast focus on the issue at hand and not "avoiding the work" are primary acts of exercising leadership. Avoiding the work in the context of leadership includes avoiding uncomfortable discussions of conflicting values and priorities among individuals and groups with a vested interest in the direction of the decision or a proposed policy that may alter the "way things are done."

When managing self, the following types of questions may help:
- When occupying positions of senior authority, what pressures you to do the leadership work yourself, instead of giving the work back to the people affected by the problems?
- What are your default settings (what behaviors do you gravitate toward)? In what situations do these defaults help you? In what situations do they hinder your exercise of leadership?
- What role have you taken on in the dental school, and to what effect? Note that, in the context of this question, "role" does not refer to your job or position.
- What is your level of informal authority? How can you gain or lose informal authority?
- What story are you telling yourself? Does it reinforce your default way of thinking? How can you facilitate letting in data and interpretations outside of your default range? Are you more interested in making progress on adaptive challenges or maintaining your default settings?
- How much of your passion do you bring to your leadership work? How much of your self are you willing to put into this work?

Facilitating Interventions

How effectively can we take action within the group, organization, or system to mobilize others to make progress on difficult issues? At its core, leadership is an activity—an intervention into the system intended to move an issue or adaptive challenge forward. An intervention can be a planned, constructed proposal or an in-the-moment improvisation. Regardless of its style, an effective intervention has several attributes. First, it is critical to gain attention for the adaptive issue at hand; typically, this is accomplished through the degree of informal authority we hold. For an intervention to "take," we must be influential within the group, organization, or system. Our degree of informal authority has little to do with our formal positional authority. Another attribute of an effective intervention is identifying the adaptive work to be done. The most common "leadership error" is in not distinguishing technical from adaptive work.[9] Thus, making this distinction becomes an important criterion of an effective intervention. Because adaptive challenges invariably involve competing values, which most often go unacknowledged, an effective intervention will identify potential losses to stakeholders and, in fact, orchestrate meaningful conflict across factions. Conflict, of course, raises the degree of disequilibrium ("raising the heat"); an effective intervention discerns the appropriate degree of disequilibrium, either raising or lowering the heat, necessary to make progress. Finally, an effective intervention places the responsibility for the work with the people who have the stake in the problem.

When facilitating interventions, the following types of questions may help:

- Have you adequately diagnosed the situation (making observations and interpretations)?
- Are your interventions purposeful?
- What choices do you make to keep everyone included? What are the costs of keeping everyone included?
- Have you distinguished what people "need" from you versus what they "want" from you?
- How will you bridge competing values expressed by competing factions? What values and operations may be left behind (i.e., no longer remain as a part of the institutional culture)?

Energizing Others

What does it take to get others engaged in adaptive work where the outcome is not predetermined? It becomes important to focus the work at a purposeful and meaningful level. We tend to define problems at such a high level of abstraction that no one can disagree; problems defined in this manner will generate little meaningful conflict and people can exist without having to do anything differently. In other words, no one is forced to give up anything they care about. For example, consider the Macy Study Principle 3, "Dental schools must have the resources needed to . . . ."[6] If viewed technically, this problem results in virtually no meaningful engagement. Defining this as a technical problem often results in a collective whining about why we aren't receiving more resources (i.e., providing more resources represents a technical solution to an abstractly defined problem). But if the problem becomes less abstractly defined—for example, looking at reallocation of resources, inefficiencies in our current way of operation, different approaches to meeting educational goals—then stakeholders may appreciate that they have something to lose in the adaptive work. Competing values come to the surface, conflict emerges, loss becomes real, and individuals have to change what they are doing and how they are thinking. Clearly, making progress

on identified adaptive issues lies at odds with our culture of individualism in dental schools and in higher education in general.

Because of resistance to loss, creating an environment in which others begin to engage becomes essential. Heifetz and Linsky refer to this as the "holding environment," where tough issues can be discussed in a safer, organized way. It takes intentionality to create such an environment, where conversations have a different feel from elsewhere in the dental school. We strengthen the holding environment by pacing the work of the group and enlisting others in making interventions. Creating a holding environment is extremely difficult, which is why external consultants are often used to facilitate these discussions. To exercise leadership, we must communicate an optimistic and shared vision centered on an orienting purpose. Heifetz and Linsky state, "Purpose is an orienting force in the exercise of leadership."[9]

When energizing others, the following types of questions may help:

- What is the orienting purpose around which adaptive work can be accomplished?
- How can we create a holding environment to engage uncommon voices?
- What is each individual's responsibility for mobilizing others to make progress on difficult issues? How can we diffuse responsibility for the exercise of leadership beyond those people in positions of authority?
- How does the dental school's valuing of "comfort" affect its progress (or lack of progress) on adaptive challenges?

One of the more intractable changes in dental education that would do well to be addressed with the competencies above is curriculum and its relationship to the delivery of contemporary, quality health care. How much do educational settings fail to resemble the care delivery systems in which graduates will practice? Nothing can be more pressing to the leadership of the dental school than the challenge of the curriculum, the clinical education setting, and the school's system (i.e., budget model) for financing dental education. Work on this problem is work done each and every day the doors of the school and its clinics are open. Yet, how well is the funding challenge understood by all stakeholders?

Disentangling stakeholders from beliefs and values that tie the outcomes for either survival or innovation (depending on your local situation) to limited, technical solutions may well require a different daily routine for those in charge of change. Imagine, for example, an effort to introduce a comprehensive curriculum and clinical change to reflect the growing need for the integration of oral health with systemic health. The vision is to not only change what is taught, but how it is taught and how it is practiced in the clinics. Imagine that changes include infrastructure related to patient records and how the faculty is organized. You are not only one of the deans or chairs in charge, but a faculty member with relationships to departments. Colleagues who stand to be affected by the change were your teachers a decade ago, or they may have been your classmates in dental school. Understanding where you are in relation to the change is key to self-management. If the curriculum were redesigned to integrate, in part, diagnosis and primary care, would organizational structures change and thereby change your formal role—as dean, say, or chair? How does structural change influence how you see yourself and how you manage yourself through the change process?

On the face of things, facilitating interventions and energizing others may seem like the competencies needed to "work a plan" once a plan has been established and accepted. The plans, however, rarely specify the daily expression of values and beliefs that camouflage as "but we've tried that" and "the regulations won't permit it." There have been numbers of plans that have yielded some change. The changes we are being called upon to make now are inextricably tied to financial viability and institutional vitality. Changing how we teach and in which venues or settings, such as school-based or community-based clinics, may present unique opportunities to examine long-standing institutional, locally derived beliefs and values. Taking these two competencies to their fullest meaning must be done with a mindfulness and acceptance of adaptive change for dental education and research to sustain and advance its leadership role in the health professions.

Developing Leadership Expertise (Eminence)

The frameworks provided by Heifetz and Linsky and the Kansas Leadership Center are helpful for understanding the longer term challenges of leadership and change. We would also like to draw attention to the development of expertise, beyond basic competencies for adaptive leadership. We should

strengthen our resolve to develop dental faculty, staff, administrators, and, ultimately, students to become adaptive leadership experts. Hundreds of studies over a wide variety of domains show that expertise takes a minimum of ten years to develop, but that experience alone does not lead to expertise.[13] To develop leadership expertise, we must be committed for the long haul.

What will it take to create a critical mass of leadership expertise within our dental schools, a cadre of individuals, not necessarily in positions of authority, who can mobilize people to make progress on dental education's adaptive challenges? Let's consider where, along the beginner-to-expert continuum, our current leadership practice falls. Thomas distinguishes three levels along this continuum: novice, adept, and eminent leadership performers.[14] Novice performers in any field are beginners who need a lot of guidance. Although there are some novices in positions of authority in our dental schools, the important leadership distinction we want to make here is between adept and eminent performers. Adept performers repeat the same patterns of behavior over their entire careers. They are rarely successful when forced to develop new skill sets beyond their current capacity.[13] Most current leadership in dental schools resides in individuals who hold positions of authority and, according to this framework, are adept performers. Eminent performers, on the other hand, excel in times of turbulence and change. They refresh and renew themselves and their organizations. Eminent performers are prepared, and prepare others, to address adaptive challenges. Thomas lists four distinguishing aspects of eminent performers,[14] which we believe apply to dental education:

1. *Grasp of method*—Expert leaders have acquired a vast toolkit of leadership knowledge and techniques. They understand the practices of leadership and the processes for leading change. They are well versed in exercising leadership in adaptive environments through the competencies we have described.

2. *Ambition*—Expert leaders have committed years of deliberate, intentional practice to achieve expertise. Most people practice on skills they are already adept at. But deliberate practice requires ongoing efforts to engage in the leadership work we *can't* do well. We believe that aspiring expert leaders must experiment, take risks, and act improvisationally, especially in situations in which they don't really have existing competence.

3. *Instruction*—Expert leaders seek great teachers and coaches. They never stop learning. Coaches and mentors accelerate the learning process; they also help develop expertise by encouraging independence and self-coaching.

4. *Feedback*—Expert leaders seek and use feedback, not only for themselves, but also for the organization. For instance, 360-degree assessments, in conjunction with coaching, provide critical leadership feedback. In their work, Heifetz and Linsky use debriefing sessions to gather feedback relevant to the individuals exercising leadership as well as the group as a whole. By providing intentional space for observations and interpretations, reflection itself can be considered a leadership activity.

We must commit to developing a cadre of adaptive leaders within our dental schools. Many health professions organizations at the national level have embraced this critical need for leadership development, but have focused primarily on preparing educators for positions of authority in academic settings. For example, the American Association of Colleges of Nursing offers an executive leadership fellowship tailored for new and aspiring deans. The Association of American Medical Colleges offers an Executive Development Seminar designed for associate deans and department chairs, and the Executive Leadership in Academic Medicine (ELAM) Program has trained over 500 mid-career women for senior leadership positions in medicine, dentistry, and, recently, public health. Through its Leadership Institute, ADEA has provided year-long training to 150 dental educators since 2000, and many Leadership Institute fellows have assumed roles of senior leadership within their institutions. These programs have raised awareness regarding the importance of leadership and, indeed, helped many individuals build their own leadership toolkits. However, without greater emphasis on and support for addressing adaptive challenges, will these trained individuals have the needed impact?

We believe that adaptive leadership capacity building will best be accomplished at a local level. Nearly thirty distinct executive education/leadership development programs are offered at U.S. medical schools.[15] While some of these programs provide intensive skill-based training, nearly all of them target educators aspiring to positions of authority in medical education settings.

The College of Health Professions at Wichita State University has taken a different tack by creating the Leadership Academy to promote and enhance leadership growth among faculty and staff to advance the vision and mission of the college and university. The Leadership Academy seeks to provide faculty and staff with opportunities to transform their capacity to exercise leadership in a challenging adaptive environment, foster a culture of leadership within the college, and reward faculty and staff work for advancing the goals and strategic vision of the college. After serving a year-long fellowship, academy fellows become senior coaches and mentors for faculty and staff who are incoming fellows. Academy fellows meet as a peer consultation group, which allows practice in diagnosing cases of personal adaptive challenges written by the fellows themselves. Academy fellows experience a two-and-a-half-day orienting program in adaptive leadership and meet weekly throughout the year to reinforce and practice these concepts. Ultimately, though, academy fellows are expected to exercise leadership across existing factions within the college and university to address adaptive challenges. With five to six new fellows accepted into the academy each year, over time a significant portion of the college's faculty and staff should be poised to promote adaptive leadership work.

Closing Comments

Throughout this article, we have purposefully not used the term "leader" in descriptions and explanations of what is needed for change, innovation, and vitality in dental education. Leadership, distinct from "the leader," is a conscious act, a choice we make daily or even in the moment, seemingly without notice. To be sure, the work of adaptive leadership is very difficult and can be both complicated and complex.

We cannot leave our discussion of leadership without acknowledging that the most valuable asset our institutions hold is people—our faculties and staffs and their connection to leadership. We recall the guidance of Peter Drucker,[16] who argued that our faculties and staffs are "knowledge workers," who should be treated as though they were volunteers. Drucker asks us to remember that volunteers are committed to what they do, and if they don't see results, they usually leave the organization. Without adaptive leadership, we are squandering this very precious resource.

Clearly, the leadership competencies developed by the Kansas Leadership Center overlap and are interrelated with much of what is described in the work of Heifetz and Linsky. From this body of work on change, leadership, and organizational dynamics, we know that there are casualties: ideas, values, and people are left behind. Adaptive work requires that we be prepared for what may well be experienced as casualties. With adaptive work, we are asking people, at times, to see the gaps between values and behaviors, between training under one set of historical principles and the need for new training environments, because materials, technologies, and economies have changed. Being adept at "authority" does not equate to being or becoming eminent at "leadership." We should be aspiring to leadership, not to being *the* leader.

REFERENCES

1. O'Neil EH, Barker BD. Pew National Dental Education Program: developing an agenda for change. J Dent Educ 1989;53(8):469–74.
2. Field MJ, ed. Dental education at the crossroads: challenges and change. An Institute of Medicine Report. Washington, DC: National Academy Press, 1995.
3. DePaola DP, Slavkin HC. Reforming dental health professions education: a white paper. J Dent Educ 2004;68(11):1139–50.
4. Donoff RB. It is time for a new Gies report. J Dent Educ 2006;70(8):809–19.
5. Pyle M, Andrieu SC, Chadwick DG, Chmar JE, Cole JR, George MC, et al. The case for change in dental education. J Dent Educ 2006;70(9):921–4.
6. Formicola AJ, ed. New models of dental education: the Macy Study report. J Dent Educ 2008;72(2 Suppl).
7. Kassebaum DK, Hendricson WD, Taft T, Haden N. The dental curriculum at North American dental institutions in 2002–03: a survey of current structure, recent innovations, and planned changes. J Dent Educ 2004;68(9):914–31.
8. American Dental Association. Report of the Special Committee on the Future of Dentistry. Strategic plan: issue papers on dental research, manpower, education, practice, and public and professional concerns and recommendations for action. Chicago: American Dental Association, July 1983.
9. Heifetz RL, Linsky M. Leadership on the line: staying alive through the dangers of leading. Boston: Harvard Business School Press, 2002.
10. Kansas Leadership Center. At: www.kansasleadership center.org/index.html. Accessed: October 2008.
11. Kouzes JM, Posner BZ. The leadership challenge. 4th ed. San Francisco: Jossey-Bass, 2007.
12. Kotter JP. Leading change. Boston: Harvard Business School Press, 2006.
13. Ericsson KA, Charness N, Feltovich PJ, Hoffman RR. The Cambridge handbook of expertise and expert performance. New York: Cambridge University Press, 2006.
14. Thomas RJ. Crucibles of leadership: how to learn from experience to become a great leader. Boston: Harvard Business School Press, 2008.
15. Medical school-based career and leadership development programs. Washington, DC: Association of American Medical Colleges, 2006. At: www.aamc.org/members/facultydev/leadershipprograms.pdf. Accessed: October 2008.
16. Drucker PF. Managing knowledge means managing oneself. Leader to Leader 2000;16(Spring):8–10.

What the ADEA CCI Series of Articles Means to Me: Reflections of a Mid-Career Dental Faculty Member

Karen F. Novak, D.D.S., M.S., Ph.D.

Abstract: In this reflection article, Dr. Karen Novak, a mid-career faculty member at a U.S. dental school, identifies important messages and insights she gained from a series of twenty-one articles about the future of dental education published in the *Journal of Dental Education* from October 2005 to February 2009. This article addresses four questions: 1) What influence have these articles had on an academic dentist's perspectives about her role and priorities as a dental school faculty member and her own career plans and future directions? 2) What are the key messages in these articles for other dental educators who are at similar places in their careers? 3) What additional topics concerning the future of academic dentistry should be covered in future articles? and 4) What issues and priorities should receive the most attention from academic dentistry in the next decade? The American Dental Education Association's Commission on Change and Innovation in Dental Education (ADEA CCI) was established to provide a mechanism for stakeholders in academic dentistry to meet and consider future directions in the education of the nation's dental workforce. Along with ADEA, these stakeholders included dental schools, the American Dental Association (ADA) Board of Trustees, the Commission on Dental Accreditation (CODA), the ADA Council on Dental Education and Licensure (CDEL), the Joint Commission on National Dental Examinations (JCNDE), the dental licensure community, the ADA Foundation, and advanced dental education programs. The ADEA CCI was created to build consensus within the dental community for innovative changes in the education of general dentists. One outcome of this process was a series of articles intended to raise awareness and stimulate dialogue about issues and forces shaping the future of dental education. Collectively, this series of articles is known as the Perspectives and Reflections in Dental Education (PRIDE) series to acknowledge the commitment of the academic dental community to reflect on current practices and future directions and also to represent the pride of dental school faculty members in their educational responsibilities and accomplishments.

Dr. Novak is Associate Professor, Director of Graduate Studies, and Interim Associate Dean for Academic Affairs, University of Kentucky College of Dentistry and the 2008 ADEA/Gies Foundation Education Fellow. Direct correspondence to her at the University of Kentucky, College of Dentistry, 414 Health Sciences Research Building, Lexington, KY 40536-0305; 859-323-8705 phone; 859-257-6566 fax; knova2@uky.edu.

This article is one in a series of invited contributions by members of the dental and dental education community that have been commissioned by the American Dental Education Association's Commission on Change and Innovation in Dental Education (ADEA CCI) to address the environment surrounding dental education and affecting the need for, or process of, curricular change. This article was written at the request of the ADEA CCI but does not necessarily reflect the views of ADEA, the ADEA CCI, or individual members of the ADEA CCI. The perspectives communicated here are those of the author.

Key words: American Dental Education Association, Commission on Change and Innovation in Dental Education, dental education, change, leadership, curriculum, faculty development

The American Dental Education Association's Commission on Change and Innovation in Dental Education (ADEA CCI) was established in 2005 to serve as a "facilitator of change and innovation" in dental education. Through this group, ADEA brought together individuals representing the major stakeholders in dental education: dental schools, the American Dental Association (ADA) Board of Trustees, the Commission on Dental Accreditation (CODA), the ADA Council on Dental Education and Licensure (CDEL), the Joint Commission on National Dental Examinations (JCNDE), the dental licensure community, the ADA Foundation, and advanced dental education programs.[1] The purpose of the ADEA CCI is to "build consensus within the dental community by providing leadership and oversight to a systemic, collaborative, and continuous process of innovative change in the education of general dentists."[1]

As part of the process, the ADEA CCI commissioned a series of articles to address a variety of issues relevant to the future of dental education. This collection of articles is known as the ADEA CCI Perspectives and Reflections in Dental Education

(PRIDE) series. Published from October 2005 to February 2009 in the *Journal of Dental Education,* these articles covered topics including a historical perspective on the development of the ADEA CCI, the rationale for change in dental education, the challenges associated with introducing change, the emerging picture of the educational and practice environments, evolving educational strategies for training practitioners of the future, standardized assessment of student achievement, and issues of faculty recruitment, development, and retention.

This article is one of the two final ones in the PRIDE series. Its purpose is to present the reflections of a mid-career academic dentist on this series. In doing so, I will address the following questions:

1. What influence has this series had on my perspectives about my role and priorities as a dental school faculty member and my own career plans and future directions?
2. What are the important messages in this series for other dental educators who are at similar places in their careers?
3. What additional topics should be covered in future articles about curriculum and change?
4. What issues and priorities should receive the most attention from academic dentistry in the next decade?

Influences on My Professional Role and Priorities

This section addresses the following question: What influence has this series had on my perspectives about my role and priorities as a dental school faculty member and my own career plans and future directions?

Each of the topics covered by the series has influenced my perceptions of my own career responsibilities and goals. Perhaps most important has been in understanding the role of the ADEA CCI and many of the factors associated with changing the face of dental education. First, although I had heard of the ADEA CCI before the series began to be published, I really did not understand the rationale for the development of this group and the leadership role it was to play in fostering change in dental education. Therefore, reading the first article in the series, "ADEA Commission on Change and Innovation in Dental Education,"[1] provided me with a brief, but very informative,

- The Institute of Medicine (IOM) report provided the rationale for change, but did not provide a roadmap. The ADEA CCI is providing dental education with a roadmap.

- Change is difficult, but even as an individual faculty member I can make a difference.

- As I made the decision to become involved in change, I found these articles to be an excellent resource.

Figure 1. Summary of my own perspectives on the ADEA CCI PRIDE series

overview of the role of the Commission and the series of events that led to its development. This article also highlighted the breadth of expertise represented on the Commission, helping me understand that this effort represents a serious commitment on the part of ADEA, as well as the other stakeholders represented, to provide comprehensive leadership and oversight in issues related to dental education. In reading this first article, I also gained a new appreciation for the commitment ADEA is making in providing tools and resources to the dental education community as we move forward in implementing changes that will direct the future of dental education.

The issue of where we are in the change process was introduced in the second article in the series, "The Case for Change in Dental Education."[2] Of all the articles I subsequently read, this one had the greatest impact on me. Having spent several years as a faculty member, I had often heard discussions on the significance of the findings of the Institute of Medicine (IOM) report *Dental Education at the Crossroads: Challenges and Change.*[3] This report was always cited as the landmark publication that should have served as a catalyst for change in dental education. As such, I assumed that significant change was occurring at the national level. After all, we had moved to competency-based education, worked to improve integration of basic and clinical sciences, and developed and implemented better teaching and assessment methods to promote critical thinking and lifelong learning. To realize that it was still necessary to make the "case for change" eleven years after publication of the IOM report was surprising to me. This took me back to the lead sentence in the first article in the series, which stated, "It's easier to move a cemetery than to change a curriculum."[1] Following this lead statement was a discussion about the difficulties and frustrations that have been encountered by schools and individuals attempting to create significant change in their institutions. I realized that while the IOM report provided the rationale for change, perhaps it did not provide a "roadmap" for accomplishing change. After reading the series and becoming more aware of the ADEA CCI's principles and initiatives, I now believe that the Commission is trying to provide this roadmap.

Let me return to the first question regarding the impact of these articles on my priorities as a mid-career faculty member. After reading the first two articles in the series, I decided that although creating change is difficult, I would try to be an agent of change at two levels—first in my own individual teaching and mentoring, and, second, in our institutional curriculum evaluation. My knowledge in these areas was enhanced by reading the articles that focused on the educational strategies we need to employ, and the culture we need to create, to graduate dentists who are competent in critical thinking, adept at linking basic and clinical sciences, committed to practicing evidence-based dentistry, and eager to be lifelong learners.[4-6]

The information in these articles served as a rich resource as I assessed my own teaching and mentoring activities. As a result, I began to reevaluate the content and structure of a second-year course in which I serve as the course director. This reevaluation led me to make several changes. In an attempt to bridge basic and clinical sciences, I began pairing sequential lectures that directly link a basic science content area with a clinical correlate. Typically, two faculty members who present the information are guided to work together in order to organize the two lectures so they complement and reinforce each other. During the latter part of the course, the students are divided into small groups to assess and discuss interdisciplinary cases designed to further reinforce the concepts presented in the didactic portion of the course. The course information and cases are presented in a web-based format, with small-group discussions being managed through online interactions. However, the details of what I did and how I did it to redesign my course are not the point I wish to make. What I would like to emphasize is that the information in the series of ADEA CCI articles provided a knowledge base and also helped me realize that change can start with one person trying something different. Change does not have to be earth-shattering or even hugely innovative. However, even if what we do as individual faculty members in our courses

most likely will not transform an entire curriculum, it can be a step towards incremental change that may ultimately have a broader impact.

In the bigger picture of institutional change and innovation, the same articles[4-6] were also important to me because they provided information about principles that are critical in shaping the dental curriculum of the future. I have been fortunate to have been given an opportunity to put these principles in place by serving as interim associate dean for academic affairs at my institution. In this role I am chairing a Curriculum Task Force that has been charged with evaluating our current curriculum and developing recommendations for future directions. I have already learned that curriculum evaluation and revision are complicated tasks and that the very words "change" and "innovation" are not always regarded as necessary and/or positive. The article in the October 2008 *JDE* titled "Managing Change in Dental Education: Is There a Method to the Madness?"[7] has been a valuable resource as I try to understand the issues related to organizational change. This article covers topics such as different types of change and the principles of managing change, with much of the information coming from the higher education literature. This article has helped me put curriculum change in the broad context of organizational change, where basic concepts of organizational development are important. With both the principles of dental education and the principles of change in mind, the ADEA CCI series of article has thus provided me with an excellent overview of the issues being addressed as the Commission's roadmap is developed. In doing so, these articles have served as an essential resource as I become more involved in change and innovation at my own institution.

Messages for Other Dental Educators

This section addresses the following question: What are the important messages in the ADEA CCI PRIDE series for other dental educators?

In addressing this second question, I would like to highlight my perceptions of several general messages introduced in the ADEA CCI series that at first glance may seem somewhat disconnected. To do this, I must put these articles in the context of another personal experience I have had over the past year—serving as the 2008 ADEA/Gies Foundation

Education Fellow. How does this activity relate to the series and my personal priorities and career directions? There are two main ways: the gift of time and the gift of exposure. As the recipient of this fellowship, I have spent three months of cumulative time at the ADEA headquarters. This gift of time, away from the daily activities that consume each of us as faculty members, has allowed me to focus on issues in dental education and to actually read and reflect on the ADEA CCI series. Without this opportunity, would I really have been able to do these two things? Maybe, but it certainly would not have been as easy. Therefore, to be agents of change we need time to reflect on and react to ideas presented in venues such as this series.

The second gift—that of exposure—was received from both the series and the staff of the ADEA Center for Educational Policy and Research, who were my colleagues during the fellowship. Each of these individuals has a strong background in higher education. Exposure to them has helped me recognize the value of interacting with individuals at our own institutions representing these broader educational backgrounds. Doing so will expose us to a different set of perspectives that may enhance our dental education programs. The concept of exposure links to the broader issue of the role of faculty development in initiating and implementing curricular change and innovation. Two articles in the ADEA CCI series focus on this issue.[8,9] The first highlights the role of faculty development in creating a culture that is ready for curriculum change and in subsequently preparing faculty members to teach and assess learning in the new curriculum. The second provides "information and insight about faculty development that may be useful to dental schools in designing professional growth opportunities for their faculty."[9] Both articles helped me realize that those of us who are mid-career faculty members need to be proactive in identifying the new tools and skills we need to be effective teachers and mentors in a new curriculum. Once those needed tools and skills are identified, we need to communicate those needs to our administrators responsible for faculty development and encourage them to identify resources, and time, to help us meet those needs.

Several articles in the ADEA CCI series focused on another area I believe is relevant to mid-career faculty members: development of future faculty and satisfaction with academic careers.[10-12] These three articles highlighted the differences in perception and expectations of careers among the

- To be agents of change, we need not only a roadmap for change, but also the time to focus on the roadmap and the tools to implement it.

- We need to recognize and appreciate that new, young faculty members represent a new generation and therefore may approach their careers differently from most mid-career faculty members.

- We need to maintain enthusiasm for our careers and project this enthusiasm to both our students and our new, young faculty members.

Figure 2. Summary of general messages for dental school faculty members regarding the ADEA CCI PRIDE series

generations, students and faculty, and faculty of various academic ranks and status (e.g., part-time versus full-time). First, the information on generational differences was of particular interest to me as a mid-career faculty member who is part of the baby boomer generation. I knew the term "Generation X," but did not really appreciate the characteristics of that generation that could influence their perceptions and actions as faculty members. Described as individuals desiring "portable careers," "freedom," "self-command," and "work-life balance" from the very beginning of their careers, Gen Xers don't fit the mold of academicians who are accustomed to continuous service at one institution, wanting "money, title, and a corner office," and willing to sacrifice quality of life until attaining a certain level of rank and recognition in their careers.[10] Given that the majority of faculty members and administrators in dental schools are more boomer than Gen Xer, a culture clash may exist that will need to be overcome. In reading these articles, I recalled hearing discussions about the outspoken nature of new, young faculty members and how bold they can be in expressing their opinions to their more experienced colleagues. These articles helped me understand that they aren't being rude or out of line; they are just representing cultural differences that as a boomer I need to learn to appreciate. So as a mid-level academician, the next time I hear those conversations I need to remember that our new, young faculty members represent a new generation that may have different perspectives on their careers than those of most mid-career faculty members.

This same group of articles highlighted work-life questions for academic dentists. I was pleased to read that, even in times of increased workloads and expectations, the majority of dental school faculty members are satisfied with their careers and work-life balance.[12] In trying to encourage students to consider academic dentistry as a career option, I think it extremely important to convey this message. For those of us who have been in academics for several years, we need to let our students and new, young faculty members know why we have chosen to be academic dentists for our careers. That means showing how much we enjoy the teaching, research, and service activities that make our careers challenging and exciting. It also means being a good mentor for both of these groups. The article in the series titled "Creating the Dental School Faculty of the Future: A Guide for the Perplexed"[13] describes the characteristics of a good mentor. To me, it described individuals who project that they are confident in, happy with, and proud of the career path they have taken. This is demonstrated by their positive interactions with students and colleagues, which is an essential component of being a good mentor and role model. Therefore, an additional message I took from these articles is that we need to maintain enthusiasm for our careers and project this enthusiasm to both our students and our new, young faculty members.

Future Issues and Priorities in Academic Dentistry

This section addresses the following questions: What additional topics should be covered in future articles about curriculum and change? What issues and priorities should receive the most attention from academic dentistry in the next decade?

- How can we facilitate better alignment between standardized benchmark examinations, such as the Dental Admission Test and the National Board Dental Examination Parts I and II, and the goals of a new curriculum?

- How successful are new educational models in training culturally competent clinicians who are addressing access to care issues?

- What educational models can we embrace that will encourage students to choose academic dentistry as a career?

Figure 3. Summary of issues on curriculum and change to be addressed in the future

Although I have highlighted several articles from the ADEA CCI series in the previous sections, future articles might introduce topics that will continue to be discussion points in the academic dentistry community. One is the impact that standardized exams, specifically the Dental Admission Test (DAT) and the National Board Dental Examination (NBDE), have on the dental school curriculum. Future articles also could expand on discussions of the relationship between the prerequisite courses for dental school admission, the DAT, and the basic science courses currently taught in the curriculum. In addition, with the expanding knowledge in basic sciences and a focus on translational research and patient care, a discussion of strategies to transition the NBDE to a more integrated, case-based format would be of benefit to the education community. Another area of interest is the decision of the Joint Commission on National Dental Examinations (JCNDE) to report the results of the NBDE as pass/fail. Future articles should focus on the development of new assessment tools designed to assist postgraduate program directors in identifying applicants who best match the goals of their programs. These same articles on assessment tools would be of value in identifying the best means to assess the overall didactic and clinical competence of our predoctoral dental students. The article on assessment of dental student competence in the December 2008 issue of the *JDE* is a starting point for closer consideration of how we determine our students' readiness for entry into unsupervised practice in the community.[14]

Beyond the issues of curricular change and new methods of assessment, future topics also could include expanded discussion on the role of dental schools in access to care issues. Qualitative and quantitative analyses of the impact that new community-based dental school curricula have had on developing students who are culturally competent and dedicated to addressing access to care issues would be of interest. Similarly, analysis of the impact that new dental schools and the new patient care models they represent are having on alleviating oral health disparities could be of benefit to dental schools that are considering moving their clinical programs in similar directions. Finally, the topic of how we can attract students into academic careers will continue to be an area of focus. Recognizing that current approaches are not as successful as one would hope, creative models that address financial issues facing graduates, as well as the image of academic dentistry, must be developed.

These are both challenging and exciting times in dental education. The issues facing us as dental educators, while not new, remain of great importance as we strive to prepare our students to be the practitioners and dental academicians of the future and to maintain our dental schools as financially viable academic institutions. The work of the ADEA CCI and the information provided in its series of articles have provided the dental education community with a useful roadmap to address these issues as we begin the process of innovative change in dental education.

REFERENCES

1. Kalkwarf KL, Haden NK, Valachovic RW. ADEA Commission on Change and Innovation in Dental Education. J Dent Educ 2005;69(10):1085–7.
2. Pyle M, Andrieu SC, Chadwick DG, Chmar JE, Cole JR, George MC, et al. The case for change in dental education. J Dent Educ 2006;70(9):921–4.
3. Field MJ, ed. Dental education at the crossroads: challenges and change. An Institute of Medicine Report. Washington, DC: National Academy Press, 1995.
4. Hendricson WD, Andrieu SC, Chadwick DG, Chmar JE, Cole JR, George MC, et al. Educational strategies associated with development of problem-solving, critical thinking, and self-directed learning. J Dent Educ 2006;70(9):925–36.
5. Haden NK, Andrieu SC, Chadwick DG, Chmar JE, Cole JR, George MC, et al. The dental education environment. J Dent Educ 2006;70(12):1265–70.
6. Iacopino AM. The influence of "new science" on dental education: current concepts, trends, and models for the future. J Dent Educ 2007;71(4):450–62.
7. Crain G. Managing change in dental education: is there a method to the madness? J Dent Educ 2008;72(10):1100–13.
8. Licari FW. Faculty development to support curriculum change and ensure the future vitality of dental education. J Dent Educ 2007;71(12):1509–12.
9. Hendricson WD, Anderson E, Andrieu SC, Chadwick DG, Cole JR, George MC, et al. Does faculty development enhance teaching effectiveness? J Dent Educ 2007;71(12):1513–33.
10. Trower CA. Making academic dentistry more attractive to new teacher-scholars. J Dent Educ 2007;71(5):601–5.
11. Trotman CA, Haden NK, Hendricson W. Does the dental school work environment promote successful academic careers? J Dent Educ 2007;71(6):713–25.
12. Haden NK, Hendricson W, Ranney RR, Vargas A, Cardenas L, Rose W, et al. The quality of dental faculty work-life: report on the 2007 dental school faculty work environment survey. J Dent Educ 2008;72(5):514–31.
13. Bertolami CN. Creating the dental school faculty of the future: a guide for the perplexed. J Dent Educ 2007;71(10):1267–80.
14. Albino JEN, Young SK, Neumann LM, Kramer GA, Andrieu SC, Henson L, Horn B, Hendricson WD. Assessing dental students' competence: best practice recommendations in the performance assessment literature and investigation of current practices in predoctoral dental education. J Dent Educ 2008;72(12):1405–35.

What the ADEA CCI Series of Articles Means to Me: Reflections of a Dental School Dean

Huw F. Thomas, B.D.S., M.S., Ph.D.

Abstract: In this reflection article, Dr. Huw F. Thomas, a U.S. dental school dean, identifies important messages and insights he gained from a series of twenty-one articles about the future of dental education published in the *Journal of Dental Education* from October 2005 to February 2009. This article addresses three questions: 1) What influence have these articles had on a dental school dean's perspectives about his role and priorities? 2) What important messages are contained within these articles for fellow deans? and 3) What messages do these articles send to dental education in general? The American Dental Education Association's Commission on Change and Innovation in Dental Education (ADEA CCI) was established to facilitate change and innovation in dental education. Through the ADEA CCI, ADEA brought together stakeholders in academic dentistry: dental schools, the American Dental Association (ADA) Board of Trustees, the Commission on Dental Accreditation (CODA), the ADA Council on Dental Education and Licensure (CDEL), the Joint Commission on National Dental Examinations (JCNDE), the dental licensure community, the ADA Foundation, and advanced dental education programs. The goal of the ADEA CCI is to provide a forum to build consensus within the dental community for innovative changes in the education of general dentists. As part of the consensus-building process, the ADEA CCI commissioned a series of articles, published in the *Journal of Dental Education,* to raise awareness and stimulate dialogue about issues and forces shaping the future of dental education and propose strategies to achieve desired enhancements. Collectively, this series of articles is known as the Perspectives and Reflections in Dental Education (PRIDE) series to acknowledge the commitment of the academic dental community to reflect on current practices and future directions and also to represent the pride of dental school faculty members in their educational responsibilities and accomplishments.

Dr. Thomas is Dean, School of Dentistry, University of Alabama at Birmingham. Direct correspondence and requests for reprints to him at School of Dentistry, University of Alabama at Birmingham, SDB 406, 1530 3rd Avenue South, Birmingham, AL 35294-0007; 205-934-4720 phone; 205-975-6544 fax; hft@uab.edu.

This article is one in a series of invited contributions by members of the dental and dental education community that have been commissioned by the American Dental Education Association's Commission on Change and Innovation in Dental Education (ADEA CCI) to address the environment surrounding dental education and affecting the need for, or process of, curricular change. This article was written at the request of the ADEA CCI but does not necessarily reflect the views of ADEA, the ADEA CCI, or individual members of the ADEA CCI. The perspectives communicated here are those of the author.

Key words: American Dental Education Association, Commission on Change and Innovation in Dental Education, dental education, change, leadership, curriculum, faculty development

This reflection article is intended to provide a dental school dean's perspective on the series of articles commissioned by the American Dental Education Association's Commission on Change and Innovation in Dental Education (ADEA CCI) and published in the *Journal of Dental Education* from October 2005 to January 2009. This collection of articles is known as the ADEA CCI Perspectives and Reflections in Dental Education (PRIDE) series. This series of twenty-one articles was developed to address a variety of issues relevant to the future of dental education. As part of this reflection, I will address three questions. First, what influence have these articles had on my perspective about my role and priorities as a dental school dean? Second, what important messages are contained within these articles for my fellow deans? And third, what messages do these articles send to dental education in general? In my responses to these questions, it is not my intent to reiterate the facts, figures, and discus-

sions contained in this outstanding series. Rather, I will endeavor to emphasize those issues that I feel are most cogent to a present-day dental school dean.

Influences on My Professional Role and Priorities

This section addresses the influence of the ADEA CCI PRIDE series on my perspectives about my role and priorities as a dental school dean.

The case for change in dental education was emphatically made in the Institute of Medicine (IOM) report published in 1995.[1] The findings and recommendations contained within this report were underscored in two further seminal publications: the report of the U.S. surgeon general, *Oral Health in America,*[2] published in 2000, and the future of dentistry report[3] published by the American Dental Association in 2001. Building on these reports, the rationale underlying the need for change was adeptly summarized in the second article of the ADEA CCI series, "The Case for Change in Dental Education."[4]

It should be emphasized at the outset that the changes being considered will not result in a new static curriculum, but one that will involve constant evolution. We should also not be lulled into a false sense of security that the changes we are contemplating will result in a "new" curriculum that will serve us for as long a period as the revolution engendered by William Gies in the 1920s, but rather will lead to a framework that will serve as an infrastructure for the foreseeable future.

I was appointed dean of the School of Dentistry, University of Alabama at Birmingham (UAB) in January 2004. Previous to that, I had spent twelve years as a department chair at the Dental School at the University of Texas Health Science Center at San Antonio (UTHSCSA). Soon after arriving at UTHSCSA, I had the opportunity to meet and be interviewed by the IOM committee led by then-HSC president, Dr. John Howe III. Looking back, I think that was the first time I had seriously considered the issues surrounding the dental educational process—I was after all a product of the traditional curriculum, and it had seemingly worked for me and had allowed me to develop into a productive, successful dental academician. Although my research training had imprinted within me the importance of research within a clinical academic dental school department, I had paid little heed to the need for change in the overall educational process. However, following publication of the report (which was for UTHSCSA faculty members required reading!) and over the intervening years, my ideas about the need for change coalesced, so that by the time I assumed the deanship at UAB my overarching priority as dean was to engage our community (faculty, staff, students, alumni, and university administration) in the process of curriculum reform. We embarked on this process in July 2005 with the first of a series of ongoing faculty advances. The timing of the ADEA initiative and the formation of the ADEA CCI was most fortuitous in this regard. The articles in the ADEA CCI series have been instrumental in shaping, guiding, and justifying our thoughts and progress. The issues discussed in them encompass the entire gamut of our reform process, and while they have not dictated our pathway, they have served as a roadmap and delineated the challenges, pitfalls, and opportunities that lie before us.

Important Messages for My Fellow Deans

This section will consider the following question: What important messages are contained within the ADEA CCI articles for my fellow deans?

Of all the articles in the series, I think that there are two critical ones that contain important messages for all faculty members and, in particular, deans of dental schools, and these should be given careful consideration. The first article[5] addresses the management of change in dental education, and the second[6] discusses how leadership must be best exercised for that change to occur. These articles detail historical and theoretical perspectives of organizations, the change process and its management, and the many principles involved in the change process itself. The role of the individual (be it dean, department chair, course director, or faculty member) in contemplating, directing, and critically observing change is discussed and exemplified. We cannot simply change for the sake of change; we must understand and commit to the need for change, while still understanding that there is much that is good about our current process. In other words, we must not throw out the baby with the bathwater!

Many of us directly involved in dental education have had little training in managing significant change and are not well prepared for this process. ADEA (through its Leadership Institute and other initiatives) has taken a significant step forward in fostering this training, but while the ADEA CCI has focused the attention of the educational community on the need for change, we are only now beginning to realize the magnitude of the task before us and the roles that each of us needs to play. The critical role that ADEA must play in educating and guiding faculties and leaders cannot be overemphasized. We must also learn from our fellow health professional organizations and institutions of higher learning. We must interact with them and learn from them in our educational environment as well as in our professional environment. Our educational milieu cannot afford to maintain the "cottage industry" mentality that is so often used to describe the practice of dentistry.

While the admonition in the IOM report[1] that "most deans would rather take a daily physical beating than try to make significant changes in the traditional curriculum" or the observation about educational reform in the first article in the ADEA CCI series[7] that "it's easier to move a cemetery than to change a curriculum" both have a ring of truth, they imply a situation in which leadership is considered more as a top-down directional activity than an all-inclusive team approach. I prefer the following sentiment: "Whatever you can do, or dream you can, begin it. Boldness has genius, power, and magic in it."[8] I recommend that principle to all my fellow dental educators.

Messages the ADEA CCI PRIDE Series Sends to Dental Education

There are many important messages that this series sends to dental education in general. A few of the articles discuss important issues external to the school environment: the changing face of the health care system,[9] and the function and particularly the structure and timing of the National Board exams,[10,11] which were surely designed to mirror our traditional curriculum. The uncertain future of funding streams for universities in general and dental schools in particular will have a profound effect on our progress. Another article[12] illustrates the need for all aspects of the dental community to engage and participate in the process of reform, an area in which dental schools would do well to engage their alumni and state dental organizations. Yet another article[13] discusses issues related to the development of educational strategies for the new curriculum. Paramount in these strategies is the development and use of methods to encourage and promote problem-solving, critical thinking, and self-directed learning. Finally, the all important area of student assessment is considered.[14]

While all of these articles contain messages that are vital, it is not coincidental in my opinion that the majority of the articles in the series deal with issues related to dental school faculties,[15-22] for that is the area in which I believe most of our challenges lie. This is even more important today in the current climate of economic uncertainty, with the inevitable budget cuts to spending on higher education. Most current dental educators are products of the traditional dental curriculum. How well prepared are they to foster a new paradigm in pedagogy? How can they be encouraged (incentivized) to develop new teaching strategies? How does the promotion and tenure process need to change to accommodate them? Where is the next generation of dental educators coming from? How much longer can we survive

as the poor cousins of our practicing colleagues? And what stresses will we impose on that relationship if we enter more significantly into the competitive marketplace of patient care?

Given an appropriate educational environment[15] (including the development of specific tracks within dental schools to foster the development of academicians), whether for clinicians, researchers, or clinician-researchers, I believe that an academic career is an attractive choice for a graduating dentist provided that adequate compensation mechanisms can be instituted. Although these mechanisms must include expansion of provisions for loan repayment in exchange for a period of public service (which could have the added benefit of addressing some access to care issues), it must also include enhanced opportunities for generating income through patient care. I rarely hear my academic physician colleagues complain about their remuneration. Granted, most of them have the safety net of hospital environments and federal and state support mechanisms to help fund their salaries, but patient care is a routine, expected, and often significant component of their appointments and provides their primary forum for teaching and role modeling of professional practice for medical students. Dental schools must provide contemporary patient care facilities where faculty members have an opportunity to generate significant income streams. These practice environments can also serve an important educational role for students who should be able to participate in the practice environment, develop much-needed business and practice management skills, and observe dentists "in action" with patients, which dental students rarely see in the current curriculum. Doubtless, this initiative will occasion some friction between the schools and the practicing communities, particularly in times of economic distress. However, I would estimate that because most dental school faculties are about the size of an average department in a medical school, the impact of increased patient care within the dental school environment on the surrounding practicing community would not be intolerable.

The importance of scientific enquiry and discovery to the profession and to the dental school's standing within its parent university is well appreciated and has significant implications for the composition of our faculties. Traditionally, dental school faculties have been composed of clinicians and researchers, the latter often being members of a medical or graduate school faculty. Unfortunately, in the past these two groups of individuals often remained separate, and although a new breed of clinician-researchers is slowly making its way into the fray, the importance of integrating clinicians and researchers, especially in the context of student education, should not be underestimated. Because many dental schools do not have a cadre of individuals who can perform the multiple academic roles—combining teaching, research, and professional service—fulfilled by clinical scholars in other disciplines, a much closer relationship needs to be forged with various individual groups throughout the university campus to accomplish these goals. And we cannot confine our thoughts to simply the integration of basic science and clinical faculties. Faculty members from schools of behavioral and social sciences, education, public health, nursing, and business (to name a few) all need to be included at significantly greater levels than at present. These relationships will reduce the need for dental schools to expend resources to recruit individuals to our ranks and will serve to further weave the dental school into the overall fabric of the university.

The same case can be made for other important new initiatives that are fundamental to our ability to promote change within our curricula. Information technology and faculty development programs are two additional examples in which broader interactions with our parent universities are essential. Most of us are now engaged in environments where some degree of university support exists in both areas. But despite this, I would emphasize the need for engaging dental school faculty members in programs in which they can acquire the skills to teach and participate in the "new" curriculum. It behooves us to remember that most of us have been trained in the traditional curriculum and old habits die hard. Unless we appreciate the need for change, appreciate the value of that change, and provide the time and incentives (fiscal and promotional) to effect that change, we will fall short of our goal.

To summarize, I salute the American Dental Education Association and its then-president, Dr. Eric Hovland, for their concern, courage, and vision in assembling a diverse group of individuals under the auspices of the Commission on Change and Innovation in Dental Education.[7] That initiative and the development of the document "Competencies for the New General Dentist"[23] must serve as a catalyst for all of us in dental education to embrace the changes that are inevitable in our society and our profession so that we can best serve the oral health needs of all Americans for the future.

I will close with a question that continues to shape my thinking throughout this journey. If you had four years to take your daughter or son as qualified college graduates and shape them into caring, competent entry-level general dentists, what would you wish for them to learn on the first day, the first week, and the first year of that process? What traits, skills, learning methodologies, and experiences would you wish to instill in them? Our students and the subsequent generations of practicing dentists deserve no less a consideration.

REFERENCES

1. Field MJ, ed. Dental education at the crossroads: challenges and change. An Institute of Medicine Report. Washington, DC: National Academy Press, 1995.
2. Oral health in America: a report of the surgeon general. Rockville, MD: U.S. Department of Health and Human Services, National Institute of Dental and Craniofacial Research, National Institutes of Health, 2000.
3. American Dental Association. Future of dentistry. Chicago: American Dental Association, Health Policy Resources Center, 2001.
4. Pyle M, Andrieu SC, Chadwick DG, Chmar JE, Cole JR, George MC, et al. The case for change in dental education. J Dent Educ 2006;70(9):921–4.
5. Crain G. Managing change in dental education: is there a method to the madness? J Dent Educ 2008;72(10):1100–13.
6. Cohen PA, Tedesco LA. Willing, ready, and able? How we must exercise leadership for needed change in dental education. J Dent Educ 2009;73(1):3–11.
7. Kalkwarf KL, Haden NK, Valachovic RW. ADEA Commission on Change and Innovation in Dental Education. J Dent Educ 2005;69(10):1085–7.
8. Murray WH. The Scottish Himalaya expedition. London: J.M. Dent & Sons Ltd., 1951.
9. Anderson MH. Dentistry and dental education in the context of the evolving health care system. J Dent Educ 2007;71(8):988–93.
10. Neumann LM, MacNeil RL. Revisiting the National Board Dental Examination. J Dent Educ 2007;71(10):1281–92.
11. MacNeil RL, Neumann LM. Realigning the National Board Dental Examination with contemporary dental education and practice. J Dent Educ 2007;71(10):1293–8.
12. Roth K. Dental education: a leadership challenge for dental educators and practitioners. J Dent Educ 2007;71(8):983–7.
13. Hendricson WD, Andrieu SC, Chadwick DG, Chmar JE, Cole JR, George MC, et al. Educational strategies associated with development of problem-solving, critical thinking, and self-directed learning. J Dent Educ 2006;70(9):925–36.
14. Albino JEN, Young SK, Neumann LM, Kramer GA, Andrieu SC, Henson L, Horn B, Hendricson WD. Assessing dental students' competence: best practice recommendations in the performance assessment literature and

investigation of current practices in predoctoral dental education. J Dent Educ 2008;72(12):1405–35.

15. Haden NK, Andrieu SC, Chadwick DG, Chmar JE, Cole JR, George MC, et al. The dental education environment. J Dent Educ 2006;70(12):1265–70.

16. Iacopino AM. The influence of "new science" on dental education: current concepts, trends, and models for the future. J Dent Educ 2007;71(4):450–62.

17. Trower CA. Making academic dentistry more attractive to new teacher-scholars. J Dent Educ 2007;71(5):601–5.

18. Trotman CA, Haden NK, Hendricson W. Does the dental school work environment promote successful academic careers? J Dent Educ 2007;71(6):713–25.

19. Bertolami CN. Creating the dental school faculty of the future: a guide for the perplexed. J Dent Educ 2007;71(10):1267–80.

20. Licari FW. Faculty development to support curriculum change and ensure the future vitality of dental education. J Dent Educ 2007;71(12):1509–12.

21. Hendricson WD, Anderson E, Andrieu SC, Chadwick DG, Cole JR, George MC, et al. Does faculty development enhance teaching effectiveness? J Dent Educ 2007;71(12):1513–33.

22. Haden NK, Hendricson W, Ranney RR, Vargas A, Cardenas L, Rose W, et al. The quality of dental faculty work-life: report on the 2007 dental school faculty work environment survey. J Dent Educ 2008;72(5):514–31.

23. American Dental Education Association. Competencies for the new general dentist (as approved by the 2008 ADEA House of Delegates). J Dent Educ 2008;72(7):823–6.